MEANINGS IN TEXTS AND ACTIONS: QUESTIONING PAUL RICOEUR

STUDIES IN RELIGION AND CULTURE

MEANINGS IN TEXTS AND ACTIONS: QUESTIONING PAUL RICOEUR

Edited by
DAVID E. KLEMM *and* WILLIAM SCHWEIKER

University Press of Virginia
Charlottesville and London

THE UNIVERSITY PRESS OF VIRGINIA

First published 1993

Library of Congress Cataloging-in-Publication Data

Meanings in texts and actions : questioning Paul Ricoeur / edited by
David E. Klemm and William Schweiker.
p. cm. — (Studies in religion and culture)
Includes bibliographical references and index.
ISBN 0-8139-1411-6
1. Ricoeur, Paul—Congresses. I. Klemm, David E., 1947– .
II. Schweiker, William. III. Series: Studies in religion and culture
(Charlottesville, Va.)
B2430.R554M43 1993
194—dc20 92-34072
CIP

Printed in the United States of America

CONTENTS

Acknowledgments ix

Meanings in Texts and Actions: Questioning Paul Ricoeur
DAVID E. KLEMM and WILLIAM SCHWEIKER 1

PART I
FUNDAMENTAL ISSUES IN INTERPRETATION

The Textuality of Texts
ROBERT P. SCHARLEMANN 13

Against Poetry: Heidegger, Ricoeur, and the Originary Scene of Hermeneutics
GERALD BRUNS 26

PART II
ESSAYS ON HISTORY AND NARRATIVE

"As Real as It Gets": Ricoeur and Narrativity
HANS KELLNER 49

Traces of the Past: From Historicity to Film
PHILIP ROSEN 67

The Cinematograph: A Historical Machine
ANDRÉ GAUDREAULT 90

Visconti Read through Ricoeur: Time in *Ludwig*
MICHÈLE LAGNY 98

History and Timelessness in Films and Theory
DUDLEY ANDREW 115

Jesus between Fiction and History
JOHN VAN DEN HENGEL 133

PART III
THE NATURE OF EXISTENCE AND THE BEING OF GOD

Ricoeur's Contribution to Contemporary Political Thought
BERNARD P. DAUENHAUER 157

Politics and Power: Ricoeur's Political Paradox Revisited
FRED DALLMAYR 176

Narrative Identity and the Mythico-Poetic Imagination
PAMELA ANDERSON 195

Imagination, Violence, and Hope: A Theological Response to Ricoeur's Moral Philosophy
WILLIAM SCHWEIKER 205

"Face to Face with Ricoeur and Levinas"
HERMAN RAPAPORT 226

Ricoeur, Rorty, and the Question of Revelation
MARK I. WALLACE 234

Theological Hermeneutics and the Divine Name: Ricoeur and the Cross of Interpretation
DAVID E. KLEMM 255

PART IV
CONCLUDING REFLECTIONS

Individuality: The Principle of Ricoeur's Mediating Philosophy and Its Bearing on Theology of Culture
DAVID E. KLEMM 275

Hermeneutics, Ethics, and the Theology of Culture: Concluding Reflections
WILLIAM SCHWEIKER 292

Response to Robert Scharlemann
DAVID JASPER 314

Response to Gerald Bruns
DONALD G. MARSHALL 318

Response to Hans Kellner and Herman Rapaport
MORNY JOY 326

Response to Pamela Anderson, William Schweiker, and Fred Dallmayr
JAMES F. MCCUE 335

Response to John Van Den Hengel, David Klemm, and Mark Wallace
MARY GERHART 343

Select Bibliography 353
Notes on Contributors 359
Name Index 363
Subject Index 366

ACKNOWLEDGMENTS

THE SYMPOSIUM that formed the context for the present volume grew out of long-standing theological conversation between the editors, David E. Klemm and William Schweiker. However, many persons were important in making the symposium and the book possible. Dudley Andrew, Donald Marshall, Steven Ungar, and Jay Semel, director of the University House of the University of Iowa, worked with us in planning the symposium. As always, Kate Neckerman, and the Executive Committee of the Project on the Rhetoric of Inquiry (POROI), especially John Nelson and Donald McCloskey, provided energy and vision for the symposium. We thank all these persons. We also thank our sponsors: the University House Humanities Symposium Award, the School of Religion, the Institute of Cinema and Culture, the Project on the Rhetoric of Inquiry, the Department of Philosophy, the School of Art and Art History, and the Department of English at the University of Iowa, as well as the Divinity School of the University of Chicago.

Finally, we thank Gwen Barnes and Lyone Fein for their help with the preparation of the manuscript. We especially wish to thank James J. Thompson and Lois Malcolm, who also prepared the index and the bibliography. Without their diligence, critical insight, and care the completion of this volume would not have been possible.

David Klemm
William Schweiker

MEANINGS IN TEXTS AND ACTIONS: QUESTIONING PAUL RICOEUR

DAVID E. KLEMM and

WILLIAM SCHWEIKER

MEANINGS IN TEXTS AND ACTIONS

Questioning Paul Ricoeur

THIS VOLUME of essays stems from the symposium entitled "Meanings in Texts and Actions: The Questions of Paul Ricoeur," held at the University of Iowa from March 29 through April 1, 1990. The symposium brought scholars from a variety of disciplines into conversation about how meanings and the interpretation of meanings enter language and existence in religion and culture. Participants in the symposium came from a variety of disciplines—including literary theory, comparative literature, theology and religious studies, history, film studies, political philosophy, ethics, and global studies—and from diverse universities in the United States, Canada, France, and Great Britain. Participants were bound together into a common enterprise by their shared conviction that any reflection on meanings and the conditions of meaningfulness in human life leads to the tradition of thought known as *hermeneutics*—the theory and practice of understanding meanings in language and existence. The central question of hermeneutics is: What does it mean that understanding is the primary mode of human being in the world?

Guided by that question, the goal of the symposium was to reflect on the meaning of being human in the world, given the thoroughly historical and linguistic character of any reflection upon the human condition. Since to be human means to grasp and receive meanings, participants were asked to consider the ways in which they understand meanings in texts and actions from their different disciplinary viewpoints. For a number of reasons, we chose to focus the cross-disciplinary conversation on questions concerning Paul Ricoeur, who, along with Hans-Georg Gadamer, is largely responsible for the emergence of a new hermeneutics in the decades of the 1960s, 1970s, and 1980s. Two basic reasons present themselves for questioning Paul Ricoeur among hermeneutical thinkers.

First, Ricoeur's thought commends itself for conversation across disciplinary boundaries. In its cross-disciplinary dimension, Ricoeur's work stands as one of the most significant contributions to humanistic scholarship of the postwar era.[1] Ricoeur's work constitutes an original synthesis of philosophical, literary, and historical inquiries. During a time when powerful forces in our world are fragmenting the discourse of humanistic studies, Ricoeur's theoretical program helps provide a coherent framework in which to raise the major question confronting us: What happens to thinking when we recognize radical historical consciousness and the fact that we have no access to the reality we talk about in language except through linguistic signs themselves? Ricoeur brings traditional philosophical concerns to this question, informed by critical readings of Aristotle, Kant, and the other major figures in Western philosophy and theology. In his pursuit of this question, Ricoeur has engaged in critical debates with major thinkers in virtually every humanistic discipline, and he has helped create a conversation across the disciplines. In other words, not only has Ricoeur's work fed into multiple disciplines, but his writing has additionally allowed scholars from the various disciplines to talk with one another about meanings in texts and actions. Herein lies one contribution by Ricoeur to the human sciences. Without losing the focus of humanistic study, he has provided a hermeneutical theory that, on grounds intrinsic to understanding itself, demands both explanatory methods and interpretative engagement. This enables scholars from fields previously dominated by analysis, like political science or positivist historiography, to enter hermeneutical reflection and thereby to enrich inquiry. Conversely, Ricoeur's hermeneutics requires that thinkers who seek to interpret complex and ambiguous patterns of meaning draw on the resources of any number of explanatory methods. In a word, Ricoeur's hermeneutics seeks to mediate debates about the place of method and explanation in the human sciences. He does so while insisting on the priority of understanding and the question of truth.

Second, Ricoeur has made a particularly important impact in the field of religious studies and theological reflection. That was an important consideration for the symposium, which intended to bring scholars of religious studies and theology into interaction with scholars working in cultural criticism in a broader sense. The intention was to uncover connections between meanings in religion and in culture as more broadly defined. Ricoeur's thought is particularly helpful for such a task. Ricoeur is a philosopher working in the phenomenological tradition whose interpretations of the meaning and structure of myth, symbol, and ritual, and whose analyses of the religious dimensions of human thinking, willing, and feeling, have made him one of the most influential figures in current theology.

Ricoeur's contribution to theological studies is readily understandable in historical terms. Prior to World War II, German theology clearly dominated the field. With the debacle in Germany and the rise of religious studies in the United States after the war, new initiatives in theology arose in this country. The emigration of Paul Tillich to the United States in 1933 had energized these initiatives. Under Tillich's guidance, theology in America emerged as a nonecclesiastical and nondogmatic study of the interrelations between symbolic meaning and the structures of human existence. Tillich's conception of a "theology of culture" led by a "method of correlation" captivated the interests of a generation of American-trained scholars. After Tillich's death in 1965, Ricoeur filled the vacated position in philosophical theology and led the field farther in the direction charted by Tillich. With Ricoeur's influence both in the United States and in Europe, theology has increasingly understood itself as hermeneutical reflection on the religious dimensions of texts and practices, informed by both practical philosophy and literary criticism. To the field of theology, Ricoeur presents phenomenological and literary methods, as well as a theory of interpretation, that can bring categories of existence and text into correlation.

On the one hand, Ricoeur has articulated a phenomenological analysis of human existence and its threefold structure of thinking, willing, and feeling.[2] He is insistent on two points regarding this analysis. First, he claims that the human being is aware of its openness to a dimension of being that transcends and grounds it.

In mediating between thinking and perceiving, sense and reference, meaning and being, human beings become aware of the unconditioned unity that is presupposed by the mediating activity. According to Ricoeur, as mediating beings we become aware of our identity with and our dependence upon a reality that transcends the self. Second, while human being is open to transcendence at the limits of its being, the symbols, myths, and rituals that speak of this transcendence nevertheless must be interpreted. None speak directly of the transcendent ground of human being. To interpret such expressions means to comprehend again what has already been comprehended about the meaning of being human in the symbolic form of myth and ritual. In other words, the interpretation of symbols, myths, and rituals is to be correlated with a hermeneutic of existence. Ricoeur's hermeneutical theory provides the categories for interpreting religious discourse in its own voice without reducing it to expressions of the repressed human psyche, the will to power, or the social structure.

On the other hand, Ricoeur claims that a Word can be and has been spoken to the human being. Ricoeur speaks of himself as a philosopher who listens to the Christian message as such a Word. In some of the writings in which he interprets the biblical word, Ricoeur critically appropriates the Word of God theologies that dominated dogmatic and ecclesial theological reflection earlier this century; in other such writings, he appears to approach more current forms of narrative theology.[3] Symbols and myths, such as we find in the Bible, open up a possible way of being in the world in which I can dwell. Symbols and myths speak to the human situation and thus demand critical interpretation. That we have always already been "spoken to" means for Ricoeur that we do not have cognitive clarity concerning who or what the human being is, since to be human is in part to be constituted by what is spoken to us. Moreover, the hermeneutics of text and the various explanatory methods an interpreter uses in examining religious symbols and myths do not exhaust the possible import of these discursive forms for understanding the human condition. In fact, they provoke further detours of interpretation on the way to understanding the truth of the ambiguity we are. That truth, it seems, is bound up in the Word spoken to us.

Ricoeur has argued throughout his career that self-understanding within different strata of worldly contexts is the goal of reflection. Hermeneutical theory is needed in part because direct reflection on the self as the subject of thinking is as empty as it is irrefutable, according to Ricoeur. However, unlike many postmodern theorists, Ricoeur does not on that account abandon or undercut the notion of subjectivity. While disputing the classical notion of the subject as transparent cogito, Ricoeur attempts to demonstrate the existence of an opaque subjectivity, which expresses itself through the detour of countless mediations—signs, symbols, texts, and actions. It is these mediations that require humanistic and religious study. We know the self through its embodiments in cultural artifacts of all kinds, including religious ones. Ricoeur's questions cut across disciplinary boundaries and to the heart of humanistic study. Following Kant's four basic questions, Ricoeur's writings ask: What is human being? What can I know? What ought I to do? What may I hope? The orientation of Ricoeur's project is philosophical anthropology, from which basis he considers the interpretation of texts and actions. Most recently his questions have led him into the world of time and narrative. He asks: How do fictional narratives shape collective and personal memory? How do historical narratives account for the problem of sequence in human life? How does human temporal experience enter into narratives so as to shape and orient human action? How do cultural symbols interpret human time and inherited narratives? How can new symbols refigure human temporal possibilities and narrative understandings? Ricoeur has helped to provide a common vocabulary for reflecting on these and similar questions that arise in every humanistic field.

The narrative turn in Ricoeur's work coheres with and yet extends the direction of his previous philosophical project. It does so in ways important not only for philosophy, but for all of the humanistic studies and religious scholarship and theology as well. Ricoeur's hermeneutics shows how time is the horizon of meaning and how narrative gives time a specific human form. Thus the philosophic turn to time initiated in this century by Heidegger is continued by Ricoeur, but in his own distinctive way. Specifically, he explores the mediation between cosmic time and lived time by historical and fictive narratives. The import of his reflection, we can now say, is to undergird at the most basic philosophical level—that is, reflection on the meaning of being in time—concern for explanation and understanding as well as the focus on the human as the subject matter of philosophy. That is, the dual perspective on time (cosmological and phenomenological) means that explanatory methods dominated by the search for causal laws must join forces with interpretation and its search for the meaning of human events and actions. Likewise, these accounts of time cannot lose their humanistic, or reflexive, focus, since it is *we* who are oriented to time as conscious beings and as beings in the physical universe. It is this dual orientation that gives rise to our most basic questions.

Ricoeur's philosophical project continues the dominant themes in contemporary thought and indeed in the whole sweep of the Western intellectual tradition. He has provided a cross-disciplinary and theologically informed interpretation theory that enables scholars to see connections between religion and culture within a common humanistic discourse. Given these considerations, the organizers of the University House Humanities Symposium decided to focus on Ricoeur and his project. We asked participating scholars to reflect on the ways in which Ricoeur's thought has advanced thought within their own disciplines and to communicate their thoughts to an audience made up of individuals from diverse disciplinary fields. Given the synthetic nature of the questions he has raised, however, we also encouraged participants to take up the cross-disciplinary nature of this questioning. Ricoeur is a philosopher in the traditional sense of one who loves wisdom and strives for a standpoint from which one looks to bring coherence and meaning into experience. His personal generosity of spirit has created situations in which cross-disciplinary conversation really happens. Although Ricoeur was unable to attend the Iowa Humanities Symposium, his spirit of inquiry guided the conference. The editors believe that the essays herein published, along with critical responses to them, display that spirit.

For readers who are introducing themselves with this volume to Ricoeur's thought and its influence on humanists, we shall make some further remarks about Ricoeur and his program in which to situate the concerns articulated in the essays.

Paul Ricoeur was born in 1913 in Valence, France. He studied philosophy at the Sorbonne under Gabriel Marcel, and was deeply influenced by the phenomenology of Edmund Husserl. Marcel gave Ricoeur his philosophical theme—the ontology of human finitude. But Ricoeur found his methodological mentor in Husserl. During the Second World War, Ricoeur served in the French army in 1936–37 and from 1939 to 1945. Most of these years, 1940–45, were spent as a prisoner of war in Germany. His German captors allowed Ricoeur to read the works of Husserl, Heidegger, and Jaspers, so his years in internment were spent reading German philosophy. Following the war, Ricoeur established himself as a leading Husserl scholar, and he wrote book-length studies on Jaspers and Marcel. In 1948, Ricoeur was called to the philosophy faculty at the University of Strasbourg. Each year he immersed himself in the works of one great thinker and taught a seminar on those works. In this way, he worked through the tradition from Plato to Nietzsche.

In 1950, Ricoeur published *Freedom and Nature,* the first volume of his *Philosophy of the Will,* which he conceived as a comprehensive and systematic study of the volitional and affective core of human existence. With that work, he established his name as a leading figure in French phenomenology. As professor of philosophy at the University of Paris X (Nanterre), he published the second volume of the *Philosophy of the Will,* called *Finitude and Guilt* (1960), in two parts. The first part, *Fallible Man,* lays out Ricoeur's reflection on human existence. Ricoeur describes the conflicts that vex human beings in the domains of knowing, willing, and feeling. These discontinuities mark the loci of human fallibility: the disproportion between perceiving and conceiving in the theoretical syntheses of knowing; the noncoincidence between the situatedness of character and the open horizon of the drive for happiness in the projected practical syntheses of doing; and the unmediated rift between the trivial drives toward possession-power-worth and the spiritual feelings of joy-anxiety-courage in the affective life. By isolating the structure of human being as a fragile noncoincidence of the self with the self, Ricoeur displays human fallibility as a condition of the possibility of fallen existence.

In the second part, entitled *The Symbolism of Evil,* Ricoeur reflects, not on the general features of existence that make humans fallible, but on concrete expressions of fallen and disrupted existence. In making the transition from the pure reflection on the possibility of evil to the actual occurrence of evil, Ricoeur discovered the necessity to work out a hermeneutics of symbol and myth. The transition from fallibility to fault is inscrutable to a pure reflection conducted by an isolated individual thinker. To understand evil, one reflects hermeneutically on given and contingent cultural expressions.

Following *The Symbolism of Evil,* Ricoeur articulated his philosophical hermeneutics more precisely through such works as *Interpretation Theory, The Conflict of Interpretations,* and *On Interpretation: Freud and Philosophy.* Throughout these studies, Ricoeur continues the modern tradition of reflexive philosophy from within the horizon of an ontology of human finitude. Against the Cartesian and Husserlian stream of this tradition, Ricoeur argued that the I of self-reflection is not transparent to itself; human existence can be viewed only in the mirror of its external manifestations in texts and actions. Moreover, the I of self-reflection can harbor illusion and mystification; therefore self-understanding calls for a hermeneutics of suspicion (such as Marx, Nietzsche, and Freud present) alongside a hermeneutics of belief in the power of traditional meanings to speak again. The examined life is the life worth living, and Ricoeur argued that self-examination is only possible through a general hermeneutics capable of interpreting the fullness and diversity of various uses and layers of language and existence. In his mature interpretation theory, Ricoeur expanded his definition of hermeneutics from "a work of understanding that aims at deciphering symbols" by discovering how the problem of double meaning inheres not only in symbols but in the nature of discourse as such.[4] Ricoeur redefined hermeneutics as the theory and practice of "the decoding of messages based on polysemic words."[5] Incorporating into his theory of discourse the results of linguistic science and structuralist criticism, Ricoeur accounted for both semantic and semiotic dimensions of discourse. In so doing, Ricoeur resisted reducing discourse to the system of signs forming its semiotic structure and claimed that language in use always retains a synthetic structure of someone saying something about something in an event of discourse. At the same time, he conceded that structural analysis has an important role to play as a moment within a complex process of understanding.

Most basically, the process of understanding has three moments, which are best isolated and exemplified in the interpretation of texts, according to Ricoeur. The initial moment in reading a text is defined by naive understanding: we guess at the meaning of the text and form a prereflective understanding of its sense and reference through the event of reading itself. The second moment is defined by a critical explanation of what was prereflectively understood: the initial impression can be validated or corrected by recourse to the objective structure of the text. The third moment is defined by appropriating a meaning the reader interprets himself or herself in light of what the text has to say and thus is changed by the dialogue with the text. Understanding, explanation, and appropriation together form a "hermeneutical arc" in which "understanding precedes, accompanies, closes, and thus envelops explanation. In return, explanation develops understanding analytically."[6]

With this hermeneutical program, Ricoeur engaged in specialized applications in biblical theology, legal philosophy, philosophy of history, political theory, philosophy of language, aesthetics, literary theory, structural anthropology, and the like. In *The Rule of Metaphor,* Ricoeur made a comprehensive study of the rhetorical tropes to show how metaphoric predication works to create new meaning in language and existence through the breakdown of literal meaning. The theory of text built on the theory of metaphor: fictional texts redescribe reality by projecting a world of the text as referent through the formal structure of the text as work.

Ricoeur has recently completed a three-volume magnum opus entitled *Time and Narrative.* In it Ricoeur expands his interpretations of meanings in human existence through detailed studies of the experience of time, and he expands his interpretations of meanings in language through careful analysis of the structures of historical and fictional narratives. A fundamental thesis joins the themes of time and narrative: "Time becomes human," Ricoeur argues, "to the extent that it is articulated through a narrative mode, and narrative attains its full meaning when it becomes a condition of temporal existence" (1:85).

Time and Narrative is the culmination of Ricoeur's philosophical anthropology in relation to his general hermeneutical theory. Focusing on the classic speculations on the nature of time in Augustine's *Confessions* and Aristotle's *Physics,* Ricoeur shows a fundamental discordance between the phenomenological experience of time and the cosmological measure of time. Theoretical speculation on time leads to unsolvable aporia to which the productive imagination can respond through the narrative activity of composing or following a plot as a synthesis of episodes. Narrative activity renders the theoretical aporia productive in a practical way: the reader or writer of narrative can give coherence to time and self-identity through the poetic activity, which in turn gives rise to deliberation and action in a return from the text to life.

On the occasion of the publication of *Time and Narrative,* the organizers of the symposium deemed it salutary to consider and to assess the contribution Ricoeur has made to humanistic reflection. The authors of the essays included in this volume differ in their degree of proximity or distance to Ricoeur's project—some of them work very closely with his ideas, others resist them. But they all are enriched and stimulated by the questions of Paul Ricoeur. In these essays the contributors take up Ricoeur's questions and pose questions to him in return. The editors bring them to publication in the hope that they will contribute to the ongoing task of understanding meanings in texts and actions.

NOTES

1. Paul Ricoeur's bibliography numbers into the hundreds. See the bibliography at the end of this volume for the major works by and about Ricoeur. Major books include contributions to the philosophy of the will (*Freedom and Nature: The Voluntary and the Involuntary,* trans. Erazim Kohák [Evanston, Ill.: Northwestern University Press, 1966]); philosophical anthropology (*Fallible Man,* trans. Charles A. Kelbley [Chicago: Henry Regnery, 1965; rev. ed. with an Introduction by Walter Lowe, New York: Fordham University Press, 1988]); studies of myth and tradition (*The Symbolism of Evil,* trans. Emerson Buchanan [New York: Harper and Row, 1967]); historiography (*History and Truth,* trans. Charles A. Kelbley [Evanston, Ill.: Northwestern University Press, 1965]); ethical and social thought (*Political and Social Essays,* ed. David Stewart and Joseph Bien, trans. Donald Siewert et al. [Athens: Ohio University Press, 1974]); interpretations of Freudian psychoanalysis (*Freud and Philosophy: An Essay on Interpretation,* trans. Denis Savage [New Haven, Conn.: Yale University Press, 1970]); theories of literary interpretation (*The Conflict of Interpretations: Essays in Hermeneutics,* ed. Don Ihde, trans. Willis Domingo et al. [Evanston, Ill.: Northwestern University Press, 1974]; *The Rule of Metaphor: Multi-Disciplinary Studies of the Creation of Meaning in Language,* trans. Robert Czerny with Kathleen McLaughlin and John Costello, S.J. [London: Routledge and Kegan Paul, 1978]); *Interpretation Theory: Discourse and the Surplus of Meaning* [Fort Worth: Texas Christian University Press, 1976]); methodology in the humanistic disciplines (*Hermeneutics and the Human Sciences: Essays on Language, Action, and Interpretation,* ed., trans., and intro. John B. Thompson [Cambridge: Cambridge University Press, 1981]); critical theory (*Lectures on Ideology and Utopia,* ed. George H. Taylor [New York: Columbia University Press, 1986]); and theological construction (*Essays on Biblical Interpretation,* ed. Lewis S. Mudge [Philadelphia: Fortress Press, 1980]).
2. The central work in this regard is *Fallible Man,* which has been supplemented by the recent *Soi-même comme un autre* (Paris: Editions du Seuil, 1990).
3. For details, see the essays below by Robert Scharlemann, John Van Den Hengel, Mark I. Wallace, David E. Klemm, and William Schweiker.
4. Ricoeur, *Freud and Philosophy,* p. 9.
5. Ricoeur, *Conflict of Interpretations,* pp. 71–73.
6. Ricoeur, "Explanation and Understanding," in *The Philosophy of Paul Ricoeur: An Anthology of His Work,* ed. Charles E. Regan and David Stewart (Boston: Beacon Press, 1978), p. 165.

PART I

FUNDAMENTAL ISSUES IN INTERPRETATION

ROBERT P. SCHARLEMANN

Beings

THE TEXTUALITY OF TEXTS

For this paper, I should like to focus attention on a matter that Ricoeur's hermeneutics seems to leave out of account. That matter can be designated by the word *textuality,* and a consideration of it will take us somewhat beyond both Ricoeur's and Heidegger's conceptions of hermeneutics on two points: the status of a text, and the question of the world we are in through the reading of texts or, generally, of literature. The setting of the discussion here is defined in part by Heidegger's distinctions in the modes of being. They will be familiar to Heidegger readers, but they can be enumerated here to make the background of the discussion explicit. The modes include: (1) the way in which tools are tools (they are not observed or contemplated but used); (2) the way in which objects are objects (they are set over against us for observation, inspection, analysis); (3) the way in which human being is human being (it is just "there," *Dasein*); (4) the way in which other human beings are other human beings (they are "there too with" us); (5) the way in which a work of art is a work of art (it is a "worlding" of the world); and (6) the way in which a poetic word is a poetic word (it is a self-annunciation of the meaning of being as being). It is particularly the third to the sixth modes that are pertinent to the present discussion; for the thesis that I shall develop is that a text is "there too with" us differently from the way in which other human beings are "there too with" us, because texts are there in the materiality of linguistic signs rather than that of a physical body. This is to say that the mode of being of texts, indicated by the word *textuality,* is not among the modes enumerated from Heidegger but that it can be defined by comparison with the "being there too with" us that does appear in Heidegger.

The two points of the status of a text and of the world we are in when reading literature can be formulated in two questions:

1. Is Ricoeur's definition of *text* as "any discourse fixed in writing" sufficient to bring into view the phenomenon of textuality?[1]
2. Is the definition of temporality contained in the experience of time and in the narrative timing that Ricoeur traces from Augustine and Aristotle to a contemporary historical consciousness sufficient to make intelligible the possibility of an existence that is other than a *Sein zum Tode* (being-toward-death)?

Particularly if we are thinking of questions at the intersection of *biblical* theology and literature, it is striking that Ricoeur's reflections do not incorporate a consideration of the sense in which, for example, the Apostle Paul can write to his readers that they have already died. Ricoeur's discussion of time in the most recently completed of his major works, the three-volume *Time and Narrative,* is oriented to the experience of time recounted in his confessions by Augustine and to the temporal structuring that Aristotle defines as *mythos* and sets over against timeless logos. It culminates in a notion of historical consciousness—Ricoeur's retrieval in temporal form of the Hegelian absolute knowledge—as a unity of the expressions of lived time, as in Augustine, and the time of poiesis, as in Aristotle and in fiction. But it does not ask whether there is a consciousness, perhaps other than historical, for which the relation of future and past is different from what it is in existential and historical time. It does not, in other words, ask whether any sense can be made of a text such as Paul's letter to the Colossians when he writes to recipients, who can themselves read or have read to them what he writes, that they have already died and been buried: "If then you have been raised with Christ, seek the things that are above, where Christ is, seated at the right hand of God. Set your minds on things that are above, not on things that are on earth. For you have died, and your life is hid with Christ in God. When Christ who is our life appears, then you also will appear with him in glory" (Col. 3:1–2). For such a being beyond death fits neither with existential time nor with the time of historical consciousness, nor does this excerpt from a Pauline letter fit into any of the genres that Ricoeur discusses in his biblical hermeneutics, which culminates in the theological mediation of religious expressions.

I should like to treat these questions by suggesting how, on one side, Ricoeur's own work in hermeneutics, including *Time and Narrative,* and, on another side, Bultmann's notion of kerygma both lead toward a concept of textuality that lies beyond Ricoeur's definition of a text as discourse fixed in writing, toward a concept of textuality that might make sense of a text that counterreads the existential understanding and presents a mode of being in the world wholly that is other than the *Sein zum Tode,* or always having to end, that is the being whole of *Dasein* in Heidegger's analysis—in other words, a mode of existence other than a being-here-now that is a being in view of the possibility of having no possibility of being in the world. Ricoeur's hermeneutics will not explain either the full novelty of Bultmann's conception of kerygma within the context of historical criticism and the rhetorical tradition or the way in which a poetic work has more to it than what Ricoeur calls a redescription of reality. A text's world is not just a redescription of the real or existential world but, we can say, a being there of another world (a "worlding" of the world, in Heideggerian language) and another voice just as each human person is a being-there of the self in the world of concern; and, if that is the case, then the textuality of a text is an articulated body that localizes a being in the world just as the human flesh and bones are an articulated body that localizes, or gives a here-and-now to, a being in the world.

Reflection and Poetic Mediation

There is a common pattern in Ricoeur's "Biblical Hermeneutics" (1975) and his three-volume *Time and Narrative.* It is the pattern in which the function of poetic creation is to redescribe the reality that is initially described in the prereflective, or ordinary-language, descriptions of reality. Ricoeur relocates metaphor by taking it out of the context of naming and putting it into the context of predicating. Metaphors are not, then, rhetorical figures in which one noun is substituted for another because of certain resemblances. They are, rather, operations in discourse. They apply to word units only by first applying to sentence units, and they function because of the way sentences, in which contradictory or impertinent predications are made of a thing, give a twist to the meaning of the word so as to disclose a new dimension in the reality to which the discourse refers. Initially there is a suspension of reference in the poetic creation. This is most evident in purely fictional works. But in the metaphorical process the suspension is in the service of making a new reference to reality by way of the metaphorical redescription, showing this reality in a dimension that is new when compared with the dimensions shown in the ordinary descriptions. This is as true of Ricoeur in the three-volume *Time and Narrative* as it is of the earlier hermeneutical works. Of the three strands that are woven together in this latest work, two have to do with an impasse in the effort to understand time in the Augustinian meditation on time and in the Aristotelian notion of myths as the temporal structuring of narrative; the third strand has to do with Husserl and Heidegger.

The aporetics of the Augustinian and Aristotelian conceptions lies in the fact that the one cannot show how cosmic time is derivable from psychological time and the other cannot show how psychological time is derived from the cosmological. From the Augustinian "present" we cannot get an Aristotelian "instant," nor conversely. Augustine's own perplexity about time is that he cannot define what he can understand. He can readily understand what is meant by time when anyone talks about it. But he cannot find a concept to define what he thus understands. Time eludes definition; we cannot conceive what it is because we cannot get into view the measure that time means. The future cannot be the measure because there is no extension to the future; the past cannot be the measure because there is no extension to the past; and the present cannot be the measure because, by the time the "now" has become a now with extension, it is already past.[2]

There is—to put it in Kantian terms—no sense-intuition of time. Augustine can arrive at an answer only when he relates time to the measuring that is done by the soul that is distended between its memory and its expectation in the present attention. When I am reciting a memorized canticum, a psalm or a song, "I," who attend to my reciting, am stretched between the part I have already recited and the part I am still to recite; but I as I must be capable of that distension, of being with the past and with the future in the present. But this will explain cosmic time, or the history that occurs outside the self, only by recourse to a mind that does for the whole of history what the individual self does in its own recitation of a verse. Augustine can account for cosmic time only by the intermediate step of a divine mind that is related to the whole of history as an individual reciter is related to the recitation of a verse, but that otherwise does not appear in the experience of time itself. This, it should be added, is not a perplexity for Augustine himself, for he comes upon the question of time only with a sense of the immediate presence of the Eternal.[3]

From Augustine, Ricoeur traces a line, which I shall not retrace here, through Kant to Husserl and Heidegger.[4] The second route that he follows is that of "verbal" experience in Aristotle's notion of myths, or narrative. Myth is a kind of recitation, or telling, but not the lived order of the recitation of a memorized verse. It also shapes material, but it does so differently from the nontemporal sequence in logos. Logos—propositions, syllogisms, sorites—does have sequence but without respect to time; myth is a temporal sequence. In explicating the theory of time involved in such narrative shaping, Aristotle has recourse to the counting and measurement connected with the ability to divide a continuum ad infinitum. Because of the possibility of dividing infinitely, the concept of the now, which divides past and future, is not that of the present, as in Augustine, but that of the infinitely divisible instant dividing any past and any future. But just as Augustine cannot derive cosmic from psychic time, so Aristotle cannot derive the psychic from the cosmic. As his own hypothesis, Ricoeur develops the theme that, although there is no ground common to these psychological and cosmological times, there is a poetic mediation between the two. Though neither can be derived from the other, nor both from a common notion of temporality, the two can be mediated by a work of imagination that bears a relation to both the world and the self. In a poetic narrative there is a unity of the lived and the created, but this is a unity of the two in a new medium rather than in something common or generic. In one direction, it is historical consciousness as the soul's consciousness of a passage of time outside the soul; and, in the other direction, it is real world history, the telling of a passage of time in cosmic reality through a narrative poiesis.

Hence, Ricoeur's own answer to the question "What is time?" is contained in the notion of historical consciousness as related not just to the distension of the soul but also to real world history. But that is not the complete answer. The other part of it, having to do with the inscrutability of time, is related to the pattern in which Ricoeur, here as in his other works, moves from the reflective to the hermeneutical or, more exactly, to the hermeneutics of myths and symbols and of prereflective rhetoric. We can find our way into this aspect of Ricoeur's theme by recalling the Kantian distinction between a rational idea and an aesthetic idea suggested in the Third Critique but not elaborated systematically. A rational idea is defined as a concept for which an adequate intuition can never be given.[5] There are three such ideas in Kant—the self as free, the world as a spatiotemporal totality, and God as unconditioned or absolute. None of these ideas can ever be presented in an intuition, because each of them contains an inner, insoluble dialectic of opposite intuitions; each is an infinite idea. The idea of the world as a totality, for example, is such that we have to think of the world as having boundaries in space and as unbounded in space or as having a beginning in time and not having a beginning in time. The insolubility of the dialectic lies in the fact that, whichever of the two positions we take as a thesis for an argument or proof, we are inescapably led to proving the antithesis as well. This dialectic lies in the rational idea, and it is the reason why the idea can never be given in an intuition, like an empirical object, or constructed as a representation of the intuition, like geometric objects.

An aesthetic idea, by contrast, is defined as an intuition for which no concept can be adequate.[6] Such an idea has the function of giving occasion to think, that is, of eliciting an attempt to conceive what it is an idea of, but of doing so in such a way that no concept can ever be adequate to the intuition the idea provides. The aesthetic idea, as Kant put it, *veranlaßt zum Denken,* gives us a lot to think about. Heidegger expresses the same meaning with *gibt zum Denken,* and Ricoeur with *donne à penser.* Whether one calls it an aesthetic idea, along with Kant, or a symbol, along with Ricoeur, the phenomenon in both cases is the same. A symbol differs from a reflective concept as an aesthetic idea does from a rational idea; the one is an intuition in an unending search for a concept to interpret it, and the other is a concept in a similar search for an intuition to fill it. An aesthetic idea presents something to view, but what it presents can never be adequately grasped in a concept of what it is; it always elicits a further effort to think it through.

That is the Kantian background of the Ricoeur who once described himself in his hermeneutics as being "in an ironical manner" a "post-Hegelian Kantian."[7] One example of this is contained in *Fallible Man* (part of a still-incomplete project under the title *Philosophy of the Will*) in the gap between fallibility and fault. Reflection can grasp the possibility of failure or of fault on the basis of an analysis of the human synthesis of infinite and finite—infinite verb and finite perspective in the theoretical, infinite happiness and finite character in the practical, and infinite happiness and finite pleasure in the affective synthesis. But it cannot retrace the movement from the possibility of failing to its actuality. In the aporetics of time brought out in *Time and Narrative,* a similar turn is made, but not until the very end of the work and as a kind of postscript. In the end it turns out that one cannot say what time is, one can only express indirectly in the language of praise, lamentation, and hope the phenomenon of time. This is, in effect, a turning from reflection on time to another kind of discourse, like the interpretation of symbols. Before reaching that point, however, Ricoeur undertakes to show what can be resolved by a poetic reprise of lived history. His hypothesis is that, for historical consciousness, world history is the poetic refiguration of the temporally lived experience by means of the imaginative, or the creative. Historical consciousness is a consciousness both psychological and cosmological. It can be such, however, only if existential history is more than what it is in Heidegger's account of historicality: it is more than the effect of the past that endures in the present consciousness because it depends in part upon the phenomenon of the document as a trace of the past—or of what really was so, unremembered, and outside of the present consciousness of it—in order to distinguish real historical consciousness from existential historicality alone.

Time and Narrative is a richer and more differentiated discussion than in Ricoeur's other treatises on similar questions. But it preserves the same pattern of poietic mediation between the unreflected language of lived experience and the language of fiction. The concept of text, as discourse fixed in writing, comes in by the way in which a poetic work, when written, becomes independent of an author's intention so that its meaning can speak anonymously. But Ricoeur does not advance to what would seem to be the next step, that is to say, to a full concept of the textuality of texts. I want to take up this matter by a detour through Heidegger's *Being and Time,* which will, I think, make somewhat clearer what is at issue in the concept of textuality.

Dasein, *Work, and Text*

Whether one regards the later development of Heidegger as still belonging to phenomenology or as going beyond it (as Heidegger himself indicated), there is in any case a change of direction when attention is shifted from ordinary talk to poetic words. In *Being and Time,* the aim of arriving at an understanding of being through an analysis of being-there, or existence, remained unaccomplished; for nothing in the analysis of the being of *Dasein* made it possible to show that temporality, which is the meaning of the being of *Dasein,* is also the horizon against which the meaning of being as such appears and is intelligible. The being of *Dasein* is, according to this existential analysis, care (*Sorge, cura*), in the sense that everything one does to be in the world is an expression of caring—taking care of, caring for, caring about, and, finally, just caring about being at all; and the meaning of this being is temporality, in the sense that the reason why we care is given by the way in which the self is stretched between its having been and its about to be. But the analysis that thus culminates in temporality as the meaning of being in the world cannot disclose whether this temporality is also the horizon for the appearance of the meaning of being as such. If the being of being-in, of indwelling the world, has the form of care, what form has being as such? Nothing in the understanding of the meaning of being-in makes it possible to leap from there to an understanding of being as being. Hence, some beginning other than analysis of *Dasein* is required.

Is it only one other beginning or two other beginnings? The answer depends upon the question whether we are to distinguish between artworks and poetic works in the later Heidegger. Let me choose, without arguing the case here, that in the later Heidegger *Dichtung* (poetry) and *Kunstwerk* (artwork) are to be distinguished from each other and not only from *Dasein*. The distinction is this: an artwork shows the meaning of "being-in" in a "worlding" of the world, and it is thus a direct parallel to the meaning of "being-in" shown in the care of *Dasein;* but a poet's word shows the meaning of "being" itself through a meaning that says the meaning of being as being. Thus Heidegger, citing Hölderlin, can describe the philosopher and the poet as dwelling in closest proximity on mountains farthest apart.[8] The one says what the other asks; but the philosopher who asks cannot hear what the poet says, just as the poet who says cannot grasp what the philosopher asks. The messenger from the one to the other is Hermes, and hermeneutics becomes the medium of a conversation between asking about the meaning of being and saying the meaning of being, or naming the holy. Thus we have, in both the earlier and the later Heidegger, being as it is shown in the careful being of *Dasein* that is a "selfing" of being there; in the playful being of the work of art that is a "worlding" constituted by the interplay of mortals and divinities, sky and earth; and, finally, in the opening of being marked by the philosopher's question and the poet's saying. None of these three, however, extends quite to the possibility that the textuality of texts, that is, the articulated materiality of their signs, is neither the careful being of human *Dasein* nor the playful being, the

Spiegelspiel ("mirror play"), of the fourfold in a work of art nor yet the self-annunciation of being as such in a poetic word, but is rather the being there of a material sign different in its materiality from the physical body. This is the possibility suggested by the development in hermeneutics associated with such Heidegger interpreters as Derrida. For here writing is accorded a material autonomy that makes of a text the materialization of an understanding of being other than that of our own being-there and other than the "worlding" of a work of art. Textuality, that is to say, is a mode of being other than that of tools that are at hand or of objects that are present to us or of other human beings who are there with us or of an artwork or, finally, of a poetic word. It is, rather, the mode of being that, like other human beings, is there with us but that, unlike other human beings, has its place materially defined, not by a physical body, but by, let us say, its textual body. To put it in less Heideggerian language, we can say that in a text we can not only indwell a world other than that of physical reality but also encounter another self, the "voice" of the text, just as we encounter another self in other human existents, and that this voice of the text need not be identical with the biographical person who is the author of the text.

If this is so, then the way in which Rudolf Bultmann used the concept of kerygma to break through the historical criticism of New Testament texts to something else signals an anticipation of the very notion of textuality. The stumbling block of New Testament criticism was, from D. F. Strauss forward, provided by the resurrection narratives; for unlike the historical criticism in the period between Semler's and his own, Strauss did not call a halt to critique at those narratives. Rather, he could lay down, for critical historical understanding, the axiom that dead people do not come back to life. A person who is dead at a certain time cannot later be seen alive; and someone seen to be alive cannot already have been "wholly dead."[9] The axiom of the finality of death separates historical from mythical time-consciousness. Yet historical critique, unlike Enlightenment rationalism, would not simply discount the resurrection narratives either. It would, rather, seek an explanation of their origin and what they are about—it would seek their *Ursprung* (source), to use the term from Heidegger on a work of art—in their mythical form. What (Strauss thus asks) would Jews of the time have done when the person they believed to be the Messiah was put to death and their hopes shattered? "His death, which [the disciples] were unable to reconcile with the messianic ideas, had for the moment," Strauss writes in the *Life of Jesus*, "annihilated their belief." When that happened, his followers did what they might be expected to do in order to understand what had taken place. They read again the prophecies of the coming of the Messiah, for "to comprehend [an event] meant nothing else than to derive [its occurrence] from the sacred scriptures."[10] As they then came to see that the prophecies concerning the messianic reign and those concerning the suffering servant of the Lord pertained not to two but to one event, they came to understand that the death of Jesus, far from being a refutation of his messianic character, constituted its fulfillment; and it was this understanding that turned their disappointment into joy and turned them into heralds of the resurrected Jesus.

The resurrection narratives do, of course, tell of Jesus' being raised from the dead. They do not report that the disciples, upon rereading their bibles, gained a new understanding of Jesus' death. (Nor, of course, do they report that the disciples, having lost their tenure as teachers in the school of Jesus, proceeded to set up a school of Christ in its place.) Peter, according to the Book of Acts, tells his Pentecost audience that God had raised the very Jesus whom they had put to death and, moreover, that it was necessary for this to happen (Acts 2:22–23). But historical criticism evaluates such reports from the standpoint of the manner in which myth and dogma are involved in human understanding.[11] Myth is a way of telling certain truths; and dogma is the speculative recovery of the myth whose empirical interpretation criticism destroys.[12] But Bultmann, admirable New Testament critic though he was, adds something quite new to this historical account in his assertion that Jesus was resurrected into the kerygma. "In the word of preaching and there alone," he writes in the famous essay of 1941 on demythologizing, "we meet the risen Lord."[13] There is no indication that Bultmann was only using a rhetorical figure, a metaphor even, when he wrote such words. The aim of existentialist interpretation, as Bultmann practiced it, goes beyond historical critique, Bultmann's own as well as others'. For its intention is to make possible an encounter with the same reality of which the disciples spoke when they told of the resurrection. It may be true that Bultmann, at least now and then, too readily equated the mode of being made possible by such a kerygmatic encounter with what Heidegger called *Eigentlichkeit*, or authenticity. For there is an important difference between an existence that has death behind it and one that (like authentic existence in Heidegger's analysis) has death ahead of it. But the intention of the concept of kerygma is clear. If Jesus was resurrected into the kerygma, then the kerygma is the materiality of his living presence, and the word of preaching is not concerned with interpreting the meaning of the words of a text but with mediating the living reality in them. The preaching of the cross, Bultmann said, has the aim of issuing anew the summons to take up one's own cross and follow. Barth may not have been far off the mark when he detected in Bultmann's hermeneutics a trace of Lutheran sacramentalism, although the category of the sacramental is surely misplaced here. There is no continuation or restoration or representation of the flesh-and-blood person who was Jesus of Nazareth, a contemporary of his first disciples. There is, rather, a textual embodiment of an "I am" and "Follow me!" that was embodied in the person of Jesus and can be heard as the living voice, the kerygma, of the text. Bultmann bound the kerygma to the biblical text, at least as far as Christian preaching was concerned. One could read this position as nothing more than a restoration or continuation of a certain Protestant biblicism, and Bultmann's abrupt termination of his dialogue with Karl Jaspers over the question of the uniqueness of the biblical text might feed that suspicion.[14] But it is also likely that there is a different motive at work. For if the very textuality of a text is taken into account, then the unique voice of a text, any text with such textuality, cannot be abstracted from the text itself any more than the individuality of a person can be abstracted from the organism that is that person's body. There can be similar voices and similar texts, just as there are similar characters and similar bodies among human beings. But the uniqueness of any real self is defined by the body that is its articulated here-and-now, the *Da* (there) of its *Dasein* (being-there). If texts have textuality in this sense, then their voices are inseparably joined with the ordered words that uniquely articulate a here-now of the voice of the text. In this way it would be true that the New Testament kerygma is bound with the articulation that is the textuality of New Testament texts.

This has now brought us to the point I wish to reach. If a text like Colossians 3:1–3 can read the existence that is *Dasein* contrary to *Dasein*'s understanding of its own being, if the voice of that writing can be "there too with" us just as much as other human beings, it can do so because its textuality localizes the voice of another way of being in another world just as our psychical and physical bodies localize our existential being. In that other way of being, the self in its futurity—its possibility of having no possibility of being in the world—comes to itself in the actuality of its here-and-now and the temporality of care is converted into the temporality of carefree being (like the lilies of the field that neither toil nor spin). If the being of *Dasein* is care, and the meaning of that being is temporality, then the being that is the textuality of such texts is a freedom beyond care, and the temporality that is its meaning is one in which the future—namely, the self in its own impossibility—has become the past.

Textuality means, in other words, that the literary work, this structured whole of words and sentences, is not only a redescription of the reality of being there in the world, as it is in Ricoeur's theory of metaphor, but another form of being there in the world. If this is so, we can ask not only what world is displayed in a work of imagination but also who is the self, who is the voice, that is there in the textual inscription. Ricoeur's hermeneutics does not extend so far as to make such a question possible. Nor does Heidegger's. I have suggested here that the reason lies in the absence of the essential concept of textuality.

NOTES

1. "Appelons texte tout discours fixé par l'écriture. Selon cette définition, la fixation par l'écriture est constitutive du texte lui-même" (Paul Ricoeur, "Qu'est-ce qu'un texte?" in *Hermeneutik und Dialektik,* ed. Rudiger Bubner, Konrad Cramer, and Reiner Wiehl [Tübingen: J. C. B. Mohr Paul Siebeck, 1970], p. 181).
2. "In quo ergo spatio metimur tempus praeteriens? Utrum in futuro, unde praeterit? Sed quod nondum 'est' non metimur. An in prasesenti, qua praeterit? Sed nullum spatium non metimur. An in praeterito, quo praeterit? Sed quod iam non 'est' non metimur." (We cannot measure time in the future because the future is not anything yet; nor the present because the present has no extension; nor the past because the past no longer is [Augustine, *Confessiones,* Leipzig: B. G. Teubneri, 1934, book 11, part 21, line 27]). My translation.
3. "Numquid, domine, cum tu sit aeternitas, ignoras, quae tibi dico, aut ad tempus vides quod fit in tempore? Cur ergo tibi tot rerum narrationes digero? (Since, O Lord, you are eternity, is there really anything of what I say to you that you do not already know? Do you see temporally what happens in time? Why then do I range so widely in telling you so many things?" [Augustine, *Confessiones,* book 11, part 1, line 1]). Again: "Quisnam ille modus est quo doces futura, cui futurum quicquam non est?" (What is the manner in which you, for whom there is no future, teach future things? [book 19, line 25]). My translation.
4. Attention might, however, be called, first, to the way in which Husserl's *Zeitobjekt,* a sound as it is heard, together with the distinction between retention and recollection, does provide a way of identifying an extension in the now, and, second, to the way in which Heidegger associates the question of time with understanding (rather than with intuition) and changes the meaning of the

modes of time when he interprets the future as the *Zukunft* (the coming-to, or advent) of the self to itself.

5. A rational idea is "a concept to which no intuition (representation of the imagination) can be adequate" (Immanuel Kant, *Kritik der Urteilskraft* [Hamburg: F. Meiner, 1959], A 190, B 193; see also A 237, B 240). My translation.
6. "By an aesthetic idea I understand that representation of the imagination that gives a lot to think about [*viel zu denken veranlaßt*] without its being the case, however, that a definite thought, i.e., concept, can be adequate to it, an idea that consequently no language completely reaches or can make understandable. It is easy to see that such an idea is the counterpart of a rational idea, which, conversely, is a concept for which no intuition (representation of the imagination) can be adequate" (Kant, *Kritik der Urteilskraft,* A 190, B 192, 193). My translation.
7. Ricoeur, "Biblical Hermeneutics," in *Paul Ricoeur on Biblical Hermeneutics,* ed. John Dominic Crossan (Missoula, Mont.: SBL, 1975), p. 142: no. 4 of *Semeia: An Experimental Journal for Biblical Criticism.*
8. "We may know something about the relations between philosophy and poetry, but we know nothing of the dialogue between poet and thinker, who 'dwell near to one another on mountains farthest apart' [Hölderlin, "Patmos"]." So Heidegger wrote in the Postscript of 1943 to his "What Is Metaphysics?" in *Existence and Being,* trans. Douglas Scott, R. F. C. Hull, and Alan Crick, with an introduction by Werner Brock (Chicago: Henry Regnery, 1949), p. 360.
9. David Friedrich Strauss, *The Life of Jesus Critically Examined,* trans. from the 4th German ed. (1840) by George Eliot, ed. Peter Hodgson (Philadelphia: Fortress Press, 1972), p. 736.
10. Ibid., p. 742.
11. Ibid., pp. 86–92, 757–58.
12. Ibid., p. 757: the task is "to reestablish dogmatically what has been destroyed critically."
13. Rudolf Bultmann, "The New Testament and Mythology," in *Kerygma and Myth,* ed. Hans Werner Bartsch (New York: Harper Torchbook, 1961), p. 43.
14. Karl Jaspers and Rudolf Bultmann, *Myth and Christianity: An Inquiry into the Possibility of Religion without Myth* (New York: Noonday Press, 1958).

GERALD BRUNS

AGAINST POETRY

Heidegger, Ricoeur, and the Originary Scene of Hermeneutics

> But there is another side to literature. Literature is a concern for the reality of things, for their unknown, free, and silent existence; literature is their innocence and forbidden presence, it is the being which protests against revelation, it is the defiance of what does not want to take place outside. In this way, it sympathizes with darkness, with aimless passion, with lawless violence, with everything in the world that seems to perpetuate the refusal to come into the world. In this way, too, it allies itself with the reality of language, it makes language into matter without contour, content without form, a force that is capricious and impersonal and says nothing, reveals nothing, simply announces—through its refusal to say anything—that it comes from night and will return to night.
>
> —MAURICE BLANCHOT,
> *"Literature and the Right to Death," 1949.*

MY TITLE is meant to take us back to the quarrel between philosophy and poetry that Socrates already regarded as ancient. My sense is that every hermeneutical situation has the structure of this quarrel, which is governed by a logic that is by turns exclusionary and allegorical. Plato's idea seems to have been that poetry embodies something, we're not sure what, that interferes with the sort of discourse that Socrates is trying to set up and that he seems to be practicing in texts like the *Republic,* where one statement follows another more or less justifiably or according to some principle of internal necessity. Call this saying what has to be said. Poetry is somehow not this sort of saying. Whatever it is, poetry seems subversive of justice and necessity. It seems to be on the loose in our talk, or in our world, causing things to go out of control. It is of course in the nature of words to run around loose, we are never really able to pin them down. But poetry seems to institute this ambiguity or misrule, as if poetry were some sort of antiprinciple principle, or as if there were some internal or even metaphysical link between poetry and anarchy, say of the sort that Artaud imagined when he said that whenever "the poetic spirit is exercised, it always moves toward a kind of seething anarchy, a total breakdown of reality by poetry."[1] Philosophy at all events is principled; it stakes itself on saving us from precisely such things as "the breakdown of reality by poetry." It seeks, among other things, a world in which things are just so and not otherwise. Moreover, it is the sort of discourse that helps to produce such a world by keeping things straight and getting them down exactly. Philosophy is that discourse that makes a point of keeping itself under control and works to make the world behave likewise, teaching every discourse to be ever watchful, as if to bring the world under its claim. In a world presided over by philosophy's kind of self-control—in a world instituted by the propositional style of philosophical discourse—it's hard to see how poetry, according to Plato's (or Artaud's) description of it, could be tolerated.

The *Republic* is, of course, a principal chapter in Plato's story about the self-sufficiency of philosophy. It is in the nature of philosophy, or of reason, to seal itself off from whatever is not itself, or, much to the same point, to convert whatever is not itself into some simulacrum or facsimile answerable to its norms. The logic of appropriation is simply a working out in another form of the logic of exclusion, rather in the sense that Aristotle's *Poetics* is not so much a reversal of book 10 of the *Republic* as an extension of it. Aristotle understood that a less Draconian method of getting rid of poetry would be to redescribe it so as to make it a systematic part of philosophy. Martha Nussbaum has shown that already in Plato's *Phaedrus* the possibility of a philosophical poetry is worked out more or less as a lesson in how to take up the challenge Socrates lays down in the *Republic,* namely, that having heard the case against her, all lovers of poetry should now come to her defense.[2] But it was Aristotle who actually made a place for poetry in the organon or general theory of the logos, which we might think of as a sort of republic of discourse. Here the idea is, first, to read poetry so as to count it, in some sense, as knowledge, that is, as connecting us up, in some hypothetical fashion, with reality, and, second, to lay bare poetry's deep structure so as to say that it has a kind of necessary consecutiveness about it and therefore can be made to work as a kind of reasoning, say a logic of discovery. So it is no trouble to get poetry to meet the claims of justice and necessity. The concepts of mimesis and plot, one might say, have no other justification.

In thinking this way about poetry, giving it a logic and a power of cognition, Aristotle was following the ancient and abiding rule of allegory, which is that if a poetic text is scandalous with respect to reason, we must rewrite it or, much to the same point, find a way of reading it that removes the scandal. Western culture has always been deeply allegorical in its operations and results; it has a special genius for constructing ways of reading poetry, or any alien discourse, so as to make that discourse consistent with its own prevailing cultural norms. It was nothing to convert Homer and the Hebrew Bible into foundational texts. Aristotle's achievement was to make tragic poetry a branch of moral philosophy, and doubtless he did much the same for comedy—although maybe not, since comedy, being so completely at home with anarchy and misrule, is probably unphilosophizable.

Historically there are two faces of allegory: one formal, the other transcendental. On the one side there is the tradition of poetics, whose task has always been the demystification of divine madness, the restraint of genius by rules. Poetics turns poetry to rational account by seeming to make it teachable, even though it is still theoretically mad. This is the classical or sober Latin view that reigned from Roman antiquity to Milton. Poetry is poiesis, a craft of language, a branch of rhetoric concerned with versification and the use of figures: in short, a school subject. Poetry has no matter intrinsic to itself but draws its meaning from philosophy, theology, and history. The modern version of this idea comes down to us from Kant in the form of a theory of aesthetic differentiation and, more recently, in the history of literary criticism, where poetry is set apart as an object of various competing forms of analytic, strategic, instrumental, or calculative reasoning. In structuralist poetics this instrumental approach is expanded to a global interest in the rules by which texts as such are constituted. Whatever it is on the surface, poetry has a lawlike deep structure or textual logic continuous with the logic of culture itself, whence it is but a short step to convert poetics into a general cultural analytic in which all discursive and nondiscursive modes of production can be examined from within the conceptual frame of a single methodological outlook. Richard Rorty summarizes a general view when he says that we would be better off dropping the distinction between poetry and philosophy altogether and speaking instead of a "general undifferentiated text."[3]

One could describe this idea as a sort of postmodern Aristotelianism in which the quarrel between philosophy and poetry is not so much resolved as absorbed into a total organon of discourse or the theory of vast networks of weaving and reweaving vocabularies.

On the other hand, there is the idea, sometimes underwritten by appeals to Plato's *Phaedrus*, that poetry is more vision than craft and that, at a certain level, philosophy and poetry are identical: that is, they are expressions of the same transcendental spirit. Marx turned this romantic idea more or less on its head and so recovered something of the original radicalism of Platonic hermeneutics. Louis Althusser, for example, sees Marx as antiallegorical, dissipating "the religious myth of reading" that has always tried to save texts by integrating them into an "expressive totality" organized around a transcendental logos.[4] Henceforward the constitution of a culture free from mental bondage requires the exclusion of the text that, however beautiful in itself, is nevertheless an ideological instrument; and perhaps the more beautiful it is, the more sinister. Like the Platonist, the historical materialist cannot contemplate poetry without horror or, at the very least, without cautious detachment.[5] Like Aristotle, the historical materialist will allow only a poetry of realism, plenty of Balzac but no *Finnegans Wake*, narrative logic but no lyrical density. But naturally there is some question (which Althusser readily acknowledges) as to whether such a constitution of an ideology-free culture is possible. The idea of a true consciousness or a consciousness purified of whatever is not itself is just what Nietzsche ridiculed with his idea that Western culture is poetic all the way down. It is Nietzsche who reminds us of what embarrassed Socrates, namely, that the Republic has to be founded, if founded at all, on the repressed or forgotten lie. Nietzsche parodies the visionary politics of romanticism, where poetry is transcendental and foundational, no longer the art of making verses but a theory of world making in which, in

Friedrich Schlegel's view, the human spirit creates the world as its work of art. Neitzsche just gives this idea a Nietzschean interpretation.

Schlegel and Nietzsche come together in Heidegger's theory of poetry as a sort of primordial discourse that is both foundational for the world and at the same time a constant danger to it. In his Hölderlin lectures, Heidegger says that, contrary to the metaphysical tradition, language is not to be understood as any sort of linguistic or conceptual system; rather, it is an event in which all that is is summoned for the first time into openness of being; and this event is what Heidegger calls poetry (*Dichtung,* not *Poesie*). "The poet," Heidegger says, "names the gods and names all things in that which they are. This naming does not consist merely in something already known being supplied with a name; it is rather that when the poet speaks the essential word, the existent is by this naming nominated as what it is. Poetry is the establishing of being by means of the word." And Heidegger continues: "The speech of the poet is establishment . . . in the sense of the firm basing of human existence on its foundation."[6] However, this foundation is not the logical foundation of the philosophers. Rather, it is entirely historical and contingent, an opening into time and the future rather than onto some absolute antecedent ground. The world opened up in poetry is not (or not yet) a Kantian world answerable to the laws of reason. The poet's naming is not conceptual determination but a calling of what is singular and ungraspable as such. In the history of the West, philosophy originates as that which tries to rationalize this naming, that is, to interpret or make sense of it; but poetry can never be part of this interpretation. Philosophy tries to stabilize the world conceptually by means of the logical determination of what poetry brings into the open, but poetry itself refuses to be stabilized in this way. Philosophy's task is to preside over the open, taking the measure of what is, fixing it in place, but poetry is a turning loose. Or, in short, poetry is foundational, but it is not philosophical: it does not try to bring things under control; rather, it lets them go, lets them turn this way and that, luxuriates in ambiguity. But philosophically this is madness. Which is just to say once more that there is a primordial opposition between philosophy and poetry that cannot be done away with. Heidegger is foursquare with Plato on this point. But for Heidegger it is not so much that philosophy must therefore summarily banish the poet according to the old story; it is rather that poetry, although an event of world making, is not itself a worldly sort of speaking—that is, it is not a speaking that the world can contain. Poetry cannot be brought into the light of being; there is no place for it in the clearing that it opens up. As Heidegger puts it, the excessive brightness of the world drives the poet into the dark. As if exile, or blindness or madness, were the poet's natural condition. For Heidegger anyhow, the poet is always set apart, a Cain-like wanderer, both founder and exile.

It is possible to see in the Hölderlin lectures something like Heidegger's version of Plato's *Republic.* One can see this even more clearly in "The Origin of the Work of Art," with its strange, almost Gnostic opposition of world and earth.[7] Heidegger says that the *work* of the work of art, its truth, is to set up a world, but this event does not occur within an absolute or transcendental space. On the contrary, the world is finite, surrounded everywhere by what is not itself. Its disclosure occurs within the horizon of that which refuses disclosure, refuses the open: and this refusal is what Heidegger calls earth. Now if the work of art makes manifest the world, it also makes manifest the refusal of the earth. Indeed, the conflict of world and earth, what Heidegger calls the rift (*Riss*), is inscribed in the very structure or gestalt of the work. This rift shows itself in the withdrawal of the work, its self-refusal with respect to the world. The work is uncontainable within the world, resistant to its reasons, excessive with respect to the boundary that separates world from earth. The paradox of the work of art is that there is no place for it in the world it works to establish. Its sort of speaking, its words, cannot be made sense of in worldly terms. With respect to the light, it is all materiality and density (*Dichtheit*). For indeed the work of art is not an object that we can possess and that we can visit on pilgrimages to caves or museums or antique ruins. To be sure, the world can seem to appropriate the work, to find places and uses for it. This is just the basic allegorical task of criticism, aesthetics, and the philosophy of art (to name only these three). The work of art can be made part of the world's equipment. But in every appropriation of the work we will find that the work has withdrawn, that it no longer works its work. For the word *work* means both being and event. It has a double inflection as both the work and the *working* of the work, that is, its work as art. For the mode of existence of the work of art, its work, the happening of its truth, is a movement (Heidegger does not hesitate to call it a "struggle" or "strife") of disclosure and concealment, of self-showing and self-exile, of the lighting or clearing of beings and the self-refusal or withdrawal of all that exists into ambiguity and darkness. As if the work of the work of art were not just a world making but also a limit of the world and an encroachment upon it; as if the work not only opened up the world but also exposed it to what is not itself or to what refuses it, namely, the self-secluding earth. "The world," Heidegger says, "in resting upon the earth, strives to surmount it. As self-opening it cannot endure anything closed. The earth, however, as sheltering and concealing, tends always to draw the world into itself and keep it there."[8] The work of the work of art opens a world, but the work, as a work, is self-closing; it remains of the earth—belongs to it, as Heidegger would say, primordially. And, this is why the world, as self-opening, cannot, finally, endure the work of art.

The work, indeed, is nothing but trouble to the world. In "The Origin of the Work of Art" Heidegger speaks of the "createdness" of the work, which is not so much a formal condition as rather a condition of its singularity and refractoriness within the world. In the world, the work is solitary, enigmatic, unapproachable, not for us, inhuman. The work of art opens a world, and it remains within the world as a breach, a rupture, a shaking that allows nothing to settle into place. "All art," he says, "as the letting happen of the advent of the truth of what is, is, as such, essentially poetry. . . . It is due to art's poetic nature that, in the midst of what is, art breaks open an open place, in whose openness everything is other than usual." In this breach, nothing seems to remain: "everything ordinary and hitherto becomes an unbeing."[9] It would not be too much to say that the task philosophy sets for itself is to interrupt this event, to close the breach, to preserve the identity and selfsameness of the world, that is, to set logical limits to the opening of the open, to establish the measure and boundary of the world, to settle the world and civilize it, bringing it under control. If the work of the work of art is to set up a world, the task of philosophy is to stabilize this event, perhaps to cut it off as if to prevent the endless dissemination of worlds. This is, in effect, the work of the logos, namely, to intervene in the work of the work of art, to master its effects, and render it accessible to reason, thereby instituting the world as a Republic. If there is a quarrel between philosophy and poetry, it begins here.

And here, one might say, is where Paul Ricoeur is to be found vis-à-vis Heidegger. We can think of Paul Ricoeur's hermeneutics of the text or his hermeneutics of narrative as philosophy's attempt to get on top of the event of art that Heidegger describes; it is to overcome the struggle of world and earth and to establish the world, not to mention the work of art, on properly philosophical foundations, freeing it, one might say, from the earth. Aristotle-like, Ricoeur's approach is not so much to banish poetry as to appropriate it, or anyhow to take over in the name of philosophy the worldly project of the poetic work.

The starting point of Ricoeur's hermeneutics of appropriation is the well-known distinction between system and history, structure and event. This distinction derives from an encounter between existentialism and structuralism, that is, between a tradition that concerns itself with the ontological condition of belonging to a concrete historical situation and a tradition that is concerned, Kant-like, with the formal or logical conditions that make things intelligible. The structure-event distinction, Ricoeur says, gives us two ways of thinking about language—the way of linguistics and the way of what he calls hermeneutics, where the one is concerned with langue, or with how language works as a system of signifiers, and the other is concerned with what is said, or parole.[10] Thus we can think of language in terms of signs or in terms of saying; that is, we can think of what words mean in relation to other words in any linguistic or semiotic system, or we can think of what they mean when they are used in actual speech, say in sentences. Somewhat loosely, Ricoeur maps onto this difference Frege's distinction between *Sinn* (ideal meaning), which has no internal connection with how things are in the world, and *Bedeutung* (actual meaning), which is always the product of assertion, of something said about something. Sometimes Ricoeur refers to the connection between these two orders of meaning in terms of a dialectic of semiotics and semantics, where semiotics has to do with the differential character of signifying systems and semantics with the referential meaning of sentences. For Ricoeur, the importance of the semiotic approach to language is that it disconnects meaning from the speaking subject.[11] Meaning is entirely internal to the linguistic system; it is not the product of consciousness or intentionality or any activity of the spirit. It is no longer anything occult; it is not anything that requires to be reconstructed or reproduced. On the other hand, for Ricoeur semiotics has one weakness, that it also disconnects meaning from the world, because if meaning is internal to the system—that is, simply a function of a chain of signifiers—then it becomes impossible to speak of anything outside the system. This is why Ricoeur wants to go beyond the semiotics of signifying systems to what he calls a semantics of the sentence, because it is in the *use* of language—in the making of predications in the world of everyday discourse—that language is reconnected to reality. Speaking does not occur inside a system; it is a practice that belongs to the environing world of circumstances in which human life runs its course, and it cannot help being about this world. In speaking, the meaning of signs is predicated of the world in which we find ourselves.

However, what happens when we shift discourse from the level of the sentence to the level of the text? In the first place, the situation of discourse is obliterated. A text is never the cry of its occasion. It is not anything one engages in a conversation. It does not have an inside and an outside like a speaking subject; it does not express itself like a "thou." A text is a structural object with its own intrinsic intelligibility; it is never an utterance. It can only be addressed by means of formal analysis. Moreover, the obliteration of the situation in which speakers discourse about the world also means that the referential movement of discourse is suspended by the text. There ceases to be a world referred to by the text. The text is not only self-contained but autotelic, closed off to its author and to the world of its composition, existing only for itself. This "leaves the text," Ricoeur says, "'in the air,' outside or without a world. In virtue of this obliteration of the relation to the world, each text is free to enter into relations with all other texts which come to take the place of the circumstantial reality referred to by living speech. This relation of text to text, within the effacement of the world about which we speak, engendered the quasi-world of texts or *literature.*" Literature is external to the world, and not only external. As Ricoeur says, "The role of most of our literature is . . . to destroy the world."[12]

I want to come back to this last line. But for now it is enough to say simply that texts are always alienating in the nature of the case; their autonomy means that they are always estranged from whatever is not a text—so that, indeed, formally speaking, it could only be by translating ourselves into texts that we could enter into the region where intelligibility, not to say self-understanding, is possible—a thought that Ricoeur pursues, for example, in "The Question of Proof in Freud's Psychoanalytic Writings," where the "truth" of psychoanalysis is the product of "constructing or reconstructing a coherent story or account from the tattered remains of our experience."[13] More important, however, the text's power of estrangement makes possible the reintroduction into hermeneutics of the historical, aesthetic, and critical distance that the ontological condition of belonging calls into question. We are always outside the texts that come down to us from the past or from alien cultures; these texts always project before us a difference from the situation in which we find ourselves. For Ricoeur, this difference, or what he calls "distanciation," restores the possibility of something like a critique of ideology. Ricoeur rejects the possibility of critique as someone like Althusser understands it, namely a critical analysis conducted from "a non-ideological place called science." The "critique of ideology," Ricoeur says, "never breaks its link to the basis of belonging," that is, it can never emancipate itself from its own historicality.[14] But this does not rule out the possibility of a "critical hermeneutics" that would be able to situate itself analytically outside that to which it nevertheless belongs ontologically. Tradition, after all, is always textual; it is not a "thou." In this respect the encounter with tradition would never be simply an act of recognition and acceptance; it would always require a critical appropriation of otherness, which is what Gadamer has in mind when he speaks of horizons that are fused but never unified or identical or subsumed into a higher or wider perspective. Horizon for Gadamer is not a perspectival concept.

For Gadamer, of course, this appropriation of the Other is radically unstable; one is always in danger of going to pieces in the encounter with alterity. This is not Ricoeur's view at all. For Ricoeur, the critical appropriation of otherness is methodological, more logical than ontological, anyhow without any dark side. In order to understand what Ricoeur means by *appropriation*, one has to go back to the inaugural distinction between the semiotics of signifying systems and the semantics of referential discourse. Ricoeur elevates this distinction into what he calls a second-order dialectic of structural explanation and hermeneutical understanding, where understanding fulfills itself in action in the world rather than in intellectual agreement with intentions, truth claims, concepts, or states of affairs. For Ricoeur, the text that comes down to us, say in tradition or from another culture, is, before everything else, a structural object that possesses its own intrinsic sense, its own laws of formal intelligibility. Its meaning is not anything that lies behind it in the form of an original intention or even an original reference to the time and place of its composition. Its meaning *is* its textuality. Textuality obliterates intentionality and referentiality in the process of objectifying itself. This is so particularly with literary texts where, Ricoeur says, "language seems to glorify itself at the expense of the referential function of ordinary discourse."[15]

Now what Ricoeur wants to argue is that the power of estrangement that texts exhibit nevertheless allows for the reconnection of discourse and a world outside of the text. "My thesis," Ricoeur says, "is that the abolition of first order reference, an abolition effected [for example] by fiction and poetry, is the condition of possibility for the freeing of a second order reference, which reaches the world not only at the level of manipulable objects but at the level that Husserl has designated by the expression *Lebenswelt* and Heidegger by the expression 'being in the world.' " For Ricoeur, the meaning of a text does not lie behind it in the region of intention and ostensive reference but *in front of it* in the space of interpretation. He writes as follows: "If we can no longer define hermeneutics in terms of the search for the psychological intentions of another person which are concealed *behind* the text, and if we do not want to reduce interpretation to the dismantling of structures, then what remains to be interpreted? I shall say: to interpret is to explicate the type of being-in-the-world unfolded *in front of* the text." This explication is not something to be worked out on paper. It is not an analytical project. Following the early Heidegger and Gadamer, Ricoeur emphasizes that understanding is a mode of being rather than simply an act of consciousness. "The moment of 'understanding,' " he says, "corresponds dialectically to being in a situation: it is 'the projection of our ownmost possibilities,' applying it to the theory of the text. For what must be interpreted in a text is a *proposed world* wherein I could project one of my ownmost possibilities. This is what I call the world of the text, the world proper to this unique text."[16]

What Ricoeur proposes is something very like a magical-looking-glass theory of textual meaning. The discourse of texts is phenomenological rather than logical or semiotic in the sense that reference means disclosure, bringing-to-appearance, rather than designation or representation. Texts mean, not by corresponding to states of affairs, not by satisfying truth conditions, but by manifesting or opening up a region of existence whose reality is not simply matter for analysis but is, on the contrary, matter for appropriation, that is, for intervention and action. The task of discourse in this sense would not be merely to picture reality but to throw light on the situation in which we find ourselves historically and to open up a path for us to follow in the way of action and conduct. The looking-glass theory of meaning presupposes an ontological turn away from epistemology toward a hermeneutics of praxis and action. It presupposes that our relationship with the world is not simply one of knowing but is one of being-with-others in states of affairs that require our intervention. *World* here is to be understood in its Heideggerian sense of ontological horizon rather than in the Kantian sense of objective representation. Thus the world that is disclosed in the text is to be thought of, not as discontinuous from our world, but as an enlargement of it, a movement of our world into the future; it is, however, a movement that can be actualized only to the extent that we act on what the text proposes, bring the text about by entering into our actual world in light of the world proposed by the text.

So we should think of ourselves as standing *before* the text and not only outside of it in some purely analytical space. The space of interpretation is always historical, always political and ethical as well as analytical—as it is, for example, in the case of legal interpretation, where we are always within the jurisdiction of what we seek to understand, whence our understanding is necessarily more than just the construction and analysis of legal propositions or more than the logical application of rules: it is a way of construing human social and political situations with respect to the action we are called upon to take in them. This interpretive action is always an intervention in reality; it alters reality for better or for worse—but always in the positive or negative light of the law. The law is a text that always projects consequences for those who find themselves before it or within its jurisdiction; its meaning lies, therefore, in its fulfillment in the future, not in the logical analysis of its internal structure or in the reconstruction of its originating intention. The law is always utopian. It projects a world; that is, a mode of being that bears upon our present existence in a historical time and place. Our relationship to the text, therefore, like our relationship with the world, is not merely theoretical; it is not just a relationship of knowing, or what we think of as knowing. The understanding of a text—any text, whether literary or legal, political or scientific—only begins to show itself in action.

Now it seems to me that what we have here is your basic Aristotelian theory of the text, and what is Aristotelian about it is just the way the text is saved or justified by being systematized and then reconnected to reality according to an up-to-date conception of mimesis—a looking-glass theory of mimesis that is, so to speak, beyond representation. As Ricoeur says in *Time and Narrative,* mimesis "takes on its full scope when the work deploys a world that the reader appropriates."[17] Were there time, I would go on to mention a number of very interesting versions of this theory developed by people like Arthur Danto, Martha Nussbaum, and Fredric

Jameson (good, cloth-coat Aristotelians one and all). But in fact one could trace the idea back through Luther and Augustine to the earliest beginnings of scriptural hermeneutics, where the idea is to interpret a text by understanding oneself and one's own historical situation in its light. The intelligibility of a text lies in its potential for fulfillment in the oncoming world of conduct and action, not in the reconstitution of an original message or state of affairs. In its heart of hearts hermeneutics is prophetic rather than nostalgic. So for Ricoeur, even mythic narratives cannot simply be framed as imaginary or aesthetic; they are not simply traces of a vanished world but are texts that expose our own actual world to alternative possibilities, and as such they cannot help bearing upon our world in critical ways, not just exposing us to the world's limits but exposing these limits as historical and contingent. The idea that poetry makes nothing happen could only be true in a nonhistorical world. The world that recovers an ancient or alien text is always altered by it: in Western culture this is just an enduring fact of historical experience.[18]

Obviously this is a very satisfying way of thinking about texts and interpretation, and I think one will never understand hermeneutics either philosophically or historically unless one works out an idea roughly along these Aristotelian lines. However, I also think that one will always fall short of grasping the hard reality of hermeneutics if one simply stops where Ricoeur and others seem to stop, without asking whether this way of thinking does not entail a reduction of the literary work of art to what one might call the bare narrative function of projecting a possible world onto the space of interpretation. Ricoeur himself acknowledges, always impatiently and on occasion derisively, that the literary work of art, and particularly the modern avant-garde text, is always excessive with respect to this narrative or mimetic function. For Ricoeur, whatever is written, considered materially as a text, remains in suspension, in the air, outside the world, mere literature, until it is appropriated in a certain way, the way one appropriates a legal or a sacred text, a philosophical argument or a political constitution or a scientific model or an ethical narrative. The literary text, by contrast, is that which resists appropriation or withholds itself from our hermeneutical tasks. The literary text is one whose looking glass remains opaque. Ricoeur does not hesitate to say that the task of the reader in such an event is to clean and polish the glass in order to render it transparent. The literary work of art, after all, is only an incomplete sketch, a fragment of what needs to be translated into a complete world by the appropriative act of reading. As Ricoeur puts it in *Time and Narrative,* the literary work, considered as a text, "consists of holes, lacunae, zones of indetermination, which, as in Joyce's *Ulysses,* challenge the reader's capacity to configure what the author seems to take malign delight in disfiguring. In such an extreme case, it is the reader, almost abandoned by the work, who carries the burden of emplotment," that is, the burden of allegory, or of reconstructing from the textuality of the text the narrative that projects a world.[19] The point is always to rewrite the literary text as if it were, in its deep structure, a philosophical, legal, sacred, or political text. This recomposition of the dark or recalcitrant text is all that allegory has ever meant.

But what would it be for the reader to engage the text at the level of its resistance to philosophy, that is, prior to reduction, in its refusal of allegory? What would it be to engage the text in its excess and in its density—or as Ricoeur says, in its disfigurement and Joycean malignancy? This is the unasked question, the unthought thought, of Ricoeur's philosophy, and of philosophy generally, and for that matter of the university study of literature, which remains basically an Aristotelian scholasticism despite its recent theoretical adventures.

The question here is one that Heidegger tried to formulate in his later writings on language, poetry, and thinking, where language is no longer conceivable as a logical or linguistic system, but is an irreducible, untheorizable place or region or event that Heidegger calls Saying (*Sage*); that is, prior to their formal reduction as Literature and Philosophy, prior to their logical construction as modes or institutions of discourse, poetry and thinking already confront one another, are exposed to one another, within the event of Saying. What sort of happening is this? What is the site or event of poetry and thinking? What does this mutual exposure entail? What are its philosophical consequences?[20]

These are the basic questions of a Platonic hermeneutics. In order to get a sense of these questions (for it is not clear that we know how to ask them), we need to take a step back from Aristotle and Ricoeur and to imagine something like the following. Suppose you grant all that Plato says about poetry; suppose that what Plato says is true, namely, that poetry belongs with darkness and ambiguity, outside the philosophy of light, therefore outside the domain of justice and necessity—not just radically unstable but linked metaphysically to anarchy and the derangement of the senses and of reason, not only external to the world, uncontainable within it, but set against it, a danger to it—suppose you grant all of this, but instead of banishing the poet, or instead of making her write philosophical novels, you just linger in her company. What then? What happens to philosophy (or the world) in this event?

A paragraph from Emmanuel Levinas's *Otherwise than Being, or Beyond Essence* might help to clarify these questions, or at least to make them less rhetorical.

> Philosophy is disclosure of being, and being's *essence* is truth and philosophy. Being's essence is the temporalization of time, the diastasis of the identical and its recapture or reminiscence, the unity of apperception. *Essence* does not first designate the edges of solids or the moving line of acts in which a light glimmers; it designates this "modification" without alteration or transition, independent of all qualitative determination, more formal than the silent using up of things which reveals their becoming, already weighted down with matter, the creaking of a piece of furniture of the night. This modification by which the same comes unstuck or parts with itself, undoes itself into this and that, no longer covers over itself and thus is disclosed (like in Dufy's paintings, where the colors spread out from their contours and do not rub up against them), becomes a phenomenon—is the *esse* of every being. Being's essence designates nothing that could be a nameable content, a thing, event, or action; it names this mobility of the immobile, this multiplication of the identical, this diastasis of the punctual, this lapse. This modification without alteration or displacement, being's essence or time, does not await, in addition, an illumination that would allow for an "act of consciousness." This modification is precisely the visibility of the same to the same, which is sometimes called openness. The work of being, essence, time, the lapse of time, is exposition, truth, philosophy. *Being's essence is a dissipating of opacity,* not only because this "drawing out" of being would have to have been first understood so that the truth could be told about things, events, and acts that *are;* but because this drawing out is the *original dissipation* of opaqueness. In it forms are illuminated where knowledge is awakened; in it being leaves the night, or, at least, quits sleep, that night of night, for an inextinguishable insomnia of consciousness. Thus every particular knowledge, every factual exercise of understanding—ideology, faith, or science—every perception, every disclosing behavior whatever it be, would owe their light to essence, the first light, and to philosophy, which is dawn or its twilight.

> Temporality, in the divergence of the identical from itself, is *essence* and original light, that which Plato distinguished from the visibility of the visible and the clairvoyance of the eye. The time of the essence unites three moments of knowing. Is the light of essence which makes things seen itself seen? It can to be sure become a theme; essence can show itself, be spoken of and described. But then light presents itself in light, which latter is not thematic, but resounds for the "eye that listens," with a resonance unique in its kind, a resonance of silence. Expressions such as the eye that listens to the resonance of silence are not monstrosities, for they speak of the way one approaches the temporality of the true, and in temporality being deploys its essence. [*italics mine*][21]

Here Levinas tells, or retells, ambiguously, the story of philosophy's genesis in "an original dissipation of opaqueness," that is, being's departure from Chaos and Old Night. Philosophy *discloses* this event—but what does this mean, exactly? Levinas has it that philosophy preserves being from the nonidentical, not so much by grasping being as such, since being is unnameable, as (oddly) by determining its essence as so many oxymora—modification without alteration, mobility of the immobile, multiplication of the identical, the self-estrangement of the punctual, and (more strangely still): *lapse,* as of time, when "the same comes unstuck or parts with itself, undoes itself into this and that, no longer covers over itself and thus is disclosed . . . , becomes a phenomenon." This phenomenon is like a phenomenon "in Dufy's paintings, where the colors spread out from their contours and do not rub up against them." This reference to Dufy is worth a moment's study, since in his writings Levinas only very rarely gives examples of any sort. Raoul Dufy (1877–1953) was a French painter usually numbered among the Fauvists, who championed the motto "color for color's sake." He is perhaps most famous for a splendid and massive mural—some two-hundred feet by thirty-five feet—called *The History of Electricity,* which he painted at the request of the Paris Electrical Supply Company and which was exhibited in the firm's pavilion at the 1937 World's Fair in Paris. But given the context in which he appears in Levinas's reflections, it seems most important to know that Dufy followed very closely, and made use of, the experiments of Jacques Maroger, a chemist who attempted to rid pigments of their opacity, thus to produce radiant colors, or colors through which light seems to shine.[22] So perhaps *The History of Electricity* is allegorical of the history of philosophy.

It is by ridding things of their opacity that philosophy enables them to appear, not as things, but as beings, that is, not in the materiality of their existence (furniture creaking in the night) but in their translucent essence, as if dematerialized or spiritualized, all thickness dissipated, so that nothing about them is hidden. Whereas by contrast (following Heidegger's analysis) poetry discloses or, more accurately, summons things, not as beings, but precisely as things—earthly, singular or nonidentical, opaque, refractory to the light, impenetrable to analysis, always withdrawing from view. Likewise, as if executing a classical decorum, poetry itself is thinglike discourse: material, dense (*dicht*), the dark saying where nothing is ever itself or capturable but is always interpretable otherwise, forever running loose, anarchic and dangerous.

Hence the idea, basic to a Platonic hermeneutics, that poetry's natural or, rather, originary condition is one of exile. On this condition one can learn most from Maurice Blanchot.

> The poem is exile, and the poet who belongs to it belongs to the dissatisfaction of exile. He is always lost to himself, outside, far from home; he belongs to the foreign, to the outside which knows no intimacy or limit, and to the separation which Hölderlin names when in his madness he sees rhythm's infinite space.
>
> Exile, the poem then, makes the poet a wanderer, the one always astray, he to whom the stability of presence is not granted and who is deprived of a true abode. And this must be understood in the gravest sense: the artist does not belong to truth because the work is itself what escapes the movement of the true, eludes signification, designating that region where nothing subsists, where what takes place has nevertheless never taken place, where what begins over has never begun. It points to the realm of the most dangerous indecision, toward the confusion from which nothing emerges. This eternal outside is quite well evoked by the image of the *exterior* darkness where man understands that which the true must negate in order to become possible and to progress.[23]

Thoughts of this character tend to turn people into Aristotelians—or, in more up-to-date fashion, either Kantians or Hegelians. Literary critics on the whole interpret the idea that poetry "escapes the movement of the true" by following Kant in resolving questions of truth procedurally, so that the "truth" of the poem (its point, say) becomes a function of the strategy used to approach it. Philosophers meanwhile mostly follow Hegel's "death of art" idea, namely that poetry may once have determined "the movement of the true" but it has since been superseded by philosophy: "art, considered in its highest vocation, is and remains for us a thing of the past."[24]

On closer examination, there may be little to choose between Kant and Hegel. Hegel goes on to say that "What is now aroused in us by works of art is not just immediate enjoyment but our judgement also, since we subject to our intellectual consideration (i) the content of the art, and (ii) the work of art's means of presentation, and the appropriateness of one to another. The *philosophy* of art is, therefore, a greater need in our day than it was in days when art by itself as art yielded full satisfaction. Art invites us to intellectual consideration, and that not for the purpose of creating art again, but for knowing philosophically what art is."[25] The point is that we have distanced ourselves from art; it can no longer do us any harm—this being, from a certain point of view, as Danto suggests, the whole definition of philosophy, or at least "the reason philosophy was invented," as if "philosophical systems [were] finally penitentiary systems [or] labyrinths for keeping monsters in and so protecting us against some deep metaphysical danger." Naturally, as Danto says, one cannot help asking "what power finally is that philosophy is afraid of."[26]

Perhaps the answer is: whatever turns people into poets, that is, wanderers, people incapable of philosophy, people suffering, as Blanchot says, "the inability to abide and stay. For where the wanderer is, the conditions of the definite here are lacking. . . . The wanderer's country is not truth, but exile; he lives outside, on the other side which is by no means a beyond, rather the contrary. He remains separated, where the deep of dissimulation reigns, that elemental obscurity through which no way can be made and which because of that makes its awful way through him."[27] One has only to recall the status of wandering in Plato's texts to understand what is at stake here for the philosopher who goes astray into the "wanderer's country."

It seems right to think of Derrida in this context. Derrida says that the central task of his philosophical work has been to find a nonphilosophical place in which "philosophy as such can appear to itself as other than itself, so that it can interrogate and reflect upon itself in an original manner."[28] Derrida is of two minds as to whether literature can provide such a nonphilosophical place. It doesn't seem that it can, because literature is, from the beginning, saturated with philosophy: that is, it has already, under the rule of poetics, transformed itself into a discourse of lucidity, a selfallegorizing or self-interpreting, self-justifying text. It has made itself over from something earthly into a worldly and even heavenly good. It is at all events something stable, something recognizable and not apt to unravel us. Anyway, insofar as this is true, there would be no getting around behind Aristotle and Ricoeur, or Kant and Hegel, to recover that originary hermeneutical situation that Heidegger characterizes as a rift of poetry and thinking, before Literature and Philosophy are stabilized or established as discursive institutions or systems of discursive constraint. Poetry, as such—as *Dichten*, Heidegger's strange word for poetry—does not exist. There is, one might say, no such thing; anyhow, we are hardly or barely in a position to recognize such a thing. There are only philosophical constructions of poetrylike objects—epics and tragedies, novels and lyrics whose transparency avant-garde writers like Mallarmé and Artaud and Joyce and John Cage interfere with by means of their bizarre disfigurations of art and language. But whereas for Ricoeur these disfigurations are indeed aberrations, interferences with philosophical reading and its projects of world making, for Derrida they are exactly what must be appropriated, taken up and put into play, precisely because they are external to the philosophy of light. In other words, they are what the philosopher must throw in with—as a philosopher. For what interests Derrida is resistance to philosophy as such. It is this resistance that he wants to act out within the institution of philosophy itself in order to unseal it, to expose it to what is not itself, exposing its limits as historical and contingent, showing it how to become different things—showing, as Wittgenstein might say, that the extension of the concept of philosophy cannot be closed by a frontier. As if wandering were not just poetic madness but something else—for example, a side of philosophy concerned, not with the movement of the true, but with another sort of movement that one could call freedom.

But how far this movement can be made intelligible by further reflection remains open to question.

NOTES

1. Antonin Artaud, *Antonin Artaud: Selected Writings*, ed. Susan Sontag, trans. Helen Weaver (Berkeley and Los Angeles: University of California Press, 1976), p. 241.
2. Martha Nussbaum, *The Fragility of Goodness: Luck and Ethics in Greek Trag-*

edy and Philosophy (Cambridge: Cambridge University Press, 1986), p. 200–233.

3. Richard Rorty, "Deconstruction and Circumvention," *Critical Inquiry* 11, no. 1 (September 1984): 1–23.
4. Louis Althusser and Etienne Balibar, *Reading Capital,* trans. Ben Brewster (New York: Pantheon, 1971), p. 24.
5. Walter Benjamin, "Theses on the Philosophy of History," in his *Illuminations,* trans. Harry Zohn (New York: Schocken Books, 1969), pp. 256–57.
6. Martin Heidegger, "Hölderlin and the Essence of Poetry," in his *Existence and Being,* trans. Douglas Scott (Chicago: Henry Regnery, 1949), p. 281–82.
7. Martin Heidegger, "The Origin of the Work of Art," in his *Poetry, Language, Thought,* trans. Albert Hofstadter (New York: Harper & Row, 1971), p. 49.
8. Ibid.
9. Ibid., p. 72.
10. See Paul Ricoeur's "Structure, Word, Event," trans. Robert Sweeney, in Ricoeur, *The Conflict of Interpretations: Essays in Hermeneutics,* ed. Don Ihde (Evanston, Ill.: Northwestern University Press, 1974), pp. 79–96.
11. Ricoeur, "The Hermeneutical Function of Distanciation," in his *Hermeneutics and the Human Sciences: Essays on Language, Action, and Interpretation,* ed., trans., and intro. John B. Thompson (Cambridge: Cambridge University Press, 1981), pp. 132–36.
12. Ricoeur, "What Is a Text? Explanation and Understanding," ibid., pp. 141, 148–49.
13. Ricoeur, "The Question of Proof in Freud's Psychoanalytic Writings," ibid., p. 267.
14. Ricoeur, "Science and Ideology," ibid., pp. 232, 245.
15. Ricoeur, "What Is a Text? Explanation and Understanding," ibid., p. 141.
16. Ibid., pp. 141, 142.
17. Ricoeur, *Time and Narrative,* vol. 1, trans. Kathleen MacLaughlin and David Pellauer (Chicago: University of Chicago Press, 1984), p. 50.
18. Michael Shapiro, who thinks of himself as "antihermeneutical," nevertheless brings out this "Aristotelian" character of hermeneutics in a very fine study ("Literary Production as a Politicizing Practice," *Political Theory* 12, no. 3 [August 1984]: 387–422). "Literary discourse," Shapiro says, "particularly in its modern guise, is hyperpoliticizing. By producing alternative forms of thought *in* language, it makes a political point" (p. 410).
19. Ricoeur, *Time and Narrative,* 1:75.
20. I go into these questions in more detail in *Heidegger's Estrangements: Language, Truth, and Poetry in the Later Writings* (New Haven and London: Yale University Press, 1989), and I mean to address them still further in "Poetry and the Philosophers: A Study in Darkness, or Freedom" (in progress).
21. Emmanuel Levinas, *Otherwise than Being, or Beyond Essence,* trans. Alphonso Lingis (The Hague, Boston, London: Martinus Nijhoff, 1984), pp. 29–30.
22. A print of Raoul Dufy's *The History of Electricity* appears in *Raoul Dufy* (New York: Harry N. Abrams, 1970), p. 149.
23. Maurice Blanchot, "Literature and the Original Experience," in his *The Space of Literature,* trans. Ann Smock (Lincoln: University of Nebraska Press, 1982), pp. 237–38.
24. Georg W. Friedrich Hegel, *Hegel's Aesthetics: Lectures on Fine Art,* trans. T. M. Knox (Oxford: Clarendon Press, 1975), 1:11. See also Arthur Danto, "The End of Art," in his *The Philosophical Disenfranchisement of Art* (New York: Columbia University Press, 1986), pp. 81–115.
25. Hegel, *Hegel's Aesthetics,* 1:11.

26. Danto, "The End of Art," p. 12.
27. Blanchot, "Literature and the Original Experience," p. 238.
28. Jacques Derrida, *Dialogues with Contemporary Continental Thinkers: The Phenomenological Heritage,* ed. Richard Kearney (Manchester: Manchester University Press, 1984), p. 108.

PART II

ESSAYS ON HISTORY AND NARRATIVE

HANS KELLNER

"AS REAL AS IT GETS"

Ricoeur and Narrativity

THE SHEER MONUMENTALITY of Paul Ricoeur's *Time and Narrative* makes it an extraordinarily difficult work to confront directly on the issue of historical reflection, which is rarely characterized as a mode of thought by the sort of sinuously indirect direction practiced so skillfully by Ricoeur. In many ways, the work mimics its vast subject, the transfiguration of time: its scope and breadth of reference not only dwarf the reader's stature but also account for it, as the reader plays a vital, if only partial, role in the process outlined by *Time and Narrative.* It is not difficult to feel like Hansel and Gretel in the woods, who discover that the bread crumbs they have dropped behind them to mark their way have been eaten up by birds; we have no way to go but forward, without complete certainty as to where we have been, despite the frequent summaries and resting along the way. With so many trees, how can we be sure what the forest actually looks like?

From the point of view of historical reflection, the central assertion of *Time and Narrative* is the union of history and fiction in a grand narrative, which is severed or divided only at great cost. Only the readerly narrative understanding inherent in the poetics of fiction makes possible our understanding of all properly historical thought, while the link of historical consciousness with a time that is more than merely human makes fictional worlds exist in a way that would be otherwise impossible. The interdependence of these narrative modes, history and fiction, is total. They lean upon each other like the two parts of the Christian Bible, the latter part of which is proven true because it fulfills the former, the former part of which is proven true because it prefigures the latter. The language by which the church fathers welded together these two canons into one is the language of figure, or so we have been taught by Erich Auerbach, Northrop Frye, and many others.[1] It is also to *figure* that Ricoeur appeals in his welding job: prefiguration, configuration, refiguration. The figure of speech that authorizes our narrative understanding is thus *figure* itself.

If Ricoeur's figural merger of history and fiction works like the technique used to justify the unity of the Christian Bible, it also resembles those scriptures in its cultural function. Both the Old and the New Testaments privilege memory. The Deuteronomic injunction, *Zakhor,* ("remember"), plays a specific role in Ricoeur's argument; and while the anamnestic imperative of the New Testament, "This do in remembrance of me," is not explicitly cited in *Time and Narrative,* the moral commandment of commemoration is certainly present. As we shall see, a great deal of Ricoeur's strategy involves keeping things in mind, regaining what has been excluded or forgotten. This is his phenomenological work of remembering. Most discussions of *history* sooner or later founder on the double meaning of the word: *history* as past event differs markedly from *history* as written report. It is hard to discuss these things without forgetting or bracketing one or the other sense of the word. Yet Ricoeur finds this double meaning, which is almost invariably a source of confusion regarding any discussion of historical matters, as an advantage to be exploited, a linguistic happenstance that, properly understood, reveals the nature of things through its very duplicity. In fact, from the point of view of history, *Time and Narrative* has no other task than to bring the two meanings of the word into a higher accord, preliminary to bringing history and fiction into the higher accord of the "great narratology." *History* as a word refers to the events of the past, things done, res gestae; on the other hand, it refers to representations of these things, that is to say, to historiography, texts, objects, narratives of one sort and another. What we find in *Time and Narrative* is a subtly protracted move from what would seem to be a discussion of the latter—namely, a discussion of narrative objects or substances—to a discussion of the former, the past as human experience. This is notoriously rare and difficult to do. It is also clearly dangerous, because the two sides of our word *history* are sworn enemies of one another, each with devoted partisans.[2] The field is strewn with mines, both academic and philosophical. Ricoeur seems to have taken note of this by traveling very slowly, with great circumspection. Hence, the bewildering nature of his discussion. Again, how can we get above his text, avoid its traps and evasions, even on this single issue of historical reflection?

One way to enter *Time and Narrative* is to look for some point of intersection or crossroads, some place where the representation of history, history as textual object, crosses over into the matter of history as real events that once took place. Such points rarely occur in traditional historical discussion; historians will not grant the idea that something in the subject matter invades and determines the text in some way. The historian speaks of "mastery of the sources," but this notion, Freudian in origin, suggests that the sources may turn the tables.[3] In Ricoeur's work, we find this involvement of subject in text consciously thematized, so to speak, in a most peculiar spot, specifically in a comment in volume 1 of *Time and Narrative* in which Ricoeur speaks of those French historians who have written about the history of death. Ricoeur refers to their work as possibly the farthest that historical consciousness can go. This can only be the case because something about the subject matter, death, reaches into and grasps the form of its representation, historical narrative as produced by professional historiography. Now death, of course, strictly speaking, has no history of its own, nor is it something that anyone can experience in a threefold sense of time. It would seem to be the most completely natural of phenomenon, the one least likely to intervene into the historical scene at any point. It is given. However, it is also clear that the historians Ricoeur mentions, namely Michel Vovelle, Pierre Chaunu, and Philippe Ariès, are not speaking of death in this sense at all. They are speaking of something else, namely social representations, ceremonials, showmanship regarding the theater of dying, the scene and plot of dying, not death itself. To confront death historically leads us back immediately into the world of representations; it is like time itself in this regard. In *The Magic Mountain*, which is a novel of time as well as a novel of death, Thomas Mann writes: "Can one tell—that is to say, narrate—time, time itself, as such, for its own sake [*an und für sich*]? That would surely be an absurd undertaking."[4] Death is in the same situation; it cannot be narrated "for its own sake." In that sense, its history is a boundary zone, and the point at which the content of a historical reflection begins to invade and undermine its form.

Heidegger, in *Being and Time*, finds that death is what makes possible the understanding of the whole of *Dasein*'s being in time. Related to the threefold essence of time (which is central to Ricoeur's vision), death, in Heidegger's words, "finalizes my past, cuts off my future, and invades my present as the perspective from which *Dasein* is seen in its wholeness and conclusive meaning." Further: "As potentiality for being, *Dasein* is unable to surpass the possibility of death. Death is the possibility of the utter impossibility of *Dasein.* Thus death reveals itself as the (ownmost, nonrelational, unsurpassable possibility)."[5] Ricoeur insists that we must bring to light those experiences where time is thematized. This cannot be done without introducing into the discussion the phenomenology of internal time-consciousness. In doing so, he is ostensibly signaling to us his principle of selection in discussing both history and fiction.[6] It will be chronographies, writings about time, that will ostensibly merit his attention. Braudel's *The Mediterranean and the Mediterranean World in the Age of Philip II* is the locus classicus, and gets full attention in volume 1.[7] More telling, however, for Ricoeur's case in *Time and Narrative* are the mortographies (I think I have coined a word here), the histories of death—whether the typology of deaths listed by Philippe Ariès, the study of testaments by Michel Vovelle, or the serial analyses devised by Pierre Chaunu, Ricoeur's identification of these works as "not . . . just the farthest point reached by serial history, but perhaps by all history, for reasons that I shall discuss in volume 2" (*TN,* 1:111), is cryptic in several ways. For one thing, if these reasons are discussed in volume 2, it is by considerable indirection (the actual discussion coming in volume 3), yet there is a great deal of interest for our purposes in his discussion in volume 2 of *The Magic Mountain,* the great *Zeitroman,* or novel of time (and death).

For Ricoeur, *The Magic Mountain* is the work in which the aporias of time are not speculatively resolved, but are instead heightened in their tensions, "elevation to a higher level" (*TN,* 2:129). Yet by thematizing time, death, and culture, the novel nevertheless performs its own assigned tasks of mediation between the opposed internal experience of time and the external form of time "down there." This inner experience is the "zero degree of the thought experiment undertaken by Hans Castorp" (*TN,* 2:129). Although Ricoeur identifies the Walpurgisnacht and the "Snow" chapters as the two crucial turning points of the novel, he denies to *The Magic Mountain* and its hero "the test of action, the ultimate criterion of the *Bildungsroman*" (*TN,* 2:129). It would apparently be too ironic for Ricoeur to find the final descent of the novel to be an elevation, which is the proper goal of the bildungsroman. In Ricoeur's reading, the magical seven years at the Berghof can only be broken catastrophically by the eruption of "la grande histoire"—*der Donnerschlag* ("the thunderbolt") in Mann's words, "the universal feast of death"—because the hero has not been involved in action.[8]

The "elevation" (*Steigerung*) that *The Magic Mountain* as text provides to the discourse on time and its aporias is exactly that elevation that Hermann Weigand attributes to Hans Castorp in his discussion of *The Magic Mountain* as a bildungsroman, but which Ricoeur does not.[9] By denying the young man this badge of elevation through action, denying that *The Magic Mountain* is a bildungsroman, and awarding the crown of elevation instead to the text or *Zeitroman* in which he lives, Ricoeur repeats a characteristic move that refocuses meaningful action considered as a text, the allegorical transfer of material to a higher level of discourse. Let us turn back to the first volume of *Time and Narrative,* chapter 4, "The Eclipse of Narrative," footnote 36, where a similar move occurs from another direction, the direction of historical discourse. In this note Michel Vovelle is quoted. The historian of death also writes about a death—but not human death, not the death of men and women. Vovelle allegorically transfers the category to a textual level. The "death of a certain historicising history is an accomplished fact," admits Vovelle, "yet the essence of such history, history, the event, allegedly so scorned by Braudel and the generation of historians that immediately followed him, lives on, even in the *longue durée.*"[10] This death and its transfiguration is transferred to a higher level of discourse, again allegorically, through narrative.

From the beginning, Ricoeur's working definition of *narrative* emphasizes dynamic functionality and aesthetics. Ricoeur calls a narrative "exactly" what Aristotle called mythos, the force that emplots events into a humanly comprehensible order (*TN,* 1:36). By presenting narrativity as that which turns straw into gold—that is to say, discord into concord—he has told us implicitly that his entire method in *Time and Narrative* is an enormous allegorical narrativization of all possible reflections on time and its representations. The ever-more-totalizing mediations of *Time and Narrative* progress relentlessly, repeatedly identifying opposing visions, repeatedly naming the "price" that each entails by reason of its inevitable partiality, which places it in a position of discord in a field of concepts strewn about like straw. Repeatedly, a mediator, or a bridge, or that which somehow conjoins, appears in his discourse, and a new concordance is earned. Because all nonnarrativized views exact a price, and because one of the purposes of *Time and Narrative* is to escape the charges of partiality, and because Paul Ricoeur has done his job with overwhelming skill and industry, there seems to be scarcely any space within *Time and Narrative* where its walls may be breached, even if one had enough time to try. In other words, the major difficulty in confronting this work is found in the attempt to pose a paradoxical question: What is the price of narrativization? Or, put another way, What is left out by an intellectual approach, narrativity, that both strives to be all-inclusive and is itself the mode of inclusiveness? After *Time and Narrative,* how might we resituate narrative so as to "see" it, or think it, in a way that is not already narrativized? Can this be done?

Let us begin by asking the basic question about the narrative form of *Time and Narrative:* What is its plot type? The genre of *Time and Narrative* is naturally a quasi genre; like the work of Hegel and the Christian Bible, it is a tragicomedy. The tropological world of *Time and Narrative* is the world of part/whole relationships, of metonymically delineated partial visions and synecdochically integrated revisions that are larger, more adequate, and, as we shall see, more beautiful; its movement is to transform the former into the latter, a literal transfiguration of these figures. Nowhere is the tragic cost of all metonymic reductions better portrayed; nowhere are the hopeful, but fragile, reconciliations of partial visions better fashioned. I say fragile because the devices used for the many provisional reconciliations depend on a technique that carries considerable dangers, the technique of the "quasi." The "quasiness" of Ricoeur's discourse grows steadily as it progresses. It begins in noting the very sensible suggestion by Paul Veyne to the effect that all change enters historical reflection as a quasi event. Consequently, even nonnarrative histories have quasi plots, quantitative social histories have quasi characters, and any meaningful action may be read as a quasi text. The ultimate interweaving of fiction and history leaves each a quasi version of the other (*TN,* 3:190), the plots of the former having become the quasi plots of the latter, the past of the latter having become the quasi past of the former. In all of this, what Ricoeur calls the "Sign of the Analogous" (*TN,* 3:151) works brilliantly in its engineering project of bridge building. It is certainly the most revealing systematic consideration of the relationship of history and fiction within narrative language that has been produced to date. All of this quasiness reminds us that the "Sign of the Analogue," under which the ship sails, certifies the figurative process, which is the lifeblood of *Time and Narrative;* its destination, after all, is a refiguration of time by narrative. Each step of the way involves a turn, a tropological allegorization, by which apparently different pieces of reality (the Signs of Same and Other) are resolved provisionally, into analogues, "quasis" (*TN,* 3:151). In this phenomenological strategy, narrative acts as a middle-level tropological process, mediating parts into wholes, without looking over either shoulder at the lower and the higher level protocols of language. Narrative is thus the quintessence of Ricoeur's vision of humanity. In *Fallible Man,* Ricoeur sketched out the mediating nature of human beings: "Man is not intermediate because he is between angel and animal; he is intermediate within himself, within his selves. He is intermediate because he is a mixture, and a mixture because he brings about mediations. His ontological character of being-intermediate consists precisely in that his act of existing is that of bringing about mediations between all the modalities and all the levels of reality within him and outside him."[11]

Man as mediator lives in the realm of the quasi. However, there is one more quasi, back in volume 1, that is more bothersome to me. "Artisans who work with words produce not things, but quasi-things; they invent the as-if" (*TN,* 1:45). Although I am not competent or disposed to debate the issue of "What is a thing?" with any professional metaphysician, I cannot help wondering how a thing can be "quasified." A quasi thing is just as much a thing as any other thing; thinghood seems to envelop any attempt to fragment it or to quasify it. This observation leads me to ask and pursue another question. What if existence were already refigured by the simple human (Adamic) act of naming things in the world? And what is the nature of the thinghood of the historical text? I think that here, in the thingfulness of naming and language rather than in the figural mediations of narrativity, a split or fracture appears in *Time and Narrative* (to use some of its own frequent metaphors) that escapes its endlessly bridging power. But in another sense, this point is not a fracture at all, because it comes, not from within the realm of argument of *Time and Narrative,* but from without, from an angle of vision too low, to be engaged by narrative as such, which, as I have said, operates for Ricoeur at a middle level—the level of grammar and syntax, so to speak, where plots are born. For all the optimism of its unlimited subsumptions and mediations, the book is built upon anxiety. The central concern of *Time and Narrative* is what might happen if narrative should be eclipsed. I find the most significant of the references in *Time and Narrative* that in which Ricoeur cites Walter Benjamin's fear, in his essay on "The Storyteller," that we may have reached the end of an era in which storytelling has a place because people no longer have experiences to share (*TN,* 2:28). Like Vovelle writing about the history of events, Ricoeur speaks of this as a "certain death," the death of *contant,* telling, as well as of *racontant,* storytelling, using just the same figure as that Vovelle had used to note the demise of a certain sort of history. Death here is an analogue, it would seem; to speak of the end—as in the end of the art of storytelling, which is the rubric under which this discussion takes place—naturally brings the metaphor of death to us as an implicit quasi. But this metaphor is clearly more than a metaphor, because the "death of narrative" is a boundary situation closely related to the narratives of death that Ricoeur studies so intently. Real human death is implicated in the death of narrative, not only because some special narratives like those by Mann, Vovelle, or Ariès, take death as their subject, but because narrativity itself has a certain relationship to death. Literary narratives keep us from the death that would be our lot if we looked directly at nothingness. The Apollinian veil that narrative throws over the "Dionysian fascination for chaos" is Nietzsche's diagnosis of the fear of death at the heart of narrative; and as usual, Ricoeur does not fail to discuss it (*TN,* 2:27). Even the confrontation between the eternity of the classical universe and the scarcely alterable span of human years has a gentleness, a veil of elegy, that taught the ancients important lessons and was repeated for long ages. "Would we speak of the shortness of life if it did not stand out against the immensity of time? This contrast is the most eloquent form that can be taken by the twofold movement of detachment whereby the time of Care, on the one hand, tears itself away from the fascination with the carefree time of the world and, on the other hand, astronomical and calendar time frees itself from the goad of immediate concern and even from the thought of death" (*TN,* 3:93).

Historical as well as literary narrativity also has death at its heart. Both the idea of the calendar upon which historical order is built and, more especially, the idea of generations thematize death. Like the elegy, the idea of the generation contrasts and reassuringly veils the contrast between the limits of a human life and the broad expanse of historical time.

"In history, death bears an eminently ambiguous signification that mixes together the intimacy of each person's death and a reference to the public character of the replacement of the dead by the living. These two references meet in the idea of anonymous death. Under the saying "they die," the historian recognizes death obliquely, and only to go immediately beyond it" (*TN*, 3:115). Generationality supersedes death in a bittersweet elegiac cheer. "The historical actor is dead. Long live the historical actor!" we might say. Like a vacant fief, our places in this world are left in escheat, to be reassigned to new vassals. At this point in *Time and Narrative*, as so often, a footnote of great import appears (*TN*, 3:302–3 n. 25). In it Ricoeur recalls his discussion in volume 1 of Braudel's *Mediterranean*. Yet the focus of Ricoeur's consideration has changed considerably, for in this note Ricoeur actually makes of Braudel's masterpiece a history of death like those of Vovelle, Chaunu, and Ariès. The chronography becomes mortography. It seems to have for him the form of an elegy. The elevation of Braudel's *Mediterranean* to the center of Ricoeur's discussion is a recognition that only mortals die, not things. Yet ironically, the great pain of human suffering, in Ricoeur's reading, comes, not in section 3 of Braudel's book, which deals with the wars and events of life and death that mortals use to comfort themselves that their lives have meaning, but rather in Braudel's famous section 1, the glacially paced "Role of the Environment," closest to eternity. Even the "Collective Destinies" of Braudel's Section 2 mask for Ricoeur the individual fate of the martyrs—he cites the Moors and the Jews—who confronted *la grande histoire.*

"That is why, when Braudel, reflecting upon the meaning of his work, asks if in minimizing the role of events and individuals he may have denied the importance of human freedom . . . , we may ask instead if it is not death that history mishandles, even though it is our memory of the dead. It cannot do otherwise inasmuch as death marks the lower bound of that microhistory that the historical reconstruction of the whole seeks to break away from" (*TN*, 3:303).

Here we have found yet another reference to death as a boundary—the lower boundary, to be precise, of historical reflection. If, at the top level, the drive of historical reflection seems to lead toward an inexorable totalization that refuses to privilege anything but the whole and is symbolized by the anonymous passing of generational roles, this process snags on the lowest and most banal, unavoidable, of events—individual human death, our most purely creatural experience. To narrate death, whether with graphs and charts, as in Vovelle, or with poems and photographs of monuments, as in Ariès, is thus a war on two fronts: to dwell on the individuality of death with its pathos and banality is to regress to the elegiac anecdotalism that history has wanted to overcome; to transform the event of death into the serial data of quantitative historiography is to lose death itself, to reduce what we intuit to be irreducible, to commit a murder. In Ricoeur's view, it is the "whisper of death" that makes Braudel grant an oddly ambivalent acceptance of the level of human events, and that prompts Braudel's denial that he is a structuralist of the abstracting sort (*TN,* 3:303). Perhaps it is this "whisper" that guides Ricoeur in his work as well.

Still, there is one death in Braudel's *Mediterranean* that has little poignancy. Although Ricoeur refers to it as "sumptuous" in volume 1 of *Time and Narrative,* he clearly chooses to minimize it—as does Braudel, in a sense—in discussing *The Mediterranean* (*TN,* 1:214). It is the death of Philip II, the death that in effect ends the book, despite the brief epilogue. This death is not the physical description of the course of the blood disease that killed the king over those long summer months of 1598, nor is it an *Annales* type discourse on the mentalities reflected in the representations and ceremonials surrounding the death of the king, nor is it in any way a psychological portrait of Philip confronting the end of his life and examining his soul. On these three points, essential to the histories of death as practiced by modern French historians, there is not a word. Braudel has instead elected to end his book with an allegorical erasure of Philip II, sense by sense, so as to underline the strict limits of human comprehension, which, I believe, is the point of his book. We read that Philip was a silent man both to ambassadors and to future historians, that he was not a man of vision, and had never thought of the word *Mediterranean* in our sense of that word. And so forth. Philip's death, as recounted by Braudel, points to the great and self-conscious paradox presented by that book, the inability of humans to capture reality in language. For the tension of *The Mediterranean* is between section 1, where genuine and permanent historical significance lies but where naming is always inadequate and misleading, and section 3, where naming (King Philip, the Battle of Lepanto, the duke of Alva) is perfectly clear and referential but the material is ephemera, dust, "victories that led nowhere." If the hero of Braudel's book is the Mediterranean, how could Philip II never have heard of it, at least not with the meaning we now give it. Look back to section 1, with it endless ironic figures—the Sahara is the second face of the Mediterranean, there are other Mediterraneans in the Baltic and North seas, there are two Mediterranean worlds (with a fine mesh filter between them), but later "a succession of small seas." We find "liquid plains," "watery Saharas," "islands that the sea does not surround," and on and on.[12] By defamiliarizing the language of reference at the same time he stresses the unique historical significance, the stability, of the environment, Braudel has made of *The Mediterranean* a satire on language. In short, what language can capture is dust; what is significant can only be approached ironically, by pointing out the failure of language to represent it.[13]

Ricoeur's understanding of Braudel's masterwork is not the same as mine, but he certainly addresses in *Time and Narrative* the issue of language and our discontents within it. Nevertheless, while Ricoeur's vision of pre-, con-, and re-figurations must operate under "the Sign of the Analogous"—is this not another way of describing the "rule of metaphor"?—for all of its recognition of the debts owed to Sameness and Otherness, his powerful dialectic does not always grant or recognize that the price of all analogical thinking is an ironic attention to language and to the fragile, temporary nature of all analogical mediation. At the lower limit, analogous to Ricoeur's history of death, the concern with language is that crisis of naming that I believe to be satirized in Braudel's Mediterranean but ignored in Ricoeur's reading of that work. Ricoeur has identified an upper level of linguistic operations as well: the abstracting tropological analysis associated with Hayden White. Chapter 6 of volume 3 is an abbreviated version of the lectures delivered as *The Reality of the Historical Past;* in these lectures Ricoeur comes to terms with White, as always, by placing him in a mediating position (in the sense that the Analogous mediates Same and Other), which exacts an unacceptable price by failing adequately to recognize White's position as mediator. The theory of tropes employed by White becomes, as Ricoeur puts it, "a relay station" in his own road of argument (*TN,* 3:152–54). Despite his respect for White's argument, particularly insofar as it foreshadows his own notion of the "interweaving of history and fiction (*TN,* 3:181)," Ricoeur is most uncomfortable with the essential tropological point, which he cites once again in a footnote, that any movement from one meaning to another meaning occurs tropologically "with full credit to the possibility that things might be expressed otherwise" (White, quoted in *TN,* 3:311 n. 36). If the sequence of generations supersedes the individual death at the upper level of historical reflection by pointing to the endless replaceability of human material, always different, always the same, so tropology supersedes the sort of satirical language used by Braudel, who himself notes that his book may be seen as an hourglass, throwing the idea of directionality of narrative into disarray. White suggests that there are no properly historical reasons for choosing one version of the past over another, assuming that the important but decidedly secondary constraints of evidence and factuality have been respected. Choosing a version of the past—and here White follows Kant—is a moral and an aesthetic choice; it is the choice of a future. This is White's version of the aporia of time, the discordant concord of the threefold present, but it is quite different from Ricoeur's. Both Braudel, at the lower linguistic boundary of naming, and White, at the upper limit where choices among full world images obtain, stress the materiality of language. Like death, language is a grimacing image of human limits. Braudel's language satire also satirizes human intentionality—the blind suffering of section 3, which he says he recounts because the actors in it believed it to be important—but the world of real meaning must be created in language by the historian, who finds it always escaping him as he tries to constitute its objects by naming them. By the same token, historians enter, not a world of traces reflecting the past intentionality of human actors, but rather a world constituted by a population of dead and living narratives, other histories. This, one could maintain, is historical reality. It is within this population of other texts that a historical text must define itself, be named, acquire an identity, engender other histories.

Ricoeur writes that the privilege of the reality possessed by historians over that possessed by writers of fiction lies in the fact that only the former speak about something that was observable to witnesses in the past. Thus, "between the 'reality of the past' and the 'unreality of fiction,' the dissymetry is total" (*TN*, 3:157). (Total, that is, before the act of reading begins its provisional mediating function.) Now, I hope I have adequately suggested that, in this notion of what constitutes the "reality of the past," Ricoeur seems to be in disagreement with his own principal example of historical discourse, Braudel's *Mediterranean.* Even without pressing further my own reading of the text as a satire on the language of historical representation, I think it evident that the "reality of the past" is exactly what is invisible to contemporary witnesses, who live in a world of illusion that the historian represents almost as a sentimental reminder of their blindness. Ricoeur, in fact, cites Tolstoy as a narratological counterexample to Braudel, suggesting that the Russian would have interwoven into a unity the temporal materials that the Frenchman arranged on his three separate levels (*TN,* 1:212). Yet a reading of *War and Peace* also confirms that Tolstoy and Braudel agree on the lack of awareness of the historical actor. Tolstoy's Napoleon, like Braudel's Philip, is scarcely necessary to the vast migration of men from West to East and back again in 1812. Kutuzov's wisdom is an ironic wisdom; he knows that all the calculations, based on the experience of thoughtful people in real situations, are in vain, and that what matters are things like the role of the environment, as Braudel would say, and fate, which both Kutuzov and Tolstoy (and perhaps Braudel too), would define as God's will. He knows that there is no reality there to be calculated, that the historian will make it real. In *Narrative Logic,* F. R. Ankersmit chooses to focus on the wholeness of the historical text, what he calls the *narratio,* or narrative substance. It is the whole of the narration, rather than individual statements within it, that gives identity to a historical vision. Translation rules do not exist for reality; there are no mediating bridges, no quasis to turn the discordance of parts into the concordance of wholes. It is the text that creates meaning by giving a rounded vision of something; and narrativity is the property of the text itself. A vision of history can only exist in a world of alternate visions. To focus on the whole identity of a historical text, its narrative substance, is to discover its network of relationships spreading, not to the past nor to the inner consciousness of humanity, but to other historical visions; it is to emphasize the ironic necessity of discordant visions. When one vision of the past prevails, we have in fact no vision of the past.[14] Only the existence of alternate narratives can give contours to any *narratio.* In this sense, Braudel's confrontation is not with the Mediterranean world or Philip II but with the *narratios* of Henri Pirenne, Francois Simiand, Lucien Febvre, and so on. To choose, as Ankersmit does, the narrative as a whole, rather than mediating processes within narrativity, as the object of historical reflection highlights the same problems that appear when we focus on the lowest-level matters of historical naming, an ironic attention to the scarcely limited possibilities and purposes of historical thought itself.

E. H. Gombrich has pointed out that realism is based, not upon a representative model, but rather upon the notion of substitution for a purpose. A broomstick hobbyhorse resembles an actual horse hardly at all, and will pull no plow and win no race, but it will serve the child's *purpose* admirably. The most poignant image of the substitutive aspect of history is also drawn from childhood toys. It is Jules Michelet's statement that "the child is serious while rocking the doll in her arms (even sincere), she kisses it and loves it, but knows very well that it is made of wood."[15] Michelet, the greatest of resurrective historians, who wanted to make the dead come forth from the dust of his archives and speak through him, at last recognizes that the past is gone. The "standing-for" and *Gegenüber* that Ricoeur uses so well in his argument to overcome his difficulties with the notion that the historian reconstructs something, *Wie es eigentlich gewesen war* ("as it actually happened") is taken up into his system, but not in an ironic way (*TN*, 3:184, 185). There is no question about the power of Ricoeur's narrativity to make partial any vision, but only in the interest of an eternal making whole, an ever-renewed healing.

From start to finish, *Time and Narrative* is based upon the ancient analogy of history and human memory. The aporias of human time-consciousness, the threefold time of Augustine, the traces and archival institutions, are all presented as modes of memory. Because memory is endowed with a tremendous moral weight, the anamnestic imperative—"This do in remembrance of me"—stands as the justification for the morality of the historical enterprise. The lowest boundary is the pathos of "anonymous death"; the upper boundary is the cycle of generations and infinite human replaceability. Nietzsche's challenge to the morality of memory is considered late in volume 3; and his advocacy of forgetfulness in the interest of life against the paralyzing totalization of an always-encompassing historicality is noted, in a footnote, as an "ironic nostalgia" (*TN*, 3:331n.). But human forgetfulness cannot, properly speaking, be considered in *Time and Narrative* as the overwhelming presence (absence) that it is. Historical consciousness is as profoundly discontinuous as human consciousness; the archives are monuments to what is there, like the great forgetting machine that is the human mind, which is designed far more for the destruction and repression of information than for the conservation and recall of it.

"The moment when literature attains its highest degree of efficacity is perhaps the moment when it places its readers in the position of finding a solution for which they themselves must find the appropriate questions, those that constitute the aesthetic and moral problem posed by a work" (*TN*, 3:173). The reader of *Time and Narrative* is surrounded on all sides by a play of mirrors—each angled slightly so as to reflect the entire image of the previous glass in the series, plus a bit more—and is denied at last his own independence from the text. The role of the reader is already there in the dialectic; this we must strategically forget if we are to gain any ground from which to survey *Time and Narrative* at its highest degree of efficacity. As I have indicated above, the morality of *Time and Narrative* is the morality of memory, the anamnestic imperative. The aesthetic dimension of *Time and Narrative* is, however, equally crucial. *Time and Narrative* operates in the interest of the beautification of a category that, in and of itself, is frightening, the sublime. Interest in the beautiful, Kant reminds us, is characteristic of sociability, the work of a good soul. The painfulness of the sublime flows from the discordance of the imagination with reason—in short, from the existence of aporicity itself.[16] The mediation operated by *Time and Narrative* is between the sublimity of time itself (and the aporias of its internal experience, whether drawn by Augustine or Husserl) and the beauty of its representations. The mediation, however, is not an entirely innocent one, because it is made necessary in the first place by the gap between the internal and the external realities of time, a gap embodied in the first instance by the confrontation between Augustine and Aristotle, but reincarnated frequently thereafter in a number of guises. This gap in itself, however, cannot ever be made into the locus of a mediation; it is never between the two concepts. Neither can mediation serve as a truly mediate concept, one in the middle. Because it is precisely the unmediated abyss of experience, the imponderable uncertainty of our reality, that is sublime, mediators always slip to the side of the beautiful, even when they mediate between the beautiful and the sublime. I suspect that this is what Ricoeur has in mind when he speaks at the end of *Time and Narrative* of the new aporias arising from his discussion. Operating under the Sign of the Analogous already puts my commentary in the aporetic position of mediator when it is mediation itself that I wish to examine, but this cannot be helped and must be willfully ignored, forgotten. The pain and pleasure that accompany the discordance and concordance of the narrative transformation suggest that the principal aesthetic process in narrative is the beautification of the chaotic straw of existence, a chaos that can be aestheticized only as pain, as the sublime. In this view, to think about—that is, to think outside of—*Time and Narrative* is to think about the sublime, to ponder its costs and to reflect on what might be lost by sublating loss itself into an optimistic phenomenology of emplotment such as *Time and Narrative.*

The repeated ternary movement of *Time and Narrative,* with its three forms of mimesis, its three figurations, its threefold version of time, its salute to Hegel, even its three physical volumes, reminds me of Ricoeur's discussion of "The Theme of the Three Caskets," an essay in which Freud demonstrates the "integration of death into life." The third, leaden, casket in Shakespeare's *Merchant of Venice* corresponds for Freud to Cordelia in *King Lear.* The third woman is the fairest, but also the one who is silent. Her dumbness signifies death. In choosing her, the hero chooses death, Mother Earth, as he must, but in the form of a substitute, which is beauty. Choice replaces necessity, Ricoeur tells us, and beauty replaces death.[17] In my opinion, this is what Ricoeur has done in *Time and Narrative.* The beauty of memorializing narrative replaces the necessity of death. One should say, quasi-replaces.

The great merit of *Time and Narrative* is both to demonstrate and to perform the abilities of narrativity to resolve any aporia under the Sign of the Analogous, the "quasi." This invokes the middle-level functions of grammar and syntax, while tactically forgetting the lexical and semantic functions of language, which ironize transformations. *Time and Narrative* does more or less what it says. It performs the mediations of narrativity in its own text until we finally want to ask: Is there any other way? Is narrative the very form of thought itself? At first glance, narrative is the very form of knowledge itself, if we are to respect the common, if distant, etymological root of narrative and gnosis. The very process of thinking through, dia-gnostic, as it were, is revealed as narrative in its core. Of course, a turn from narrative to the French *récit* takes us into a quiet different genealogy of naming. And, if Pellauer and Blamey had chosen to translate *Temps et récit* as *Time and Tale,* a perfectly defensible (but by no means superior) choice, we should have been led into a different, more Teutonic world of telling (*erzählen*). In this world of naming, as Braudel made unusually clear, ironies abound, as does the awareness of alternate possibilities that Hayden White often stresses. Yet in spite of this, narrative remains secure because it is the domain of parts and wholes, apart from the process of naming parts and interpreting wholes. Narrative, we might say, is what does *not* get lost in translation.

There can be no question but that *Time and Narrative* represents an enormous step forward in the discourse regarding time, narrative, historical discourse, realism, and many other things. We will still be chewing on these volumes years from now, and finding new nourishment. Limits must exist. As Ricoeur wrote in his Freud book: "A limit, as Kant has taught us, is not an external boundary but a function of a theory's internal validity."[18] Still, I feel that the power of Ricoeur's theory is also its weakness, its unapproachability. It does not give way easily to frontal assaults, because the gap in narrativity is its inability to represent gaps. Narrative always remembers, even when it remembers forgetfulness. This seems to be the blind spot of narrative: that, in a sense, it cannot narrate itself. My feeling, in other words, is that while there seem to be no aporias that cannot be resolved within the realm of narrative, there is nevertheless an outside that cannot be narrativized because the elements are too basic or too whole.

NOTES

1. See Erich Auerbach, *Scenes from the Drama of European Literature*, trans. Ralph Mannheim (Minneapolis: University of Minnesota Press, 1984).
2. One need only cite the savage response of J. Hillis Miller to *Time and Narrative* in *Times Literary Supplement* October 9, 1987, pp. 1104–5.
3. See Patrick Mahony's fine discussion in *Freud as a Writer* (New York: International Publishers Press, 1982), p. 94.
4. Thomas Mann, *The Magic Mountain*, trans. H. T. Lowe-Porter (New York: Vintage Books, 1969), p. 541.
5. Martin Heidegger, quoted in David E. Klemm, *The Hermeneutic Theory of Paul Ricoeur: A Constructive Analysis* (Lewisburg, Pa.: Bucknell University Press, 1983), pp. 41, 42. For a discussion that attempts a synthesis of Heidegger and Ricoeur on history, see Bernard Dauenhauer, "History as Source: Reflections on Heidegger and Ricoeur," *Journal of the British Society for Phenomenology* 20, no. 3 (1989): 236–47.
6. Paul Ricoeur, *Time and Narrative*, vol. 1, trans. Kathleen McLaughlin and David Pellauer (Chicago: University of Chicago Press, 1984); vol. 2, trans. Kathleen McLaughlin and David Pellauer (1985); and vol. 3, trans. Kathleen Blamey and David Pellauer (1988). Subsequent quotations are from this edition, and volume and page numbers will be cited in text to *TN*.
7. Fernand Braudel, *The Mediterranean and the Mediterranean World in the Age of Philip II*, 2 vols., trans. Siân Reynolds (New York: Harper & Row, 1972–74).
8. Mann, *The Magic Mountain*, p. 716, quoted in *TN*, 2:129.
9. "If we now ask what resources *Der Zauberberg* is capable of bringing to the refiguration of time, it appears most clearly that it is not a speculative solution to the aporias of time that we are to expect from the novel but, in a certain way, their *Steigerung*, their 'elevation to a higher level' " (*TN*, 2:129).
10. Michelle Vovelle, "L'histoire et la longue durée," in *La Nouvelle Histoire*, ed. Jacques Le Goff, Roger Chartier, and Jacques Revel (Paris: Retz-CEPL, 1978), p. 318, quoted in *TN*, 2:249 n. 36 (Ricoeur's translation).

11. Paul Ricoeur, *Fallible Man,* trans. Charles Kelbley (Chicago: Henry Regnery, 1965; rev. trans. with an Introduction by Walter Lowe, New York: Fordham University Press, 1988), p. 3.
12. Braudel, *The Mediterranean,* quotations from section 1.
13. This procedure is discussed at length in Hans Kellner, "Disorderly Conduct: Braudel's Mediterranean Satire," a chapter in Kellner, *Language and Historical Representation: Getting the Story Crooked* (Madison: University of Wisconsin Press, 1989).
14. F. R. Ankersmit, *Narrative Logic: A Semantic Analysis of the Historian's Language* (The Hague: Nijhoff, 1983), p. 240.
15. Jules Michelet, *Histoire de France,* 12:290–91, quoted in Linda Orr, *Jules Michelet: Nature, History, and Language* (Ithaca, N.Y.: Cornell University Press, 1976), p. 204.
16. Immanuel Kant, *Critique of Judgement,* trans. J. H. Bernard (New York: Hafner, 1951), pp. 139, 141.
17. Ricoeur, *Freud and Philosophy: An Essay on Interpretation,* trans. Denis Savage (New Haven, Conn.: Yale University Press, 1970), pp. 330–32.
18. Ricoeur, *Freud and Philosophy,* p. 176.

PHILIP ROSEN

TRACES OF THE PAST

From Historicity to Film

IN HIS MAGISTERIAL *Time and Narrative,* when Paul Ricoeur finally puts forward his own view of the work of history, the notion of the trace is central. While he conceives of historiography and fiction as complementary narrative refigurations of time, the most specific difference of historiography is the trace as vestige of the past. The presence of the trace in historiography is preeminently the authority of references to primary documents in the historian's practice.

Ricoeur presents the trace as one of several connectors that serve human culture by publicly mediating the fundamental antinomies that produce the aporias of time explored in phenomenological philosophy, such as the antinomy of psychic and physical time, or of phenomenological and cosmological time. Other such connectors are the calendar, which establishes a measured, bidirectional linear temporality to negotiate the divide between the restricted time of human mortality and the unlimited time of the cosmos; and the succession of generations, which connects the distant past and the future through a biologically defined "we." The trace, a survival from the past, establishes a mutual "contamination" over the fissure between the limitations of the present and the virtually unlimited extent of the past. This is because, as a preserved materiality from the past, the trace is an object submitted to laws of causation, but it also has the effectivity of a sign. Thus bridging nature and culture, the trace overlaps the existential and the empirical to produce an impossibility for a historicizing intentionality: a presence of the past.[1]

The invocation of the document, then, becomes the historian's proof for whatever claim his or her discourse lays, in Ricoeur's phrase, to constructing a reconstruction, that is, of a special relation *to* an actual past in the relating *of* that past. Ricoeur explicates this relation as a dialectical synthesis of Same, Other, and Analogous. These stand for three theoretical accounts of historiography that Ricoeur inflects to his own purposes: history is available as identifying reenactment, after R. G. Collingwood; as differentiating otherness, after Michel de Certeau; and as metaphorization, after Hayden White. Ricoeur thus emphasizes the *as* in Ranke's famous 1824 slogan—to show the past "as it actually happened" (*Wie es eigentlich gewesen*).[2] In its quest to secure the actuality of the past, even the modern critical historiography based on systematically careful use of documents that Ranke supposedly promoted cannot avoid a certain minimum of otherness, hence insecurity in its relation to a real past. But instead of destabilizing historiographic ambition, this leads to Ricoeur's bedrock argument: such claims of valid contact with past reality will always be through refiguration. (This refiguration occurs in connection with another dialectic among past, future, and present elaborated in phenomenological philosophy.) Nevertheless, any historiography remains definitionally grounded in the trace, because the trace is the only kind of sign by which historical narrative is distinguishable from a fictional figuration. This grounding evinces a debt to the dead in the face of the otherness of the past—that is, a responsibility to render the past in such a way that it is rendered its due. As the unavoidable split between past and present is mediated in the overlap of the trace, so the gap between identity with and the otherness of past reality finds its discursive response in a figurative emplotment derived from traces.

The notion of the trace in this sense is not foreign to the theorization of cinema. In the same decade that Ranke contended for a history based on what actually happened, Niépce and Daguerre were experimenting with chemicals and a camera obscura to produce the earliest surviving photographs. When we in 1990 look at Niépce's *Set Table,* we see silverware, bowl, and glass that actually existed in 1827, chemically "traced" onto a photographic plate from these objects by light. The preservative function of photography and later sound recording as components of cinema was most influentially celebrated after World War II by the phenomenological film theorist André Bazin. It has occasionally been taken up by others, some of whom have reread Bazin as founding a film theory on what C. S. Peirce might have called "cinema as indexical sign" (in his second trichotomy of signs). In Ricoeur's terms, it seems to me we can say that in such preservation of sights and sounds from the past, photography, cinema, and most recently videotaped television always present themselves to us as some kind of iconicized trace of the past.[3]

Naturally, then, those of us engaged in the study of media might notice that Ricoeur does not deal with traces that are, strictly speaking, nonlinguistic. True, in passing, he occasionally acknowledges the interest of ruins and monuments to his account of figurations of temporality. Yet in his summary of history as "a knowledge by traces," he only cautions that his emphasis on written documents is not meant to denigrate the oral tradition—but there is nothing said about nonverbal traces. Yet, as the rough coincidence in time between Ranke and Niépce suggests, in a consideration of traces of the past there may be some "historical" basis for investigating connections between historiography and such indexical media as photography and cinema, an argument that can be found most recently in work of Stephen Bann.[4]

My contribution here, then, is a simple one: to probe aspects of some less verbal configurations of temporality. This will serve to indicate that historiography as knowledge by traces may be positioned in socioeconomic and cultural processes greatly diffused and expanded in the nineteenth century, which is sometimes called the age of history. I will begin with extended examples of appeals to the trace (in the straightforward sense of survivals from a past) in projects that, like historiography, value contacts with pastness and purport to reconstruct a past, but whose products do not consist in linguistic writing. Then, I will move to some illustrative points revolving around the idea of temporal control as a socioeconomic project. This is where film, as a major twentieth-century enterprise of the trace, can serve as a revelatory example. I will conclude with brief remarks on a perspective on historiography that can deflect Ricoeur's concern with the trace in a somewhat different direction.[5]

I

A path is suggested by Bazin's bon mot in praise of a film by Robert Bresson based on Bernanos's novel *Diary of a Country Priest:*

"After Bresson, Aurenche and Bost are but the Viollet-le-Duc of cinematographic adaptation."[6] This pejorative allusion to the nineteenth-century architectural historian, theorist, and practitioner famous for the restoration of cathedrals such as Notre Dame in Paris refers us to the problematic of architectural restoration established during his lifetime.

By the nineteenth century, when the disposition of old edifices had become a central architectural issue in Western Europe, many buildings, especially churches, dating back to the Middle Ages and further, included additions and alterations constructed by those who had used them in succeeding eras. Many such edifices had not been completed by the generation that originally designed them, and as succeeding generations continued the construction, the original plan was modified to accord with current practices. As a result, a revered old building might appear, by standards of an organicist aesthetic, to be a stylistic hodgepodge. In such a common situation, given what appeared from the perspective of the nineteenth century as a virtual continuum of architectural work and adjustments from a large segment of the past, precisely what should be the principles guiding the rapidly increasing number of projects commissioned to renovate, say, a medieval cathedral? In his major theoretical essay on restoration, Viollet-le-Duc notes that this was a completely modern problem, arising only in the first quarter of the nineteenth century—that is, as historical studies ascended to the status of a master discipline. It was necessary to invent principles to guide the architect, and Viollet-le-Duc became associated with the general tendency whose slogan was *l'unité de style.* With historical learning and research, the architect could ascertain the dominant style in which the building had originally been intended, or at least that which was likely in the period of the original construction. The building could then be made into an aesthetically valid entity according to those stylistic tenets, derived from a periodization of architectural history. In practice this doctrine could lead to the razing of more recent, yet centuries-old, components of the building in order to reconstruct it with stylistic unity. In fact, in many cases this meant unifying the building according to such an "original" period ideal *even when the building had itself never previously existed in that style.* In addition, restoration on this principle also justified the use of new materials and modern methods to construct ideal substitutes, even for those aspects of the building, "original" or otherwise, that had been worn down over the centuries (a common restoration practice).

Now, this is an extremist summary of the sometimes vaguely formulated rationales for restorationism in the first half of the nineteenth century, and in his writings Viollet-le-Duc was often not an extremist. He intermittently inveighs against hypothetical renderings and repeatedly provides examples that require pragmatically balanced choices between constructive stability, current usefulness, respect for original remains, and the historical or aesthetic value of parts of the building originating in different periods. Nevertheless, he begins his article on restoration by proclaiming, "To restore a building is to reestablish it to a completed state which may never have existed at any particular time."[7] Not only the famous restorations he directed, but such a definition, along with the pragmatic concern in his writings for beauty and stability in the present, have also enabled commentators to align him with the view that restoration could mean to construct, on the shell of the old, a modern ideal substitute for an ancient thing.

By the second half of the century, notably in England, there had appeared a resistance to the dominant attitudes in architectural restoration. The most famous early spokesperson of the opposition was John Ruskin. This resistance is often said to have achieved a lasting ideological victory spearheaded by the Society for the Protection of Ancient Buildings founded in 1877 under the leadership of William Morris, who summed up its attitudes toward refinishing old surfaces by nicknaming it "the Anti-Scrape Society." Put briefly, the Ruskin-Morris position was that in restoration, a new construction becomes destruction: to replace what succeeding ages have added to a building in order to make it match a supposedly "original" style, which was too often only a hypothetical ideal anyway, was in effect to evacuate historical actuality. Historical actuality consisted in a continuity of effectivities between any such origin and the present. The proper response to the aging of buildings was, not restoration, but *preservation:* maintaining the old, prolonging the existence as long as practically possible.

The arguments and rhetoric by which the Ruskin-Morris line appealed for preservation as opposed to restoration have interesting resonances. When Ruskin sounds the battle cry in 1849, he compares the impossibility of duplicating ancient buildings to that of raising the dead, and insists instead on something like Ricoeur's debt to the dead. On the one hand, the past is Other to the present: "Another spirit may be given by another time, and it is then a new building; but the spirit of the dead workman cannot be summoned up, and commanded to direct other hands, and other thoughts." On the other hand, respect for the remains left by the dead enables contact with the past. Any newly constituted replica of the old, no matter how skillful the attempt at faithfulness, is deficient with respect to the continuous passage of time. Ruskin finds "the greatest glory of a building" in its age, which makes its walls "lasting witness against men, in their quiet contrast with the transitional character of all things . . . , [which] connects forgotten and following ages with each other, and half constitutes the identity, as it concentrates the sympathy, of nation." This emphasis on the appeal of time's passage leads him to value the wear on the surface that marks a building as genuinely old:

> As for direct and simple copying, it is palpably impossible. What copying can there be of surfaces that have been worn half an inch down? The whole finish of the work was in the half inch that is gone; if you attempt to restore that finish, you do it conjecturally; if you copy what is left, granting fidelity to be possible (and what care, or watchfulness, or cost can secure it?), how is the new work better than the old? There was yet in the old *some* life, some mysterious suggestion of what it had been, and of what it had lost; some sweetness in the gentle lines which rain and sun had wrought.[8]

Thus, restoration cannot bring the dead back to life, but preservation can maintain that of the dead which still lives. Ancient buildings should remain untouched, as monuments to the dead, preserving their spirits in a kind of architectural afterlife. The genuine surface of the old building is here treated as an indexical sign, or trace, of the passage of a real temporal span, a "mysterious suggestion" that can permit us in the present to experience the past, the preexistent.

In a landmark 1877 polemic, William Morris articulated the implications of this line of argument.

> In earlier times . . . [i]f repairs were needed, if ambition or piety pricked on to change, that change was of necessity wrought in the unmistakable fashion of the time: a church of the eleventh century might be added to or altered in the twelfth, thirteenth, fourteenth, fifteenth, sixteenth, or even the seventeenth and eighteenth centuries; but every change, whatever history it destroyed, left history in the gap, and was alive with the spirit of the deeds done amidst its fashioning. The result of all this was often a building in which the many changes, though harsh and visible enough, were by their very

> contrast interesting and instructive, and could by no possibility mislead. But those who make the changes wrought in our day under the name of Restoration, while professing to bring back a building to the best time of its history, have no guide but each his own individual whim to point out to them what is admirable and what contemptible; while the very nature of their task compels them to destroy something, and to supply the gap by imagining what the earlier builders should or might have done. Moreover, in the course of this double process of destruction and addition the whole surface of the building is necessarily tampered with; so that the appearance of antiquity is taken away from such old parts of the fabric as are left, and there is no laying to rest in the spectator the suspicion of what may have been lost; and, in short, a feeble and lifeless forgery is the final result of all the wasted labour.[9]

To begin with, Morris makes it clear that a radical preservationist position is willing to subordinate organic order to the disordering work of time. The promotion of a disjunctive series of period styles in the same building might seem like a strange precursor of postmodernism, but since the styles actually come down from their various periods, this promotion is an affirmation rather than an ironic negation of authenticity in time. Furthermore, this position also involves a theory of reception or, using Morris's term, a theory of the spectator, for it promotes engaging the imaginative faith of an onlooking subject in the historical actuality of the building, based on an apprehension of the materials and style(s) of the building as indexical markers or traces. He explicitly describes Ruskin's empathy-inducing "mysterious suggestion" of being in the presence of the past as an appeal to the imaginative faith of an onlooker that enables a kind of contact with the past. The restorationist's alleged substitution of a theoretically beautiful, hypothetically reconstructed, "original" is a negation of the continuous work of time *for a subject in the present.* Paradoxically, stylistic disunity draws the spectator into a more authentic encounter with the past as the work of time.

The opposition between the restorationist tendencies often associated with the name of Viollet-le-Duc and with Ruskin-Morris preservationism, which the latter claims is an opposition between a substitute and the real thing, is thus an opposition between the abstractly ideal and the concrete, between a priori organicized conceptions of a building and a posteriori respect for what the building is and has been in time—and therefore, we might say, between the building's hypothetical essence and its actual, historical existence. It appears that for the Ruskin-Morris line the existence of a medieval cathedral precedes its essence.

But it is also necessary to note that the Ruskin-Morris preservationist rationale shares its basic assumption with its restorationist opponents, namely, the exceedingly high value placed on a recovery of the past. This can remind us that the nineteenth-century debates over building restoration define more than opposing schools. Both sides of these debates embody a pervasive premise of much of Western culture and intellectual work during this period: concern with the past is basic and desirable. It would, in fact, be possible to trace out the force of these controversies in institutions, laws, and even language (including shifts in meaning of the word *restore*).[10] To stay with the example of Western European architectural theory and practice, the relation of *new* to older building styles was a central issue from at least the mid-eighteenth through the nineteenth century. This was the period of "revivals"—again the figure of resurrection: Elizabethan, Jacobean, Romanesque, and, above all, the reaction of the Gothic revival against Classicism. Consequently, recent textbooks can label the dominant architectural impulse of this era Historicism, an attitude whereby "architectural scholarship abandoned aesthetic theory and concentrated on historical research."[11]

Thus, the extremes of restoration and preservation are polar alternatives within an overall historiographic problematic. At stake is the status and configuration of the trace as well as its impact on the spectator—conceived as consciousness attracted by and/or seeking the past. My next major point is that this problematic is not restricted to the nineteenth century. Its power into our own century can be illustrated by another exemplary phenomenon, the genre of the so-called museum village, or outdoor museum, or living-history museum. The spread of the public museum per se in the nineteenth century is, of course, more evidence of an institutionalized concern with the trace closely akin to that which Ricoeur discusses under the rubric of the archive. However, the museum village attempts not just to display elements and fragments from the past but to construct a more or less overall environment from the past for the present-day spectator.

Consider one member of the genre, in Sturbridge, Massachusetts. Pay an admission fee, and you enter Old Sturbridge Village, which purports to be an authentic display of New England village life from the first half of the nineteenth century. You can walk through a small water-powered gristmill and a sawmill; a cooperage, kiln, schoolhouse, bank, and so forth; and a farm with livestock, worked with early-nineteenth-century implements. In so doing you encounter a number of peripheral details such as horse-drawn carriages and proper period costumes worn by those working at the various trades. It is claimed that, to the extent possible, the place is self-contained (for instance, barrels used in some of the village undertakings come from the cooperage, where you can watch barrels being made), and the major activities are seasonally correct (tourists coming in the spring can see planting; in the summer, haying; in the fall, harvesting and harvest festivals).

Throughout, there is respect for the ideal of preservation, an invitation for the tourist to engage in a kind of relation with the past envisioned by Ruskin and Morris. This is especially the case with the buildings making up the village. A number of them are actual nineteenth-century edifices moved from their original sites, repaired, and reassembled at Old Sturbridge Village. Their authenticity is communicated in a number of ways, from the claims of the tourist literature to more immediate manifestations. For example, on the schoolhouse walls are generations of names and graffiti carved by students. The schoolhouse originated in 1800 in New Hampshire, but its walls—and the traces left in the wall by those long since dead—have been preserved for us to see and touch.

Yet it is a given of this project that compromises must be made. For one thing, there are the legal constraints of current building codes, health regulations, and so forth. A portion of what we see, including certain buildings or parts of them and perhaps costumes, has been fabricated with modern methods. We can engage in conversation with what are called (appropriately in the present context) "interpreters" in roles of people from the past, but they also slip out of their roles to answer questions from a twentieth-century viewpoint, like good guides to any kind of exhibit. So their dress is, not just an invitation to imagine them as authentic figures from the past, but also one more exhibit of what the past looked like. To some degree, then, this is a substitute, something like a restoration. Or rather, the invitation of Old Sturbridge is less to a pure restoration or pure preservation than to a fluctuating mix of the two or, from another perspective, a dialectic that is the grounds for this construction of a reconstruction.

Farm livestock provides an irresistible example (and one, incidentally, that is reminiscent in an intriguingly off-center way of themes important to Ricoeur on history and pastness, including the relation of the trace to death and the succession of generations). Sheep raised on an early-nineteenth-century New England farm would probably have been a breed called Wiltshire-Dorsets, but this type is now extinct, having disappeared because of interbreeding with other types. In the name of authenticity, Old Sturbridge has bred phenotypes, sheep that resemble physically this now-nonexistent breed from the past.[12] Such breeding extends the preservation-restoration problematic from built environments to the biological. Genuine preservation would provide us with an individual animal of a certain appearance because it was produced from a gene pool extending continuously back to the early nineteenth century. But faced with this unbridgeable gap between past and present, Old Sturbridge has proceeded on a restoration of Wiltshire-Dorsets, producing a replica lacking the continuity with the past and hence the authenticity of a trace, but at least indicating what the past would have looked like. It is important that this goes beyond verisimilitude in the sense of avoiding conflict with a tourist/spectators' sense of the real, for how many visitors would recognize the deviation from the correct type of sheep? The attention to detail, the desire for absolute accuracy here evinced, begins to border on compulsion. In one sense, the preservationist goal of mysteriously and imaginatively *being* in the presence of the past remains significantly dominant: it would have been better to have actual Wiltshire-Dorsets. In their absence, however, that goal has been subtly diverted into a restorationist satisfaction of *seeing* what the past should have looked like. But, as Ricoeur points out with respect to Ranke, the word *like* opens the gates to a multitude of slippages, since it continually evinces the resort to resemblance rather than being, iconicity rather than indexicality, breaks between past and present rather than continuity; hence, perhaps, the compulsive attention to detail that most claims to mirror the past in the face of failed identity with it.

Old Sturbridge is interesting here only as a member of a genre. This genre was unique as a significant national phenomenon in the United States during the interwar period, when Old Sturbridge was conceived. A forerunner was the outdoor museum of Skänsen in Stockholm, which collected various Swedish buildings, artifacts, and craftspeople, and became a model that spread throughout Europe. In its promotion of the crafts practices of prior periods, the Skänsen movement allied itself with fascinations presumed by the historic-preservation movement. This kind of alliance occurred most influentially in the United States in the 1920s, when both John D. Rockefeller, Jr., and Henry Ford became personally involved in projects that established the genre: Colonial Williamsburg in Virginia and Greenfield Village in Michigan. Since World War II, the idea of the living-history museum developed in the U.S. has in turn been taken up in other Western countries.[13]

Colonial Williamsburg and Greenfield Village can be used to argue that the poles of preservationism and restorationism became a generic axis for the museum village. In the construction of Colonial Williamsburg, Rockefeller enthusiastically participated in the restoration of an American town of the 1790s, insisting on precisely accurate detail. Ruskin's dictum that restoration is destruction was literalized. While pre-1800 buildings still extant were preserved as much as possible, hundreds of post-1800 buildings were razed in order to allow twentieth-century contractors to restore eighteenth-century edifices over their original foundations in an organically totalized reconstruction of the town. Under the banner of historically correct restoration of an original, Rockefeller in effect eliminated the architectural history of the postcolonial United States. Ford, on the other hand, was not interested in a perfect reconstruction of a totalized environment, but in preserving the tools, artifacts, and edifices associated with admirable figures and types of actions from the past. In addition to his accumulation of outmoded mechanical devices, he actually preserved buildings where virtuous industry supposedly occurred, ranging from an 1939 doctor's office to the courthouse where Lincoln practiced law and Thomas Edison's Menlo Park Laboratory. As a result, Greenfield Village is more like the kind of museum that houses genuine, preserved artifacts, but from a jumble of disjunctive times and places. We might say that the experience of an ideal tourist here is not of what an actual town is supposed to have looked like at a specific point in time, but rather (to make the point through oversimplification) of a movement from one preserved trace to another.[14]

Thus, this comparison also reproduces the opposition established in earlier preservationist polemics: extreme respect for the force of time embodied in preservationism leads to spatial and temporal disjunction in the representation of the past, something for which Greenfield Village has been criticized; on the other hand, a unified reconstruction in the name of an ideal based, not on the trace, but on a hypothetical original can lead to a totalizing unity that can be criticized as stifling, artificial, and even false, charges sometimes made against Colonial Williamsburg.

In this context, Old Sturbridge—whose moving consciousness

was yet another industrialist, A. B. Wells—appears as a compromise formation, a version between the extremes of preservationism and restorationism represented by these other most influential of early museum villages. As we have seen, it includes preservationist components and appeals, but in its drive to construct an accurately detailed and completely typical nineteenth-century New England village, it necessarily includes restored elements. Consequently, in conceiving of the genre of the museum village, it is possible to treat Old Sturbridge as generically the most indicative of the three, in the practical and intellectual issues its reconstructions confront and in their solutions.

II

At this point, we can turn the discussion to another enterprise centrally concerned with the trace, film. One way to do this is at the level of cinematic images and texts. As a medium of the iconicized trace—a mechanical presentation of sights and sounds from the past—cinema as such is historical insofar as it participates in the concern for making the past present. It seems to me that it is possible to treat cinema as yet another variant on the dialectic of preservation and restoration. Within film history, this approach at first seems to lean toward an opposition between fiction film and film as a kind of document of past events, what is now vaguely but indicatively called documentary. The argument would be that even a single shot in a documentary, in comparison with one in a fictional film, presumes a fascination with seeing something that had actually happened in the past. From the exhibition of motion pictures in 1894 until around 1908, the so-called actuality film, often consisting of one shot, was a common and popular film genre. Of course, the documentary film as we now know it, composed of many shots ordered for rhetorical, explanatory, and/or aesthetic purposes, itself takes on some characteristics of a restoration in its impulses toward a totalizing unity. Again, preservation does not eliminate restoration but is instead its opposite pole in a dialectic.

This works both ways. In this perspective the establishment of fiction film as the norm of filmmaking after 1908 would seem to be a victory of restorationism. Instead of film as a document that recovers the past, we have since had the reenacted true story, the historical film, the docudrama—all of which (I would argue) condition other kinds of mainstream filmmaking. But this victory of restorationism has its preserved traces, not of original events, but of everything arranged in front of the camera to restore an event. Suppose we watch *Birth of a Nation* in 1990. Of course, to take one scene, we are well aware we are not seeing the actual assassination of Lincoln. However, we do see the now-dead Raoul Walsh as John Wilkes Booth jumping out of a boat seat onto a stage within a set that looks like a replica of Ford's Theater; Walsh actually did this for the filming of *Birth of a Nation.* Thus, again, the preservation-restoration construction is a dialectic, with varying intermixings of the two poles. Clearly this could lead to a long and complex discussion regarding the place of pastness and historicity in the history of filmic textuality.[15]

There is also a second kind of possible discussion stemming from the dialectic of preservation and restoration in which cinema can also stand as an important example. It would place that dialectic in some kind of more comprehensive view of temporality in its socioeconomic implications. To begin this discussion, let us return to the museum village.

All three of the museum villages discussed above were major enterprises bankrolled by wealthy twentieth-century industrialists who believed there were values in the past that are now lost. The experience they wanted to give touring spectators was one of the presence of a past embodying the spirits not just of the dead but of the virtuous dead. In Michael Wallace's convincing class-based analysis, both Williamsburg and Greenfield Village provide an experience of the past whose mix of preservation and exact restoration authorizes the display of a utopian social order. Ford's Greenfield Village highlights individualized technological innovators who rose from an industrious common people to make history. Rockefeller's Colonial Williamsburg froze time in the 1790s, in Wallace's words "just before that junction at which artisanal production succumbed to capitalist social relations." This becomes a mythical moment when a beneficent planter elite—as forerunner of a twentieth-century corporate elite—presided over a harmonious society based on an order of craft production free from socioeconomic discontent and conflict, in short, free from historical forces. This could be quite explicit. A. B. Wells expressed Ruskinian concerns with recovering the spiritual values of those now dead. But in establishing the rationale for the compromise formation of Old Sturbridge, he stated that even authentic preservation and material accuracy was only a means that could occasionally be violated in light of the ultimate goal:

> The purpose, briefly, will be to preserve the ever-good things of New England's past in a manner that will teach their usefulness to the people of the present and future. By "good things" of the past is meant not merely antique objects, but rather everything these objects imply—how they were made, how they were used, what the people and conditions of life were that made them necessary and influenced their designs; above all, how virtues and ideals expressed in them can be applied to life and work today.

What seems at first to be an anthropological concern with lifeways has in fact a more utilitarian significance. Wells seems to have envisioned a stream of potential industrial workers first serving as crafts apprentices in Old Sturbridge and then being educated in nineteenth-century virtues, thus echoing Ford's and Rockefeller's concerns with inculcating values from a mythical good old days of allegedly greater craftsmanship—and social harmony—into the labor force. In a more general sense, then, Wells's ambition for Old Sturbridge applies to all of these museum villages: the resurrection of the spirit underlying a productive community of some superior, harmonious past era arises against a disordered present lacking that spirit; and this translates into an anxiety about social order and control. In a number of ways, this description could be extended to the development of the preservation movement as a whole, which was nurtured and supported by a range of powers, from high-status social groups and wealthy individuals to the foundations they endowed.[16]

On the one hand, fascinated by the past, and on the other, disavowing conflictual historical processes and contemporary change, these ideological attempts by dominant social types to freeze time highlight the corrosive, disordering effects of a radical emphasis on temporality. We have already encountered such corrosiveness in the disjunctive aesthetic that is the logical extreme of a Ruskin-Morris preservationism. Here, however, the threats of coherence and stability posed by temporality are experienced as socially disordering. Now, some such defensiveness may be implicit in any attempt to recover the past. An extreme preservationism in its insistence on the value of the continuous integrity of the trace through time implicitly involves a submission to time, so that the spectator/tourist is to experience the past by confronting the force of duration, what Ricoeur calls passage. Yet, since the attraction of the past must, by definition, in some way involve its otherness to the present, this submission can never be complete; that is, since the past can never be present in its actuality, the present can only encounter the past by constructing it and saying something about it from the present. An extreme restorationism is one relatively pure form of this rebound; "looking like" is not a simple submission to the past but also embodies the power to reconstruct it for purposes and benefits in the present, as Viollet-le-Duc knew. The impulse to gain some purchase on pastness and thereby on time, to control it implicitly or explicitly from a present, is recurrent. It is evinced in Ford's preservationist variant on the museum village, and even Ruskin asserts the benefit to the nation of preservationism.

Put abstractly, the problem is a theoretically familiar one. The modern emphasis on temporality can lead to an insistence on unending flux and therefore change. This threatens to become characteristic of the present moment from which the past is to be apprehended. It is often based on such an emphasis that modernist and postmodernist challenges to arguments from or to identity appear as destabilizing and disordering. However, the social stake in the past felt and expressed by the powerful also suggests that there are social facets in defenses that appear in reconstructions of the past. There is a social, and even a political, stake in controlling and ordering temporality. Cinema, the model mass medium of the twentieth century, provides an important illustration. We have seen that cinematic textuality can be schematized along a polar opposition between preservation and restoration, and that the balance and intermixing on this axis can shift historically. From this perspective, the institutionalization of narrative film as the textual norm that occurred most influentially in the United States between 1909 and 1917, with its movement away from the preserved actuality as a commercial genre, appears as a means of regulating mass-produced indexical images or traces. To put it differently, this institutionalization regulates a key Ricoeurian "connector," establishing textual parameters that control the mass production of traces and submitting them to a unifying (classical cinematic narrative) order, which delimits narrational and consequently spatial and temporal configurations of film images and (later) sounds. Over the past two decades, this kind of textuality has been much analyzed by film scholars, though only occasionally from a notion like indexicality or the trace.[17] But an exploration of temporal control in cinema must also be considered at a socioeconomic level, with attention to the consumption as well as the production side of institutionalized mainstream film-making. Here, we depart from the textual dialectic of preservation and restoration in order to illustrate the social stake in temporal order underlying that dialectic.

As a condition of its existence, the film industry assumes a mass audience with a certain minimum of disposable income and what has been called leisure time, for mainstream films provide a leisure time activity. Now, the very notion of leisure time—and therefore cinema as the socioeconomic institution we know—assumes the weekly and daily scheduling that came to govern the activities of working masses during industrialization. In previous, nonfactory (home manufacture, farm) kinds of production, workers were often able to determine their own daily work schedules. Or rather, constraints on the use of time tended to revolve around completion of whole tasks, such as the fashioning of a garment or the ploughing of a field. Furthermore, such labor tended to be scheduled in comparatively vague and sometimes variable periodicities associated with categories of natural temporalities that cultures had marked with calendars from time immemorial, such as days, months, years, and seasons; and, insofar as daily work was subject to more detailed time constraints, even some of these might be associated with naturalized needs such as food and sleep. The gradual introduction of wage-manufacturing labor that began in England in the late seventeenth century, along with an accretion of technological shifts implemented especially in the second half of the next century, entailed a concomitant intensification in the division of labor. The growth of productivity and commerce associated with the increased need for detailed coordination between different subtasks in the production process eroded the importance of both the natural cycle and the unity of the task as temporal markers for labor. Manufacturers found it desirable to regularize labor time by other modes and on other grounds, in the interest of the economic efficiency of a rationalized industrial capitalism. This process was quite normalized by the mid-nineteenth century, but not before labor experienced its development as the subjection of a naturalized temporal freedom to the requirements of the centralized factory and the manufacturer.

E. P. Thompson has emphasized that the shift from task-oriented to temporally disciplined labor involved the regulation of something that had not previously been ordered on this scale, the hour-by-hour activities of employees. The employer's interest in temporal control and surveillance and hence the measurability of time had, by the end of the nineteenth century, led to a constellation of temporal mechanisms and devices governing the workplace, from time signals and the very concept of "overtime" to Taylor's time-motion studies. At first such innovations often engendered resistance, but the ultimate success of the manufacturers resulted in profound cultural changes—cultural because they affected lifeways and even conceptions of life. That is, the emphasis on temporality extended well beyond the workplace. It should not be surprising that an increase in time awareness was felt throughout industrialized culture, including its intellectual and scientific strata. For example, Taylor's experiments presupposed prior technological advances in the accurate measurement of time that had been stimulated in part by needs of navigation and astronomy and that provided new tools, evidences, and conceptual inspirations for less immediately pragmatic natural sciences like physics.

But here I would emphasize the social and economic spheres. The growth and success of industrial capitalism was inseparable from the need to organize unprecedentedly large combinations of production, markets, and labor forces, which meant the economically induced ordering of time had to be instituted in a wide variety of activities. Temporal calculation was required for communication and commerce at modern speeds, as is demonstrated by the universal standardization of worldwide clock time and time zones toward the end of the nineteenth century—about the time of cinema's appearance. And this, in turn, reinforced the ever-increasing expectations that less expansive, more individualized activities be scheduled and timed. Technical problems in the factory mass production of personal watches were solved in the 1860s, and according to an 1875 report, worldwide watch production was 2.5 million per year as opposed to 350,000 to 400,000 around 1800. By 1902, the personal timepiece was so universal in the West that Georg Simmel illustrated the interdependent nature of modern metropolitan life by imagining the effects if every pocket watch in Berlin suddenly went wrong: "all economic life and communication of the city would be disrupted. . . . the technique of metropolitan life is unimaginable without the most punctual integration of all activities and mutual relations into a stable and impersonal time schedule."[18]

The rapid expansion of the film industry that firmly established the cinema as a leading mass medium was dependent on this intensification of time awareness and temporal control at the level of the day symbolized by the universal profusion of the watch. On the production side the mass production of narrativized traces, like other mass manufacture industries, required highly rationalized methods, which assume relatively predictable regularities with respect to labor, production, and marketing schedules. On the distribution and consumption side, it required an audience whose leisure time was regular enough to make volume of film viewing calculable and reasonably predictable. Consequently, in its socioeconomically dominant forms, cinema could only exist in a society that regulated the week and the day so that, as a relief from or reward for work, there were a certain number of hours regularly allotted to "leisure." (This also assumes something famously recognized by Henry Ford with respect to autoworkers, that the audience must have access to a requisite minimum of "disposable income" to fuel the production of mass entertainment with capital.) Note that this also affects the textual; for example, one constraint on the length of film programs and hence texts would be the need to coordinate offerings with society-wide norms of available leisure time. Thus, not only might we find a special relation between cinema and temporality through its technical and textual claims to re-present a past, that is, as preservation and restoration; it simultaneously and relatedly bears a special relation to modern temporal constructions and organizational matrices through its status as mechanized mass medium. As a junction of indexical trace and rationalization, cinema is one crossroads in the emphasis on controlled ordering of time throughout culture after industrialization.

III

The writing of history is also an ordering of time. In the first instance, there may be unexpected and odd connections between historiography and film. To return to Ricoeurian emphases, if the institution of cinema is a site where the trace meets the clock, the institution of history is a site where the trace meets the calendar in the datable document. Such an aphoristic formulation is immediately insufficient in the face of the obvious and wide differences between the two, such as the distinctive nature of their respective traces and of the kinds of institutions that produce films and histories. Yet, a general point is here broached, namely, that both can be interrogated as orderings of the trace and hence temporality. Motion pictures were a development of nineteenth-century technology that both registered and exploited aspects of the heightened time consciousness that came to pervade modern life. Another aspect of nineteenth-century culture was the rise of history as master discipline, its importance in the development of the modern university, and its ideological prestige. As we have seen, however, concern with the past could be disordering. As the production of texts asserting knowledge and as institution, the discipline of history registered awareness of the pervasiveness of temporality in human affairs, the order of which was now to be studied as a "human science." This is much too large a topic to develop here, but let us move to a conclusion with just two schematic comments on historiography.

The first is that the approach developed here is not one easy to envision within Ricoeur's framework for historicity, for as much as he would accommodate social and ideological considerations, his phenomenology appears to preclude self-historicization. For example, Darwinism is one of the most obvious emblems in the tension between time as corrosive and the control of time, for Darwin exposed once and for all the destabilizing aspects of the vast expanse of time and mutations of species, yet submitted them to human reason. It is not unusual in intellectual history to focus on Darwinism to illustrate the pervasiveness of an impulse to historicize in the nineteenth century. Interestingly, however, when Ricoeur follows Collingwood in distinguishing between historiography as a human science and the natural sciences, he specifically excludes evolutionary biology from historiography. This is ultimately because as philosopher Ricoeur seeks to integrate into his theory of history some proportion of a humanist view of agency against strong currents in contemporary theory, so he restricts historical accounts to the mimesis of human actions. But if instead of seeking to save a residue of the concept of an active consciousness for philosophy we seek a historical understanding or historical consciousness, Darwinism must appear as the historicization of nature. Thus, when Stephen Toulmin and June Goodfield chart out a historical sequence of ideas of time, they point out that evolutionary thought and the geological constructions on which it depended followed on and from the establishment of the modern discipline of history and specifically appealed to some of the latter's principles. Darwinism claimed to reconstruct inferentially a comprehensible overall development in time from traces of the past. Aside from the fact that its traces were fossils, this sounds very much like what a historian does.[19]

This leads to a second comment, having to do with the relationship of the textualization of the past in historiography to some of the broad sociocultural processes outlined above with respect to cinema. According to Reinhart Koselleck, on whom Ricoeur draws, modern historiography initially appeared with the attribution of epic unity to sequences of historical events. The conception of reality as *internally* related sequences of events was stimulated by Enlightenment notions of progress and the concept of revolution after 1789. This belief that there were principles of change internal to history is what Koselleck calls the temporalization of history. As an a priori ideology, the idea of progress could soon be challenged by another aspect of the new discipline of professional historiography, critical examination of documents, the trace par excellence for the historian according to Ricoeur. This is where we began. But the notion of a time with its own, transnatural internal development, a development susceptible to rational analysis and demonstration, had also taken hold. From now on, historiographic disputes would be both over the authenticity and pertinence of documents and over principles for unifying developmental sequences evidenced by those documents.

The temporalization of history was thus implicated not only in a historian's working methods but in theoretical and institutional considerations. It meant that there was such a thing as history per se, which could be the object of theory or philosophy. The identification of this distinctive object also provided the basis for a professional scholarly discipline, hence university departments, professorships, and journals. But, in addition, the principle that genuine historical change is possible meant that disputes over principles of development were imbricated with political and social understandings. As the French Revolution confirmed, history could produce something radically new instead of constituting a set of repetitions that served as lessons to the present, or a constant reference to an eschatology. The specter of history as production of the new is what we have seen encountered as threat—the ever-present social threat of history—and disavowed in enterprises such as the genre of the museum village. This suggests that more-formal, prestigious written historiography, as the disciplined rational understanding of human affairs in time, could well embody similar disavowals and defenses in its own orderings of temporality.

Pertinently here, Koselleck emphasizes that the new vision of the past and of historical temporality necessarily posited relationships between past and future—in his terms, between the space of experience and the horizon of expectations. But rather than fastening on the roots of this idea in phenomenology and/or reception aesthetics, I would here emphasize Kosellek's insistence on connecting the modern definitions of history to sociopolitical concerns. Thus, for example, he links the new concept of history to the notion of the forecast. If a statesman or politician understood the internal principles driving a sequence of events, he or she might act to accelerate or retard historical development. We could substitute *social planner* or *business entrepreneur* for *politician* in order to make a point. The desire for rational control of temporality, its organization and manipulability, are not so distant from modern structurings of historicity. The temporalization of history basic to historiography presented itself as a means of gaining control over the passage of time, ordering temporality. But, again, this temporalization should not be separated from social, economic, and political imperatives. It may not be too tendentious to connect it to planning and rationalization procedures, the profusion of the clock, and all that is associated with these factors. A good starting (though not ending) point for developing this position remains the mutual imbrication of epistemological constructions and socioeconomic practices in Horkheimer and Adorno's *Dialectic of Enlightenment* (an approach that, incidentally, includes its own account of phenomenology and its aporias).[20]

In this paper, beginning from the idea of the historical trace, I have touched on a number of practices concerned with historicity and temporality, such as the dialectic of preservation and restoration, cinema as mass-produced narrativization of the trace, and the socioeconomic rationalization of labor and daily life. As distinct as they all are, they intersect in their relations to the problem of ordering time, which has become central to social and intellectual life since the onset of modernity. From all of these emerges a gestalt of a pervasive time awareness, which includes a cluster of anxieties with respect to the aspects of temporality that posed various kinds of threats to social, cultural, conceptual, and economic practices. While this time awareness was widely diffused in the nineteenth-century West, its vicissitudes and consequences are still strong in the twentieth century. With professional historical studies as just one leading edge, it seems possible not just to conceive of a temporalization of history but to subsume this under the temporalization of modern culture and society. So this becomes in part an explanation of the epistemic importance of history.

Since I began with Ricoeur, it is worth emphasizing that phenomenology might also be included; for example, its concern with the great expanse of cosmic time in existential contradiction with mortal time was only validated by geological research in the eighteenth century, and awareness of that expanse of time was widely disseminated as fact and problem with the later nineteenth-century influence and popularization of Darwinism. Cinema, history, and phenomenology itself—all in different ways discourses marked by concern with the trace—probably cannot be easily separated from this massive temporalizing impulse with its concomitant concern with temporal control. Hence, the preservation of our interest in the genealogy and theory of history today, which this paper evinces.

NOTES

1. Paul Ricoeur, *Time and Narrative,* vol. 3, trans. Kathleen Blamey and David Pellauer (Chicago: University of Chicago Press, 1988), pp. 105–23.
2. Ricoeur, *Time and Narrative,* vol. 3, chap. 6, esp. pp. 154–56.
3. See Peter Wollen, " 'Ontology' and 'Materialism' in Film," pp. 120ff. in his *Signs and Meaning in the Cinema* (Bloomington: Indiana University Press, 1972), rpt. in his *Readings and Writings: Semiotic Counter-Strategies* (London: New Left Books, 1982), and Philip Rosen, "History of Image, Image of History: Subject and Ontology in Bazin," *Wide Angle* 9, no. 4 (1987): 7–34. For major writings of Bazin, see André Bazin, *What Is Cinema?* vols. 1–2, trans. Hugh Gray (Berkeley: University of California Press, 1967–71).
4. Ricoeur, *Time and Narrative,* 3:221–23. Stephen Bann, *The Clothing of Clio: A Study of the Representation of History in Nineteenth-Century Britain and France* (New York: Cambridge University Press, 1984). See also Siegfried Kracauer, *History: The Last Things before the Last* (New York: Oxford University Press, 1969), pp. 50–61, 191–92.
5. Much of what follows draws on my forthcoming book, *Past Present: Theory, Cinema, Historicity.*
6. Bazin, *What Is Cinema?* 1:143.
7. Eugene-Emmanuel Viollet-le-Duc, *The Architectural Theory of Viollet-le-Duc: Readings and Commentary,* ed. M. F. Hearn (Cambridge: MIT Press, 1990), p. 269–79, quoted sentence on 269. Cf. his 1843 letter about Notre Dame, pp. 279–88. For the general nineteenth-century debates, I have relied on Stephan Tschudi-Madsen, *Restoration and Anti-Restoration: A Study in English Restoration Philosophy* (Oslo: Universitetsforlaget, 1976).
8. John Ruskin, *The Seven Lamps of Architecture* (New York: Farrar, Strauss and Giroux, 1988), pp. 186, 177, 184. See also chap. 5, "The Lamp of Life."
9. William Morris "Restoration," *Athenaeum* (1877), reprinted as an appendix in Tschudi-Madsen, *Restoration,* pp. 144–45.

10. Tschudi-Madsen, Introduction to *Restoration,* pp. 24ff. Cf. Nikolaus Boulting, "The Law's Delays: Conservationist Legislation in the British Isles," in *The Future of the Past: Attitudes to Conservation, 1174–1974,* ed. Jane Fawcett (London: Thames and Hudson, 1976).
11. Nicholas Pevsner, *An Outline of European Architecture,* rev. ed. (New York: Penguin, 1982), p. 377; see also pp. 375–89. On the development of architectural historiography during this period, see David Watkin, *The Rise of Architectural History* (Chicago: University of Chicago Press, 1980).
12. "Sheep as They Used to Be 150 Years Ago," *Providence Journal Bulletin,* October 30, 1986, sec. B, p. 4.
13. Useful accounts of the establishment of the genre include Charles Hosmer, *Preservation Comes of Age: From Williamsburg to the National Trust, 1926–1949,* vol. 1, chaps. 1–2 (Charlottesville: University Press of Virginia, 1981), and Michael Wallace, "Visiting the Past: History Museums in the United States," in *Presenting the Past: Essays on History and the Public,* ed. Susan Porter Benson, Stephen Brier, and Roy Rosenzweig (Philadelphia: Temple University Press, 1986). The bibliography on the idea of living museums is rapidly growing. See, e.g., Tony Bennett, "Museums and 'the People,'" in *The Museum Time Machine,* ed. Robert Lumley (New York: Routledge, 1988), and Patrick Wright, *On Living in an Old Country: The National Past in Contemporary Britain* (London: Verso, 1985).
14. See Wallace, "Visiting the Past," pp. 142–49, 151–53, 156–57.
15. See my *Past Present: Theory, Cinema, Historicity* (forthcoming).
16. Wallace, "Visiting the Past," p. 382 n. 60 (see also pp. 142–49, 151–53, 156–57, and Michael Wallace, "Reflections on the History of Historic Preservation," in *Presenting the Past*). The Wells quotation is from A. B. Wells, *Old Quinibaug Village,* quoted in Hosmer, *Preservation Comes of Age,* 1:114.
17. For samples of seminal post-1970 discussions of narrative and textuality in classical cinema, see Philip Rosen, ed., *Narrative, Apparatus, Ideology: A Film Theory Reader* (New York: Columbia University Press, 1986). The standard work relating industrial constraints to textual practices in the U.S. is David Bordwell, *The Classical Hollywood Cinema: Film Style and Mode of Production to 1960* (New York: Columbia University Press, 1985).
18. Georg Simmel, "The Metropolis and Mental Life," in *The Sociology of Georg Simmel,* ed. and trans. Kurt H. Wolff (New York: The Free Press, 1950), p. 413. E. P. Thompson, "Time, Work-Discipline, and Industrial Capitalism," *Past and Present,* no. 38 (Dec. 1967): 56–97. Cf. Ricoeur on the calendar and natural cycles in *Time and Narrative,* 3:104–8, 123. On increased "time awareness," see David Landes, *Revolution in Time: Clocks and the Making of the Modern World* (Cambridge: Harvard University Press, 1983), pp. 227–30; on the mass production of watches, see chap. 19 and, for the production figures used here, p. 287. On temporal standardization and regulation, see also Michel Foucault, *Discipline and Punish: The Birth of the Prison,* trans. Alan Sheridan (New York: Vintage, 1979), esp. pp. 149ff.; Wolfgang Schivelbusch, *The Railway Journey: Trains and Travel in the Nineteenth Century,* trans. Anselm Hollo (New York: Urizen, 1979), pp. 48–50; and G. J. Whitrow, *Time in History: The Evolution of Our General Awareness of Time and Temporal Perspective* (New York: Oxford University Press, 1988), pp. 158ff.
19. Ricoeur, *Time and Narrative,* 3:90; Stephen Toulmin and June Goodfield, *The Discovery of Time* (Chicago: University of Chicago Press, 1982), p. 238.
20. Reinhart Koselleck, *Futures Past: On the Semantics of Historical Time,* trans. Keith Tribe (Cambridge, Mass.: MIT Press, 1985); see pp. 31–37 for a summary. See also Max Horkheimer and Theodor Adorno, *Dialectic of Enlightenment,* trans. John Cumming (New York: Herder and Herder, 1972); and on phenomenology, see esp. Theodor Adorno, *Against Epistemology: A Metacritique,* trans. Willis Domingo (Cambridge, Mass.: MIT Press, 1983).

ANDRÉ GAUDREAULT

THE CINEMATOGRAPH

A Historiographical Machine

I WOULD LIKE TO NOTE, in beginning, that my essay is not, as Michèle Lagny's is, aimed at making an evaluation of the purely historical scope of Ricoeur's theory, nor does it evaluate the validity of using analogies or symbols for reducing the difference between the historical and the fictional narrative. Rather, my paper examines how Ricoeur's fundamental postulates regarding historical and fictional narratives can be appropriated as categories for analyzing the medium of cinema.

In order to do so, I have chosen to analyze a film from the early period of cinema, a period of time when, to paraphrase Phil Rosen's essay in this volume, the indexical moving image had just been innovated and was not yet normalized. This film shares some features with the film studied by Lagny. Its main character is also a king from a European country, and the action involved in it also concerns his coronation. Furthermore, it also tells, as Lagny puts it for *Ludwig,* a "true" story.

My film is a rather famous one, at least for people familiar with cinema studies. It is called *The Coronation of Their Majesties King Edward VII and Queen Alexandra* and was made in 1902 by the famous French film director Georges Méliès, following an order by the American-born English film distributor Charles Urban. I am examining this film in order to explore the problem of historical narrative, that is, to examine in what ways a documentary film might serve the function of historical narrative in cinema.

In fact, this curious object, made in 1902, is a short film that, in a

A production still from *The Coronation of Edward VII* (Mélies, 1902), an unanticipated "newsreel"! It seems here that we are, some ninety years later, witnessing the coronation ceremony of the king of England, or, at least, the trace that this ceremony left on the film track.

documentary fashion, narrates the story of the coronation of the king of England. Our analysis of it will enable us to examine some of the questions that arise when one tries to apply Ricoeur's concerns to another narrating medium, the medium of cinema.

It seems here that we are, some ninety years later, witnessing the coronation ceremony of the king of England or, at least, the trace that this ceremony left on the film track. But, in fact, when we look at a film like this, what do we have in front of us? Is it a trace of a historical reality (*réel historique*) or is it some sort of fictional unreality (*irréel de fiction*)? In order to answer this question, it will be necessary for us to consider how the film was made, and to analyze the nature of the trace left on the image track.

Let us start our investigation at a somewhat abstract and theoretical level, focusing our analysis on the relationship between film and history. A genuine documentary of the coronation ceremony is, in principle, supposed to establish a relationship of representation (*représentance*), or of *lieutenance* (standing for or taking the place of),[1] with the real past depicted in the film, the real past reproduced on the film track. Such a film should indeed be considered as constituting the traces of the abolished past of the coronation.

In the present case, however, we are not in the presence of a genuine documentary of the coronation ceremony. Indeed, Méliès acted the same way as Visconti will, seventy years later, in making his *Ludwig:* he hired an actor to play the role of his king. The difference, however, is that Méliès's actor is a contemporary of the king he is impersonating; this is obviously not the case of the actor in the Visconti film. But there is a second difference between these two films as well: the actor playing the role of the king in the Méliès film was crowned before the king himself, thus making that film, not the "usual" reconstituted newsreel, but an anticipated one. There is also a third difference between Méliès's and Visconti's films. As far as I know, the first criterion for Visconti's choice of an actor was not his strict resemblance to the impersonated king. In the case of Méliès, however, the resemblance between his actor and the king was important because one of the major purposes for making this film was to use it as a *tenant-lieu* (taking the place of), as we say in French, of the genuine documentary that Méliès could not secure, primarily because of technical difficulties filming with the poor lighting of Westminster Abbey. In a word, and here we draw on Ricoeur, it is because of the unrepresentability of the event for the camera that Urban was able to combine his historiographical will with the skills of the French director Georges Méliès, who specialized in fiction.[2]

One of the conclusions, then, we may draw from this coronation film is that, while making the film, Méliès acted, in part, as a historian, even though he made his historical narrative prior to the actual event. In fact, by anticipating what would have happened, he acted in a manner similar to a "retrospective" historian who has to, in a somewhat experimental fashion, reconstruct what actually occurred by means of documents and other traces from the past; as everyone knows, such reconstruction is the fate of any historian, since history would not have to be made if all traces from the past were present. Méliès, indeed, gathered for himself a number of documents in order to prepare his "historical" film. He allegedly went to London in order to record, by drawing sketches, a number of traces of the general look of the interior of Westminster Abbey so that he could reproduce this interior on the painted sets of his studio. As for the activity of the coronation itself, Méliès not only consulted, as he puts it himself, the "great master of ceremony" in person[3] but referred to various documents in order to ensure the authenticity (or at least the appearance of authenticity) of the numerous props and details (such as "uniforms, dresses, decorations, crowns, diadems, jewels" that were reproduced with accuracy, according to the *Daily Telegraph* of June 20, 1902[4]). In preparing for this film, Méliès acted in many ways like a historian, the only difference being that instead of asking his sources: "What happened and how did it happen?" he asked: "What will happen and how will it happen?"

But unluckily—unluckily, that is, for the sake of historical "truth"—Méliès, was not able to have access to one very important piece of information. Of course, he could not have had access to this information, since at the time he made his film the event had not yet happened. In other words, he could not have access to any important document that would inform him that there would, in fact, be, in the story of the king, a reversal of fortune (a *metabolè,* as Aristotle would call it), which, according to Ricoeur, gives to the plot its dramatic turn and constitutes the threshold of the historical event.[5] Indeed, the king fell sick just before the coronation ceremony, and it was decided that the coronation should be postponed; yet, the "reproduction" concocted by Méliès had already been made! It had, in fact, been prepared in order to be "premiered" the very night of the actual coronation—on June 26. In itself, the postponement would induce only minor consequences; the so-called historical truth of Méliès's film was not really threatened. The real problem, rather, was that the king's illness was prolonged to such an extent that the actual coronation did not take place until August 9.

So, as mentioned earlier, the Méliès film was intended to be a *tenant-lieu* of a genuine actuality. Note that *tenir lieu* in French means "to take the place of" something. And here, if we invert *tenant-lieu,* we form the word *lieutenant,* which forms the root for the important concept of *lieutenance* proposed by Ricoeur for understanding historical narrative. The general consequence, then, of this situation is that, when we are looking at the coronation film, we are not in the presence of a trace of a historical reality (*réel historique*); instead, we are in the presence of some sort of fictional unreality (*irréel de fiction*). But, to my eyes, the Méliès film does not lose, for all that, its capacity to narrate a historical occurrence. It is simply, like any other historical discourse, an interpretation of historical reality. And the discursive nature of the film is yet more evident if we take into consideration the fact that Méliès decided, in order to make a long story short, to select which, among the predicted actions of the ceremony, were to be included in the filmic *représentance.*

Indeed, Méliès constructed a "montage" of these actions by compressing, profilmically, the temporality of the ceremony. As the catalog announces: "Only such portions of the ceremony as would admit of action have been selected for purposes of this representation, thus greatly reducing the duration of the actual performance, and blending the same into a consecutive series."[6] This means that some of the actions that would occur in the real ceremony are missing from the film. We are then obliged to come to the conclusion that the Méliès film makes a rather obvious incursion into the realm of fiction. In fact, as we are going to see, this film is, in many respects, a rather good example of a cross-reference [*référence croisée*] between fiction and history. Indeed, the following remark by Ricoeur applies perfectly to this case: "it is a question of the role of the imaginary in intending the past as it actually was." The question has to do with the "unique way the imaginary is incorporated into the intended having-been, without weakening the 'realist' aspect of this intention. The empty place to be filled by the imaginary is indicated by the very nature, as nonobservable, of what has been."[7]

The historiographical consequences of Méliès's activity include such effects as the use of unreal things in order to signify real things (a worker in a washhouse—that is, the actor hired by Méliès—is not a king). But Méliès's use of the unreal had another, far more impressive, consequence. By using the unreality of a coronation ceremony not yet accomplished, the filmmaker was taking some risks, and what had to happen happened: his rather historiographical pretensions had to give way to more and more fiction! Indeed, historical reality contradicted the historiographic will of anticipation and, because the king's illness did not leave him, it was decided that the ceremony should be performed on August 9, although this meant eliminating less-necessary aspects of the ceremony in order to accommodate the king's fatigue. The following result was to be expected: not only does the film miss portions of the ceremony that were performed in actual reality (because of Méliès's decision to exclude some aspects of the coronation), but it also presents portions that never occurred (because of decisions made by the master of ceremonies).

So, Méliès's film does not place us in the presence of a genuine coronation. Rather, we are in the presence of a simulacrum of it. Nevertheless, are we not fundamentally in the presence of a kind of historical narrative, in as much as the Méliès film has recorded, has kept the traces of, a genuine simulacrum of the coronation, that simulacrum constituting, in itself, the traces of the genuine coronation, even though the coronation in question would still have to occur at the time of the shooting?

What I want to stress here is the apparent coalescence between the medium of cinema and what we would call historiographicity. If a fictional *written* narrative does not have to deal with the various constraints of reality, is not a fictional *filmic* narrative necessarily compelled to give an account of some sort of reality—that is, the one that appeared in front of the camera—even though it has been disguised in a fiction in order to be recorded? The pioneers of cinema were not all deluded on this matter when they decided to call their own cinematographic apparatus a historiograph.[8]

If, as Ricoeur says, "in an ontological sense, we mean by historical event what actually happened in the past,"[9] then the cinematographic apparatus is nothing else than a historiographical machine. The camera is, undoubtedly, a machine to record events that occurred in the past and a filmic narrative is made up of the fragments—that is, photographs—of these events from the past. This is the reason why what Ricoeur says of the written narrative cannot be applied in an unqualified manner to the filmic narrative: "the time of the fictional narrative is released from the constraints of paying it back [*de le reverser*] to the time of the universe."[10] In some respects, it is indeed by using portions of historical time that cinema builds up *fictional* time, hence the always-already-given historiographical character of cinematographic time. Unlike the characters of written fiction, the characters of filmic fiction do not make a completely unreal experience of time because it would not be true to say of them that (as Ricoeur puts it for the written fictional narrative) "the temporal marks of this experience do not have to be connected to the single spatial-temporal network constitutive of chronological time."[11]

In a way, then, one of the peculiarities of the cinema is the fact that a film always constitutes the history, the documentary of its fiction. As Alain Lacasse puts it in his thesis: "As a recording, a film constitutes a real past. Filming is always giving an account of history and fiction *simultaneously.*" And Lacasse goes even further: "The cinema, by its nature as a language, already holds, inscribed in itself, this intersection of the referential of history and fiction; hence, it certainly contributes to enabling the filmic narrative to participate in the refiguration of human time in a particularly unique fashion."[12]

But this is not to say that written narrative fiction cannot also be considered a kind of documentary or, consequently, a historical narrative. Both the written and the filmic narrative fiction would be, in my view, historical, although in a different manner.

I understand from Ricoeur that written narrative fiction is a kind of documentary. He writes: "So it is that the hard law of creation—which is to *render,* as perfectly as possible, the vision of the world that impels the artist—matches in every respect the debt of the historian or of the reader of history toward the dead."[13] In my reading of Ricoeur, I understand him to say that one of the reasons why one should consider that fiction intersects with reality is because fiction is, in some respects, a kind of a documentary of that part of reality that exists in a kind of extrafictional reality. That is, it records the past of the "soul" of the author of any fiction (Ricoeur talks of this past as a "quasi-past." The text of the fiction that is "embodied" in the narrative voice of the implied author who is, according to Ricoeur, a fictitious disguise of the real author[14] can, therefore, be considered as a mediator between that soul and the reader. We thus may conclude that cinema simply adds one more mediator to the process. If we come back to our Méliès film, we may conclude that the fiction scenically or profilmically set up by Méliès in front of the camera is a first mediator between his soul and the reader (in that case, a viewer) and that the film itself is a mediator of a second degree. In that sense, is one not justified to say for a filmic narrative what Ricoeur applies solely to a written narrative? "We can say that fiction is quasi-historical, just as much as history is quasi-fictive. . . . Fictional narrative is quasi-historical to the extent that the unreal events that it relates are past facts for the narrative voice that addresses itself to the reader. It is in this that they resemble past events and that fiction resembles history."[15]

Is it not true, then, that in cinema unreal facts are twice-past facts for the narrative voice: once as they have been imagined, or pictured, by the author-as-screenplay-writer and one other time as they have been staged by the author-as-director (or, to use the term I proposed recently,[16] by the author-as-profilmic-monstrator)?

NOTES

1. Paul Ricoeur, *Time and Narrative*, vol. 1, trans. Kathleen McLaughlin and David Pellauer (Chicago: University of Chicago Press, 1984); vol. 2, trans. Kathleen McLaughlin and David Pellauer (1985); and vol. 3, trans. Kathleen Blamey and David Pellauer (1988).
2. Ricoeur, *Time and Narrative*, 3:151.
3. Méliès quoted in Jacques Deslandes and Jacques Richard, *Histoire comparée du cinéma*, vol. 2 (Tournai: Casterman, 1966), p. 460.
4. Ibid., p. 456; my translation.
5. Ricoeur, *Time and Narrative*, 1:43.
6. Quoted in English in Deslandes and Richard, *Histoire comparée du cinéma*, 2:455.
7. Ricoeur, *Time and Narrative*, 3:181.
8. This is the case with (among others) Henry de Grandsaignes d'Hauterives, who at the turn of the century made traveling film shows in Canada and in the U.S.A. with his "historiograph." See Germain Lacasse (with the collaboration of Serge Duigou), *L'Historiographe (Les débuts du spectacle cinématographique au Québec)*, Les Dossiers de la Cinémathèque (Montréal: Cinémathèque québécoise, no. 15, 1985).
9. Ricoeur, *Time and Narrative*, 1:96.
10. Ibid., 3:128.
11. Ibid.
12. Alain Lacasse, "Temps et récit: Essai d'application de la thèse de Paul Ricoeur au film Huit et demi de Federico Fellini," master's thesis, Québec, Université Laval, 1988, p. 89; my translation. French text: "en tant qu'enregistrement, le film constitue un réel passé. Filmer, c'est toujours rendre compte de l'histoire et de la fiction *simultanément*. Que le cinéma, de par sa nature même de langage, possède déjà inscrite en lui cette croisée des pouvoirs référentiels de l'histoire et de la fiction, ceci contribue certainement à faire en sorte que le récit filmique participe à la refiguration du temps humain d'une façon particulièrement unique."
13. Ricoeur, *Time and Narrative*, 3:177.
14. Ibid., 3:190: "The idea that narrative has to do with something like a fictive past seems more fruitful to me. If narrative calls for an attitude of detachment, is that not because the past tense of the narrative aims at a temporal quasi-past? . . . the events recounted in a fictional narrative are past facts for the narrative voice, which we can consider here to be identical with the implied author, that is, with a fictive disguise of the real author. A voice speaks, recounting what for it has taken place. To enter into reading is to include in the pact between the reader and the author the belief that the events reported by the narrative voice belong to the past of that voice."
15. Ibid.
16. See André Gaudreault, *Du littéraire au filmique. Système du récit* (Québec/Paris: Presses de l'Université Laval/Méridiens Klincksieck, 1988).

MICHÈLE LAGNY

VISCONTI READ THROUGH RICOEUR

Time in *Ludwig*

Translated by Charles O'Brien

In this essay, I would like to examine the temporal configuration of Luchino Visconti's *Ludwig* in its filmic organization. The interest of the film resides, in effect, in the complexity of the relations that its central character establishes with time: a hero who completely refuses the world, Ludwig escapes from a history he rejects in order to take refuge in myth, and to find a realization in death. *Ludwig* is a biography—that is, a historical narrative; but it is also, because of Ludwig's involvement with great mythical narratives as well as with cosmic forces (the stars, the night, the water), a fable about time. The film is like such literary fables as Thomas Mann's *Magic Mountain* and Marcel Proust's *Remembrance of Things Past,* which Ricoeur has analyzed and from which Visconti drew inspiration.

For Ricoeur, historical time and mythical time are two ways of connecting lived and cosmic time. With respect to the heterogeneity of these different temporalities, only narrative is capable of realizing a synthesis by "refiguring" the time whose aporetic character philosophy can only indicate. This is because the "cardinal trait of narrative time" is precisely "its aptitude to combine, in variable proportions, the chronological component of episodes and the non-chronological component of configuration"; through the play of concordances and discordances, narrative has the capacity to take account of the nonlinear aspects of time as well as its inexorable temporal progress at the same time.[1] In order to develop his hypothesis, Ricoeur proposes an "extended" conception of narrative that is manifest in several "narrative forms that we do not yet know how to name" (2:48); this conception postulates "a functional unity between the multiple modes and narrative genres"[2] that authorizes the reintegration into modern narrative theory of texts in which the struggle against the linear representation of time facilitates a deepening of our understanding of narrative temporality (1:53).

It is thus as a narrative form testifying to Ricoeur's extended notion of narrative that I will consider *Ludwig*. Why? First, because it raises the question of a film's competence to narrate, which has been questioned by some, notably Gerard Genette; next, because although the film's events unfold chronologically, according to a naive model of narrative, the film adopts, at the same time, a procedure of fragmentary exposition and imposes significations through a play of multiple references. To take account of the film's temporal organization will thus mean exploring the manner in which the time of the narrating produces narrated time. That is, we will try to determine the procedures through which a narrative temporality is organized, and how this temporality constructs the two modalities (historical and mythical) through which lived time is reinscribed into cosmic time. This will involve, first, examining the cinematographic combination or disjunction of verbal, visual, and musical elements whose imbrications produce temporal effects. Then, by taking the film as a node in a network that involves other texts, we will measure the contribution of "the narrative intelligence, forged by the frequentation of the narratives transmitted by our culture" (1:13).

By means of a study of this film's subtly interwoven temporalities, we will be able to evaluate how Ricoeur's "expanded narrative" fulfills the function that he assigns to it: that of authorizing "the synthesis of heterogeneity," particularly with respect to time (1:302).

I

A biography of the last king of Bavaria, *Ludwig* postulates a return to history, to the testimony of witnesses, to a chronological organization of events. An integral, episode-by-episode breakdown (*découpage*) shows above all that the film constitutes a veritable challenge to the historical time that authorizes the narrative of history.[3] This third, chronological time has for Ricoeur a double function: at the level of human experience, where it articulates together different forms, it serves as a mediator between cosmic time and lived time (3:147); but at the level of narrative, it also constitutes the grounding of historical narration, the hidden law of the writing of history that Michel de Certeau considers unavoidable.[4]

Historical time is constructed thanks to connectors, none of which function correctly in *Ludwig.* The role of connectors involves, on the one hand, a chronological organization, and on the other, the process of a succession of generations. The first operation consists in establishing definite marked dates, certified as factual by the traces left by the past and measured by the conventional, institutionally fixed scale of the time of the calendar. It enables the fixing of an order of events and the measurement of relative durations. The second operation displays the movement of generations, which do not so much succeed one another as accumulate. This accumulation thus makes possible (excluding the case of exceptional, chance events) the continuity of social time, in which tradition founds innovation, thanks to the phenomenon of contemporaneity, which has the additional advantage of establishing bridges between the individual experience of lived time and time experienced collectively.

First and most obviously, Ludwig does not belong to the line of succession of generations: he is a descendant, certainly, but of a dead father and a foreign mother (note that she undergoes a religious conversion), incapable, much like his insane brother Otto, of transmitting the tradition, as is evident in his decision to cancel his betrothal and his homosexuality. Moreover, he is disconnected from his era, non-contemporaneous, as is apparent in the growing incomprehension between him and his ministers, a phenomenon that signifies madness (because if the king is not crazy, the ministers must be). This gap between the individual and the social group that he is supposed to lead permits an explanation of the monarch's failure at the level of historical rationality, and a justification for the widely developed theme of Ludwig's decadence in the domain of aesthetic judgment.

To say that the king does not occupy the same time as his ministers, who seem to follow the sense of history (since they embody it), entails an examination of the manner in which the text configures (according to what Ricoeur calls mimesis$_2$) historical time in its chronological dimension. What are the events and

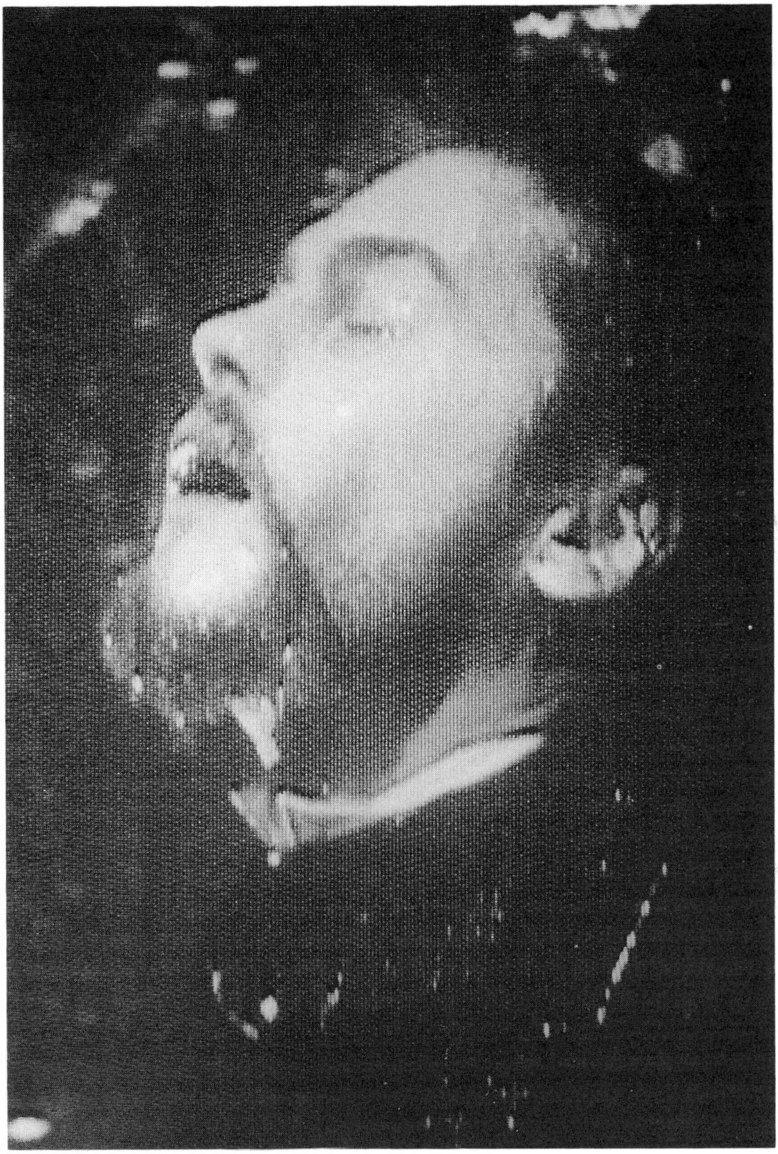

A production still from *Ludwig.* Ludwig's madness signals his "disconnection" from his era, his "non-contemporaneity."

actions that constitute a story that Visconti selects, and how does he arrange them?

The film unfolds in a linear order, but one made up of very loosely connected episodes. These form a succession of forty sequences, from Ludwig's coronation to his death. One could regroup these segments in divisions comparable to those of a novel except for the irregular interventions of several types of cinematic punctuation whose very different functions accentuate an impression of fragmentation. Some of these perform a traditional role, as does the fade-to-black that typically indicates the end of an episode and the beginning of a temporal ellipse. On the other hand, fifteen cases of filmic punctuation have a singular status. Each of their interventions breaks the continuity of the narrative: all appear in a manner that makes it impossible to locate the character presented within the episode in progress.

These shots are all close-ups of ministers, pages, or the doctor, who seem to be testifying at an inquest whose result will be the dismissal of the king. Dethronement effectively intervenes at the end of the film (segment 35 to 38 of the *découpage*). Each framing isolates, on a black background (outside of any context), a face rendered moonlike by a lighting that divides it in two (one part lit, the other in shadow) and whose look to the camera constitutes a direct address to the spectator. Although we recognize many of the characters from previous episodes, the isolated shots show literally only their talking heads, removed from the space and time of the narrative.[5] In effect, the supposed inquest may never have taken place; one sees, in the film, only its consequence: the reunion of the counsel (segment 34) that organizes the regency, followed by the last of these isolated shots, in which the psychiatrist Van Gudden declares the king afflicted with paranoia.

These shots thus have an extradiegetic allure, which gives to the characters represented an "excess" that signifies power.[6] The function of these isolated shots is essential, since they appear to serve as narrative connectors. Their serial organization allows for the possibility of a narrator with several voices, a sole master of the advance of a narrative that he shapes to his taste. This narrative is that of history, since these shots provide the chronological indications that produce an effect of reference and thus organize the calendarlike linearity of the third historical time. The narrated time seems much more that of history, because the system puts in the past, through the use of the successive flashbacks, all the activity, presented as madness, of the king of Bavaria.

A production still from *Ludwig*. The isolated shots show only the characters' "talking heads," removed from the space and time of the narrative.

Moreover, it is clear that the isolated shots, which imply a time of narration different from that of the diegesis, serve to indicate that the king's destiny has been historically fixed since the beginning of the film, controlled by the ministers and the force that they represent, the Bavarian bourgeoisie. These shots give to the king's entourage not only the real power in history, but also control over the historical narrative: history is rationalized and interpreted by the vision of the conquerors. This is marked in the short, reedited version of the film with a simplifying exaggeration, in the form of a global flashback, which by condensing the successive flashbacks returns to a familiar, even classical form of fictional as well as historical narrative. But things are not as simple in the complete version, in which a variety of cinematic devices prevent such a clear interpretation.

First, the ministers and other witnesses provide only an intermittent and fragmented narration. The essence of Ludwig's story escapes them, and the organization of the narrative is troubled, on the one hand, by the importance of the ellipses, and, on the other, by the growing uncertainty of the references to the dates of history: the activity of the film's narration consists in contradicting that of the narrative instance represented in the film. The ellipses are all the more unsettling since they have several functions. They perform the classical role of abridging the duration of the event told by the narration. But they also clearly serve to erase from the diegetic development events important from the point of view of traditional history.

Moreover, they imply sequential alternations, provoking a kind of interlacing that ruins the linearity, and often the coherence, of the narrative proposed by the ministers. These crosscuttings produce false narrative relations that are doubled at the level of montage in even the most apparently continuous sequences. A minute analysis could track them shot by shot, in, for example, the scene of the coronation or that of the riding school.[7]

The difficulties increase as the film advances, since it becomes harder to identify a chronology in either the order or the duration of the diegetic development, where the time of disorder and contradiction predominates. To be sure, dates are recited by the ministers in the isolated shots, especially at the beginning of the film. But these are gradually replaced by some vague allusions, in which the sequence of events is frequently inverted, the result being that the order of the text often contradicts that of the events of reference. Besides, once having entered the history that they have made by provoking the failure of the king, the narrators are no longer able to master it, and consequently to tell it. The isolated shots effectively disappear in the last forty minutes of the film. During this time, the ministers, pages, and doctor are nothing more than ordinary characters held in the same temporality as the king, over whom they no longer have control. At first temporarily imprisoned, they are on the verge of losing their heads (in both the literal and figurative senses, in segment 37); then in the chateau at Berg, they allow Ludwig to escape, if not physically at least mentally (segments 40 to 41).

This change requires that we return to the notion of contemporaneity. A connector constitutive of the third historical time, necessary in the construction of the rationalizing narrative of history, contemporaneity comes apart for the ministers as well as for Ludwig. This is because, first, if we agree with Ricoeur, contemporaneity, "the structure of mediation between the private time of individual destiny and the public time of history," exists only "in virtue of the equivalence between contemporaneity, anonymity

A production still from *Ludwig*. The ministers, pages, and doctor become figuratively imprisoned in the chateau at Berg.

and ideal-typical comprehension" (3:167). The ministers grasp, during the inquest, only the typical role of the king, the one assigned to him by institutions; once engaged in action, it is to the individual that they must attend; their own ideal-typical representation must be abandoned in order for them to become individuals submitted to meteorological elements or to human needs. At this point they are literally put into equivalence with the king by montage: segment 35 presents them to us first at the table and then outside under a hard rain, in alternation with Ludwig enclosed in the somber chateau of Neueschwanstein.

The notion of contemporaneity supposes a placement within the past. If Ludwig remains always in the time of the diegesis, it is because he fails to take the necessary distance, by referring either to a past (which would allow him to conform to a traditional model, like that represented by his mother), or to a future (the one of innovation, to which, in fact, the ministers belong): he thus exists in a present with neither a before not an after, an untimely present that makes historical evolution difficult. But by acting, the ministers serve to enclose themselves in the same immediacy, which prevents them from the escape that would make an interpretation possible. By the time they make a decision, they are too late: they give a version, which satisfies them, of Ludwig's non-contemporaneity. On the other hand, when their coup succeeds, they find themselves in the same untimely present as Ludwig and are reduced to acting like him, proceeding blow-by-blow, almost as madly: they show fear (when they are enclosed), comprehension (on the part of the psychiatrist), and finally a probable complicity in murder.

In other words, one is never directly contemporaneous with the time of the action, and if the notion of contemporaneity has a meaning, it is only a posteriori. It is a category that functions only in the domain of historical narration: useful in the narrating of history, it hardly seems so with respect to taking action in lived history. In the latter case, the untimely present prevails, but without the positive function that is attributed to it by Nietzsche, or by Ricoeur in his rereading of *The Uses and Abuses of History* (3:339–46). Here the historical present is, not the line of intersection between "the ultimate end of an accomplished history" and "the inaugural force of a history to be made" (3:345), but a time of disorder, incapable of opening onto the horizon of expectation of the future.

In the final analysis, history is very much a matter of what is narrated (at the inquest, perhaps; for posterity, no doubt; for the spectator, of course), and what we are given are very much narratives proposed by witnesses who explain its course, organizing linearly by relations from cause to effect a discourse that produces a historical rationality. But the manner in which the film presents its own narrative challenges chronology and contemporaneity, that is, two of the connectors constitutive of historical time. Thus it shows how history is able to narrate itself, and therefore to rationalize itself, if only from the outside and after the fact—outside of any truth—and without authorizing a rational action.

What Visconti indicates, then, by disarranging without deconstructing historical time, is precisely the duplicity of the narrative of history. He underlines how lived time, whether that of history in the making or that of the individual who lives or dies there, remains irreducible to the time of the history of the historians. The new mode of telling outlined here is simultaneously a narrative and a critical discourse on narrated history: if the act of narrating enables comprehension, it is only when it puts itself in question, precisely by assuming the incompatibility of lived-with narrated time.

II

But it is not this history that the film tells, and it is not in historical time that Ludwig belongs. *Ludwig* has been several times described as a cinematographic novel.[8] Like those biographies that constitute for Ricoeur a literary genre connected to history, *Ludwig* would enable us to mark the differences and common points between historical narrative and the narrative of fiction. The weakness of the film's historical time suggests that here a time reconstructed by fiction predominates. Its advantage is that of being able to perform imaginative variations on phenomenological time, by liberating itself from the constraints of cosmic time.

Thus the disorder of the chronology, which we have underlined, derives from the fictional narrative: the latter organizes the order of its own events in function of the necessity of staging the intrigue, whereas the historical narrative is supposed to follow the order of the attested events. The ministers tell history; the film tells *a* history, that of Ludwig, and organizes it as a function of the internal logic of the character that it presents.

The tendency toward privatization testifies to this. The systematic elision of the great historical events is accentuated by the fact that any evocation of a public fact—even a lengthy one, like the coronation—is manifest only in its personal dimension (the confession and the preparations of the young prince). All of the meetings with Elizabeth and with Wagner are intimate, even when they are "official" (with the empress at Bad-Ischl or with the composer in the palace). This results from an insistence on a rupture between the king and his time (which is far from being in conformity with the traditional historiography: Ludwig II had been actually involved, whether for better or worse, in the affairs of his kingdom). And without doubt it is also a question of a formal choice, one that gives to Ludwig an allure more theatrical than novelesque, and thus, to follow Lukács, a dimension more symbolic than historical.[9]

Fiction especially is able to play on the effacement of standards of measure and thus is able "to confront a non-measurable time with an incommensurable time . . . : interior time, freed from chronological constraints, enters into collision with a cosmic time exalted by contrast" (3:197). By neutralizing historical time, Ludwig reconnects private time to another form of public time, that of myth, a ". . . grand time that . . . *encloses* all reality . . . [and whose] function . . . is that of ruling the time of societies—and of people living in society—according to cosmic time. . . . In effect . . . it initiates a unique and global *scansion* of time by ordering the one through relation to the others by means of cycles of different durations, the great celestial cycles, biological recurrences and the rhythms of social life" (3:154). The remythicization of time at work in the fables on time would be therefore another mode of organization of the film.

It is primarily music that inscribes the time of myth in the day-by-day activity of Ludwig: the musical fragments utilized establish, in effect, thematic indicators of those "grand narratives" constitutive of our narrative intelligence that are called myths, reactualized here by the intermediary of the Wagnerian operas.

The musical citations, often inscribed within the frame of the narrative world (as is the case with those concerning Wagner—in particular, the creation of *Tristan*) have several functions in the film. They are, first of all, the expression of the time of the affective conscience: it is entirely within the private sphere, whose dominating role we have noted, that they manifest themselves.

On the other hand, music serves to individualize the characters: each has his affinity, because as Wagner says, while playing some particularly ironic measures of *La Perichole* (pertaining to the letter sent by the heroine to the lover whom she had abandoned for the viceroy "Oh, my dear love, I pledge to you . . ."): "This is the music that the German people like." The characters are thematized in different registers: while Wagner offers to Cosima the *Siegfried Idyll,* Elizabeth is given a "Schumanian" theme and is thus inscribed in a "musical time" very different from that of the "Wagnerian" Ludwig. Related to the childhood dreams that she actualizes through her permanent fugues, Elizabeth is also, like this music of classical structure, profoundly socialized, mastered, conscious of her role as lure ("We other kings, we are window displays").

It is through a play of crossed references that the figure of Ludwig is constructed. The return to myth is effected through the intermediary of the Grail, with the first measures of Prelude 1 of *Lohengrin,* but the leitmotif themes, notably that of the "Liebestodt" ("Love-Death"), come from *Tristan,* and the "Romance of the Star" of *Tannhauser* occurs several times. The music thus manifests the aspirations of Ludwig, a circumstance commented upon emphatically by the extracts from the great mythic roles like *Hamlet,* that the king asks the actor Kainz to perform.

This time of myth, evoked musically, is also literally incarnated by the relation of Ludwig to certain characters—specifically, Wagner, Elizabeth, and Kainz—who are substituted for each other in succession in order to symbolize the romantic aspiration to love and grandeur. As Ricoeur states apropos of *Remembrance of Things Past* and *The Magic Mountain,* "time needs a body in order to manifest itself, to make itself visible" (3:197).

In this way the film designates the great relational phases that construct as well the temporality in which the king functions. This temporality has a cyclical aspect whose interest derives from its negotiation of the relation between the linear time of events—public or private—that marks the present of the king, and the "incommensurable" time of the imaginary. We can identify three successive phases, three cycles, that mark, first, the attempt to inscribe the ideal in the real, then that of the adaptation to the world, and finally the fight outside of both the real and the world. These cycles function elsewhere according to a complete tripartition/bipartition that one would be able to relate to the system analyzed by Georges Duby in *Les trois ordres ou l'imaginaire du feodelisme.*

These three great cycles that encompass the collapse of the king evoke, through the intermediary of an enveloping narrative, the schema of the fall (which is, of course, present in the film through the failures of the flesh and the physical deterioration of Ludwig). This schema of the fall is one of the great permanent symbolic faces of time, which one discovers thematically in the film through the recurrence of the horse, the insistence on water, or the obsessive theme of the night that is accentuated throughout the film.

Moreover, everything in the film—image, music, montage—formally constructs the ambivalence of a king whose imagination seems to be the prisoner of the contradiction between antithetical images of time, between the somber chasm of forgetting and the luminous hope of eternity. The relation of the king to the time of myth inscribes him thus in the *longue durée* (long time span) that affects the anthropological structures of the imaginary and whose interest for Ricoeur lies in its capacity to become "one of the paths through which historical time is returned to cosmic time." But the film indicates clearly that lived time is no more extensible to the time of myth than it is reducible to that of history.

Thematically, everything necessary has been said concerning the portrait of Wagner incarnated by Trevor Howard (and inspired by Thomas Mann and perhaps Nietzsche[10]): his need of money and his megalomania, denounced by the ministers, but also his taste for the easy life, his adulterous games, his infantile behavior (as in the long scene with the dog) or his social conformism (as at the Christmas party). Much like the tune of the charlatan of *The Elixir of Love,* which grotesquely introduces the director of *Bellissima,* the caricatured scenes with Kainz accentuate the derision accorded to the "artists" who produce myths. The problem is that the artists are themselves creators, and that behind the apparent judgment is the thesis that only the separation of art and life enables creation. It is necessary to eat and to sleep in order to be able to beseech the wives of his friends for support to write the sublime *Siegfried Idill* or another "Liebestodt." To live in myth as Ludwig does is a regressive behavior and impossible. The narrating instance itself maintains an ironic relation with myth, and the effects of derision that result from a contamination due to the filmic organization do not spare the more romantic themes.

Certainly, "beyond his tragedy, the last king of Bavaria continues to exist for us as a dreamer, an immense and poetic visionary," as Enrico Medioli, the coscenarist of the film, has claimed. This is evident in the "Ludwig Clubs," whose existence in Bavaria has been mentioned by Laurence Schifano.[11] Ludwig is among those who, to quote Nietzsche, "are on the route that leads to immortality and to monumental history." "Such individuals strive to raise themselves to Olympian laughter, or at least to a sublime disdain." It is true that "their descent into the tomb will be ironic—because who among them could be buried? What alone had always oppressed them, waste, vanity, animalism, now falls forgotten. . . . But one thing will live, the monogram of their most intimate essence . . . a singular clarity . . . because no posterity would be able to do without it."[12]

The film, however, does not develop this idyllic image that could function as a model (although it invokes such an image, which is precisely the difficulty). It challenges the monumental history that returns to the time of myth, just as it challenges the "critical history" constructed in the time of history: facing the king are either subsidized gnomes like Wagner and Kainz, who can create only because they live trivially, or salaried workers like the ministers or pages, who form judgments in order to extricate themselves from that which prevents them from acting.

III

If there is a time that cannot be measured by the clock or the calendar—although it has certain constraints, through the play of intervals, rhythmic cuts, and choices of accents—it is very much musical time; it remains for some, like Stravinsky, the time of consciousness, but it could also be what Ricoeur, among others, suggests is the time of narrative. By limiting our analysis to musical citations, we have remained until now in an especially thematic dimension, which has returned us to the time of myth. But it is possible to go beyond this by identifying a certain number of filmic facts that relate the structure of the narrative time of *Ludwig* to that of its musical time, notably through the system of relative durations. The film could thus be described as a polyphonic form of narrative capable of articulating together different temporalities. The temporal respiration of the text is produced through the work of the camera, evident especially in the recurrence of ascending and descending movements, the anchorage of the sound track to the image track, the appearance of musical citations and impressive play of silences, and the rhythm of the editing, both at the level of the relations between shots and those between sequences. It is impossible here to go into fastidious analytical detail; we will limit ourselves to a study of the reciprocal relations between the successive episodes.

On the one hand, the sequences are structured in a way that often accords more time to the beginnings (with the very long, elaborated arrivals) and ends of scenes than to their central parts; on the other hand, a dialectic short time–long time is added to the ellipses discussed above, providing the means through which moments where the myth develops extend their duration, while those that return from myth to reality are imposing through their brevity. The film thus constructs a particular rhythm (which the short version eliminates by suppressing anything that seems dispensable for understanding the story). To the long, cyclical, repetitive time of myth is opposed the brief, nervous, choppy time of history—to the detriment, at least it would seem, of the former: although the alternation occurs to the benefit of the slow time of myth, this time disappears in the last part of the film, when the time of action (that of the ministers) becomes linear without becoming completely homogeneous (the alternations of the montage during this part of the film no longer indicate anything other than simultaneity). The event comes to overtake the imaginary: history irrupts within myth, and engenders precisely the earthly fall of Ludwig, allowing him only a return to the whole of things, a transposition into eternity affected by the last shot. It is with the defeat of 1866 that the ideal dream ends (in segment 18), and with that of 1870 that the flight from the world begins, already hinted at by the renunciations of Otto and the queen-mother (in segments 27 to 29), in much the same way the inquest of 1886 signs the king's death warrant. Certainly the film shows us none of these "facts," but their narration a posteriori serves to constrain the flux of mythical time. In fact, the film marks less the possibilities for arrangement of the different times in relation to one another than the difficulty of their articulation, their nonconcordance.

An attempt to discern the original characteristics of narrative in *Ludwig,* by systematically taking into account its polyphonic procedures, its narrative ruptures and contradictions in the play of references, enables us to illustrate the notion of "expanded narrative." The question is one of knowing if the film's narrative responds to Ricoeur's demand: to assure "the synthesis of heterogeneity" (1:302).

If we follow the inclination of the philosopher himself, we would adopt a synthesizing posture that involves favoring the concordances of the narrative and minimizing the discordances: "As far as I am concerned, the search for concordance is among the unavoidable presuppositions of discourse and communication" (2:47). These concordances are necessary for permitting the articulation together of the various times, to the point, moreover, that Ricoeur, in his own analyses tries to bring forth (under the term *quasi-intrigue*) a virtual intrigue in the texts of those who challenge such an articulation (as Braudel does for history). To accomplish this, he privileges everything that can play the role of a "relation," neglecting to the utmost the disjunctive procedures. It is from a synchronic point of view, which accords "precedence to narrative intelligence" (2:231), as well as to the "sense of an ending," to use Frank Kermode's phrase (Ricoeur discusses Kermode's work at length in 2:39–47), that we will read *Ludwig.* The last shot of the film, marked by the overexposure of its lighting and the return of the music of the "Liebestod," is an image of transfiguration: the impossibility for Ludwig of living in the time of history and the incompatibility of the times of history and of myth are confirmed by the triumph of death, which has become the only possible connection between lived time and cosmic time. From this point of view, the film stages a spectacle of victimization that "reunites between the negation of illusion and the non-being of reality all of the themes of decadence,"[13] and that by means of antithesis supports the philosopher's position: the incapacity to master time prevents being in the world and the participating belonging that precedes any relation of a subject to an object.

On the contrary, to accord primacy to the diachronic reading of narrative time leads to an insistence on the procedures of disjunction, of discordance, which operate at all levels of the text. An examination of these shows that what is important reveals itself in the palimpsest, between the interstices more than in the final synthesis. By rejecting one after the other of the "histories" (monumental and critical), whose simultaneous danger and necessity Nietzsche has underlined, Visconti's film suggests the total inability of historical narrative to take account of lived experience, to organize the chaos of the world. History, whether it is told on the monumental scale of myth or according to the restrictive standards of critical interpretation, is only a trompe-l'oeil and pretense. Yet, paradoxically, whether one denies history (as Ludwig does) or knows that one cannot represent it in its truth (as Visconti claims), it nonetheless constitutes the determining mechanism of lived time. Thus, if narrative can still constitute a "hermeneutic of historical consciousness" (3:151), it does so when it can provide the means of its own negation dialectically: by refusing to narrate what can be understood only through the deficiencies that limit the examination and analysis of contradictions and impossibilities.[14]

On the other hand, the attention given to the relation of narrative time to the diverse times that it configures shows that *Ludwig* maintains, without excluding punctual concordances, the autonomy, and probably the incompatibility, of the different temporal strata, in the domain of narrated time as well as in that of lived time. Is it necessary to envisage the specificity of the mode of expression? Would not film be, not as Genette says, incapable of narrating, but particularly apt at realizing, through the diversity of its materials of expression, the play of times, each in relation to the others? Would this not lead us to admit for once that all kinds of narratives (and particularly filmic narrative) do not lead to the "synthesis of heterogeneity," but that some find their force in heterogeneity itself, by accepting paradoxes, particularly those that manifest themselves through the aporetic character of time?

NOTES

1. The references in the body of the text are to Paul Ricoeur, *Temps et récit*, 3 vols. (Paris: Editions du Seuil, 1983–85). Volume and page numbers for quotations from this title will hereafter be cited in the text to this edition.
2. See Ricoeur, "Ce qui me préoccupé depuis trente ans," *Esprit* 8–9 (August–September 1986): 230–31.
3. The original four hours and twenty minutes of the film has not only been shortened (to around three hours) but re-edited. An even shorter version exists that differs according to country (with English and German prints shorter than the French and American). Constructed as a flashback, the re-edited version places in succession the coronation and the deposition of the king, giving in advance the parameters of the biography, and thus imposing a retrospective view. It suppresses certain sequences, as well as shots of witnesses and the beginnings and ends of scenes that had been judged too long. Even the original version of the film is incomplete, since Visconti himself removed certain scenes initially filmed (notably the premiere of *Tristan*, the funeral of Wagner, a scene in which Elizabeth learns of the death of her cousin, as well as the testimony of a servant who claimed to have seen the traces of bullets in the vest of the king). The even shorter version, constructed by a team led by Suso Cecchi d'Amico and presented in Venice in 1980 and then in France in 1983, is not absolutely identical to the original; it lacks in particular a flash-forward showing Elizabeth on her deathbed. It is this most recent version of the film that we will use, to the extent that the original is unavailable. For a comparison of the *découpages* of the new and original versions, see Alain Menil, "Ludwig roman," *Cinématographe* 91 (July–August 1983): 3–7.
4. Michel de Certeau, "L'óperation historique," *Faire de l'histoire*, vol. 1, ed. Jacques Le Goff and Pierre Nora (Paris: Gallimard, 1974), pp. 3–41, quoted in *TN*, 3:309 n. 25.
5. An exception occurs in shot XIV, in which Elizabeth, alone in the carriage, seems to hear the offscreen echo of the cries of despair of her abandoned husband.
6. For Ricoeur's appropriation of the Aristotelian notion of *diegesis*, see *TN*, 1:36. See also Aristotle's *Poetics*, intro. D. W. Lucas (New York: Oxford University Press, 1968), p. 178.
7. See the meticulous articles by Georges Mourier, "Le dévoilement par une esthétique de la contradiction," and Michel Buttet, "Ludwig: L'Histoire opéra," in *Visconti, Classicisme et subversion* (Paris: Sorbonne nouvelle, 1990).
8. See Youssef Ishaghpour, *Visconti: Le sens et l'image* (Paris: Editions de la Différence, 1984), p. 80; or Menil, "Ludwig roman," 2–19. The direct literary reference is to Klaus Mann, "Vergittertes Fenester," in his *Abenteuer des Bratpaars* (Munich: Edition Spangenberg, 1976).
9. See Georg Lukács, *The Historical Novel*, trans. H. and S. Mitchell (Boston: Beacon Press, 1963).
10. See Thomas Mann, *Pro and contra Wagner*, trans. A. Blunden (London and Boston: Faber and Faber, 1985); Friedrich Nietzsche, *The Birth of Tragedy/The Fall of Wagner*, trans. W. Kaufmann (New York: Vintage, 1967).
11. Enrico Medioli, quoted in Laurence Schifano, *Luchino Visconti, les feux de la passion* (Paris: Perrin, 1987), p. 423.
12. Friedrich Nietzsche, *The Use and Abuse of History*, trans. A. Collins (Indianapolis: Bobbs-Merrill, 1967), p. 89.
13. Ishaghpour, *Visconti; Le sens et l'image*, p. 157.
14. This leads me to say, without actually contradicting myself, that Visconti does not "narrate" history, in the restrained sense of the term *to narrate*.

DUDLEY ANDREW

HISTORY AND TIMELESSNESS IN FILMS AND THEORY

How can we best explain the import and impact of individual movies and the institution of the cinema as a whole? I am ready to count this question as the prime question in my field, and to see it as a variant of the questions Paul Ricoeur has posed to philosophy and the human sciences during the past four decades. As we shall see, over the course of time and in the natural course of events, if I may say so, Ricoeur has come to answer such questions by invoking history and the historical.

I

Every five years or so, the French conduct a poll of critics, or theater owners, or filmgoers, in an effort to determine the top French films of all time. Invariably *Les enfants du paradis* (1945) comes out on top. As the longest, most expensive, and most star-studded film the French had yet made, its proportions match the romantic myth it recounts. Edward Baron Turk calls it "a film for all time," the summit of Marcel Carné's career, indeed the summit of French cinema. "*Les Enfants du paradis* marks the culmination of France's Golden Age of moviemaking . . . [it] will always retain a privileged position among film masterworks."[1] Jean-Pierre Jeancolas is still more explicit: "*Les Enfants du paradis* is an ageless film, one that concentrates, sums up, and crowns fifteen years of French cinema."[2]

What can it mean for a movie to be "for all time"? Perhaps that its sensual appeal is so immediate, so biological, that time cannot attenuate the effect of its chemistry on every human organism it comes in contact with. Viewing it today, we imagine we experience much the same hypnotic power that it exercised over its Parisian audiences in 1945. Its perennial appearance not just on cinéclub programs but at revival houses goes to confirm this. It satisfies humans the way bread and sleep do, or the sounds of a nursery rhyme, all of which are equally "for all time."

But of course this "universal" human appeal is just what scholars are drawn to understand. And so it is hardly surprising that *Les enfants du paradis* should have become the focus of attention of film theorists in their effort to explain the power of the movies in general. Such canonized, timeless, works announce themselves as the most suitable candidates for intense analysis. And *Les enfants du paradis* is indeed a joy to analyze. Every viewer is initially overwhelmed by the sheer number of its major characters and by the intricate geometry of plots their conflicting desires shape. Structural analysis goes a long way in elucidating the complexities of a film that generously initiates such an analysis by packaging itself in two acts demarcated by the rise and fall of theater curtains, and by intercalating three extensive mime shows that reflect on its dramatic action at key moments.

If the large-scale structural outline of the movie appears obvious because bold, on the microscopic level a hidden mechanism is felt to coordinate the film's subtle effects of lighting, composition, acting, costume, set design, and music. Exposing this mechanism has been the task of critics, more or less informed by semiotics.

Both the size and the intricacy of *Les enfants du paradis* call up comparisons to nineteenth-century novels, a resemblance visible most strikingly on an unconscious or psychoanalytic level. The film's first sequence signals an overt Oedipal drama when Baptiste responds to his father's kicks by expressing himself in pantomime. His quest for language parallels his search for an impossible woman, "the lost mother, incarnated in Garance," as one critic would have it.[3] A treasure chest of psychoanalytic types and situations, the film's dialogue and sets are studded with interpretable symbols, and the trajectory of its plot might serve as a textbook case of condensations, displacements, and secondary elaboration.

In fact *Les enfants du paradis* brings to the cinema the full panoply of techniques and effects associated with melodrama, and it is through this perennially powerful aesthetic that it can best be linked to Dickens and Balzac. To the extent that melodrama is ageless, then *Les enfants du paradis* will never age; and our understanding of its textual strategies should be tantamount to an understanding of much of what the cinema is capable.

II

Both the immediate appeal of *Les enfants du paradis* and the highly mediated systems that can be shown to determine it (structural, semiotic, psychoanalytic, etc.) are the direct objects of film theory. Where else should film theory begin and end except in the effort to account for the private and cultural "work" that a film like this involves? This is the question I mean to pose by glancing sideways at the questions of Paul Ricoeur.

While Ricoeur has scarcely spent time thinking about the movies, the issues and methods that arise in connection with *Les enfants du paradis* (as in the case of any powerful artwork) are precisely those that, across a complicated itinerary, he has stopped to address. An attentive listener to the positions surrounding him, Ricoeur serves as an unusually comprehensive exemplar of the shifting theoretical tendencies coming from Europe since World War II. Film studies grew to maturity during this period and, while seldom citing Ricoeur, faced many of the same problems and the same methodological options that he openly dealt with.

The phenomenology of the early phase of his thought that culminated in *Fallible Man* and *The Symbolism of Evil* sought to understand directly the need human beings have for stories of loss, like that told by *Les enfants du paradis.* Myths distinguish themselves from other representations precisely in being timeless. These early writings on the spiritual function of traditional narratives and on the psychic work of given symbols aim to elucidate the vital cultural function of perennially powerful genres like the melodrama.

No film sets out more directly to adopt the strategies, atmosphere, and mythic power of melodrama than *Les enfants du paradis.* Indeed, one might say that melodrama is itself the film's primary referent, beyond the actual plot and subplots that express this atmosphere. In the first place, the film's action opens in the 1820s, on the very Boulevard du Crime where melodrama flourished in its heyday. The heroes of the film and its primary historical anchors are the two most celebrated actors of the time: Baptiste Debureau and Frédérick Lemaître.

Debureau, as the most famous mime of all time, brings to *Les enfants du paradis* the theme of muteness, singled out by Peter Brooks as one of the essential elements of melodrama.[4] The historical Debureau turned his private life into melodrama when he found himself charged in one of the most sensational murder trials of the era. All of Paris, we are told, flocked to the courtroom as the darling of the mime shows revealed to the public for the first time the sound of his voice. Baudelaire wrote of this incident, and he wrote as well of Lacenaire, the dandy of crime who transformed his nefarious deeds into best-selling poems and ultimately into a spiteful book of reminiscences written in his prison cell. He didn't disappoint the huge crowd assembled at his execution, dramatically flinging himself upon the guillotine.

Carné and Prévert chose these colorful characters and chose the world of melodrama in general with no hint of condescension. "The greatest creators of cinema—and Carné is certainly among these—don't hesitate to make melodramas since that's where the real popular essence of their art lies."[5] Every strategy of expression at their command they mobilized to inflate the sentiments of the characters whose lives are tied together by threads crisscrossed in a fatal pattern. Each character, prop, and speech stands out as significant by its very inclusion in the film as well as by its hieratic treatment. Think of the ragpicker, Jericho, who wanders amongst all the characters crying out doom and serving as Baptiste's primary nemesis. A trader in stolen goods, a propman at the Funambules, he recites his lines in litany. Or recall the moon, the mirrors, and the flowers, sanctified by their calculated recurrence in the drama and by the words *lune, miroir,* and *fleur* so carefully pronounced by characters who sense their import. The simplicity and exaggeration of such objects and words come to construct another world, a morally and aesthetically superior one, where everything turns on a phrase, on the color of a gown, on the presence of the moon. *Les enfants du paradis* explicitly replays in the boldest manner the familiar, unavoidable, and obsessive moral situations that Ricoeur situates at the very origin of his philosophizing, indeed at the origin of philosophy itself.[6]

Later Ricoeur would put behind him the phenomenological method of direct reflection and adopt hermeneutics, the method of indirect cultural analysis of philosophical issues. In essays like "Structure-Word-Event" (occasioned by a debate with Claude

Lévi-Strauss) and in his stupendous *Freud and Philosophy*, he conceded the systematic character of symbols and myths, but nevertheless insisted on the possibility of an insurgent "surplus" of meaning welling up within any powerfully articulated textual body.[7] Although comprehensible only because of differential systems for which language is the source or prime model, such surplus meaning is capable of offering philosophy options that the system had not produced before, potentially altering the system itself. Because of his belief that texts are capable of limitlessly generating meaning and of guiding reflection, art, as a category of text, moved to the center of Ricoeur's reflections. Discussing artistic functions, he hoped to make best use of the structuralism of the era while avoiding the prison house of language to which it otherwise seems to condemn both texts and the readers of texts.

Film scholars who flirted with structural and psychoanalytic methodologies and yet who worried lest these approaches utterly smother the films they sought to interpret, could have used Ricoeur as a staunch ally. This became perfectly evident in 1977, with the appearance of *The Rule of Metaphor*—whose heart beat to the vibrant but unpredictable rhythm of creativity and art.[8] Ricoeur once again was timely, for at this very moment the most trenchant versions of cinema semiotics were on the wane and the field's leading theorist, Christian Metz, had turned to the function of figuration in films and away from a focus on language."[9]

It was during this period that melodrama moved to the center of film studies, since it strove for and supported the kind of hypnotic experience thought to represent the essence of the fiction film. "L'effet mélo," as Claude Beylie has dubbed it,[10] results from an interplay of dramatic contrivance (the coincidences, the lost identities, the pathetic reverberations of nature) and a sense of the breadth of reality within which such dramas occur. For melodrama to work, the audience must achieve an overwhelming and unquestioned identification with the entire portrayal of the fiction, that is, with the narration as such. How like this is to the notion of "primary identification" advanced by Christian Metz in *The Imaginary Signifier*, where spectators are bound primordially to the all-perceiving gaze of the camera/projector and only secondarily to the characters portrayed via this apparatus.[11] This is one way of explaining the affinity of the cinema for melodramatic material, and it certainly helps account for our experience in *Les enfants du paradis*, where we accede to a grand, exhilarating way of representing Paris out of which eddies our special attachment to

Baptiste and his longings. The cinematic apparatus and the entire genre of melodrama conspire to encourage the spectator to submit to the paternal authority of authorship; for how else can the complex, often hidden, relationships, and the multiple threads of subplots stretching across years, be sorted out?

Because of its broad appeal and incontestable emotive power, melodrama was held up by film theorists of the seventies as the form of the basic experience offered by cinema. The attractiveness of films like *Les enfants du paradis* was taken to be an ideological function based on regressive obsessions for the authority of the camera and the storyteller. This is certainly an implication that was not lost on feminists like Laura Mulvey, who, at this very time, attacked narrative authority and cinematic pleasure in the same breath.[12] For his part, Ricoeur would never have accepted the inevitable ideological effects implied by theories of the "basic cinematic apparatus" and by the parallel descriptions of the ideological force of the very form of melodrama.[13] All such views, including most retorts like Mulvey's, tend to eliminate the inventiveness of the text (particularly as a response to its historical moment) and of its potentially progressive interpretation by spectators in subsequent historical situations. Essentialism follows when theory aims to explain the power of cinema through such effectively timeless factors as technology, biology, psychology, logical structure, or language.

III

Ricoeur's involvement with phenomenology, structuralism, and psychoanalysis, hesitant and suspicious though it be, makes him a resource for the kind of theoretical undertakings that reached their apogee in cinema studies during the mid-1970s. However, his hermeneutics—which always looked to texts as potential sources of new meaning rather than treating them as local examples of universal rules—inevitably spilled over into historiography, a discipline dedicated precisely to understanding development and change.

Historiography is not merely another theoretical paradigm that has risen to prominence in the past fifteen years, following post-structuralism, feminism, and the like. It stands before us as fundamentally different in what it wants to know and in how it understands knowledge. *Time and Narrative,* the title of Ricoeur's immense treatise, names the object of this knowledge and its means. To the historical imagination, truths can never be essential; nor can they be gotten at directly through experience or deduction. All truths need to be framed within the circumstances in which they can be said to arise. Narrative is not the embellishment of a view but the creation of values in time, and philosophy's task, instead of constructing meaning from the ground up in the Cartesian manner, is to recover meanings already available in history.

Once again the artwork stands as the ideal index to this process, since its existence as art (as painting, film) depends upon the encounters in which new viewers bring it to life, and with it the values that culture has long found there. Artworks thus possess a virtual solidity, conferred on them by their rootedness in a particular past (their origin) and in the continuity of their importance (their belonging to tradition). As they stand before us in the present, they await reexperience and, in the case of fertile works, they invite the creation of new meanings capable of adjusting tradition and culture. In this way, art is both private and public, both personal and cultural. History, taken as the past and the present (or, better, the past in the present), thus bridges the two perspectives with which we began, that of the immediate (biological) effect of a film and that of the layered mediations of culture that condition experience and frame its significance.

Paul Ricoeur has ever urged us to take the road between the public and the private, which represent the poles of subjectivity and objectivity that it was phenomenology's task to dissolve. In film studies, this would mean not only demoting film appreciation (as private, subjective, often narcissistic), but also questioning the priority of what used to pass as pure (objective) film theory. In their place hermeneutics would support the engaged pursuits of criticism and history, both of which negotiate the plasmatic space of interpretation lying between immediate, subjective experience and the putatively objective laws that determine it.

As hermeneutic enterprises, criticism and history presume the condensation of the past in the present. Every screening of an old film thrusts this fact in our face, in that we must interpret it in our own moment but in such a way that it leads us to then interpret the past that gave it birth. Moreover, and as if as a bonus, movies maintain a dual allegiance to fiction and to history, for even the most outlandish entertainment retains on its celluloid traces of some past that has been concocted or manipulated by the storyteller.

And so film scholars have much at stake when volume 3 of *Time and Narrative* climaxes with Ricoeur declaring history and fiction to be equivalent enterprises in the pursuit of human understanding, alternative enterprises to systematic or nomological disciplines.[14] While they appear free of the a priori laws that make psychology, sociology, and other sciences of man the disciplines that they are, fiction and history alike are subject to an inner rule that regulates their composition and interpretation. The internal organization that controls fictional plots, and especially the onus felt by poets and novelists "to be true to their work," has its counterpart in the imaginative restraint imposed on historians by the traces unearthed in documents and archives. The historian must conjure up a version of life that is faithful to those traces, that brings them to life in a way that pays back to them what we owe to the past. In both practices "we reach the point where discovering and inventing are indistinguishable, the point, therefore, where the notion of reference no longer works."[15]

Ricoeur gives to us film scholars a spectacular latitude by revising the concept of unreality so that we no longer need answer to criteria of reference (How much is this film like the world I know?) but to those of application or appropriation (In what ways is this film relevant to the life I lead?). This rhetorical understanding of history and fiction doesn't erase the work of "poetics" that pursues the laws of composition that confer the feeling of timelessness on a masterpiece like *Les enfants du paradis;* however, such rhetorical understanding does complicate it with a historical dimension. As David Bordwell has repeatedly claimed and shown, the laws of composition make sense only in relation to their systematic development through a process of transgression and normalization.[16] I mean to go further, as does Ricoeur, by insisting that composition and its poetic laws form only one part of the rhetorical system that must also include the spectator and the context of a transaction that comes to closure, not in the act of understanding, but only in the act of appropriation whereby the spectator confers significance on a text whose meaning has been impressed on him or her.

And so if *Les enfants du paradis* strikes some scholars as the "timeless" instantiation of the melodramatic imagination, it has every right to signal to others its "timeliness," its "rootedness" in a peculiar period, that of the Occupation and Liberation.[17] From this perspective *Les enfants du paradis* stands at the summit of traditional French filmmaking and particularly of poetic realism. Rather than being treated as some vehicle that lifts itself off its historical base like a balloon rising into the cloudless sky, it can stand as a monument solemnly crowning, by representing, the tradition that made it possible. This solidifies the view that Vichy cinema, and above all its most famous masterwork, be treated as an outgrowth of prewar movies;[18] but it does so at a cost, for how can a film made under modestly different industrial conditions and immensely different cultural ones fulfill a style that by all rights should have slid into the past? If André Bazin is right in claiming that poetic realism instinctively expressed France's prewar malaise, in what sense can an "ageless" film from another period come to crown it? Did not the vicissitudes of social and artistic history that the Germans brought with them cause the melodramatic heart of poetic realism to change rhythm between 1939 and 1945?

Les enfants du paradis indisputably shares with *Le jour se lève,* to take the essential poetic-realist example from the 1930s, a team of creative personnel and shares also the theme of the impossibility of the survival of pure love. Yet *Les enfants du paradis* spoke to an audience seeking quite different experiences at the cinema from those offered by *Le jour se lève,* and consequently it spoke in a different manner.

Whereas most of the key films of the Occupation evince a calculated innocence of expression that marks the height of artistry and that certainly deserves the admiration it solicits, *Le jour se lève* aims to provide an experience so immediate that the spectator has no wits left with which to admire anything, artistry included. Two centuries ago Friedrich Schiller made an analogous distinction between what he called "naive and sentimental poetry." Naive writing seems at one with nature; it is simple and instinctive. At a later, more sophisticated time a poetry of calculated effects comes to take its place, a sign perhaps "of the exhaustion of genres, of a growing self-consciousness, or of an increasingly complicated life generally."[19] André Bazin would use different terms to suggest the trajectory of Carné's career, calling the 1930s work "classical" (meaning both natural and realist) in relation to a more and more "baroque" direction taken later on.[20] One might go so far as to suggest that poetic realism existed naturally until such a time as it recognized its nature and became codified and citable. Hence *Les enfants du paradis* stands paradoxically outside poetic realism by summoning it up, then by summing it up and crowning it from above.

If poetic realism, or its parent, melodrama, is understood not only through poetics but, as Ricoeur would like, through the particular kind of rapport it sets up between spectator and text, then *Les enfants du paradis* can be said to bear the poetic-realist legacy to another cultural moment inhabited by another kind of spectator. For above all this film concerns the uses of hypnotic representation. Baptiste puts a silent spell over all who watch him, over the crowd at the Funambules, over us in the movie theater, and over Garance, who represents everything that art desires. She retains to the end an unassuming self-possession, so that when the innocent silence of Baptiste's art attracts her, we long for their perfect union. The pure spirit of the populace, she offers herself up to the purity of a transcendent yet popular artist.

When the impurities of the world intervene, Baptiste stages an allegory of unfulfilled love in a self-reflexive skit that features all the characters of his life. Dreaming beside the statue of Phoebe for whom he pines (played by Garance) Baptiste doesn't notice when Harlequin enters to steal her away. It is his wordy and worldly real-life rival, Frédérick Lemaître, who interprets Harlequin and who makes of this more than a diverting entertainment. Baptiste searches for them in vain, then plans to hang himself. As Nathalie the laundress enters (played by the girl who loves Baptiste faithfully to the end) we catch with her a glimpse in close-up of his real, not his represented, despair. Baptiste and Pierrot, actor and character, become an indistinguishable unit looking out of the skit and into the wings of the stage where Frédérick whispers flirtatiously into the delighted ear of Garance.

More than a tiny allegory about the pangs of jealousy, this skit displays the film's crucial opposition between the silent mime who loses the only audience he cares for to the loquacious actor. When next we see Frédérick, he has indeed won the heart of Paris for the bravura of his performances; yet his rapport with the audience that adores him is utterly different from Baptiste's. Frédérick intervenes in the roles he plays, whimsically toying with them until the audience cheers his personal conquest of the drama. With Baptiste the audience sits in uninterrupted wonder, locked to his gestures as though tied to a string.

It doesn't take much to extend this allegory of art and audience to the history of cinema. For if Baptiste stands for the "naive," nearly religious function drama assumed after the French revolution and Lemaître for the "sentimental" revival of sophistication on the stage, then Baptiste also represents the cult of the silent cinema losing its audience to the urbane, promiscuous talkie.

With Garance embodying the hypnotized audience, *Les enfants du paradis* is a film for all times, because it is a film about the magic of movies. In this it might be compared to Cukor's *A Star is Born*, which likewise takes a type of representation, the musical, as its intertext. Both follow a common pattern in the sociology of art whereby early examples of any genre reach outside themselves for the material they reshape. The musical originally drew on vaudeville, for example. Much later the genre may begin to feed on itself, explicitly reshaping its own cinematic form.[21] Like *A Star is Born*, *Les enfants du paradis* is such a second-degree movie, modeling the world of cinematic melodrama, constructing an allegory of it.

Les enfants du paradis represents the power of melodrama but curiously does not provide audiences with a genuine melodramatic experience. Its nostalgia for a better form of representation indicates, against its wishes, that such bare experiences are a thing of the past. A crude sociological chronology can follow from this. In the prewar years, an ungoverned, fatherless society looked to the movies for evidence of any values left in contemporary life. As their chosen sacrifice to unknown gods, Jean Gabin never reassured them, but at least he demonstrated a tight-lipped style of suffering they understood and introjected. His fidelity to himself and to an image of pure love could be said to outlast the movies that inevitably brought him to a bad end. By turns silent and explosive, Gabin was the everyman his costume and anonymous address indicated.

Then came the German Occupation with its abundance of father figures (Maréchal Pétain, foremost among them). In place of the lonely, orphaned Gabin, audiences were asked to identify with remote but appealing spectacles usually set in the past. The creators of the most important of these surely wanted to evoke the same values that the Gabin character had pursued film after film through his hopelessly private quest in the late 1930s (uncompromising honesty, pure love); only now those values were represented as cultural, not individual, achievements. One imagines the spectators of the prewar films arriving singly at the theater, putting all obstructions from their minds, and virtually climbing through the screen to join Gabin. Audiences during the Occupation, the argument goes, attended films in couples or groups, fascinated by a spectacle that literally if benevolently looked down on them. No matter that Fate and Destiny continued to haunt the Occupation films as they had the prewar works, there was something reassuring about the (allegorical and spectacular) way such themes were presented. *Les visiteurs du soir* (1943) and *Les enfants du paradis* could be viewed as models of life. Indeed the duc de Berry sets of the former were specifically meant to look like illuminated miniatures. Watching *Le jour se lève* or *Quai des brumes* (1937), on the other hand, had been like watching life itself with no model to go by, for Gabin seemed to have wrested narrative authority from the filmmakers, whose culture and paternal care never inserted itself between spectator and text. No historical references, no showcasing of sets or stars, came to deliver that spectator, who was left alone in what I might prematurely call the existential situation of melodrama.

The opposition between immediacy and model shows itself unmistakably in acting methods. To hang on every gesture and expression of an actor, to adopt his aspirations and to suffer from the gap between those aspirations and their realization in the ordinary world—this is the trigger of melodrama. In this Barrault models himself not only on the Baptiste Debureau whom we read about in books, or on the memory we hold of silent-film stars like Charlie Chaplin, but also on France's greatest film actor, Jean Gabin, who, from 1935 to 1939, developed a rapport with the critics and public of France that has never been equaled in that country. Invariably cast in contemporary working-class roles, invariably suicidal at the end, Gabin became the self-conception of an entire generation. It is with good reason that his name was virtually synonymous with poetic realism, a style that suited him and suited the era, a fully expressive style designed to bring out what Bazin would call "le destin de Jean Gabin." Listen to Bazin: "It remains for the sociologists and moralists . . . to reflect on the profound meaning of a mythology in which, through the popularity of an actor like Gabin, millions of our contemporaries rediscover themselves. Perhaps a world without God becomes a world of the gods and the fates they dispense."[22]

Of course this is precisely the world of melodrama to which Bazin refers, and which he goes on to claim is perfectly exemplified by *Le jour se lève.* French and German authorities alike censored it as decadent.

Les enfants du paradis was never thought decadent. Its retreat to the safety of another century and its wonderful evocation of the life of the theater protected it from direct confrontation with the authorities, and must have buffered its popular reception too, making it easy to digest. An enormous mime show, it playacted

An image of authenticity. Jean Gabin in *Quai des brumes* (1938). (Courtesy of the British Film Institute).

scenes and sentiments that seemed to belong literally to the films and the era of the 1930s. The discourse of *Les enfants du paradis* is omniscient and unidirectional. All of its characters play with stentorian clarity to the camera or at least to its wishes. Even Barrault's miming couldn't be more articulate, nor could the chaos of the finale be more clear.

From this standpoint, *Les enfants du paradis* is at once the apotheosis of poetic realism and a betrayal, through contrivance and theatricality, of its innocence and vulnerability and of its

Jean Louis Barrault in *Les enfants du paradis.*

quest for total identification producing an intense, unthinking involvement of audience and narrator with the world portrayed. *Le jour se lève* tries most to provide the experience of fusion that *Les enfants du paradis* merely represents. On the eve of the Nazi takeover, a sizable audience begged to be inundated completely in the fatal destiny of a fictional world. This is the ritual of melodrama, a form scorned by the intelligence and the intelligentsia, but a form that came to be appropriated by the France of 1939.

IV

We are on the brink of claiming that the blind fatalism at work in poetic realism responds to the collapse of the Third Republic in the face of the Nazi war machine. The orphan hero of these films spoke to a populace that must have felt betrayed by the fathers of that republic; note the many scandals and instances of mismanagement that had occurred there since World War I. Where could they turn? Surrounded by Fascist fathers in Spain, Italy, and Germany, and recently betrayed again by the self-proclaimed father of international communism, Joseph Stalin, the French had also been disillusioned by the brief brotherhood of the Popular Front. Their moral situation indeed seems aptly expressed by the grim finales of *Quai des brumes* or *Le jour se lève.*

This is not a question of returning to a reflection theory whereby art finds its significance by referring, even obliquely or symbolically, to social history. Ricoeur urges us to scuttle "reference" altogether in favor of "applicability," where the specific kind of unreality trafficked in by fiction and even by historical reconstruction takes on the burden of proving significant for those who need to appropriate it.[23] In his view, "appropriation" occurs only when the reader or spectator understands the appropriate questions to which the artwork stands as a response. Poetic realism was taken into a culture that understood questions of moral isolation like few other generations.

This indirect relation among producer, context, work, and audience that Ricoeur characterizes as one of question and response, is exactly what interested André Bazin when he sought to explain the waning of Carné's relevance. He had *Le jour se lève* explicitly in mind when he wrote:

> A work should not be defined only in relation to itself and without reference to its time. It would be pure abstraction to place Carné's talent on one side, the sensibility of the public on the other, and to note their accord around 1938, since this accord is not a simple passive connection but one of the indirect creative components of

> the work. In other words, Carné's inspiration, his work as an artist, participated in the period; it answered its questions, but the questions determined the direction of the responses. Now by responses I do not mean an objective content, but the expression given to this content, that is to say, a style.[24]

Le jour se lève, Bazin implies, was not alone when, in responding to the question of where to put one's faith, it turned inward to the solitary, orphaned self, to private morality based on private memory and experience. Aside from the full catalog of poetic-realist films, we can locate innumerable expressions up and down the cultural ladder that share this turn to private morality. At the bottom rung the *chansons réalistes* (music-hall songs) as well as the joyful Charles Trenet tunes so popular at this time are an index to the focus on personal sentiments and sentimentality. Like *Le jour se lève* they scarcely hint at the social or domestic framework surrounding private life. And when they do, it is in the key of nostalgia. The same myopia, this time strategically employed, shapes the insights of the developing philosophy and literature of existentialism, the most famous contemporaneous example of which is Sartre's *La nausée.* Heightened expressions of personal honesty in the face of social and cultural isolation abound; later on, they would seem inappropriate, indecent, or at least maudlin. Bazin ends his essay on the diminishing impact of Carné this way: "The director of *Quai des brumes* is not wrong in being unfaithful to his past, but only in trying to prolong it beyond that situation where the meeting of a style, a time, and his themes made perfection possible. The time has changed, the style has evolved, the themes have remained the same, and we discover that they are no longer myths."[25] Myths are ageless; but films can only appear to be myths. Instead they are thoroughly cultural and historical phenomena, even when what they express repudiates culture and history.

V

The attention Ricoeur and Bazin demand for the historical circumstances of artistic creation and reception do not eradicate the importance of poetics; style and composition are in fact raised to a consequential level where they can be expected to play into cultural expectations or needs. And so a historical approach to *Le jour se lève* and *Les enfants du paradis* tells us a good deal about melodrama taken as an abstract or theoretical mode of representation. In fact, melodrama is never abstract in the world, but surfaces in specific cultural circumstances that continually redefine it. Even a cross section of world cinema taken in, say, 1939, would reveal immense differences among films all labeled melodramatic. Think of *Le jour se lève* in France, Mizoguchi's *Story of the Last Chrysanthemum* in Japan, and *Gone with the Wind* in Hollywood. Melodramas they may be, but in every relevant respect they belong to different cultures for which they fulfill different functions in very different ways.

More important, the films (and the history they lead us to) open up forms of experience otherwise unavailable. Surely this is Ricoeur's attraction to history. More obviously even than artworks, the past is something that belongs to us (resides in us) and yet is alien. The author of the recent *Soi-même comme un autre* challenges us to seek our expanded selves in confronting and assimilating alien forms of experience that attract us for reasons that retrospectively become apparent.

Our readiness to succumb to the familiar otherness of a film, to adopt provisionally its point of view, makes it a tantalizing example of the hermeneutic process. I have argued that, taken as a trace of the past rather than as a text alive in the present, any film can likewise open onto the experiential landscape of an earlier cultural moment, revealing the questions to which it stands as a response. Here we aren't speaking of films that allude to their periods. For "the horizon of expectation peculiar to literature does not coincide with that of everyday life."[26] In passing through the trace to a reconstitution of that horizon, we understand not just the past in an intimate way but ourselves in the present in a different way. We become another kind of spectator to the films (old or new) that draw us, a more fluid spectator, an open and uncompleted self, enlarged both by the model of existence tried out in films and by that provided by our sense of other audiences for whom such films were somehow appropriate.

NOTES

1. Edward Baron Turk, *Child of Paradise* (Cambridge, Mass.: Harvard University Press, 1989), p. 219.

2. Jean-Pierre Jeancolas, *15 Ans des années trente* (Paris: Stock, 1983), p. 330.
3. Turk, *Child of Paradise,* p. x.
4. Peter Brooks, *The Melodramatic Imagination* (New Haven: Yale University Press, 1976), chap. 3.
5. Marcel Oms, "*Les enfants du paradis:* La mutation cinématographique du melodrame," *Les cahiers de la cinémathèque* 28 (1978): 143; my translation.
6. Brooks, *Melodramatic Imagination,* p. 28.
7. Paul Ricoeur, "Structure-Word-Event," translated by Robert Sweeney, in *The Philosophy of Paul Ricoeur: An Anthology of His Work,* ed. Charles E. Reagan and David Stewart (Boston: Beacon Press, 1978): pp. 79–96; Ricoeur, *Freud and Philosophy: An Essay in Interpretation,* trans. David Savage (New Haven, Conn.: Yale University Press, 1970).
8. Paul Ricoeur, *The Rule of Metaphor: Multi-Disciplinary Studies of the Creation of Meaning in Language,* trans. Robert Czerny et al. (London: Routledge and Kegan Paul, 1978).
9. The relevant texts here by Christian Metz are *Langage et cinéma* (Paris: Librairie Larousse, 1970), and *The Imaginary Signifier* (Bloomington: University of Indiana Press, 1982). The latter book appeared first in French in 1977.
10. Claude Beylie, "Propositions pour le mélo," *Les cahiers de la cinémathèque* 28 (1978): 7.
11. Metz, *The Imaginary Signifier,* pp. 49–56.
12. Laura Mulvey, "Visual Pleasure and the Cinema," *Screen* 16, no. 3 (1975): 6–18.
13. See Jean-Louis Baudry, "The Ideological Effects of the Basic Cinematographic Apparatus," trans. Alan Williams, *Film Quarterly* 28, no. 2 (1974/1975): 39–47.
14. Paul Ricoeur, *Time and Narrative,* vol. 3 (Chicago: University of Chicago Press, 1988), chap. 8.
15. Ibid., p. 158.
16. David Bordwell, *Narration in the Fiction Film* (Madison: University of Wisconsin Press, 1986).
17. See Alan Williams, *The Republic of Images* (Cambridge, Mass.: Harvard University Press, 1992).
18. Aside from Jeancolas and Turk, this view is promulgated by Jacques Siclier in his *Le France de Petain et son cinéma* (Paris: Veyrier, 1980) and by François Garcon in his *De Blum à Petain* (Paris: Cerf, 1984).
19. Walter Jackson Bate, Introduction to Schiller's essay "On Naive and Sentimental Poetry" collected in Bate's *Anthology Criticism: The Major Texts* (New York: Harcourt Brace, 1952), p. 407. Schiller's essay originally appeared in 1795.
20. André Bazin, "The Disincarnation of Carné," trans. John Shepley, in *Rediscovering French Film* ed. Mary Lea Bandy, intro. Richard Roud (New York: Museum of Modern Art, 1983), pp. 131–35. This essay first appeared in French as "Carné et la desincarnation" in *Esprit* 19 no. 9 (September 1951): 232–52.
21. For a discussion of this process in relation to the musical, see Jane Feuer, *The Hollywood Musical* (Bloomington: Indiana University Press, 1982).
22. André Bazin, "The Destiny of Jean Gabin," in his *What Is Cinema?* trans. Hugh Gray, vol. 2 (Berkeley: University of California, 1971), p. 178.
23. Ricoeur, *Time and Narrative* 3:158.
24. Bazin, "The Disincarnation of Carné," p. 132.
25. Ibid., p. 135.
26. Ricoeur, *Time and Narrative,* 3:173.

JOHN VAN DEN HENGEL

JESUS BETWEEN HISTORY AND FICTION

PAUL RICOEUR has defined his attentive listening to the Jewish and Christian texts as a philosophical, not a theological, endeavor.[1] These texts warrant a hearing by a philosopher, he says, because the text and its tradition are thought provoking. As he acknowledged in *The Symbolism of Evil,* his listening to the Jewish and Christian texts intended to bring him to a better understanding of the human and of the bond between the human and the being of all beings.[2] The interpretation of these texts gives the philosopher access through sympathy. Although the lines of demarcation between theology and philosophy are at times indistinct in his works, Ricoeur's impact on theology has not been so much his hermeneutical phenomenology as his frequent contributions to topics of interest to theologians. His concept of Original Sin, his reflections on the mystery of evil, the interpretation of parables and revelation, have been pried out of their hermeneutical context and inserted in other frameworks. Ricoeur may be partially responsible for this situation because so many of his publications are occasional writings for symposia and conferences and he has not delivered a classical text.

This article takes up one of these occasional topics: Ricoeur's hermeneutics of the Christian Gospels. In a number of articles Ricoeur has examined the narrative form of the Gospel texts and found the genre to be historicized fiction rather than history. In light of the linkage of narrative with history in *Time and Narrative,* this article examines what might be the outcome of a more historical reading or appropriation of the Gospel texts.[3] At stake in this question is the interpretation of the person of Jesus of Nazareth and the hermeneutical appropriation or, to use Ricoeur's term, refiguration of Jesus in Christian communities. Is the appropriation of Jesus mediated by way of a narrative text and hence provides Jesus with a narrative identity, or is it granted by way of a historical text and leads to a historical identity?

JESUS AND HISTORY

According to Gerhard Von Rad, at the heart of Israel's confession lies the "historical credo" of Deuteronomy (24:5–9) and Joshua (24:2–13), a liturgical remembering (*Zakhor*) of the ancestral event of Abraham, a nomad to whom God promises a people and a land. It is a confession that the Most High, Abraham's God, is agent in human history and interacts in pragmatic history. The form of Israel's existence—as Eric Voegelin has pointed out in his *Israel and Revelation*—is history.[4] The experience of God, retained in Israel's memory of Moses, reveals a transcendent God giving form to a temporality that is historical. Israel's liturgy is, for that reason, a *todah*, a prayer of praise, recalling the deeds of God in real time.[5]

The confessional form of Christianity is no less historical. The liturgy of baptism and eucharist is a sacramental remembering of the death and resurrection of Jesus. It makes operative in worship the liberating power of an event in real time. In Christian worship the appropriation of the Jewish *todah*, but now focused on Jesus, is considered essential to the Christian praise of God.[6] The historical reference to the life and death of Jesus culminating in the experience of the resurrection roots the worship of praise in real events.

It is in this context of Christian worship that the current debate on the role of history and faith in the exegesis of the Gospels and in Christology can be situated. The confession of God's activity in history in the liturgy and its translation into the doctrine of the Christian churches became an object of debate in the eighteenth century. The naive acceptance of the historical character of the scriptural affirmation was transformed into a decidedly modern critical question: "Can the confession of God's historical agency bear up under a critical historiographical inquiry of the biblical text?"[7] In Christology this translated into a critical quest for the historical Jesus, today in its third phase. The quest for the historical Jesus never was a straightforward historical inquiry. From the beginning it was tainted by the bias of the Enlightenment, which saw itself as a new origin based on the exploits of reason and which sought to forge a new "religious" worldview wrested free from the dominance of the Christian churches. Enlightenment thinkers used history to test the evidence of the Bible. For the first time in the West the Bible's authority as Word of God was drawn into the vortex of doubt and skepticism by making its events share the contingency of history. *Ein garstigen Graben* (a nasty ditch), according to Lessing, separated the historical Jesus from the necessary salvation in Christ proclaimed by the churches.[8]

From Pastor Goeze, the Lutheran antagonist of Lessing, to the quest of historians of the nineteenth and twentieth centuries, the churches have struggled to show the identity between the Christ of faith and the historical Jesus. Christologists have searched for the "real" Jesus in the scripture texts, archaeology, social history, and other related Judaic and Christian documents as the bedrock for the ecclesial Christological interpretation. The contingent and the necessary had to coincide. The quest was incapable either of reconstructing an original Jesus event or of grounding the current Christian confession.[9] Yet underlying the effort of the historical quest was the authentic perception of a historical core at the root of the Christian experience.[10]

Similar concerns for the historical factor in the Gospels explain the continuing interest in historical critical methods in New Testament exegesis despite the current popularity of synchronic and diachronic methods. These synchronic and diachronic methods have sought to bypass the aporia of the historical by restricting exegesis to the intratextual play of language. The historical character of the Jesus event as extratextual referent is perceived not to affect the meaning of the text. But these methods have not been able to dislodge the enduring value of historical criticism.

RICOEUR'S HERMENEUTICS OF THE NEW TESTAMENT TEXT

Ricoeur's venturing into this complex area of biblical hermeneutics coincided with his own linguistic and hermeneutical turn. In a number of earlier essays and in *The Symbolism of Evil* he had broached the question of biblical meaning. But an explicit approach to the understanding of the biblical text began only in the later 1960s. In one of his earliest interventions on the biblical text, Ricoeur touched on the quest of the historical Jesus. During a congress on the interpretation of the Scriptures in the Christian churches in 1966, Ricoeur examined the works of R. Bultmann and G. Ebeling, whose books were then beginning to create a theological stir in France.[11]

The underlying question of their work, as he perceived it, was the manner in which proclamation (Bultmann) or the Word of God (Ebeling) could endure as proclamation or Word of God despite the materiality of the written scriptures. Both authors sought to transcend the particularity or contingency of the historical in order to safeguard the scriptures as a living word. Bultmann proposed to retain the link with the living word by demythologizing the scriptures in order to unblock its access to modern hearers. Once retrieved from their prescientific cosmology, he believed, the scriptures could blossom again as God's word in preaching. Both Bultmann and Ebeling sought a free zone for faith, unmediatedly encountered in proclamation and inaccessible to critique, which they variously called "God as act" or "God's Word." The historical identified with historiographic inquiry was perceived as a human effort and as such too much a human achievement to give access to faith. In order to avoid the reaches of historical critique for the Word of God, both Bultmann and Ebeling insisted on a nonobjectifiable Word of God. God's Word was to remain "of God." It could be existentially experienced only in the proclamation. Nowhere does it become my word.[12] It is inaccessible, therefore, to critical history. In Ricoeur's terms, the biblical word as proclamation intends to create existence, to instigate self-understanding and to generate the human person.[13]

In his writings Ricoeur has gone a long way toward accepting this approach of Bultmann and Ebeling—perhaps because it resonated with his own Reformed background. He too seeks to unfetter the Word of God and he too designates preaching as the activity where the Word of God is appropriated and encountered existentially.[14] But Ricoeur's hermeneutics offers no free zone of pure faith or of a pure Word of God. His biblical hermeneutics engages a "disposable believable,"[15] the realm of "meaning" of the scriptural text, before a personal appropriation of faith is opened up.[16] For that reason, in his biblical hermeneutics Ricoeur has urged the application of the phases of his general hermeneutics, that is, participation, distanciation, and appropriation to biblical exegesis.[17]

The analytic of distanciation that Ricoeur has favoured for the

New Testament has been the structural and semiotic, on the one hand, and narrative analysis, on the other.[18] While he has acknowledged that the historical critical method remains indispensable,[19] he has offered no reflection on its significance. Ricoeur has exercised his hermeneutical style on only two New Testament genres: the parables[20] and the Passion narratives.[21] But placed in the light of his more programmatic essays on biblical hermeneutics,[22] we may underscore some basic orientations that shed light on Ricoeur's approach to the historical in the gospels: We will begin with his analysis of narrative and then discuss the implications of this analysis for an understanding of historical intentionality.

Narrative Form

Ricoeur has perceived narrative as the central cumulative form of the Gospels. He has accepted Perrin's thesis that an originally prenarrative kerygmatic proclamation was composed into a narrative form as we now find it in the Gospels. The announcement of the kerygma by Jesus leads to conflict and confrontation that results in the passion of Jesus. These narrative "occasions" once configured into the gospel genre have produced an intensification of the narrative genre that makes the Gospels carriers of a unique message.[23] From Robert Alter Ricoeur has adopted the analysis of the theme of biblical narrative. Alter proposes that biblical narrative conjoins a supratemporal (or omnitemporal) divine plan with an intratemporal resistance to this plan in the actions of people. The biblical narrative operates on two levels: an invisible, mysterious divine plan, on the one hand, and the pragmatic actions and passions of people, on the other. In the Gospels this interplay of the divine and human action and passion is evidenced in its narrative sequence: the Gospels begin with the announcement of the imminent "Reign of God"; this announcement provokes controversy, and the conflict leads to a challenge of God's pronounced "reign" in the suffering and death of Jesus. As a sequence of setting, change of fortune, and denouement, this is the basic stuff of narratives. The meeting point of the supratemporal and the intratemporal is in the narrative of the suffering innocent Jesus. It is a narrative, not of action, but of passion.[24] But in spite of this defeat, the effectiveness of the supratemporal plan is proclaimed.

A further characteristic of the gospel narrative is its proliferation into more than one composition. The New Testament presents us with four Gospels. The reason why the canonical Gospels have multiplied into four Gospels lies in the fact that the organizing principle or point of view is not theological but Christological. Jesus is the mediating point of the theological perspective, linking the divine plan and the human course of events. That is why the Resurrection plays such an important interpretative role, because it has shaped the narrative into its unique composition.[25] It has called forth a variety of ideological codes to interpret the figure of Jesus. These different codes allowed for the articulation of "the Gospel" in a number of gospels.[26]

What is the relation of this text to history? The Bible in its Hebrew and Christian versions contains texts that in form or genre appear to be history. Typologically they are narrative genres, but the relationship of these narratives that contain saga, legends, tales, novellas, and myths to what we might call history is tenuous. Ricoeur maintains that the genre of history is set by the Greek historiographers Herodotus and Thucydides. As a consequence, the Hebrew writings with their mixture of narrative and nonnarrative forms, and their complex relation to heroic legends and myths, he believes, do not qualify as history.[27]

This bald statement must be qualified. First of all, like Voegelin, Ricoeur has differentiated between historical self-understanding on the one hand and historiography on the other hand. This distinction is considered important in order not to confuse the issue of what is meant by history. Even in its earliest writings and traditions ancient Israel manifested a historical mindset. Von Rad, whose work—particularly his *Theology of Israel's Historical Traditions*—Ricoeur continues to consult, had insisted that Israel's credo was intrinsically historical.[28] But this historical self-understanding of Israel, Ricoeur believes, "is not exclusively, nor even principally, expressed in historiographic writings."[29] He does not make clear what relationship exists between the biblical self-understanding and the historical genre.

The issue of historiography or the historical genre, not the historical mindset of Israel, has been the focus of Ricoeur's analysis. On this score he followed the lead of the Quest historians and examined the properties and genre of the biblical text. With regard to historical genre, he notes that the biblical text does contain historical accounts, but that the overall form or genre is not historiographic. Biblical research has struggled with this question in a variety of ways. Genetically and structurally the historiographic sections or forms in the Hebrew Bible have been shown to be one form among a number of narrative forms. Exegetes have not succeeded in determining the filiation of these narrative forms. On the whole, while the narrative form predominates over the variety of other genres such as the lyrical, legislative, prophetic, and sapiential, it is governed, not by a historical, but by a theological intentionality. A theological point of view determines its form. The Yahwist document displays this character well. It encompasses events that are more recent, such as those that deal with the monarchy and are closest to what we might call history, as well as events of a more distant past that resemble legends of a heroic age, and finally mythic events and their narratives. Moreover, the Yahwist documents have incorporated not only narrative forms but also nonnarrative laws, wisdom segments, praises, and curses, which heighten the issue of genre. Intentionality analysis indicates that these texts are not historical but theological.

In summary, Ricoeur has followed the suggestion that (1) these texts are not historical in form even though the ensemble articulates Israel's historical mindset; (2) the overarching form is narrative, indicative of this historical self-understanding, but it is not exclusively narrative; (3) only texts or segments that display "a structural and thematic kinship with early Greek historiography" ought to be called history in the strict sense; (4) the other narratives should be qualified as history-like and not historical; and, finally, (5) the narrative form—outside of the historiographic concern—is capable of articulating the main intention of these texts, which is theological.

This summary begs a few comments. In his "De moeilijke weg naar een narratieve theologie," Ricoeur had indicated why he thought the historical to have become problematic. The distinction in biblical interpretation between history and fiction is a decidedly modern event. It is not consciously operative in the biblical text. Our appetite for authentification through the historical too easily transforms the historylikeness of biblical narratives into history. It is therefore our problem, and we should refrain from reading our appetite for the historical into the text. Moderns are too obviously tempted by the historylikeness of the narrative. For Ricoeur, however, these historylike narratives are neither history nor fiction.[30] But the question may be asked whether *historylike* is to be understood Platonically as having only the likeness or appearance of history but not the reality of history? Or may *historylike* be understood metaphorically, so that the resemblance of these texts to the history genre generates another logic of action and a new historical form. As Ricoeur proposed in *The Rule of Metaphor,* the interplay of *is* and *is like* can lead to a true predication.[31] Can the resemblance of these narrative texts to the historical not lead to a specifically Hebrew concept of history, and can this concept be more properly related to the genre of history?

Ricoeur appears to be unwilling to broaden the historical genre. His conviction that these texts are not to be interpreted as historical has even led him to place these larger complexes of texts and this salvation history closer to myth than to history.[32] His understanding of the historical genre comes from Greek historiography. Greek history understood itself as a kind of research into the causes of human actions (such as the causes of the Persian Wars) and investigated the responsibilities of human agency in events. Historical accounts seek to determine the identity of a culture in the agency of its people, particularly of its leaders.[33] Writers such as Herodotus did not exclude the possibility of agents or forces other than the human in history. But historiography is a secular exercise. Not divine agency or intervention, but human activity is determinative for the Greek Enlightenment history. Greek historiography created the split between the human and the suprahuman forces. Greek history has discovered human time and human agency in the face of a time of the gods and divine agency.

On this score, there appears to be a marked difference with the Hebrew perception of time and agency. The decisive difference between the Hebrew biblical texts and Greek historiography lies in the point of view. The scriptural narratives are permeated and oriented by a theological intention. Broken down into its constituent elements, as Alter has done, this theological intention is expressed in a unique model of interaction and exchange between God and humans. The most significant narratives of the Hebrew Bible articulate the supremacy of the divine intention and agency in and over history. Human agency, on the whole, is seen as obstructing this intention. But the recalcitrance of human agency does not succeed in obviating the deeper intention and effectiveness of God's plan in history. Hebrew narratives do not omit or deny human agency; they narrate its limits. Human action and passion retain their free play, even their logic of action and causal imputation. But Hebrew history presents the history of human agents within a more fundamental history.[34] Its focus is not political but theological. The experiences that it articulates are human-limit experiences of the transcendent in the course of human events. It is for that reason that this biblical history has been qualified as salvation history.

The larger complexes of biblical writings present a theology of history—more accurately "theologies" of history, because the biblical text carries more than one theological vision. But these theologies of history or salvation history unfold in human time and not in the time of the gods. As he maintained already in his treatment of biblical hermeneutics, the referent of biblical texts is not God's action but human experience.[35]

The question needs to be asked whether theological intentionality so subverts the historical that a metaphorical resemblance of the biblical text to history is too impertinent. Ricoeur obviously thinks so. He accepts the historical form of Hebrew culture and the existence of historiographical writings in the Hebrew Bible, but he insists that the relation between historical form and historical genre is incommensurate. His approach to the question is guided by his understanding of historiography as a literary genre. Because in the biblical text historiography is only one among several genres and the texts closest to historiography, such as the Books of Samuel and Kings, are sometimes overlain with mythical strains, he refuses to acknowledge these texts as historical. But how, then, are we to think of the relationship between historical form and historiography? Is their incommensurability as strict as Ricoeur holds it to be?

Eric Voegelin has made the historical form of Israel the theme of his *Israel and Revelation.* Voegelin studied the Bible from the perspective of historical forms or types of human existence. His thesis is that in Israel a significant advance in differentiation of consciousness took place that superseded the earlier cosmological, imperial organizations of the civilizations of the ancient Near East. He believes that in Israel a historical form of existence came into being because of the revelation of a transcendent God. This historical form was expressed as an account of Israel's relation with God. Such spiritual history, according to Voegelin, may not rank high as a pragmatic, critical history. Its events are evaluated, not for their political efficacy, but in relation to a revealed will of God. Although not presented with critical evidence, events such as the burning-bush experience of Moses, the Exodus, or the tribal covenant take on paradigmatic status. They are symbolic of the experience of human souls in their struggle to be at one with God. As Voegelin notes, the criteria of truth applying to paradigmatic events in this sense cannot be the same as those applying to pragmatic events. For an event, if experienced in its relation to the will of God, will be truthfully related if its essence as a paradigm is carefully elaborated. Precision with regard to the pragmatic details of time, location, participating persons, and their actions and speeches will be much less important than precision with regard to the will of God on the particular occasion.[36]

Is this paradigmatic history still history? Is Israel's account of the discovery of God as the source of order in society in and through events of their history closer to fiction than history? The paradigmatic narrative in its uniqueness is a narrative that has constituted Israel as a people politically and historically. The course of events that required a constantly revised paraenesis in the books of the Bible is important for Israel's ongoing struggle to understand the truth of its existence. The events are not fictional; they are real. If the Bible is not a record of pragmatic, critical historiography, then it is an account of Israel's identity. In relation to other national histories, Israel's history is a search for its own form of existence. When Israel's faith burst into existence and with it the historical form, the event was "an ontologically real event in history."[37]

This does not mean that the Hebrew Bible is historiography in the strict sense. But the symbolizations of the historical order—even the theological symbolization in which Israel gives an account of its genesis as a people—are not so far removed from the intentionality of the historical genre that they must be exiled to a historylike status. That would not do justice to the reality of Israel's account of the experience. It separates the historical form too cleanly from the literary genres that configure the experience of Israel. The events that Israel refers to are real events, and such symbolizations must respect the nature of these events to remain authentic. Voegelin concludes, therefore, that the account "is a symbolic form *sui generis*" that must be understood "in terms of the experiences that motivated its construction."[38] Ricoeur proposes that in the New Testament Gospels the relation between history and the text is similar to the one that exists in the Hebrew scriptures. The intention of these texts is again theological. More specifically, it is Christological as it seeks to assure the identity of Jesus with the Christ figure proclaimed by the enthusiasts and charismatics of the early communities. Ricoeur is equally specific here: Christ's identity is configured, not by a historical genre, but by a fiction in historicized prose. It is the task of this fictional narrative to express how Jesus is identified with the Christ. Again, the narrative genre of the Gospels is seen as the appropriate form to accomplish this task. Here Ricoeur has adopted the position of Hans Frei regarding the midrash.[39] For that reason, Ricoeur adduces the historical only obliquely in his various writings on the New Testament Gospels. Three specific references are useful for our consideration here.

1. Ricoeur acknowledges both the indispensible contribution of historical critical inquiry and the inability of the method to reconstruct the life of Jesus. But this method has disclosed in the proclamation texts of the early community a minimal link with the "factual" history of Jesus. It uncovered an original structure and sequence of occurrences that Perrin had called "occasions" for a narrativization (announcement, controversy, suffering).[40] But historical criticism as method cannot lead to a Christology. In the manner of a critique of ideology, it functions rather as a critical control of the Jesus question. In the hermeneutical approach, historical criticism is operationalized on the level of explanation (distanciation), and not on the level of understanding (appropriation).
2. Ricoeur has criticized the use of history in the Christologies of Pannenberg, Moltmann, and Metz. They had attempted to find the meaning of the Jesus event by linking the history of Jesus into a larger historical framework. Thus, for instance, Moltmann found the context for understanding the death of Jesus in the solidarity with the oppressed in history. For Ricoeur, however, the relation of the original event to the Gospel text is governed, not by these colligations, but by the dialectic of event and meaning. Events for Ricoeur become meaningful by being configured in language. An event crystallizes in or passes into a meaning.[41] The Gospel text sediments the event-character of Christianity into an event of meaning.[42] Accordingly, Ricoeur holds that "the relation event-testimony is the reference of the text."[43]
3. The only context where Ricoeur has recognized the existence of history lies in the reception of the New Testament text by the ecclesial community.[44] By applying a hermeneutics of historical consciousness to the Gospel reception, Ricoeur perceives history as the line of historical continuity between the original event, witness or tradition and the reprise or the chain of interpretations of the text in subsequent history. The reprise of the text by the chain of interpretations historicizes the text by linking the present community with the original witness. The importance of this effective history of Jesus has been recognized by a number of current authors.[45] The testimony locked into the text is released as history or as tradition.

Historical intentionality

This short summary of Ricoeur's position indicates that for him the historical is not part of the form of the New Testament text. The text is not a history. The Gospels remain historylike. But in the light of the historical form of the Hebrew Bible, is this all that can be said? The Gospel text like the Hebrew Bible is not devoid of a historical intentionality. If history means the account that a society gives of its own past, then the Gospels are the account of the origin and experience of the community of Christians, or the church. On a number of occasions Ricoeur states that the aim of the New Testament writers is to configure the identity of the proclaimed Christ of the churches with Jesus of Nazareth.[46] In creating the figure of Christ and the essential experiences of the new order by the religious discourse of the text, the Gospel writers interpret the person of Jesus not only as an expression of the ineffable God but also as the grounding event of a new existence in the world.[47] The Gospels intend therefore to account for the current experience and activity of Christian communities by their interpretations of Jesus. These experiences, like those recounted in the Hebrew Bible, are rooted in real events and a real person. Once again, the effort of the account is not to arrive at accuracy regarding dates, times, and places. The narrative of the Gospels and the letter genre are informed by the experience of the resurrection of Jesus. The reference of the text is, therefore, the new existence, the new justice, the reign of God, occasioned by Jesus. Jesus is only the indirect or oblique reference of the text. The account seeks to configure the new covenant, the new possibilities of life. The overall theological intentionality of the text does not exclude, therefore, a historical intentionality. That is why certain authors hold, for instance, that, despite the theological orientation of the text, Luke-Acts is history.[48] The quest for the historical Jesus may be irrelevant and inconsequential at the structural level, but in its ecclesial use and reception, the historical meaning is cointended to ground the reading in real experience and action and to give identity to the church's self-understanding. The historical can hardly be considered extraneous to the intention of the text.[49]

Without expecting the Gospel text to exemplify the same standards of inquiry as set by current historiography, one can hardly deny that the writers of the Gospel have used documentary evidence. Historical critical analysis has shown the use of sources such as parable collections, miracle stories, the sayings' source, and other materials. These sources were configured, as Ricoeur has shown, around a core that is the account of the passion of Jesus.[50] The passion account circulates around a real event in the life of Jesus. Without intending to write a factual sequence of the events (only occasions) leading to the death of Jesus, the writers were not engaged in creating a fable. The story is constructed as an interpretation of the event. The accounts of the words and deeds of Jesus, as Ricoeur has convincingly demonstrated, provide an interpretative key to the understanding of the passion. The apocalyptic, paradoxical, and metaphorical discourses and stories of the deeds of Jesus interact with the account of the passion and death to expose the symbolic or paradigmatic meaning of these events. The intensification and extravagance of the symbolic discourses and deeds not only make the passion and death of Jesus scandalous but transform it into an account of the ineffable mystery of God's redemption and justification.[51] Without these qualifiers, the story of the passion would lack the eschatological tension and would not do justice to the real story of Jesus. This is a history that does not dissociate the divine and the human but insists that the theological is historical. This is the only account the community could give of its own past and experience.

CHRISTOLOGY AND HISTORY

What difference in interpretation would occur if the form of the Bible, particularly of the Gospels, was indeed a type of history? What would the repercussions be if one applied to the interpretation of the Gospels the resources for the understanding of history assembled in *Time and Narrative?* I believe that such an attempt would prove to be fruitful in resolving some of the perennial problems encountered both in exegesis and in Christology. The historical self-understanding of Israel and the church that is presented as grounded in specific events and that in these accounts seeks to present its order of existence would then find its articulation in a linguistic form that is like the historical. If it is true that history is the most appropriate form for dealing with the issues of human temporality and action in relation to past experience, then the Hebrew and Christian Scriptures, like national histories, allow the present to be understood in a dialectic of experience and expectation.

The following points do not intend to be exhaustive; they do, however, intend to indicate how the analysis of history in *Time and Narrative* allows a break-through in a number of impasses in current Christology.

1. Ricoeur has proposed the thesis that history derives its cognition through its indirect connection or indirect derivation from narrative understanding. Historical inquiry and research into the past through documents and traces of the past are configured into a text that not only carries the quasi characteristics of narrative but also presents its argument of causal imputation by way of a structure that in form resembles the narrative. A literary approach toward the understanding of the Gospel text is, in principle, not opposed to a historical understanding. The fruitfulness of the historical critical method attests to the possibility of doing a historical inquiry and of hypothesizing the real, indirect linkage of the text to Jesus of Nazareth.
2. Such a narrative approach to the New Testament text could help break the hold that a positivistic notion of historical fact still has upon historical critical exegesis and Christology. As Ricoeur has indicated, the critique of the Ideal Chronicler by Danto has effectively deconstructed a determined, fixed, eternally irreformable past.[52] The past is not unalterable. History does not reduplicate the past but reconfigures it. The Fregean notion of reference to a real past is reformulated into a hermeneutics of narrative refiguration.[53] In that sense the Gospels configure a trace of a past of Jesus. But the reference to the past is not direct. The text does not give immediate access to Jesus but access comes only indirectly by way of the text. The text does not present a fiction or fable of Jesus, but through the account or configuration of the reported events of the past, it configures for the readers the past reality of Jesus.[54] Thus the occasions for narrativity uncovered by the analysis of the Gospel text are referred to in the text by way of textual composition and genre.[55] Here the tropological approach of Hayden White to the historical text is particularly fruitful.[56] The metaphorical refiguration of occasions into a Gospel narrative creates the indirect reference of the account to the original event. The illusive quest by Christology and historical critical exegesis for the person and life of Jesus is thereby shown to be a historical question badly put. The New Testament text as a historical document can be no more than a Levinassian trace of a past that is invented in the

text. The real Jesus is signified as being like the configured Jesus of the Gospel. The reality of Jesus is as he is said to be in the Gospel. The trace of Jesus in the Gospels stands metaphorically for the past of Jesus, resembling in dissembling him.[57]

3. To accept the historical intentionality of the Gospel text also shifts the perspective on the appropriation or refiguration of the text. The intentionality of history lies in the refiguration of the field of human action and temporality. At the level of time the historical genre, according to Ricoeur, is a mediation of human and cosmic time, the time dominated by the immensity of astronomical, physical, and biological time. Historical time forms bridges and connectors to inscribe lived, human time within cosmic time. If understood as historical, the various temporalities of the Gospel text would generate not only a narrative or ethical identity but also a historical identity.[58] Historical temporality pairs my temporality not only with the temporality of the text but also with a real past witness of an experience materialized in the text. This dimension is essential for the role of the text in the community. If understood as history, the biblical narrative brings my time in line with the flow of things as they emerge in nature.[59] The Gospel texts by their use of, for example, John's Jesus as Logos of created reality in the Prologue and Matthew's and Luke's *toldoth* of the generations, touches on cosmic time and seeks to root the Gospel in an objective temporality.
4. But also at the level of human action the historical genre would provide an orientation to Christology that may give a better operating framework, for example, to the Christologies of liberation theology. The historical genre insists more than fictional narratives on configuring the order of real action. History is a text of human action and passion. It must have a plausibility structure founded on the prenarrative structure of action and the conceptual network of action that stems from real human action.[60] History curbs utopian imaginative variations that are operative in fictional configurations by its interest in pragmatic competence. A historical genre calls for a more differentiated refiguration of human action than a fictional narrative does. Historical Christology's interest in examining the efficacy of history by communicating the real possibilities of human action, the effective "I can,"[61] can turn to Ricoeur's proposal of the hermeneutics of historical consciousness.[62] Ricoeur has proposed that history operates with a dialectic of the space

of experience generated by the past of human action and a horizon of expectation or possibility of human action. The present where past and future intersect becomes then the moment of initiative. The Gospel text provides a specific perspective upon human action and the possible space of its experience. It has an even stronger message about human passion. It relates the experience of a witness of the life and death of Jesus toward a realistic expectation of life's possibilities. On both the level of time and of action, Christology is better served by a historical mediation than a fictionalized narrative. Such a perspective would break the logjam of liberation Christology between its orientation toward practice and the traditional orientation toward the ontological identity of Jesus. A historical approach would create a more harmonious relationship between the donor of the action (Jesus) and the action itself.

5. History is not a reliving, reenacting, or rethinking of the actions of people but a discovering of the schema, the framework, or the worldview within which such actions took place and can take place again.[63] Also, in the gospel genre the actions of Jesus, in all their contingency, are inserted into an overall schema that governs the structure of the account. The New Testament schema is derived mainly through intertextuality with the figures of the Hebrew Scriptures. Placed within this framework, the second Testament is shown to have obtained its intelligibility structure from the symbolism, genres, personages, titles, and events of the first Testament. It embraces the expectations of the first readers, who had little difficulty understanding the genre of the text, and hence the promise or hope contained in it or the limits or constraints upon action and passion.[64] This logic of the probable governs also the Gospels. The Gospels make the experience of the action and passion of Jesus probable for an ecclesial community. The Gospel text makes the life, death, and resurrection of Jesus intelligible and followable.[65] As such, it gives rise to what Ulrich Simon has called the "Christian pattern" of the appropriation of the Christian message.[66]
6. On the level of entities, the New Testament text, according to source criticism, is less a history of Jesus of Nazareth than a history and proclamation of ecclesial identity. The level of its temporality is not of event but of institution. There are similarities between this ecclesial identity of the Christ with Jesus and the conjunctural, institutional time uncovered by French historiography. Conjunctural time is not the time of brief, abrupt

events but of events at the level of institutions and their longer duration. The Gospel text resembles this conjunctural configuration of the event of Jesus. The experience of the life, death, and resurrection of Jesus is configured into a worldview and life pattern of an ecclesial community.[67] It says as much about the community and its appropriation of Jesus as it does about the events of the historical Jesus. This approach to the text corresponds to the discovery of source critics and Christologists that the Gospel text is an ecclesial text and must be read from the perspective of the meaning of the Jesus event for the various communities of the early church.

7. The aligning of the Gospel text with cosmic time makes it understandable why the event character or even the quasi-event character of the conjunctural ecclesial Christ could link up with the Greek nous or logos. The cosmic pull of history opens up the possibility for incorporating a noetic, speculative differentiation that the experience of the risen Christ revealed. The encounter of Christianity with the Greek logos is, then, not a disastrous deformation of the original event character of the Gospels, but its deepening into a conceptual system leading to an ecumenical meaning structure.[68] Ricoeur himself saw this ecumenical expansion at work in Jewish Wisdom literature.[69] This thrust toward conceptualization may be understood analogously as an expansion of the Gospel text into the long duration of structural history.[70] Here too Ricoeur's warning to structural history to retain its bond with the event character of the original narrative could serve to better articulate the relation of church dogma to the original Gospel text.[71]
8. Finally, at the level of appropriation I would agree with a more recent text of Ricoeur where he proposes liturgy as the most adequate setting for the reading of the scripture text. Liturgy includes not only the proclamation of the Word in preaching but the refiguration of the death and resurrection of Jesus in a ritual reenactment as well. The configuration of the life, death, and resurrection in the Gospel text finds its fullest appropriation in its liturgical remembering. I follow here the rich suggestions of L.-M. Chauvet regarding the sacramentality of the Scriptures.[72] In line with Ricoeur's concept of history, a liturgical appropriation that makes use of the symbols of nature, regeneration, sustenance, covenanting, space, and time is more attentive to the cosmic pole of temporality. It transcends the narrative identity and appropriation and is a freer testing of the real.

This proposal regarding the historical genre within the Christological project requires further elaboration. But the case for or against the historical genre in the Bible is not yet settled. I believe that Ricoeur's magisterial *Time and Narrative* opens up a number of new ways of reflecting on history and its functioning within Christology. *Time and Narrative* is like the scriptural storehouse from which theology can extract things both old and new.

NOTES

1. Paul Ricoeur, "Freedom in the Light of Hope," in his *The Conflict of Interpretations: Essays in Hermeneutics,* ed. Don Ihde, trans. Willis Domingo et al. (Evanston, Ill.: Northwestern University Press, 1974), p. 403.
2. Paul Ricoeur, *The Symbolism of Evil,* trans. Emerson Buchanan (New York: Harper and Row, 1967), p. 347. See also "Guilt, Ethics and Religion," in *The Conflict of Interpretations,* p. 426.
3. Paul Ricoeur, *Time and Narrative:* vol. 1, trans. Kathleen McLaughlin and David Pellauer (Chicago: University of Chicago Press, 1984); vol. 2, trans. Kathleen McLaughlin and David Pellauer (1985); and vol. 3, trans. Kathleen Blamey and David Pellauer (1988).
4. Gerhard von Rad, *Theology of the Old Testament,* trans. D. M. G. Stalker (New York: Harper and Row, 1962); Eric Voegelin, *Israel and Revelation,* vol. 1 of his *Order and History* (Baton Rouge: Louisiana State University Press, 1956), pp. 111–33.
5. Harvey H. Guthrie, *Theology as Thanksgiving: From Israel's Psalms to the Church's Eucharist* (New York: Seabury, 1981); Walter Brueggemann, *Israel's Praise: Doxology against Idolatry and Ideology* (Philadelphia: Fortress, 1988).
6. See L.-M. Chauvet, *Symbole et sacrement: Une relecture sacramentelle de l'existence chrétienne* (Paris: Cerf, 1987).
7. Hans Frei, *The Eclipse of Biblical Narrative: A Study of Eighteenth and Nineteenth Century Hermeneutics* (New Haven, Conn.: Yale University Press, 1974), p. 42.
8. Gotthold E. Lessing, "Uber den Beweiss des Geistes und der Kraft," in *Lessings Werke,* vol. 7, ed. Georg Witkowski (Leipzig: Bibliographisches Institut, 1911), p. 84.
9. Peter Stuhlmacher, *Historical Criticism and Theological Interpretation of Scripture: Towards a Hermeneutics of Consent,* (Philadelphia: Fortress, 1977), pp. 21, 35. See also Ferdinand Hahn, *Historical Investigation and New Testament Faith: Two Essays,* trans. Robert Maddon, ed. with foreword by Edgar Krentz (Philadelphia: Fortress, 1983); James Barr, "Exegesis as a Theological Discipline Reconsidered and the Shadow of the Jesus of History," in *The Hermeneutical Quest: Essays in Honor of James Luther Mays on his Sixty-Fifth Birthday,* ed. Dikran Y. Hadidian (Allison Park, Pa.: Pickwick Publications, 1986), pp. 11–45.
10. See, for example, E. P. Sanders, *Jesus and Judaism* (Philadelphia: Fortress, 1985); Ben Meyer, *The Aims of Jesus* (London: SCM Press Ltd., 1979).
11. Paul Ricoeur, "Bultmann" and "Ebeling," *Foi-Education* 37, no. 78 (1967): 17–35, 36–53, 53–57.
12. Paul Ricoeur, *Les incidences théologiques des recherches actuelles conçernant le langage* (Paris: Institut d'Etudes Oecuméniques, 1969), p. 16.

13. Ricoeur, "Ebeling," p. 47.
14. See, for example, Paul Ricoeur, "Manifestation and Proclamation," *Blaisdell Institute Journal* 11 (1978): 13–35.
15. Paul Ricoeur, "Tasks of the Ecclesial Community in the Modern World," in *Theology of Renewal*, vol. 2 of *Renewal of Religious Structures*, ed. L. K. Shook (New York: Herder and Herder, 1968), p. 246.
16. Ricoeur, "Preface to Bultmann," in *Conflict of Interpretations*, p. 397.
17. Ricoeur, *Time and Narrative*, 1:91–225. See also Paul Ricoeur, "Philosophical and Theological Hermeneutics," *Studies in Religion/Sciences religieuses* 5, no. 1 (1975): 14–33, and "Temps biblique," *Archivio di filosofia* 53 (1985): 27–32.
18. Ricoeur, "Biblical Hermeneutics," in *Paul Ricoeur on Biblical Hermeneutics*, ed. John Dominic Crossan, (Missoula, Mont.: SBL, 1975), pp. 29–148, no. 4 of *Semeia: An Experimental Journal for Biblical Criticism*. See also "Du conflit à la convergence des méthodes en exégèse biblique," "Esquisse de conclusion," and "Sur l'exégèse de Genèse 1:1–2:4," in *Exégèse et herméneutique*, ed. X. Léon-Dufour (Paris: Seuil, 1971), pp. 35–53, 67–84, 85–96, 285–96.
19. Ricoeur, "Du conflit à la convergence des méthodes en exégèse biblique," p. 36.
20. See Paul Ricoeur, "Listening to the Parables of Jesus," *Criterion* 13, no. 3 (Spring 1974): 18–22; Ricoeur, "Biblical Hermeneutics," 29–148; "Le 'Royaume' dans la parabole de Jésus," *Etudes théologiques et religieuses* 51, no. 1 (1976): 15–19; and Ricoeur, "The Bible and the Imagination," in *The Bible as a Document of the University*, ed. H. D. Betz with a foreword by Martin Marty (Chico, Calif.: Scholars Press, 1981), pp. 49–75.
21. Paul Ricoeur, "Le récit interpretatif: Exégèse et théologie dans les récits de la Passion," *Recherches de science religieuse* 73 (1985): 17–38. See also Ricoeur, "Temps biblique."
22. Paul Ricoeur, "Philosophical Hermeneutics and Theological Hermeneutics"; Ricoeur, "Naming God," *Union Seminary Quarterly Review* 34, no. 4 (1979): 215–28; Ricoeur, "Toward a Hermeneutic of the Idea of Revelation," *Harvard Theological Review* 70, no. 1–2 (January–April 1977): 1–37; Ricoeur, "Myth and History," in *The Encyclopedia of Religion*, vol. 10, ed. M. Eliade (New York, London: MacMillan, 1987), pp. 273–82.
23. Ricoeur, "Le récit interpretatif," p. 17. See also his "De moeilijke weg naar een narratieve theologie," in *Meedenken met Edward Schillebeeckx*, ed. Hermann Haring, Ted Schoof, and Ad Willems (Baarn: Uitgeverij H. Nelissen, 1983), pp. 80–93.
24. This makes the Gospel narrative to be a story, not of action, but of passion. See Paul Ricoeur, "From Proclamation to Narrativity," *Journal of Religion* 64 (1984): 511.
25. Ricoeur, "Le récit interpretatif," p. 24.
26. Ricoeur, "From Proclamation to Narrativity," p. 504.
27. Ricoeur, "Myth and History," p. 279.
28. Gerhard von Rad, *The Theology of Israel's Historical Traditions*, vol. 1 of his *Theology of the Old Testament*, trans. D. M. G. Stalker (New York: Harper and Row, 1962).
29. Ricoeur, "Myth and History," p. 280.
30. Ricoeur, "De moeilijke weg naar een narratieve theologie," p. 88.
31. Paul Ricoeur, *The Rule of Metaphor: Multi-Disciplinary Studies of the Creation of Meaning in Language*, trans. Robert Czerny with Kathleen McLaughlin and John Costello, S.J. (London: Routledge and Kegan Paul, 1978), esp. pp. 216–56.
32. However, Ricoeur urges caution in the application of the term *myth* to the theological interpretation of salvation history. See "Myth and History," p. 280.
33. Ibid., p. 276.
34. Ibid., p. 280.

35. Ricoeur, "Biblical Hermeneutics," p. 92.
36. Ibid., pp. 121–22.
37. Ibid., p. 130.
38. Ibid., pp. 176–79.
39. Ricoeur, "Le récit interpretatif," p. 17.
40. Ricoeur refers to Perrin's terminology in "From Proclamation to Narrativity," p. 504.
41. Paul Ricoeur, "La parole, instauratrice de liberté," *Cahiers universitaires catholiques,* no. 1 (July 1966): 504.
42. Paul Ricoeur, "Evénement et sens," *Archivio di filosofia* 41 (1971): 25.
43. Ricoeur, "Esquisse de conclusion," p. 291; my translation.
44. Ibid. See also Paul Ricoeur, "Le Dieu crucifié de Jürgen Moltmann," *Les quatres fleuves: Cahiers de recherche et de réflexion religieuse,* no. 4 (1975): 109–14; Ricoeur, "Ipséité/Alterité/Socialité," *Archivio di filosofia* 54 (1986): 17–34, esp. pp. 32–33; and Ricoeur, "Eloge de la lecture et de l'écriture," *Etudes théologiques et religieuses* 64 (1989): 395–405.
45. Stuhlmacher, *Historical Criticism and Theological Interpretation of Scripture,* and Francis Schussler Fiorenza, *Foundational Theology: Jesus and the Church* (New York: Crossroad, 1984).
46. Ricoeur, "Le récit interpretatif," pp. 20–21, and "Biblical Hermeneutics," p. 136.
47. Ricoeur, "Biblical Hermeneutics," p. 133.
48. See, for example, Richard Pervo, "Must Luke and Acts Belong to the Same Genre?" in *SBL Seminar Papers* (Atlanta: Scholars Press, 1989), pp. 309–16; James M. Dawsey, "Characteristics of Folk-Epic in Acts," ibid., pp. 317–35; Gregory Sterling, "Luke-Acts and Apologetic Historiography," ibid., pp. 326–42, Douglas Edwards, "Acts of the Apostles and the Graeco-Roman World: Narrative Communications in a Social Context," ibid., pp. 362–77; Donald Jones, "Luke's Interest in Historical Chronology," ibid., pp. 378–87; W. Ward Gasque, "A Fruitful Field: Recent Study of the Acts of the Apostles," *Interpretation* 42 (1988): 117–31.
49. Ricoeur gives an indication of how a link between the kerygma and the event character was maintained in ancient and medieval exegesis. In "Le récit interpretatif" he refers to Erich Auerbach's concept of figura in biblical interpretation, which links pragmatic history—the history of human failure and recalcitrance—with God's providential plan. See Auerbach, "Figura" in his *Scenes from the Drama of European Literature* (New York: Meridian Books, 1959), p. 27.
50. Ricoeur, "From Proclamation to Narrativity," p. 511.
51. Ricoeur, "Biblical Hermeneutics," p. 126.
52. Arthur Danto, *Analytical Philosophy of History* (New York: Cambridge University Press, 1965).
53. Ricoeur, *Time and Narrative,* 3:51.
54. Ibid., 1:92. See also Paul Ricoeur: "The Function of Fiction in Shaping Reality," *Man and World* 12, no. 2 (1979): 123–41; Ricoeur, "Contingence et rationalité dans le récit," *Phänomenologische Forschungen* 18 (1986): 11–29; Ricoeur, "Individu et identité personnelle," in *Sur l'individu,* ed. Paul Veyne, J.-P. Vernan, et al. (Paris: Editions du Seuil, 1987), pp. 54–72; Ricoeur, "Life: A Story in Search of a Narrator," in *Facts and Values: Philosophical Reflections from Western and Non-Western Perspectives,* ed. M. C. Doeser and J. N. Kraay (Dordrecht: Martinus Nijhoff, 1986), pp. 121–32.
55. Ricoeur, *Time and Narrative,* 3:152–54.
56. Hayden White, *Metahistory: The Historical Imagination in Nineteenth-Century Europe* (1973; rpt. Baltimore and London: Johns Hopkins University Press, 1987), particularly part 3.

57. Ricoeur, *Time and Narrative,* 3:152–54.
58. Ricoeur, "Temps biblique," p. 29. See also his "Geschichte als erzählte Zeit," *Evangelische Kommentare* 18 (1984): 45–46.
59. Ricoeur, "History and Hermeneutics," trans. David Pellauer, *Journal of Philosophy* 73, no. 19 (1976): 687.
60. Ricoeur, *Time and Narrative,* 1:180.
61. Ibid., 1:92; Ricoeur, "History and Hermeneutics," p. 689.
62. See Ricoeur, "Towards a Hermeneutics of Historical Consciousness," in *Time and Narrative,* 3:207–40.
63. Ibid., 1:130.
64. Ibid., 1:154. See also Ricoeur, "The Bible and the Imagination," pp. 54–72.
65. Ricoeur, *TN,* 1:170–74.
66. Ulrich Simon, *Story and Faith in the Biblical Narrative* (London: SPCK, 1975).
67. Ricoeur, *Time and Narrative,* 1:175–92.
68. Eric Voegelin, *The Ecumenic Age,* vol. 4 of his *Order and History* (Baton Rouge and London: Louisiana State University, 1974), esp. pp. 1–58.
69. Ricoeur, "Le récit interpretatif," p. 33.
70. Ricoeur, *Time and Narrative,* 1:174.
71. Ibid., 1:193–225. See also Jean Ladrière, "Théologie et historicite," in *Une école de théologie: Le Saulchoir,* ed. G. Alberigo (Paris: Cerf, 1985), pp. 63–79, esp. p. 69.
72. Chauvet, *Symbole et sacrament,* esp. pp. 195–232.

PART III

THE NATURE OF EXISTENCE AND THE BEING OF GOD

BERNARD P. DAUENHAUER

RICOEUR'S CONTRIBUTION TO CONTEMPORARY POLITICAL THOUGHT

Paul Ricoeur has not thus far published a systematic, book-length treatise devoted solely to political philosophy.[1] But over the years he has explicitly treated political matters in numerous works. And not a few of his treatments of other topics, particularly his elucidations of the hermeneutic character of all human making, doing, and saying, have important consequences for a proper understanding both of the nature of politics and of the conditions for its responsible practice. Regrettably, Ricoeur's contribution to political thought has not received the consideration it deserves. This essay, I hope, will help in some small way to bring this contribution the attention it merits.

I will concentrate here on three major themes. The first is what Ricoeur calls the "anthropology of action."[2] Ricoeur's treatment of this theme substantially clarifies the constituent conditions for human action of any sort, including, of course, political action. The second theme to which I will draw attention is that of politics itself. I will emphasize two parts of this theme, namely, (*a*) political agency and its basis, and (*b*) the relations among politics on the one hand and both economics and ethics on the other. Dealing with these two themes leads naturally to a third, namely, the fragility of politics, its vulnerability to degradation. Ricoeur's handling of these themes brings to light crucial features of a salutary "third way" for political thought and practice. This "third way" avoids both the Scylla of the ahistorical individualism found in both classical and contemporary liberalism and the Charybdis of those contemporary postmodernist views, often inspired by

Nietzsche, that reduce both human action and its agent to nothing more than a product of the material and social conditions in which they are embedded. By guiding us toward this third way, Ricoeur makes a major contribution to contemporary political philosophy.[3]

THE ANTHROPOLOGY OF ACTION

Among the most important of Ricoeur's contributions to the anthropology of action and interaction, and hence to the understanding of the possibilities and limits of political action are (*a*) his account of the temporal conditions for action and its history, and (*b*) his analysis of the mimetic structure of historical time, the time of action and of its interpretation.[4]

Temporal Conditions for Action and Its History

No action, for Ricoeur, is possible, much less intelligible, apart from a history of actions, both those of one's own and those of others. Hence he speaks of the time of action as historical time. Historical time, when articulated narratively, becomes human time. In his words: "*Time becomes human to the extent that it is articulated through a narrative mode, and narrative attains its full meaning when it becomes a condition of temporal existence.*"[5]

Historical time presupposes at least a latent recognition of a fundamental paradox in our experience of time. On the one hand, we experience the flow of our own brief lives from our birth toward our death. This can be called lived time. On the other hand we experience the time of the cosmos, a seemingly endless succession of undifferentiated moments. There is no way, Ricoeur argues, for us satisfactorily either to hierarchically order or to make homogeneous these two times. The wisdom of the ages, he says, "has always known the disproportion between time that, on the one hand, we deploy in living, and on the other, that envelops us everywhere. It has always told of the brevity of human life in comparison with the immensity of time."[6] Thus the paradox: Though the life span both of individual persons and even of all humanity—with all their plans, hopes, and fears—is insignificant in terms of the cosmos, nonetheless, it is only during the brief duration when there are people that any question of meaning or significance can occur.

Historical time is a time "constituted at the junction of our fractured concept of time."[7] It is a bridge we throw over the chasm separating cosmic time from lived time. It is the time in which we act, interact, and discursively articulate our interaction.

In historical time, human life shows itself to be an open and incomplete interplay of an anticipation of the future, a reception of the past, and a living out of the present. In contrast to cosmic time—in which there is, properly speaking, no present but only an oriented succession of indifferent instants—in historical time, as in lived time, there is a present that enables us to distinguish *qualitatively* between a before as past and an after as future. And, in contrast to mere lived time, which could be experienced as both fundamentally detached from others and evanescent, historical time is the time in which we find it possible to develop procedures that link us both to others and to the material cosmos we inhabit. Some of these procedures show up in historiology.[8]

If, as Ricoeur encourages us to do, we turn our attention to action as a project of history to be made, we find that, in the course of the movement or passage of the future into the past, the present is the time of initiative. The present is the time when the weight of what has already transpired, both in the cosmos and in the field of previous human conduct, is suspended or open to interruption. It is likewise the time when the desires and aspirations of a history still to be made are transformed into decisions and actions by agents who are uniquely responsible for them.[9]

Ricoeur develops his interpretation of the time of action with the help of Reinhart Koselleck's distinction between the space of experience and the horizon of expectation. The space of experience encompasses the set of past individual and social actions, events, and occurrences that are remembered in the present. As the past now rendered present, the space of experience provides the point of departure for new initiatives. Correlatively, the horizon of expectation is the future rendered present. It is the unfolding of possibilities one can adopt, pursue, or seek to avoid. It is nontrivial to note that either ignorance or error or forgetfulness or all three combined ensure that our grasp of neither the space of experience nor the horizon of expectation can ever be more than partial.

The space of experience and the horizon of expectation are asymmetrical. The former tends to unify the past objects, persons, and states of affairs that are its constituents, whereas the latter tends to proliferate new possibilities as its constituents. But these two do not stand in polar opposition to one another.[10] Action, undertaken in the present, keeps them in dialectical tension. Thus we are shaped both by a past, a history we have not made, and by ourselves through the past we do make in the course of pursuing projects into the future.[11]

The historical present, as the time of action, is the time of initiatives, of beginnings. Initiatives are genuine inaugurations of new sequences and arrangements of things. They transform the mere present moments of cosmic time into beginnings that have continuations. Thus, wherever there is initiative, there is the historical present. And without the historical present there is no historical time that mediates between cosmic time and lived time.[12]

Historical time, then, is the time of the dialectical interplay among the space of experience, the horizon of expectation, and initiative. But historical time is never merely the time of an individual. It is always interpersonal, public time. It is the time in which we come to see and appreciate the sequence of generations, and particularly the traces that predecessor generations have left behind. It is the time in which one can recognize debts to those who, coming before, have shaped the space of experience that makes our own initiatives possible.

If there is to be a full-fledged historical present, then there must be not merely a human doing. There must also be someone who articulates that doing in language. Thus the initiative constitutive of the historical present "is signaled by the coincidence between an event and the discourse that enunciates it."[13] The fundamental mode of the discourse constitutive of the historical present, and hence of historical time as a whole, is narrative discourse.[14]

THE MIMETIC STRUCTURE OF HISTORICAL TIME

To flesh out the sense of action and its narrative articulation, let me turn now to Ricoeur's doctrine of mimesis. Ricoeur developed this doctrine to make sense of the relation between history and fiction. But it also sheds considerable light on the possibilities and limitations of political practice.

Following Aristotle, Ricoeur applies the concept of mimesis

only to human action or production. And with Aristotle he takes mimesis to be the productive activity of emplotment, of arranging incidents into a story, a more or less unified plot.[15]

Mimesis is analyzable into three moments, which Ricoeur labels $mimesis_1$, $mimesis_2$, and $mimesis_3$. $Mimesis_1$ refers to the fact that if human action can intelligibly be brought to words in narrative, it is because both the speaker-writer and the listener-reader are already, even if nonconceptually, familiar with the signs, rules, and norms constitutive of action. They have a preunderstanding of its order and its temporality.[16]

Whereas $mimesis_1$ consists of the *prefiguration* of action presupposed by its narration, $mimesis_2$ is the *configuration* of incidents and actions into a whole. It is the emplotting of events into an intelligible story. An event, Ricoeur says, "must be more than a singular occurrence. It is qualified as an event by its contribution to the progression of the plot. A story, on the other hand, must be more than an enumeration of events in a series. It has to organize them into an intelligible whole."[17]

As the activity of configuration, $mimesis_2$ is not itself without antecedents. It always draws upon patterns of configuration sedimented in one or more traditions of emplotment. But because each act of configuring, of storytelling, is itself an action, it stands in varying relations to the constraints imposed by this sedimentation. It is not necessarily wholly governed by them.[18]

$Mimesis_3$, Ricoeur tells us, corresponds to what Hans-Georg Gadamer, in his hermeneutics, calls "application." It *transfigures* what was *prefigured* in $mimesis_1$ and *configured* in $mimesis_2$. It does so by having the action it transfigures rebound upon the prefiguration in which mimesis as a whole originates. That is, the action transfigured in a story rebounds upon and modifies both the teller's and the hearer's preunderstanding of action. Their subsequent encounters with actions will now be informed by the transfiguration of action effected in the story. The preunderstanding with which they previously encountered action is now *refigured.*[19] Refiguration thus is "the power of revelation and transformation achieved by narrative configurations when they are 'applied' to actual acting and suffering."[20]

The stories that articulate this refiguration of time are of two sorts, namely, fictions and histories. Ricoeur argues that history and fiction make two different responses to the discordance between mortal or lived time and cosmic time. These different responses are not antithetical to one another. Rather, they complement each other. Whereas history as historiography consists in reinscribing lived time upon cosmic time by means of such devices as calendars and dated documents and monuments, fiction invents imaginative variations upon these reinscriptions and their devices. Indeed, fiction's disclosive and transformative power "is in proportion to its de-realizing power with respect to the constraints of calendar time and knowledge by traces."[21]

If fiction gets its power from the imaginative variations it performs on elements drawn from history, history, in turn, always involves a resort to the fictive. All of the devices—calendars, monuments, etc.—that history employs to reinscribe mortal time on cosmic time are inventions of the productive imagination. History, then, is no less the work of imagination than it is the work of representing or reenacting the past. Thus Ricoeur concludes: "It is in the intersection of history and fiction in the refiguration of time that we discover or invent . . . what we might suitably call human time. Human time, that fragile mix where the representing of the past of history and the imaginative variations of fiction are joined against a background of the aporias of the phenomenology of time."[22]

It is in this rich but fragile human time that we make sense out of our own existence. In telling our own stories, Ricoeur says, we come to recognize ourselves, to constitute our own identity. That is, in the very process of narrating what he/she does, an agent recognizes himself/herself and achieves what can properly be called a narrative identity. In this self-constitution, "it makes little difference whether these stories are true or false, fiction as well as verifiable history provides us with an identity."[23]

This narrative self-constitution of the agent, set as it is in the context of the aporetic experience of time as both mortal or lived and cosmic, has important consequences for political thought and practice.

THE RELATIONS AMONG POLITICS, ECONOMICS, AND ETHICS

Some critical implications of seeing human action as necessarily transpiring in a time always experienced as aporetic show up in the way Ricoeur understands the "human condition" of the political agent. They also show up in the way he construes the connections between politics and ethics, on the one hand, and economics, on the other. Though these two matters are logically connected, I will distinguish them for expository purposes.

The Political Agent

Politics, Ricoeur says, is defined in large measure by the central role that the state holds in the life of historical communities. Quoting Eric Weil, he says: "The State is the organization of a historical community; organized into a State, the community is capable of making decisions." The task for political philosophy is to account for how the reasonable liberty of the individual can issue in his insertion into politics. That is, how does one understand the constitution of the individual as citizen. Political philosophy, then, is a mediation on citizenship.[24]

Given his analysis of historical time and the narrativity associated with it, it is no surprise that Ricoeur rejects the concept of the individual subject that lies at the basis of the liberalism of a Locke, Mill, or, more recently, Nozick. It makes no sense to construe the individual as one who has powers and rights prior to and independent of society with its array of institutions. Rather, with Aristotle, Hegel, Marx, and Arendt, Ricoeur regards political involvement in a historical community to be "constitutive of the very existence of human beings as active beings."[25]

But Ricoeur also makes it clear that he does not regard individual agents as nothing more than products of some set of processes or forces, as some Marxists, structuralists, and poststructuralists might lead one to think. Even though they do not make the circumstances in which they work, act, and speak, the makers of history are real individuals irreducible to generalized processes or forces. "The only reality, in the end, are individuals who do things."[26]

These individuals are not liberalism's individualistic, ultimately narcissistic, egos. Rather, these selves who know themselves as selves are fruits of individual lives, each of which is in large part constituted by the cathartic effects of narratives, be they historical or fictional, conveyed by our culture. So self-constancy [*l'ipseité*] (self-constancy, self-identity) refers to a self instructed by the works of the culture that it has applied to itself. Without this instruction by one's culture, there is no self-conscious self capable of action, much less of political action. Thus both an individual and a community constitutes and is constituted in its identity "by taking up narratives that become for them their actual history."[27] And so the very stories through which liberalism transmits itself undercut it. Even in declaring the radical independence of each human being, they show our ties to one another.

It follows that if people become and remain full-fledged human persons capable of acting—if they become and remain citizens—only by virtue of involvement in social institutions, then they are obligated to serve and preserve these institutions. Because people are indebted from birth to institutions for having allowed them to become free agents, then they are obligated to make these institutions accessible to others. Here, Ricoeur says, "lies both the origin and the meaning of political authority. Such authority designates the counterpart to the obligation stemming from belonging to and participating in some political space. . . . Belonging and participating lead to an obligation to the extent that those capacities whose flowering is socially conditioned are themselves worthy of respect."[28]

This position does not, of course, legitimate just any political regime. It simply denies, on the one hand, that agents can be free apart from any association with others, and asserts, on the other hand, that people owe it to others to be concerned that the form of a society promote the development of the capacities that make a person worthy of respect. This position, in short, opposes both political atomism and totalitarianism. "If individuals are not originally the bearer [*sic*] of subjective rights, their social existence does nevertheless develop capacities that make them agents immediately worthy of respect."[29] It is their social existence in institutions not wholly of their own invention that makes them citizens, i.e., political agents.

Politics, Economics, and Ethics

Precisely because the individual person is the free historical agent who nonetheless owes his/her identity and efficacy and, therefore, his/her citizenship to a historical community, politics is neither reducible to nor dissociate from either economics or ethics. This indissoluble connection with economics and ethics imposes important constraints upon any politics that seeks to be responsible.

In the twentieth century there have been two significant attempts either to reduce politics to economics or to trivialize politics while exalting economics. Both of these attempts blur to the vanishing point the "distinction between economics, which regulates the group of relations with respect to work and goods, and what we could call the history of power."[30] It is politics that deals with the history of power.

Orthodox Marxists, if not Marx himself, have engaged in one form of this reductionist effort. They regard political alienation as nothing but the reflection or surface manifestation of economic alienation. Identifying political liberalism with economic liberalism, they justify the suppression of the benefits of the former as the price necessary for eliminating the injustices brought about by the latter. But the upshot of this identification is that the absence of any autonomous political thought clears the way for a political Machiavellianism that justifies recourse to tyranny on grounds that it will promote the abolition of economic injustices. This recourse to tyranny permits political experiments of all sorts, including totalitarianism.[31]

Even if the Orthodox Marxist attempt to reduce politics to economics is now widely discredited, a second form of that effort is still much with us and indeed shows signs of growing stronger.[32] Organization theorists like Herbert Simon have long argued that the fundamental task of any organization is to adapt the individuals involved in it to its requirements. The organization's objective is to achieve efficiency. And efficiency is defined as having its members make the decisions and perform the actions that best serve the organization.[33] Indeed, an individual is rational only insofar as he or she promotes the objectives of the organization. When this notion of technical rationality is applied to economics, it leaves no room for autonomous political considerations that might modify in any way the technical imperatives of a rationalized economy.

Both of these attempts to subjugate politics to economics fail to draw the distinction Ricoeur makes between the rational and the reasonable. The technical and economic sphere of life can satisfy only the demands of the rational. To seek the reasonable, to assess the *worth for people* of the requirements of economic rationality, one must turn to politics.[34] It is politics, understood as the exercise of decision making and force at the level of the community, that should determine the extent of the sway to be given to technical and economic organization and activity.

Ricoeur justifies his insistence upon keeping the political distinct from the economic by noting how the histories of these two spheres differ. The economic sphere shows a progressive accumulation of resources and sophistication of techniques and tools. The political sphere shows no comparable progression. What we learn in political experience is never a settled acquisition that we can then take for granted. In politics, unlike in rationalized economics, there can be regression as well as progression. And neither regression nor progression can be quantified or measured in politics, as they can be in economics.[35]

If politics must be protected against subjugation to economics, so too must it be protected against subjugation to ethics. It is not wrong to see what Ricoeur calls the "ethical intention" at play in resisting the reduction of politics to economics.[36] But this does not justify reducing politics to ethics.

To show the mistake of any attempt to identify the political with the ethical, Ricoeur invokes Max Weber's famous distinction between an ethics of conviction or aspiration and an ethics of responsibility. This is a distinction between the preferable, on the one hand, and the realizable in a given historical context with a restricted use of violence, on the other. Politics necessarily insists upon this distinction.

An ethics of conviction is concerned not only with values themselves but also with the justifications, motivations, and sources that support them and whence they spring. Particular cultural and intellectual groups and confessional communities support this ethics. In a real sense, in accepting an ethics of conviction one recognizes a call to change his or her entire approach to life.

An ethics of responsibility, by contrast, is satisfied with consensus about values. So long as the consensus is preserved, it tolerates disagreement about the bases of these values. Recognizing that to press for agreement about their bases is to risk fragmenting the community, this consensus refrains from doing so. Rather than demanding a thoroughgoing commitment to an entire way of life, it is content with mutual accommodation.[37]

Thus, for example, European democracies have roots in medieval Christianity, the Reformation, the Enlightenment, and elsewhere. For an ethics of conviction, how one justifies adherence to democracy makes a dramatic difference. Not so for an ethics of responsibility. There is, though, another, more subtle, way in which one might attempt to merge politics with ethics. It derives its plausibility from the ethical intention that admittedly animates politics and marks it off from economics. Whatever other decisions a state may make or objectives it may adopt, its fundamental decision and objective is the decision to strive for survival, to endure regardless of external or internal threats. To abandon this decision and objective would be to abolish the state and hence to abolish politics. But precisely what the essential contribution of the state is to the community's survival can be understood in one of two ways, depending on whether one stresses the state's form or its force.[38]

If, with Arendt and Weil, one emphasizes form, then one accents the constitutional aspect of a state and its laws. This would lead one to conclude that the reasonable function of the state is, in the final analysis, to effect a harmonization of technical and economic rationality with what the history of mores shows to be reasonable. In Ricoeur's words: "The State would then be the synthesis of the rational and the historical, of the efficacious and the just. Its virtue would be prudence in the Greek and medieval sense of prudence. By this we mean that its virtue consists in holding together the criterion of efficacious calculation and the criterion of the living traditions which give the community the character of a particular organism striving for independence and longevity."[39] The state therefore must function as educator to bring its citizens to appreciate this synthesis.

If a state could be exclusively an educator, then perhaps one might be able to abrogate the distinction between politics and ethics. A state could be unequivocally a morally good state. But no state can be exclusively an educator state. It is also, and inevitably, a force, a power. Force or power is not equivalent to violence. But history shows us no state that has eliminated the domination of some people by others and the violence connected with that domination. "Political life remains ineluctably marked by the struggle to win, keep, or retake power. It is a struggle for political domination."[40] No formal or constitutional factors can convert this struggle to a purely educative exercise. The judgments pertinent to this struggle, and hence even to the educative function of concrete states, are judgments belonging to an ethics of responsibility rather than to an ethics of conviction. That is to say, they are political and not purely ethical.

Thus, Ricoeur concludes that Weil is right both that violence has been and remains what drives history and that nonviolence is what the state always aims at. Hence, a proper estimation of a state must always reflect the ambivalence induced by the fact that it is both a form and a force.[41]

But if politics is irreducible to either economics or ethics, it cannot be disassociated from them either.[42] At least one facet of its link to economics is obvious. The survival of a state and its people is directly tied to available material resources and to the organization required both to prepare them for human use and to distribute them. No sane politics can disregard matters bearing substantially on the present and future availability of economic resources.

A second facet of the link between politics and economics is perhaps less obvious. It has to do with time. Economic resources belong, on the one hand, to the time of the world. Fossil fuel, for example, gets constituted in cosmic time, a time impervious to human decision. But material elements become fully economic resources only through decisions made in historical time. And these decisions in turn modify cosmic processes, e.g., climatic alterations induced by burning fossil fuel. Thus, politics, by reason of its indissociable link with economics, is tied to the material world. Its time, historical time, thereby confronts and transpires within cosmic time.

THE FRAGILITY OF POLITICS

The results of the reflections on the themes of the anthropology of action and of its relations with economics and ethics readily leads to a third theme of substantial significance both for understanding politics and for practicing it responsibly. This is the theme of politics' fragility. Consideration of the first two themes can readily show both that politics is possible so long as there is human action and that politics can have a distinctive nobility and excellence if it is autonomous. But when these reflections are connected to the historical record, one also sees that the autonomy of politics is intrinsically fragile. So too is the appreciation of the nobility of its possibility. Thus, politics is indefinably vulnerable to degradation and deprecation.

Consider first the fragility of human time, the time of action. Its fragility springs from its origin in our paradoxical experience of time both as cosmic, unending, and indifferent to individual concerns and as mortal, fleeting, and marked by specific human projects. One can become so impressed by the indifference of the cosmos and its time to human endeavors that one comes to regard all undertakings as ultimately trivial. Conversely, either an individual or a group can become so narcissistically infatuated with its own activities that it disregards both the larger communal context and the cosmic one that make those activities possible. An example of this narcissism is the attitude of what has been called in the United States in recent years the me generation. Each of these responses to our paradoxical experience of time leads to the denial of the seriousness and worth of politics.

The narrativity ingredient in the mimetic structure of all action, and hence of political action, is a second source of politics' fragility. Narrative cannot avoid drawing on both historical actuality and fictive possibility. The historical record shows all too many willful attempts to eliminate the tension between these two constituents of action. Reactionary attempts to eliminate this tension seek to constrict the future by wholly subjugating it to the past. They dogmatically disdain the genuinely new and the initiative that can bring it about. Conversely, revolutionary attempts to eliminate this tension so favor the merely dreamed-for that they dogmatically dismiss the abiding achievements of the predecessors. Both of these sorts of attempts inevitably debase politics: the former by despising initiative, without which there is no action, political or otherwise, and the latter by despising a constitutive feature of all political action, namely, that it have lasting consequences.[43] By its very nature as action, politics cannot be made invulnerable to these perversions.

Besides the fragility resident within it, politics is also vulnerable to degradation and deprecation by reason of its inextricable ties to economics and ethics. Overwhelmed by economic poverty or beguiled by economic wealth, people can be and have been prodded into subjugating politics, with its pursuit of the reasonable, to the imperatives of the technologically and economically rational. Efficiency becomes the ultimate criterion for what is to be done. If there is to be politics at all, concerned as it is with justice and freedom, then it is to be kept unequivocally subservient to the requirements established by technical, calculating rationality for uninterrupted economic progress. A subservient politics, though, is a debased action. It is action that has surrendered its autonomy to mechanisms of production.

No less perverse is the unqualified attempt to subjugate politics, with its ethics of responsibility, to an ethics of conviction. Such an attempt presumptuously slights the technical and economic conditions that simultaneously constrain and facilitate human action of all sorts, political and otherwise. It also slights the specific sedimented historical context within which both individuals and historical communities live and act. Historically, subjugations of politics to ethics of conviction have produced theocratic and Thermidorean dictatorships. They have thereby subjugated political reasonableness to theological-philosophical rationality.

There is, however, no way to make politics invulnerable to threats to subjugate it to either economics or ethics. If it is both to be autonomous and to respect its ineliminable links with economics and ethics, it must patiently persist in its fragility and vulnerability.[44]

Ricoeur himself sheds much light on politics' fragility by examining the language deployed in politics. Political language, he notes, is always rhetorical. Rhetoric, generally, is fragile because it deals only with opinion. Standing between the language of rational demonstration, on the one hand, and sheer sophistry, on the other, rhetoric can present only plausible, at best probable, lines of reasoning.[45] In politics, the fragility, the finitude, of rhetoric is particularly noteworthy because so much is at stake.

Political language, which is itself a kind of political action, functions on three successive levels. The first level is that of political deliberation. Here the conflicts inevitably found in any nontyrannical state call for a consensus on how to live with these conflicts. Because language at this level is both conflictual and consensual, it is vulnerable or fragile. It is unavoidably open to threats from a language that would neither countenance conflict nor seek consensus, a language, in short, that would repudiate the autonomous legitimacy of politics.

At a second level, political language deals with the ends of good government. It asks what form a state should have, and how it should display force. But each concrete state has its own distinct history and geography as constitutive conditions. Further, as Aristotle has noted in the *Nichomachean Ethics,* crucial notions like justice and equality are inherently polyvalent. Hence there can be no unique definitive answers to these questions. But because these questions are so momentous, there is always a temptation to abandon the plurivocity appropriate to political language for the univocity of either utopian or ideological propaganda and demagoguery.

Finally, at a third level, political language deals with the ageless issue of the connection between good government for a specific community and a good life for its several individual members. Here again, the language that responds to this issue is inevitably ambiguous and ambivalent. This is so because, as the case of Socrates showed, one and the same person "can love or hate the same things for good reasons . . . , can welcome or reject the same values."[46] This is particularly true when it is a question of those fundamental choices that determine the identity of a people in modern democratic regimes. Here the question is: To what kind of society will I give my allegiance and what sort of self-identity will I constitute by so doing? To escape this often painful ambiguity and ambivalence, we find ourselves regularly tempted to retreat to the comparatively simple language either of escapism or of unmitigated chauvinism.

Because political language is inevitably fragile in these ways, there can be no secure knowledge or technique with which to determine unequivocally its proper functioning. Likewise, there can be no definitive way to guarantee that it will not degenerate into sheer sophistry.[47] The fragility of political language does not, however, reduce its human importance. For, as Ricoeur concludes: "Political language is a rhetorical language, not as a result of some accidental flaw, but in essence. What makes it weak is also what makes possible its greatness, for in the last analysis we have no better instrument for interpreting ourselves as political animals."[48]

CONCLUSION

Reflection on these three themes—the themes of an anthropology of action; the relations among politics, economics, and ethics; and the fragility of politics—thus shows (*a*) that politics is always possible so long as there are people, but (*b*) that if politics is to be autonomous, then it will be fragile. In the course of doing so, it also brings to light the virtues conducive to responsible political practice. In conclusion, I wish to comment briefly on these virtues.[49]

First, responsible political practice calls for patience by its practitioners. Political action—as action performed in, by, and for a historical community—can, by its very nature, have no bottom line. Or, as Senator Eugene McCarthy once put it, politics is always in the second act. It is always, in some significant measure, action that makes room for further action, political or otherwise, that will modify its accomplishments. Without patience, one can be led to dismiss this incomplete politics as, at best, inferior if not actually trivial action, action not worthy of one's best efforts. Or conversely, without patience one can try to force completeness upon politics, either by subjugating politics to some other sort of action, economic, religious, etc., or by pursuing a utopian politics aimed at ending politics. The patience required for responsible politics, then, is the patience that permits and sustains politics as politics. It lets politics be politics.

Correlatively, responsible political practice calls for courage by its practitioners. Political action, like all action, is risky. Since it necessarily involves choice and deals with the contingent, its outcome cannot be guaranteed. No concrete political initiative can find vindication until after the fact. And then it is only a contingent vindication. But without courage, political practice stagnates, becoming ever less appropriate to its material and cultural context. And, a stagnant politics is a politics ripe for subjugation.

The historical record of the misery inflicted upon humankind by perversions of politics is enough to motivate one to promote political patience and courage. But one need not promote them only for defensive reasons. One can promote them precisely because they honor and respect human action. Indeed, one best promotes them when one positively esteems human action in its multiple forms, including political action, when one has confidence in the intrinsic worth of human action.

It is not, of course, indubitably evident that human action is intrinsically worthwhile. If it were, our experience of the immensity of cosmic time would not appear so disproportionate to lived time that it threatened to reduce lived time, and hence human action, to triviality. But no deployment of language, itself a form of action, could prove the triviality of action. Indeed, the very possibility of language, with its capacity to raise the question of significance, points in the opposite direction. And so we can hope.

The hope in question here is a hope in and for human action as *interminably* worthwhile. No action can reasonably cancel hope for more action. And since all human action about which we know anything transpires within a historical community, and since political action is part of the action of any historical community with which we are familiar, the hope in question here is a hope in and for unending politics. It is a hope that synthesizes patience, courage, and confidence.[50]

This hope in and for human action, including political action, finds support in the great stories constitutive of the narrative identity of religious traditions. So too is it supported by the stories and legends that figure large in the constitution of national identities.[51] But both because of their multiplicity and because of the irremovable fictive element in their constitution, these stories can never lead us beyond hope to certitude. However, supportive of hope in and for human action these stories may be, neither singly nor together do they so establish the worth of human action that they render this hope idle. To pretend to ground hope in any or all of the stories would be tantamount to justifying what lies at the base of politics—namely, an ethics of responsibility—by some version of an ethics of conviction.

Part and parcel, then, of all responsible political practice is its anchorage in hope, a hope that is not only global but that also is at play in all specific political performances. It is this hope—which is never more nor less than hope, never certitude and never despair—that keeps political action true to the conditions of its possibility. Political action never escapes the fragility or vulnerability to the perversion intrinsic in action, in the connections politics has with economics and ethics, and in the language in which politics is enacted. But at the same time, politics need not be perverse. Indeed, it can reasonably aspire to nobility. Hope keeps alive this aspiration.[52]

One need not look either hard nor far today to find multiple examples of the degradation and deprecation of politics. By his reflection on the three themes I have discussed here, as well as by his analyses of other social and political themes, Ricoeur has significantly clarified both the possibilities for and the limitations of politics. In so doing, he has articulated conditions that any politics seeking to be responsible must observe. He has thereby directed us toward a salutary third way of construing and practicing politics, a way between ahistorical individualism and reductionistic contextual determinism. This salutary political thought and practice requires of its participants, if I am right, a synthesis of patience, courage, and confidence. In short, it requires hope, a hope that acknowledges that the question of its own defensibility must always remain open.[53]

NOTES

1. Valuable and insightful as Paul Ricoeur's *Lectures on Ideology and Utopia* (ed. by George H. Taylor [New York: Columbia University Press, 1986]) is, it makes no pretense of being a systematic treatise. For an appreciative comment on it, see my "Ideology, Utopia, and Responsible Politics," *Man and World* 22, no. 1 (1989): 25–41.
2. Paul Ricoeur, "The Fragility of Political Language," *Philosophy Today* 31, no. 2 (1987): 37.

3. To keep matters manageable, I will discuss only a rather small number of Ricoeur's writings. With but one exception, all of the works I will take up appeared during the decade of the eighties.
4. These topics, of course, lie at the core of Ricoeur's *Time and Narrative,* vol. 1, trans. Kathleen McLaughlin and David Pellauer (Chicago: University of Chicago Press, 1984); vol. 2, trans. Kathleen McLaughlin and David Pellauer (1985); and vol. 3, trans. Kathleen Blamey and David Pellauer (1988). One should not overlook Ricoeur's "Action, Story, and History: On Re-Reading *The Human Condition,*" *Salmagundi,* no. 60 (Spring–Summer 1983): 60–72. In this piece Ricoeur sympathetically examines the connections Hannah Arendt makes among action, story, and history as part of his own effort to identify "the most enduring features of the temporal condition of man" (p. 60).
5. Ricoeur, *Time and Narrative* 1:52; italics are Ricoeur's.
6. Paul Ricoeur, "Narrated Time," trans. Robert Sweeney, *Philosophy Today* 29, no. 4 (Winter 1985): 263.
7. Ibid. My modification of Sweeney's translation.
8. For Ricoeur's discussion of some of these historiological procedures, see "Narrated Time," pp. 263–65.
9. Ricoeur, *Time and Narrative,* 3:208.
10. Ibid., 3:208–9.
11. Ibid., 3:213.
12. Ibid., 3:233–40.
13. Ibid., 3:108–9. Ricoeur acknowledges his debt here to Emile Beneviste.
14. Paul Ricoeur, *Hermeneutics and the Human Sciences: Essays on Language, Action, and Interpretation,* ed., trans., and intro. John B. Thompson (Cambridge: Cambridge University Press, 1981), p. 294.
15. Paul Ricoeur, "Mimesis and Representation," *Annals of Scholarship* 2, no. 3 (1981): 16.
16. Ibid., pp. 19–20.
17. Ibid., p. 23.
18. Ibid., p. 25.
19. Ibid., pp. 28–29. For Ricoeur's fullest explication of mimesis and its three moments, see *Time and Narrative,* 1:52–72.
20. Ricoeur, "Narrated Time," p. 260.
21. Ibid., p. 269.
22. Ibid., pp. 270, 271.
23. Paul Ricoeur, "History as Narrative and Practice," *Philosophy Today* 29, no. 3 (Fall 1985): 214.
24. Ricoeur, "Ethique et politique," *Esprit* 101 (May 1985): 5, 6. Ricoeur quotes Eric Weil from *La philosophie politique* (Paris: Vrin, 1984), p. 131.
25. Ricoeur, "The Fragility," p. 36.
26. Ricoeur, "History as Narrative," p. 216.
27. Ricoeur, *Time and Narrative,* 3:247. Though it is accented differently, Amartya Sen's "Individual Freedom as a Social Commitment," *New York Review of Books,* June 14, 1990, pp. 49–54, nicely complements Ricoeur's position.
28. Ricoeur, "The Fragility," p. 37. See also in this connection Charles Taylor, "Atomism," in his *Philosophy and the Human Sciences* (New York: Cambridge University Press, 1985), pp. 187–210.
29. Ricoeur, "The Fragility," p. 38.
30. Paul Ricoeur, "The Tasks of a Political Educator," *Philosophy Today* 17, no. 2/4 (Summer 1973): 142–52.
31. Ricoeur, "Ethique," pp. 3–4.
32. To my knowledge, Ricoeur has not explicitly dealt with the second form of the effort to reduce the political to the economic. But it is easy to see how what he does say applies to it.

33. See Herbert Simon, *Administrative Behavior* (New York: Macmillan, 1947), pp. 38–39, 79, 101–2, 109–19. See also in this connection Sheldon Wolin's critique of Simon's position in Wolin, *Politics and Vision* (Boston: Little, Brown, and Co., 1960), pp. 380–414.
34. Ricoeur, "Ethique," p. 5.
35. Ricoeur, "The Tasks," p. 145. I develop here the leads Ricoeur provides.
36. Ricoeur, "Ethique," p. 5.
37. Ibid., pp. 10–11, and Ricoeur, "The Tasks," pp. 149–50.
38. Ricoeur, "Ethique," pp. 5–6.
39. Ibid., pp. 6–7.
40. Ibid., p. 8.
41. Ibid. See also Weil, *La philosophie*, pp. 233, 281.
42. In discussion here of the indissociability of politics, economics, and ethics, I have tried to follow the logic of Ricoeur's remarks on the relations among them. He himself has given less stress to their indissociability than he has to their mutual irreducibility. See Ricoeur, "Ethique," p. 11.
43. See in this connection Ricoeur, "History as Narrative," pp. 220–21.
44. Further analysis of the complex relations among ethics, politics, and economics is unquestionably called for. But considerations of space preclude further development here.
45. Ricoeur, "The Fragility," p. 36.
46. Ibid., p. 41.
47. Ibid., pp. 38–43. Ricoeur's analysis is nicely complemented by Steven Lukes in his "Marxism and Morality: Reflections on the Revolutions of 1989," *Ethics and International Affairs* 4 (1990): 23–26.
48. Ricoeur, "The Fragility," p. 44.
49. What follows is my elaboration on Ricoeur's work. I think that it is warranted. But I, not Ricoeur, am responsible for it.
50. For detailed specification of the hope in question here and its distinction from religious and other forms of hope, see my "Hope and Its Ramifications for Politics," in *Phenomenology and the Human Sciences*, ed. J. N. Mohanty (Dordrecht: Martinus Nijhoff, 1985), pp. 453–76.
51. See in this connection, Ricoeur, "History as Narrative," pp. 214–15.
52. See in this connection, Ricoeur, *Time and Narrative*, 3:215–16.
53. My *Politics of Hope* (London: Routledge and Kegan Paul, 1986) is wholly consistent with the position of Ricoeur I have described here. But if I had as fully appreciated his position then as I do now, it would have been a notably better book.

FRED DALLMAYR

POLITICS AND POWER

Ricoeur's Political Paradox Revisited

"LIKE EVERY EVENT worthy of this name, the event of Budapest has an infinite capacity for shocking. It has touched us and stirred us at several levels of our existence: at the level of historical compassion, caught by the unexpected; at the level of ordinary political strategy; at the level of reflection on the abiding political structures of human existence." These lines have an uncanny contemporary ring; they seem to speak of events still freshly imprinted in our minds. Yet, they were written by Paul Ricoeur in 1957 in the aftermath of the Hungarian uprising that was crushed by Russian tanks (as was the Polish revolt of the same year). They are the opening lines of an essay entitled "The Political Paradox," which first appeared as "Le Paradoxe Politique" in the journal *Esprit* and which I want to use here as my guidepost—not as a compendium of settled doctrines, but as a fertile source of insights inviting further elaboration. For Ricoeur, the events of Hungary and Poland were deeply unsettling on an existential as well as a philosophical level. The essay speaks of "the flames of Budapest" in the sense a flaming signal lighting up an obscure and darkly overcast landscape. From the vantage of political thought or philosophy, the signal threw into stark relief a central and perennially troubling issue of politics: the issue of power and its possible limitation. "For my part," Ricoeur wrote, "the Budapest event, coupled with the October revolution in Warsaw, has rekindled, confirmed, inflected, and radicalized a reflection on political power." To be sure, the issue is not of recent origin—although its contours have been harshly accentuated in our time. Pondering the range of political experience and its historical trajectory, Ricoeur perceived a profound dilemma or "paradox" operating in the heart of politics—hence the title of the essay—namely, the paradox of "a twofold progress in [political] rationality and in the possibilities for perversion."[1]

Recent events have further underscored the problem and the need for political reflection. Seemingly permanent structures—in place for nearly half a century—suddenly have come to disintegrate before our very eyes. Concomitantly, the flaming signals have multiplied or proliferated: to Budapest and Warsaw we today add Prague, Sofia, Bucharest, and East Berlin. Few if any of us could have predicted these developments even a short while ago. For his part, Ricoeur acknowledged having been surprised and "shocked" by the upheaval in Budapest at that time. Still, in retrospect and in light of present occurrences, many statements in his 1957 essay exude a nearly prophetic character. Apart from broader philosophical considerations, the essay offered a number of concrete comments on Socialist (or Communist) regimes and their relation to political power. Starting from the premise that power does not simply vanish—or (in Marxist terms) that state power does not simply "wither away"—Ricoeur stressed the importance of curbing party elites, a need intensified by the extensive ambitions of Socialist regimes. More than the liberal or "bourgeois" state, he observed, socialism seems to require "a vigilant, popular control" precisely because of its expanded scope of action, which tends to encompass "sectors of human existence which elsewhere and in former times were given over to chance and improvisation." Holding that power over people was unlikely to be replaced by a simple "administration of things" (as Marx had envisaged), the essay treated the issue of "democratic control" as of paramount significance in Socialist regimes, an aspect that rendered urgent the infusion of certain features of "liberal politics" in Socialist contexts. Among these features, Ricoeur singled out judicial due process and freedom of speech and press—arguing that justice and incoercible public opinion are "the two lungs" of a politically sound regime: "Without these, there is asphyxiation." More boldly, Ricoeur emphasized the role of independent labor unions or workers' councils and also the desirability of a "pluralism of parties," the latter designed to inject contestation and discussion into political structures, thereby reducing the "tendency to abuse power."[2]

Large masses of people in Eastern Europe have in recent years tended to confirm Ricoeur's judgment in these matters. Implicitly, their actions also lend credence to his broader philosophical or political-theoretical reflections—which are my primary concern in these pages. In my view, Ricoeur's "Political Paradox" contains insights that vastly exceed their immediate occasion and deserve to be pondered anew by political theorists today. One central tenet that runs through the entire essay and buttresses its arguments is that of the "relative autonomy" of politics vis-à-vis socioeconomic conditions or underpinnings, that is, of the persistence of specifically political issues irrespective of class structure or social hierarchy. Closely linked with this tenet, and a corollary of this autonomy, is the notion of an ineluctable correlation of political rationality and nonrationality, that is, of the promise of general consensus and of the potential of repression. In a subtle choice of terminology, the essay introduces a distinction rich in theoretical implications: namely, the distinction between politics seen as polity (*le politique*) and politics viewed as policy-making or decision making (*la politique*), or between a broadly shared political framework or public space, on the one hand, and the pursuit of partisan strategies or programs, on the other. Seen as a public framework, Ricoeur notes, the polity "expresses the fundamental will of the nation in its entirety"; on this level, political experience displays "a specific type of rationality which is irreducible to dialectics based on economics." On the level of policy-making or decision making, by contrast, politics involves necessarily the rule of some groups over others, thereby conjuring up "specific evils—which are precisely political evils, evils of political power" or domination. For Ricoeur, the crux of political thought was to come to grips with this correlation. "Specific rationality, specific evil—such is the double and paradoxical originality of politics," he states. "It would seem to me that the task of political philosophy is to explicate this originality and to elucidate its paradox."[3] In what follows I shall address first the topic of political rationality (as embodied in the polity) and turn next to the domain of political power and oppression; finally, I shall offer some critical comments or afterthoughts on Ricoeur's "political paradox."

I

Seen as a framework of rational concord, polity can boast a venerable history or tradition. Ever since the time of Socrates, politics has been viewed not only as the pursuit of power and might but also as an arena of justice and mutual recognition. If the focus were placed entirely on power and domination, then public or collective life would be a synonym for oppression and irrational caprice; in this case, however, reason itself would be bound to wither. The latter consequence was emphatically and pertinaciously resisted by classical Greek philosophy, which saw politics as embedded in a cosmic order not entirely alien to reason. "What will always remain admirable in the political thought of the Greeks," Ricoeur writes, "is that no philosopher among them—with the possible exception of Epicurus—ever resigned himself to the exclusion of politics from the domain of rationality. All or almost all knew that if politics were declared evil, foreign or 'other' in relation to reason and philosophical discourse, if politics were literally given over to the devil, then reason itself has capsized." Banishing the aspect of rational concord means to invite a Manichean-style bifurcation whereby human reality, including the publicly shared reality, is radically devalued and robbed of intrinsic significance; devaluation of this kind, however, damages and undermines rational inquiry itself—for, "if nothing is reasonable in man's political existence, then reason too is not real." The unreality of reason, in turn, implies the demise or disintegration of philosophy, particularly political philosophy, which in the absence of intelligible public contexts becomes moot or unintelligible to itself.[4]

In Ricoeur's view, Aristotle was a major spokesperson of rational concord—precisely because of his linkage of politics and reason or of political and philosophical intelligibility or teleology. For Aristotle, all human pursuits, including the enterprise of philosophy, aimed at and derived their meaning from the telos of goodness and happiness (*eudaimonia*); comprising the aspirations of all citizens collectively, politics construed as *polis* or polity necessarily was geared toward "the highest and most perfect good," which Aristotle also called the "good life." Since human beings "by nature" were seen, not as isolated atoms, but rather as politically constituted and engaged creatures, the pursuit of goodness inevitably presupposed a public space or forum: that is, a properly organized *polity.* "Henceforth," Ricoeur comments, "to reflect on the autonomy of politics is to find in the teleology of the *polis* or 'state' its irreducible manner of contributing to the humanity of man." By participating in the public forum, citizens are not so much repressed or disfigured in their humanity but rather enabled to partake in the quest for moral and intellectual perfection; they are empowered "to pursue a good which they could not otherwise attain." By definition, this goal exceeds individual abilities or the range of individual competence. To this extent, the public forum of the polity is a necessary premise or prerequisite of human growth and of the cultivation of moral and intellectual virtues; in Ricoeur's dramatic formulation, "humanity comes to man by means of the body politic." As a consequence, in Aristotelian terms, the opposition between individual and polity is misleading and indeed mistaken as a theoretical starting point—given the fact that citizens are humanized and also "universalized" by their polity. As a corollary, rational concord as embodied in the polity precedes and conditions individual achievements as well as partisan strategies and designs. This precedence, for Ricoeur, entails that "the threshold of humanity is the threshold of citizenship, and the citizen is a citizen only through the polity or state." Hence, he adds, "the movement of political philosophy starts with happiness which all men pursue, moves to the proper end of the state, then to its nature as a self-sufficient totality, and from there to the citizen."[5]

The emphasis on polity and its civilizing effects militates against the center-staging of political power and might—features that, to be sure, are not missing in Aristotle's political philosophy. As presented in Aristotle's *Politics*, domination and repression are not so much constitutive features of public life as manifestations of a certain lack or deficiency of goodness; accordingly, morally "bad" or unjust regimes are treated as modes of perversion introduced after the discussion of properly ordered regimes. An illustration of this treatment is tyranny, which is regarded as the most depraved type of polity. For Aristotle, tyranny is not worthy of being called a constitution or a regime; it is, in his view, the worst of all political perversions and is only treated at the end of his analysis of different forms of government. If the accent were placed on tyranny and other perverse types of regimes, then the polity or public space could not function as a civilizing arena or as a medium of moral and rational growth; in that case, philosophy and politics would be pushed into a radical opposition (after the fashion of Koestler's antinomy between the "Yogi" and the "commissar"). Siding with the Aristotelian legacy, Ricoeur finds this antithesis politically as well as philosophically debilitating or disabling. "A meditation on politics," he asserts, "which would begin with the opposition of the 'philosopher' and the 'tyrant' and which would reduce the whole exercise of power to the perversion of the will to power, would thereby forever enclose itself within nihilistic moralism" (or moral nihilism). Hence, in his view, one of the first acts of political reflection should be "to push the figure of the 'tyrant' off to the side, allowing it to emerge only as the frightening possibility which cannot be coped with because men are evil."[6]

A further lesson to be learned from Aristotle is the distinction between *polis* (public life) and *oikos* (private economic concerns)—a lesson endorsing the relative autonomy of politics. Although this lesson was frequently forgotten and obscured in modernity—with the upsurge of commerce and industry—it was nonetheless rigorously reinstated by thinkers like Rousseau. According to Ricoeur, Rousseau recaptured the basic insight of classical philosophy regarding political rationality or the polity as embodiment of rational concord—although modernity added the emphasis on public or civic freedom; the notion of the social contract, in particular, was a powerful means of rearticulating the Greek view of the civilizing effect of the *polis*. In Ricoeur's words: "To discover and reiterate within oneself the most profound motivation of the 'social contract' is, at the same time, to discover the meaning of polity as such. The great, invincible idea of the *Contrat Social* is that the body politic is born of a virtual act, of a consent which is not an historical event but which arises only in reflection." Far from being an agreement of a commercial or utilitarian sort, the contract in Rousseau's text signifies a "pact of each individual with all" that thereby constitutes the public space and the rational concord undergirding the polity. Accepting or reflectively underwriting this pact means not only an exchange of "savage liberty for security" but also the passage from natural existence to civil freedom through the medium of a law that enjoys general consent. At this point, too, Rousseau rejoins Aristotle. The pact that engenders the body politic, Ricoeur notes, "is, in voluntaristic language and on the level of virtuality (of the 'as if'), the *telos* of the state referred to by the Greeks. Where Aristotle speaks of 'nature' and 'end,' Rousseau uses 'pact' and 'general will' "; but in both cases "the specific nature of polity is captured in philosophical reflection." While the Greek conception is more objective or naturalistic, Rousseau's is more subject centered; but the latter's "general will" occupies an objective status just as Aristotle's naturalism harbors a human or humanistic telos. In both cases, thus, it is a matter "of manifesting the coincidence of an individual or desiring will with the objective-political will, in short, of making man's humanity pass through law and civil restraint."[7]

Given its virtual or stipulating character, Rousseau's contract can readily be denounced as fictional or illusory—but only by neglecting the constitutive role of polity and the relative autonomy of the public space. For Rousseau, as well as for classical philosophy, polity or rational concord has primacy over particularizing pursuits, including economic class interests. As Ricoeur notes, Rousseau's contract "cannot be engendered by any economic dialectic; it is this founding act which constitutes polity as such." As a virtual and reflectively assumed foundation, rational concord can easily be abused as a smoke screen of harmony disguising the harshness of political oppression or economic exploitation; yet, even this camouflage still pays tribute, and owes its condition of possibility, to polity and its premise of civil equality. Before it is hypocrisy or a smoke screen hiding the "exploitation of man by man," we read, "equality before the law, and the ideal equality of each before all, is the *truth* of polity; this is what constitutes the *reality* of the polity or state," a reality that is irreducible to "class conflicts and the dynamics of economic domination." Seen in this light, polity has the character of an ideal reality or of a "reality of ideality," a character that is starkly at odds both with a fictive utopianism and with pragmatic or cynical modes of realism. In Ricoeur's formulation, which paraphrases Rousseau's argument: As soon as there is a body politic or an organized political community, "there exists the reality of this ideality." By contrast, where polity is reduced to the interests of a ruling class or elite, then "there exists no longer a political state but only despotic power." However, even the most despotic state remains a polity only by virtue of contributing indirectly or obliquely to the common good. The same holds true of class struggle and class hegemony; for, in order to seize the reins of the polity, "a class must make its interests penetrate into the sphere of the universality of law."[8]

The notions of a real ideality and of a lawful universality closely link Rousseau's text with Hegel's thought, particularly as the latter is articulated in the *Philosophy of Right.* Hegel's philosophy has frequently been taken to task for glamorizing or idealizing harsh social and economic disparities, a charge that shortchanges his political insight. "When Hegel looks upon the state as reason realized in man," Ricoeur comments, "he is not thinking about a particular state" or about any contingent political structure, but rather about the state as synonym for rational concord or as embodiment of reason or the "idea." The latter concept, moreover, was only another term for public freedom or civil liberty, more or less along Rousseauean lines. Hence, from this vantage, the state appears as "what is desired by individuals so as to realize their freedom: that is, a rational, universal organization of freedom." Granted that some of Hegel's formulations regarding the state appear today extreme or excessive in their idealism; for Ricoeur, however, these statements should be taken simply as "limit expressions" or as "advanced points of a thought determined to situate all its recriminations within the confines" of a rationally organized polity. Despite their extreme and perhaps exaggerated language, Hegel's views on the state at least recuperate the relative autonomy of the polity vis-à-vis social and economic forces or hierarchies. This recuperation even survives the Marxist attack on the "bourgeois" state, and particularly Marx's critical observations on Hegel's *Philosophy of Right*—a critique that fails to adumbrate a public space beyond the imperatives of economic class struggle. In Ricoeur's view, the strength of Western political thought—epitomized in "such giants as Aristotle, Rousseau, and Hegel" revolves around the legacy of the rational polity, a legacy "supposedly brought down in the Marxist critique."[9]

II

Polity seen as a space embodying rational concord is only one dimension of political life. The paradox of politics emerges by virtue of the fact that concord is always crisscrossed and contested by particular strategies and the need for concretely binding, though necessarily partisan, policies. Policy-making or decision making, however, defines the will or will-to-power as a counterpoint to political rationality or concord. As Ricoeur notes: "The crux of the problem of the state is that the state is will. . . . If the state (as polity) is rational in its intentions, it nevertheless advances through history by means of decisions," particularly through decisions of "historical import" that decisively alter the course of human events. This consideration throws into sharp relief the distinction lurking in the case of politics: namely, that between polity seen as public space or "rational organization" (*le politique*), on the one hand, and politics construed as policy-making or decision making (*la politique*), on the other. Couched in different language, the distinction between the two domains revolves around the contrast between permanence and flux, between rational idea and contingency, between theoretical concept and practical implementation. In the formulation of the essay: Once we proceed from polity to politics in the sense of policy, "we move from advent to events, from sovereignty to the sovereign, from the state to government, from historical reason to power." Viewed from another angle, the distinction may be said to imply a difference of temporal perspectives or modalities. As a framework of public life, we read, polity is always presupposed and carries on "without interruption," though its meaning is grasped only "after the fact, in reflection, in 'retrospection.' " By contrast, politics as policy-making is pursued "step by step, in 'prospection' or in projects"—where projects involve the analysis of concrete situations and the extrapolation of probable trends into the future.[10]

Once the focus is shifted to politics as policy-making, rational concord is replaced or overshadowed by the dynamics of power relations or the struggle for power. For Ricoeur, power is not simply a marginal adjunct but an intrinsic corollary of political life. Under the rubric of policy-making, he states, politics may be defined as "the sum total of activities which have for their object the exercise of power, and hence also the conquest and preservation of power." Political projects or decisions from this vantage include "every activity whose goal or effect is to influence the distribution of public power." An accent on power, however, also brings into view the problem of "political evil," precisely because such evil is a prominent ramification or implication of public power. The point is not—the essay asserts—that all power is always and necessarily evil, but that it is eminently and endemically "prone to evil." What is paradoxical is that this proneness is simultaneously linked with public reason—since power is also "the vehicle of the historical rationality of the state (or polity)." As one should realize, evil here does not denote an individual failing or private sinfulness but rather a public perversion or a corruption of public life. Above and beyond the level of private faults, Ricoeur insists, it is important to grasp political evil as "the evil of political power." From this perspective, it is political life with its consuming ambitions and exigencies that "confers upon sin its historical dimension, its devastating power and, I would venture to say, its grandeur." The traditional notion of sin here acquires broader and more dramatic overtones and connotations—connotations that transform all of history into a moral-political spectacle (of guilt and redemption). For, taken as political evil, sin "manifests itself in power," just as power "unveils the true nature of sin, which is not pleasure but the pride of domination, the evil of possession and holding sway."[11]

The linkage of power and political evil—or the proneness of power to corruption and domination—has been recognized by religious and secular thinkers from antiquity to the present. As Ricoeur points out, it is "well worth noting that the earliest recorded biblical prophecy," that of Amos, "denounces political crimes and not individual faults" by proclaiming divine punishment for collective or tribal atrocities. A similar concern pervaded classical Greek philosophy, as is evident in Plato's *Republic* and also in the *Gorgias.* To some extent, the whole of Socratic and Platonic philosophy can be said to spring from a reflection on tyranny and related modes of domination—that is, on "power without law and without consent on the part of subjects." In Greek thought, tyranny was closely connected with sophistry seen as corruption of language—due to the damage inflicted by both types of perversion on rational concord and public communication. For Socrates and Plato, we read, tyranny was not possible or conceivable "without a falsification of the *word*—that is to say: of this power, human *par excellence,* of *expressing* things and of communicating with men." As presented in the *Gorgias,* tyranny and sophistry were shown to form a monstrous pair. In that dialogue, Plato concentrated on one form of political evil that, though seemingly distinct, is yet an intimate corollary of power: namely, flattery or the art of manipulating and controlling people through rhetorical devices. Corruption of political power is here portrayed as an incidence, if not a consequence, of the corrupting abuse of speech and rational argumentation. Given that language is a constitutive element of the polity seen as rational order, abusive tampering with language prompts political as well as philosophical decay: "Thus the lie, flattery, and untruth—political evils *par excellence* corrupt man's primordial state, which is word, discourse, and reason."[12]

Echoes of these teachings can still be found in Machiavelli's *Prince* and in Marxist thought—although in the latter they tend to be muffled by a certain economic slant. Machiavelli has himself frequently been accused of "Machiavellism," a charge that misses the complexity of his argument. In large measure, the *Prince* focused on the constitution or founding of a new polity or state, that is, on the inauguration of a new governmental power. This focus brought to light the nontransparency or incomplete rationality of acts of political founding. In Ricoeur's words: "The *Prince* evinces the implacable logic of political action: the logic of means, the pure and simple techniques of acquiring and preserving power." From the angle of power, politics is to be dominated by the "essential relationship between friend and enemy," where the enemy may be "exterior or interior, a nation, nobility, an army, or a counsellor and every friend may turn into an enemy and vice versa." Through its accent on newly founded regimes, or on political paradigm shifts, the *Prince* is led to confront the role of coercion and violence in political life—though the concern is not simply with arbitrary or random force but with that "calculated and limited type of violence designed to establish a stable state." Once the founding act is successful, inaugural or inceptive violence transforms itself into legitimate rule, thereby placing itself "under the judgment of established legality"; however, legitimacy, lawfulness, and rational concord can never entirely blot out the birthmark of the originating force and its continued reverberations. All polities or regimes, Ricoeur comments, "are born in this way." Their initial violence later becomes "re-absorbed in the new legitimacy which they foster and consolidate"—but that always "retains a note of contingency." In the *Prince* and his other writings, Machiavelli thus exposed an important, but not always appreciated, relationship: that "between politics and violence" or power—an accomplishment that testifies to "his probity and his veracity."[13]

The embroilment of politics with power and violence is likewise recognized in Marxist thought—though with a restricted focus on "bourgeois" society. The recognition surfaces particularly in Marx's attack on Hegel's conception of the state—provided that text is read as a critique not simply of capitalism but of political idealism in general. Elaborating on a point made earlier, Ricoeur sees the "great error" besetting Marxism-Leninism as well as the concrete regimes established in its name in the "reduction of political evil to economic evil"; this reduction prompts the illusion "that a society liberated from the contradictions of bourgeois society would also be freed of political alienation." Once reductionism is put aside, however, Marx's text can be viewed as addressing a broader political point, one directly pertinent to the "political paradox": namely, that a state or polity is not and can never fully be what it claims or aspires to represent—the embodiment of reason or rational concord. In Hegel's portrayal, the state is a public arena designed to reconcile on a higher plane the conflict of socioeconomic interests operative on the level of civil society. In the *Philosophy of Right,* the state is depicted as rational arbiter or "mediator" and hence as embodiment of reason; and citizens are said to gain public freedom and legal rights by means of state authority. The nub of Marx's critique is to expose the pretense of this conception and hence the inescapability of power: by showing that the Hegelian state is not "the true world of man" but another or "unreal" world that resolves conflicts or contradictions only by virtue of a "fictive law." For Ricoeur, the core of the political paradox resides precisely in this interlacing of ideality and reality, of polity and policy, of reason and power. "The idealism of right," he affirms, "is maintained throughout history only by means of the caprice of the prince. Thus the political sphere is divided between the *ideal* of sovereignty and the *reality* of power, between sovereignty and the sovereign, between the constitution and the government or police."[14]

In Ricoeur's view, this interlacing is not restricted to a particular historical period or economic mode of production; instead, it marks the core of political life, buttressing its relative independence or autonomy. As the essay notes, no state or polity can exist "without a government, an administration, a police force"; but if this is so, then the "phenomenon of political alienation" afflicts all political regimes and is endemic to all constitutional forms. Marx's shortcoming, from this vantage, was precisely that he did not perceive the "absolute character" of the political dilemma or paradox. Contrary to both Marx and Lenin, Ricoeur asserts that "political alienation is not reducible to another, but is constitutive of human existence" and that, accordingly, political life implies intrinsically a breach "between the citizen's abstract life and the concrete life of family and work." Concern with power and political alienation, however, should not simply be seen as an expression of political pessimism or "defeatism." Recognition of political evil and its pervasiveness—Ricoeur is emphatic on this point—should not be misconstrued as entailing the radical devaluation of politics, whose rational potential persists on the level of polity or public framework. Abuse of power emerges only in the context of a shared way of life; political evil, only against the backdrop of the good life. In Ricoeur's words: "Politics can be the seat of the greatest evil only because of its prominent place in human existence"; thus, "the enormity of political evil is commensurate with man's political vocation." On these premises, politics involves an intimate commingling of power and telos, of unreason and reason; political corruption can be perceived *as* corruption only in light of the promise of rational concord. Differently phrased: political evil is serious or matters only because it is "the evil *of* man's rationality," the specific evil or derangement of the "splendor of man." If rational concord or the good life manifests the potential of human grandeur, then political evil represents literally the "madness of grandeur," that is, the "madness of what is great—grandeur and culpability of power."[15]

III

In both its content and its style of presentation, Ricoeur's essay is captivating and arresting. Viewed in the current milieu of postmodernism, his portrayal of politics and its intrinsic paradox exudes a seriousness and integrity that is rare and refreshing. In bold and often haunting language, his argument spans the broad panorama of modes of political life, from the sublime to the abject, from rationality to violence and oppression—while also showing their intimate connection. In surveying this field, his work recovers and reinstates the relative autonomy of politics and political institutions—an insight that in recent times has been so dramatically underscored in Eastern Europe (and elsewhere). His comments on power and its specific role in socialist regimes, I believe, would have been heartily welcomed and endorsed by writers as diverse in background as Hannah Arendt and Vàclav Havel. Clearly, in an age ravished by the plight of totalitarianism and despotism in its many forms, concern with power as source of distinctly *political* evil must always be in the forefront of both theoretical and practical endeavors. Yet, in Ricoeur's treatment, this concern never becomes obsessive or debilitating; as a philosopher, he never took the prevalence of political evil as an excuse for a retreat or exodus from politics altogether. Shunning philosophical elitism (or esotericism), his writings always respect the embedment of reflection in a shared matrix of life—whose destruction signals both a political and an intellectual calamity. In terms of philosophical ancestry, his essay straddles or brings together divergent and even antagonistic theoretical legacies: legacies stressing either power and political conflict or public consensus. Although not directly mentioned, the emphasis on political evil evokes Augustinian views of human corruption and of the primary need to curb such corruption in the "earthly city." This accent is offset, however, by Aristotelian and even Hegelian leanings, evident in references to the good life and to the polity as arena of rational concord.

It is primarily this linkage of divergent legacies that renders distinctive and innovative Ricoeur's conception of the political paradox. The relevance of this conception has by no means diminished in the decades since its original formulation. Still, while appreciating and applauding the basic intent of his outlook, I cannot entirely concur with all its features or accents—which leads me now to set forth some of my qualms or reservations. A major qualm concerns precisely the linchpin of Ricoeur's argument: the correlation of reason and power, of polity and policy. It seems to me that this correlation often has the tendency of shading over into a rigid bifurcation approximating a Kantian antinomy. To be sure, this tendency is vigorously resisted and contested in several passages of the essay. Thus, in broaching the notion of political paradox, the introduction immediately cautions against its dualistic construal. "It is necessary," we read, "to hold out against the temptation to oppose two styles of political reflection, one which stresses the rationality of polity, drawing on Aristotle, Rousseau, and Hegel, the other emphasizing violence and the untruth of power." Opposing the splitting of spheres (or the "doubling" of the world), Ricoeur insists on the need to keep the paradox intact: in the sense that "the greatest evil adheres to the greatest rationality" and that political alienation exists "*because* polity is relatively autonomous." Elsewhere, the same view is urged in the phrase that "polity necessarily involves politics." Yet, how is this view to be reconciled with the repeated differentiation or disjuncture between idealism and realism, between the "ideality" of reason and truth and the "reality" of corruption? As previously indicated, in discussing Marx's rebuttal to Hegel, the essay notes that "the political sphere is divided between the *ideal* of sovereignty and the *reality* of power, between sovereignty and the sovereign, between the constitution and the government or police." A little later the same thought is amplified to encompass the idea that politics involves the "external contradiction between an ideal sphere of legal relations and a real sphere of communal relations"—a conflict that is said to be matched by the "internal contradiction between sovereignty and the sovereign, between the constitution and power (or the police in critical cases)."[16]

In light of these formulations, the political paradox acquires overtones of a Kantian juxtaposition of "noumenal" imperatives and "phenomenal" conditions (or else of an Augustinian confrontation of two "cities"). To complicate matters further, Ricoeur's essay occasionally reformulates or recasts the entire issue—in a manner designed to accommodate Aristotelian and Hegelian notions of being and *Wirklichkeit* (reality, actuality). Thus, references to an "ideal reality" or a "reality of ideality" clearly point in a different ontological direction that cannot readily be squared with a Kantian framework (nor with a strict Augustinianism). Large portions of the discussion of polity seem predicated on such a different ontology—where the "reality of power" is not simply external to concord and where being (however construed) sustains both reason and unreason. To recall a phrase occurring in the commentary on Rousseau's *Contrat Social:* Before it is hypocrisy or a disguise hiding socioeconomic exploitation, Rousseau's general will—that is, "equality before the law"—manifests "the *truth* of polity"; it is "what constitutes the *reality* of the polity or state." The same commentary portrays the "reality of the polity" as irreducible in the end to "class conflicts and the dynamics of economic domination." A similar outlook pervades the treatment of Aristotelian political thought, with its focus on the telos of the good life. In Aristotle's *Politics,* the pursuit of human goodness and happiness is shown to constitute the intrinsic "nature" of the polis or polity. Yet, nature clearly cannot strictly be opposed to reality—without rendering nature and its telos entirely fictive or utopian.[17]

Whether couched in Kantian or Aristotelian language, Ricoeur's view of the political paradox in many ways pays tribute to traditional metaphysics—a tradition that today is under siege. This changed situation, to be sure, does not invalidate the notion of the "political paradox" as such; but it is bound to rearrange crucial accents as well as to bar any dualistic leanings. One aspect affected by the change is the meaning and status of reason or political rationality. In Ricoeur's presentation, the polity is largely identified with rational concord or public reason—an identification that is said to persist from Aristotle to Rousseau and Hegel. Ever since Nietzsche and Freud, however, this rationalist legacy has been called into question, mainly because of the complicity of reason—chiefly scientific or instrumental reason—with mastery or the control of (inner and outer) nature. On a broader cultural-political scale, the beneficial effects of relentless rationalization have become dubious, particularly with respect to the continuation of viable social and political modes of life. Can reason by itself, one is prone to ask, furnish the resources for political concord once the reservoir of meanings sedimented in the (prerational) life-world is eroded or depleted? Another feature affected by the postmetaphysical turn is power, particularly political power. In Ricoeur's essay, again, power tends to stand as a synonym for oppression or domination—thus representing the antipode to reason or rational concord. From Arendt to Claude Lefort, however, a string of recent thinkers has challenged this Weberian formula in favor of a broader conception making room not only for restrictive oppression but also for constructively enabling modes of power or empowerment. Particularly noteworthy in this context is Foucault's notion of "micro-powers" or "capillary powers" seen as forms of agency intersecting or crisscrossing governmental and sovereign domination. Equally pathbreaking, in my view, is Foucault's rethinking of the correlation of reason and power (and implicitly of polity and policy) in terms of the nexus of "power/knowledge" (*pouvoir/savoir*). As used in his writings, "power/knowledge"—I believe—does not denote the equation of knowledge or reason with power nor the reduction of one term to the other, but rather signifies their intimate nondualistic entwining (which stops short of coincidence). As Foucault himself stated at one point: "We are subjected to the production of truth through power and we cannot exercise power except through the production of truth."[18]

Closely connected with the center-staging of reason or rationality, and its relative distention from power, is the accent placed on the notion of the state. Throughout Ricoeur's essay, polity tends to be equated with the state, the two terms appearing virtually synonymous or interchangeable. However, given the broad scope ascribed to polity, this equation seems dubious. Clearly, the Aristotelian view of polis is vastly different from the modern administrative and territorial state—regardless of whether the latter is defined as embodiment of rational freedom (as in Hegel) or as locus of the monopoly of bureaucratic power (in Weber). Whether construed along substantive or purely procedural lines, reason or rationality is seen as chief emblem of the modern state and as warrant of public unity—an emblem buttressed by the modern metaphysics of consciousness and subjectivity. As it happens, contemporary postmetaphysics has tended to decenter these pillars of modern thought, a development that necessarily also entails a decentering of the modern state and its constitutive role in the formation of public concord or consensus. Questioning the centrality or privileged status of the state does not remove or resolve the issue of polity, but it calls for a rethinking of it. Some tentative steps in this direction have been undertaken by Heidegger in his wartime lectures, particularly in his lecture course on Hölderlin's hymn "Der Ister" ("The Danube"). As Heidegger insisted at the time, *polis* or polity should not quickly be identified with a fixed structure like the modern state—where the openness of the public space has already been stabilized or administratively settled. In his account, the term *polis* should be rendered neither as state (*Staat*) nor as city (*Stadt*), but should rather be taken in the sense of "place" or "space" (*Statt*), that is, as "the place of the historical dwelling of humans in the midst of being." As such a dwelling place, *polis* is not a stable habitat—neither the epitome of reason nor the locus of bureaucratic control—but rather an open site of questioning and search: "*Polis* then is *polos*, the pole or vortex in which and around which everything turns."[19]

Rethinking the notion of *polis* also means reassessing the correlation of polity and policy, that is, of the political paradox highlighted in Ricoeur's essay. Construed as an open arena, polity no longer denotes the citadel of reason or of a rationally transparent consensus; seen as site for the encounter with "being," polity inevitably carries in itself the seeds of contestation—not for extrinsic considerations, but because of the rift engendered by negativity, that is, by the interplay of being and nonbeing, presence and absence. Politics in the sense of partisan policy-making simply means the enactment or acting out of this contest in the confines of prevailing historical and cultural constellations. Political life, from this vantage, necessarily involves a struggle for power or, in Gramscian terms, a struggle for hegemony—which cannot be safely or completely contained in accepted public structures (given their hegemonic features). Yet, struggle for power is not and cannot be the last word—if politics is not to end in mutual destruction or a Hobbesian war of all against all. What stems or countermands violence is precisely polity: the fact that power contests are also struggles for recognition presupposing a shared public space—a space that, as a source of concord and discord, cannot simply coincide with radical dissent or hostility. Against this background, the political paradox implies indeed a correlation of polity and policy—now seen, not as stark opposition, but as mutual entwining and interpenetrating. In postmetaphysical language, *polity* signifies not merely the antithesis or else the abstract condition of possibility of politics but rather its hidden sense—a sense exceeding all partisan strategies or particular purposes. In Augustinian terms (which Ricoeur would not have spurned), the earthly city with its power struggles and conflicts is secretly permeated by, or poised in the direction of, the redemptive city—although the latter cannot be constructed through human designs. In the midst of violence and public evil—with which our century surely abounds—politics harbors in itself the promise of peace instantiated by what Ricoeur at one place calls the "ministry of reconciliation."[20]

NOTES

1. Paul Ricoeur, "The Political Paradox," in his *History and Truth,* trans. Charles A. Kelbley (Evanston, Ill.: Northwestern University Press, 1965), pp. 247–48.
2. Ibid., pp. 264, 267–70. Compare also Ricoeur's essays on "Adventures of the State and the Task of Christians" (1958) and "Socialism Today" (1961) in Ricoeur, *Political and Social Essays,* ed. David Stewart and Joseph Bien, trans. Donald Siewert et al. (Athens: Ohio University Press, 1974), pp. 201–16, 229–42, particularly this statement in the former essay: "In the period in which we must extend the role of the state in economic and social matters and to advance along the path of the *socialist state,* we must also continue the task of *liberal politics,* which has always consisted of two things: to divide power among powers, to control executive power by popular representation" (p. 213).
3. Ricoeur, *History and Truth,* p. 248.
4. Ibid., p. 249.
5. Ibid., pp. 249–50.
6. Ibid., p. 251. See also Aristotle, *Politics,* ed. and trans. Ernest Baker (New York: Oxford University Press, 1962); Arthur Koestler, *Darkness at Noon,* trans. Daphne Hardy (London: Jonathan Cape, 1940).
7. Ricoeur, *History and Truth,* pp. 251–53.
8. Ibid., pp. 252–53.
9. Ibid., p. 254.
10. Ibid., pp. 254–55. The temporal difference is also couched as one between duration and critical moments: "If polity carries on without interruption, one can say in a sense that politics only exists in great moments, in 'crises,' in the climactic and turning points of history" (p. 255).
11. Ricoeur, *History and Truth,* pp. 255–56.
12. Ibid., pp. 256–57. Compare also Ricoeur, "Violence and Language," in *Political and Social Essays,* pp. 88–101.
13. Ricoeur, *History and Truth,* pp. 257–58. In a similar vein, see also Maurice Merleau-Ponty, "A Note on Machiavelli," in his *Signs,* trans. Richard C. McCleary (Evanston, Ill.: Northwestern University Press, 1964), pp. 211–23, particularly his comment: "There is a way of praising Machiavelli which is just the opposite of Machiavellianism, since it honors in his works a contribution to political clarity" (p. 223).
14. Ricoeur, *History and Truth,* pp. 258–59.
15. Ibid., pp. 259–61. As Ricoeur adds: "Henceforth, man cannot evade politics under penalty of evading his humanity. Throughout history, and by means of politics, man is faced with his grandeur and his culpability" (p. 261).

16. Ibid., pp. 248–49, 255, 259.
17. Ibid., pp. 249–50, 252.
18. Michel Foucault, *Power/Knowledge: Selected Interviews and Other Writings*, ed. Colin Gordon (New York: Pantheon Books, 1980), p. 93. Compare Tom Keenan, "The 'Paradox' of Knowledge and Power: Reading Foucault on a Bias," *Political Theory* 15 (1987): 5–37; and see also my "Pluralism Old and New: Foucault on Power," *Polis and Praxis* (Cambridge, Mass.: MIT Press, 1984), pp. 77–103.
19. Martin Heidegger, *Hölderlin's Hymne "Der Ister,"* ed. Walter Biemel, vol. 53 in Heidegger, *Gesamtausgabe* (Frankfurt: Klostermann, 1984), pp. 100–101. The above is not meant to detract from the incisive and fruitful character of many of Ricoeur's comments on the state. As he notes at one point: "The state is, among us, the unresolved contradiction of rationality and power" (Ricoeur, *Political and Social Essays*, p. 208).
20. Ricoeur, "Faith and Culture," in his *Political and Social Essays*, p. 130. Compare Ernesto Laclau and Chantal Mouffe, *Hegemony and Socialist Strategy*, trans. W. Moore and P. Cammack (London: Verso, 1984); see also my "Rethinking the Hegelian State," in my *Margins of Political Discourse* (Albany, N.Y.: SUNY Press, 1989), pp. 137–57.

PAMELA ANDERSON

NARRATIVE IDENTITY AND THE MYTHICO-POETIC IMAGINATION

How can a meaningful unity be legitimately given to the constantly changing subject of human experience? Paul Ricoeur presents this Kantian formulation of a perennial philosophical question. Ricoeur's answer presupposes that the mythico-poetic imagination makes possible the narrative constitution of self-identity or selfsameness (*ipséité*).[1]

In this essay I intend to elucidate the tension in Ricoeur between the positive role of the imagination in constituting self-identity and the potentially negative power of myth. Essentially, for Ricoeur, self-identity involves a dialectic of personal identity as both constituted by and constitutive of communal identity. Myth presents this dialectic of self-identity by symbolically mediating a historical tradition; in Ricoeur's post-Kantian terms it constitutes a narrative configuration that is able to create a meaningful unity for the life of an individual in and beyond the identity of a community.[2]

In *Time and Narrative,* volume 3, Ricoeur makes a significant qualification concerning self-identity; this qualification becomes especially significant for his account in *Soi-même comme un autre.* It is worth citing his manner of distinguishing self-identity in the sense of *ipse,* or selfsame, from the sense of *idem,* or being the same.

> We substitute for identity understood in the sense of being the same (*idem*), identity understood in the sense of oneself as self-same [*soi-même*] (*ipse*). . . . Self-sameness, "self-constancy," can escape the

> dilemma of the Same and the Other to the extent that its identity rests on a temporal structure that conforms to the model of dynamic identity arising from the poetic composition of a narrative text. The self characterized by self-sameness may then be said to be refigured by the reflective application of such narrative configurations. Unlike the abstract identity of the Same, this narrative identity, constitutive of self-constancy, can include change, mutability, within the cohesion of one lifetime. The subject then appears both as a reader and the writer of its own life. . . .
>
> We can [also] speak of the self-constancy of a community. . . . Individual and community are constituted in their identity by taking up narratives that become for them their actual history. . . .
>
> [Yet] narrative identity does not exhaust the question of self-constancy of a subject, whether this be a particular individual or a community of individuals. Our analysis of the act of reading leads us to say rather that the practice of narrative lies in a thought experiment by means of which we try to inhabit worlds foreign to us. In this sense, narrative exercises the imagination more than the will, even though it remains a category of action. . . . Still it belongs to the reader, now an agent, or an initiator of action, to choose among the multiple proposals of ethical justice brought forth by reading.[3]

By scrutinizing Ricoeur's presuppositions, we will find that his conception of the imagination in its narrative activity of opening up actual and possible worlds assumes that a mythico-poetic nucleus of meaning resides at the center of human experience.[4] It is only in this light that the mythico-poetic imagination can be understood to function productively in constituting meaningful dimensions of personal and communal praxis. Yet a crucial question is: Who—what agency—lies behind the narrative activity of the mythico-poetic imagination?

Clearly the actual and possible worlds of human praxis, which are constituted by the author/reader of a narrative text, are never ethically neutral.[5] The worlds and so the self-identities, which are opened up by myths and by the accepted symbols of a community, determine, as well as are determined by, the norms governing human action. Yet a further question emerges: What precisely can be said about the ethical responsibility that accompanies the configurating act, as Ricoeur defines it, of opening up a world? In partial answer to this question of responsibility, Ricoeur claims that the narrative constitution of self-identity must always have the character of a judgment. This is a reflective judgment in Kant's sense of both deriving a rule of unity from a manifold and reflecting, critically, upon this unifying act of extracting a configuration from a temporal succession.[6]

To sharpen the focus I intend to reconstruct and criticize Ricoeur's ideas concerning the mythicopoetic imagination insofar as they are based upon a Kantian problematic. These ideas will reflect a critical dialogue with an opposing French intellectual tradition. Yet it is my contention that Ricoeur's contribution in proposing the narrative constitution of personal and communal identity may be best understood and appreciated in the light of his Kantian conception of the productive a priori imagination. In fact, from his phenomenological description of an affective imagination in *Freedom and Nature* and his anthropological description of the transcendental imagination in *Fallible Man* to his reflections in *Time and Narrative,* volumes 1–3, Ricoeur remains consistent in relying upon Kant's conception of the productive a priori imagination.[7]

His anthropological descriptions in *Fallible Man,* especially, recall Kant's conception of the transcendental imagination as it functions—however mysteriously—in mediating between temporal intuitions and nontemporal concepts.[8] For Ricoeur, time represents the fundamental enigma of human existence: "That is the point one can make about time, which is the medium, the *metaxu,* par excellence. . . . Time dispersed and ordered, is ultimately . . . enigmatic."[9] According to Kant's account of human experience in the first *Critique,* temporal intuitions are taken up by the imagination that orders time by bringing successive appearances under a rule of unity.[10] According to Ricoeur, human willing is always governed by the incarnation of the self within a temporally determined order. Yet, as he also states, the marks of the human self are found in the aspects of change that cannot be fully explained. These aspects of Ricoeur's Kantian conception of the mediating power of the productive a priori imagination are crucial for the freedom of human selves to re-create myths—i.e., to refigure time and so to initiate change that makes possible self-determination.[11] In Kantian terms Ricoeur presupposes that the human self must be understood as both an object that, like any other empirical object, is known by way of the forms of time and space and a subject that is involved in generating time as a plurality of discrete moments on the way to becoming united by the productive imagination.

Ricoeur's emphasis upon the human imagination should also be placed in the context of the Paris-based intellectual milieu to which his early definition in *Fallible Man* of a mediating being is largely opposed. At the very same moment in the 1960s when French structuralists such Claude Lévi-Strauss and Michel Foucault are asserting the death of man, Ricoeur, on the contrary, aims to make possible a restoration of the meaningful dimensions of human lived experience.[12] The dimension of meaning that is symbolically represented by myth is only conceivable with reference to Ricoeur's philosophical anthropology, that is, to the mediating signs of the human "effort and desire to be."[13]

As already suggested, Ricoeur is consistent throughout the corpus of his works in maintaining the conception of a mediating being that he first elaborates in *Fallible Man*. His conception is of a being placed between finite and infinite aspects of experience, between time and eternity. In *Soi-même comme un autre* it is precisely the experience of being a milieu between self and other than self that, according to Ricoeur, makes human life a quest for narrative identity.[14] In fact, self-identity depends upon the mediation, by way of signs, symbols, and myths, of a historical tradition that is both constituted by and constitutive of poetic creativity. Ricoeur insists that the re-creation of myth or, to be consistent with his later terms, the refiguration of time involves "receiving a tradition and re-creating it poetically to signify something new." For him, "The problem is . . . not to rediscover some pristine immediacy but to mediate again and again in a new and more creative fashion. The mediating role of imagination is forever at work in lived reality."[15]

My criticisms of Ricoeur pertain to both the mythicopoetic function of the imagination and the illusory nature of myth. One might call this an immanent critique in that I endeavor to follow Ricoeur in applying a twofold hermeneutics of restoration and of suspicion to his own work. For instance, consider the question of remythicization that Ricoeur poses in his reconstruction of Sigmund Freud: "Is not this remythicizing a sign that the discipline of reality is nothing without the grace of imagination? . . . Freudian hermeneutics can be related to another hermeneutics, a hermeneutics that deals with the mythico-poetic function and regards myths not as fables, i.e. stories that are false, unreal, illusory, but rather as the symbolic exploration of our relationship to beings and to Being."[16] Here Ricoeur moves beyond Freud's hermeneutics of suspicion in order to restore the positive function of the mythicopoetic imagination; I will move in the opposite direction by raising suspicion concerning this mythicopoetic function.

However the significance of Ricoeur's reconstruction of Freud needs to be acknowledged. Ricoeur claims that "Freud . . . understood the central and essential significance of conflict in human anthropology, but he . . . failed to understand its origin."[17] Consistent with what we have found to be his Kantian anthropology, Ricoeur maintains that Freud failed to seek the primary origin of conflicts in the situation of a being who is him or herself a *mediation* between the infinite and the finite aspects of experience. Ricoeur's Kantian account of human willing involves a conception of the self as being rationally free but also as being embodied and so constrained. It is on this basis that the productive imagination plays a crucial role for Ricoeur in constituting the narrative unity of a life.[18]

Unfortunately, the significance of Ricoeur's early account of human willing for his later concern with narrative identity cannot be considered in detail here. Yet I want to emphasize that Ricoeur's ideas concerning human experience continue to be developed in his proposals for narrative activity. Roughly, he proposes a threefold mimesis of experience, i.e., a prefiguration, a configuration, and a refiguration of human praxis. This threefold mimesis not only represents experience but constitutes a dynamic cognitive activity of shaping and reshaping of worlds.

Having already quoted from Ricoeur's description of the narrative activities of configuration and refiguration above, let me now add that prefiguration includes the structural, symbolic, and temporal resources that make possible the poetic composition of narrative identity. Norms that govern human action are considered to be one instance of the symbolic resources of prefiguration. Yet the three forms of figurational praxis, together, may be understood as three interrelated moments in the transformation of the dehumanizing and alienating conditions of temporal experience.

For Ricoeur the contemporary lack of authenticating individual and corporate narratives of self-identity reflects the more fundamental postmodern lack of a comprehensive account of the authentic meaning of being human. Ricoeur's very positive proposal for a comprehensive philosophical anthropology would endeavor to inform all reflective knowledge of humankind. In his own words: "Philosophical anthropology has become an urgent task of contemporary thought because all the major problems of that thought converge on it and its absence is deeply felt. The sciences of [humankind] are dispersed into separate disciplines and literally do not know what they are talking about."[19]

The question that now needs to be raised is this: In what ways does the mythico-poetic imagination in its role of constituting a narrative unity out of the discreteness and discontinuity of human experience make possible the recreation—or refiguration—of that same experience? This refiguration may be understood to develop from reflective judgment upon the norms that are embodied in traditional myths. Ricoeur is able to construct a dialectical conception of prefiguration and refiguration as mediated by narrative configuration because he sees human creativity as always a response to a regulating order. To reiterate: "the problem . . . is not to rediscover some pristine immediacy but to mediate again and again in a new and more creative fashion."[20] But does Ricoeur actually construct a *post*-Kantian account of the social and cultural constitution of human receptivity and creative activity? This account would be post-Kantian insofar as it aims to recognize the social and cultural determinants of creativity and receptivity; and so it would not suggest that the activity of the mythicopoetic imagination is simply that of an individual subject.

Let us backtrack slightly. Again we return to Kant in order to consider the manner in which we might characterize Ricoeur's philosophical anthropology. His conception of narrative configuration, undeniably, reflects a Kantian reconstruction of human experience. He builds upon the epistemological and ontological significance of the arguments concerning time in the first *Critique.*[21] The important achievement of Kant in this context is to have demonstrated the extent to which our temporal consciousness is bound up with certain features of the world. In particular the causal features of the world are necessary conditions for the objectivity of our experience and hence for subjective self-awareness as well as for the continuity of the subject in having a determinate history in which one event or experience affects another.[22] Causality, admittedly, not only performs a crucial part in the constitution of the objectivity of human experience, it also plays a determining role in the dislocation of the self.[23] That the constantly changing subject of human experience can never be temporally located constitutes a condition of self-alienation that human freedom never fully overcomes. Yet the individual subject of human experience may still have a continuity or a self-constancy—as was described by Ricoeur in the long quotation at the beginning of this essay—insofar as a determinate narrative identity is developed. So, too, in a comparable manner but at another level of reflection, we can conceive of the constancy of a community, especially with regard to the reception and the critical re-creation of traditional myths. The fundamental philosophical problem with Ricoeur's notion of selfsameness (*ipséité*) must be What exactly remains constant? What is it that can be understood to be continuous besides the maintenance of spatiotemporal laws such as that of causality?

With regard to this question of constancy, Ricoeur can now be seen to assume that a mythico-poetic nucleus of meaning resides at the center of human experience. More precisely, this nucleus of meaning both determines and is determined by the accepted norms and symbols that govern human action. Insofar as accepted norms and myths remain constant, these mediating forms of praxis are able to constitute the self-identity of individuals and communities. Of course the mythico-poetic nucleus that structures a society and renders its culture opaque must and can be criticized. In Ricoeur's words:

> No culture is wholly transparent . . . a hidden nucleus . . . determines and rules the *distribution* of . . . transparent functions and institutions. . . . It is only by the analysis of the hierarchical structuring and evaluation of the different constituents of a society (i.e. the role of politics, nature, art, religion, etc.) that we may penetrate to its hidden *mythico-poetic nucleus*. . . . [Thus in moments of crisis] a society is compelled to return to the very roots of its identity; to that mythical nucleus which ultimately grounds and determines it. . . . [Now] modern man can neither get rid of myth nor take it at its face value.[24]

Yet this notion of an enduring, hidden nucleus of meaning to human experience would not be acceptable to more radical theorists. Ricoeur maintains that mythical narratives may play a positive cognitive role in reshaping human lives and in restoring meaning to traditional symbols. This conception of mythos is directly opposed to the postmodern views of certain French theorists. For example, while Ricoeur maintains that mythos reflects the communal work of constructing an intelligible world, Gilles Deleuze finds it to be the founding rationale of the paranoia of the regime; while Ricoeur has a calm, even existentially hopeful view of the teleological structure of narrative, Jean-François Lyotard recognizes in narrative finality a coercive imposition of a last work on a potentially limitless heterogeneity; and while Ricoeur finds in mimesis a structure of care, Philippe Lacoue-Labarthe claims that mimesis embodies *la force identificatoire* of myth, whose epistemological and historical point of no return is the Nazi *Volk*. For Ricoeur, mythos—in the sense of emplotment—is, very positively, a form of human knowledge. In Ricoeur's post-Kantian terms, it is the active shaping of the otherwise formless character of pure succession. According to Ricoeur, the narrative configurations by which we shape our lives have real cognitive power.

At this stage I feel compelled to stress the major criticism that can be made of Ricoeur's point of view regarding the mythical representation of reality. That is, there exists no guarantee of the validity and the authority of cognitive categories, such as the pure, productive a priori imagination, which depend on a Kantian conception of the human subject. A further difficulty with Ricoeur's enterprise of restoring an authentic meaning to a Kantian tradition is his refusal, at one and the same time, of a strictly autonomous conception of the human self and of an ideology of individualism, both of which, nevertheless, have been thought to be presupposed by Kant's Enlightenment philosophy.[25]

Yet this difficulty may also be seen as pointing to the true originality of Ricoeur, if we return to the possibility of a *post*-Kantian project that restores a liberating meaning to human time. Ricoeur's own interpretative project is characterized by what is understood in the context of this essay on narrative identity to be a personal constancy to see the social constancy of the narrative configuration and refiguration of time. This post-Kantian reading of Ricoeur discloses the dual characteristics of human constitution. We recognize both the temporal discordance (or, as stated above, the dislocation) of the self and also its dramatic unity represented by Ricoeur's configurating acts that involve the grasping together that incorporates, as a product of time, the story of a community.[26]

At this point I will to try to conclude. Above all, I have aimed to elucidate the positive and negative aspects of Ricoeur's assumptions concerning the mythico-poetic imagination. In order to assess finally what has been found to be the crucial mediating role of the imagination in its capacity of creating authentic narratives of personal and communal self-identity, reconsider Ricoeur's own words concerning the critical and creative dimension of praxis: "we need . . . a critical and creative dimension, which is directed towards neither scientific verification nor ordinary communication but towards the disclosure of possible worlds. This third dimension of language I call the poetic. . . . [Phenomenology] . . . raised the central question of 'meaning' . . . [and] hermeneutics looks to the 'meaning' produced . . . [yet] the primary concern is with the worlds . . . authors and texts open up."[27] For Ricoeur the primary responsibility that accompanies the activity of the mythico-poetic imagination involves recognizing the nature of the worlds opened up by authors and texts or, in this case, myths. This means that reflective judgment is necessary in seeking to discern the critical difference between myths that mystify and those that give an authentic unity to the life of an individual as part of a community. Yet I am still compelled to ask: Is such judgment sufficient to ensure the truth and justice of the forms of praxis, as well as the norms governing action, constituted by what is assumed to be the mythico-poetic imagination?

When it comes to these crucial ethical and political questions of truth and justice, I believe that Ricoeur's critical reason is not radical enough. This is seen in his *Lectures on Ideology and Utopia,* where he tends to subsume reason under the power of the human imagination. Although Ricoeur recognizes the role of reason as a moment of distanciation, he maintains that the distorting function covers only a small surface of the social imagination.[28]

In the end I must conclude with a note of uncertainty concerning the potentially distorting and mystifying power of Ricoeur's transcendental idealist conception of the productive imagination in the narrative constitution of self-identity. Perhaps Ricoeur himself realizes the instability of self-identity—an instability that is due to the exercise of the imagination. After all, he concludes in *Time and Narrative,* volume 3, that "Narrative identity thus becomes the name of a problem at least as much as it is that of a solution."[29]

NOTES

1. See Paul Ricoeur, *Time and Narrative,* vol. 3, trans. Kathleen Blamey and David Pellauer (Chicago: University of Chicago Press, 1988), pp. 246–49; *Soi-même comme un autre* (Paris: Editions du Seuil, 1990), pp. 12–14.
2. See Paul Ricoeur, "The Creativity of Language," trans. Richard Kearney, in *Dialogues with Contemporary Continental Thinkers: The Phenomenological Heritage,* ed. Richard Kearney (Manchester: Manchester University Press, 1984), pp. 23–36; and *Time and Narrative,* 3:243, 247–48, 262–63, 272–73.
3. Ricoeur, *Time and Narrative,* 3:246–49.

4. See Ricoeur, "Myth as the Bearer of Possible Worlds," trans. Richard Kearney, in *Dialogues with Contemporary Continental Thinkers*, pp. 36–45.
5. See Ricoeur, *Soi-même*, pp. 193–98.
6. Paul Ricoeur, *Time and Narrative*, vol. 1, trans. Kathleen McLaughlin and David Pellauer (Chicago: University of Chicago Press, 1984), pp. 66ff.; cf. Immanuel Kant, *The Critique of Judgement*, trans. with analytical indexes by James Creed Meredith (Oxford: Clarendon Press, 1986), Introduction, pp. 18–20.
7. Paul Ricoeur, *Freedom and Nature: The Voluntary and the Involuntary*, trans. Erazim Kohak (Evanston, Ill.: Northwestern University Press, 1966), especially p. 12; Ricoeur, *Fallible Man*, trans. Charles Kelbley (Chicago: Henry Regnery, 1965: rev. ed., with an Introduction by Walter Lowe, New York: Fordham University Press, 1986).
8. Ricoeur, *Fallible Man*, p. 65ff.; cf. Kant, *The Critique of Pure Reason*, trans. Norman Kemp Smith (London: Macmillan, 1950), A 138–44/B 178–81.
9. Paul Ricoeur, "The Antinomy of Human Reality and the Problem of Philosophical Anthropology," trans. Daniel O'Connor, in *The Philosophy of Paul Ricoeur: An Anthology of His Work*, ed. Charles E. Reagan and David Stewart (Boston: Beacon Press, 1978), pp. 26–27.
10. On the productive a priori imagination conditioning all activity of the imagination, see Kant, *The Critique of Pure Reason*, A 100–102, A 118, and A 142–44.
11. Ricoeur, *Fallible Man*, pp. 65–71.
12. Claude Lévi-Strauss, *The Savage Mind* (Chicago: University of Chicago Press, 1966); Michel Foucault, *The Order of Things: An Archaeology of the Human Sciences*, trans. Alan Sheridan Smith (London: Tavistock, 1970), especially p. 386.
13. Ricoeur, *Fallible Man*, pp. 215ff.
14. Ricoeur, *Soi-même*, pp. 145n, 150n.
15. Ricoeur, "The Creativity of Language," pp. 25–26, 24.
16. Paul Ricoeur, *Freud and Philosophy: An Essay on Interpretation*, trans. Denis Savage (New Haven, Conn.: Yale University Press, 1970), p. 551.
17. Ricoeur, "The Antinomy of Human Reality," pp. 34–35.
18. Cf. Paul Ricoeur, "The Teleological and Deontological Structures of Action: Aristotle and/or Kant," in *Contemporary French Philosophy*, ed. A. Phillips Griffiths (Cambridge: Cambridge University Press, 1987), pp. 103–4.
19. Ricoeur, "The Antinomy of Human Reality," p. 20. Cf. Ricoeur, *Time and Narrative*, 1:52–77.
20. Ricoeur, *Time and Narrative*, 1:52–77.
21. Ibid., 1:66, 68, 3:44–59.
22. Cf. Kant, *The Critique of Pure Reason*, A 90–94/B 123–27.
23. Kant, *The Critique of Pure Reason*, A 155.
24. Ricoeur, "Myth as the Bearer of Possible Worlds," pp. 36–39.
25. Concerning Ricoeur's advance on a strictly autonomous conception of the human self and of an ideology of individualism, see his engagement with the hermeneutics of traditions and critiques of ideology in his "Ethics and Culture: Habermas and Gadamer in Dialogue," trans. David Pellauer, in Ricoeur, *Political and Social Essays*, ed. David Stewart and J. Bien (Athens: Ohio University Press, 1974).
26. Cf. Paul Ricoeur, *The Symbolism of Evil*, trans. Emerson Buchanan (New York: Harper and Row, 1967), pp. 168–71, 349f.; and Ricoeur, "The Narrative Function," *Hermeneutics and the Human Sciences*, ed. and trans. John B. Thompson (Cambridge: Cambridge University Press, 1981), pp. 278–79, 285.
27. Ricoeur, "Myth as the Bearer of Possible Worlds," p. 45.
28. Paul Ricoeur, *Lectures on Ideology and Utopia*, ed. George H. Taylor (New York: Columbia University Press, 1986), p. 8.
29. Ricoeur, *Time and Narrative*, 3:249.

WILLIAM SCHWEIKER

IMAGINATION, VIOLENCE, AND HOPE

A Theological Response to Ricoeur's Moral Philosophy

In this essay I will explore the way in which Paul Ricoeur's philosophy helps us think about moral identity.[1] In order to do so, I want to examine the linguistic, moral, and religious dimensions of his thought. These roughly correspond to the famous Kantian questions: What can I know? What ought I to do? What can I hope for? Yet for Ricoeur, and for most contemporary thinkers, the problem found in these questions is precisely the self who does know, may act, and can hope. How are we to speak of the self, the moral agent?

This is the question Ricoeur addresses, and his answer, I contend, calls for theological as well as ethical assessment. In making this assessment I take with utter seriousness Ricoeur's claim that he is in fact a philosopher who listens to theological discourse. The issue then becomes: To what degree, if any, does theological discourse actually bear on his ethics? This question is important for exploring Ricoeur's conception of the self, since, for him, morality, in the strict sense, is "the infinite reflective moment, the moment of interiority, which makes ethical subjectivity appear."[2] I am attempting, then, to examine the appearance of ethical subjectivity, realizing that an adequate account of this in Ricoeur's mind entails moral and even theological discourse.

As will become clear, I agree with Ricoeur that we cannot circumvent the question of the self in our discourse about the good or the divine. However, I want to show that a theological ethics cannot finally be satisfied with Ricoeur's understanding of this fact. Put differently, I agree with Ricoeur that one must trace the interconnection between ethics and theology. The dispute is over how to do so, a dispute that comes to focus on how we ought to speak of moral identity and the good. I want to begin, therefore, by specifying what is at issue in the argument of this essay. I will turn, second, to exploring in some detail the dimensions of Ricoeur's ethical thought. The essay concludes by returning to the question of the import of theology for understanding the moral self.

SPECIFYING THE ARGUMENT

We can say that to be a self entails the ability to question who one wants to be with respect to some idea of how one ought to live. If we cannot determine our lives by norms and values that are in some sense our own, can we really speak of being selves in any profound sense? Without this kind of reflexivity it is difficult to understand our normal intuitions about ourselves and the significance of our lives, let alone our discourse about moral agents. In other words, we understand ourselves and others with respect to some notion of what is good, some measure of what makes a life appreciably higher or richer than other possible ways of living. As Charles Taylor puts it, we orient our lives by "strong evaluations."[3] And we can even ask the question of what good(s) ought to determine our lives. Posing this question is putting ourselves to the test.

This fact raises an interesting problem beyond the obvious difficulties that surround evaluating the conflicting goods and norms that persons and communities hold. Is the self, the one who questions itself, the proper object of interrogation in order to understand what we mean by the good? Not all moralists have thought so. Ricoeur's moral philosophy holds that it is; his is, after all, a philosophy of the will. Yet, in making this argument, he also insists that as moral beings we face the question of whether or not we can ultimately affirm being itself. It is at this juncture that ethics dovetails in Ricoeur's thought with the concerns of ontology and religious discourse. How so?

In Ricoeur's mind the dilemma of this primary affirmation of life with respect to good and evil tells us something crucial about being human. As he puts it, "In the end, I do not know what man is. My confession to myself is that man is instituted by the word, that is, by a language which is less spoken by man than spoken to man. . . . Is not The Good News the instigation of the possibility of man by a creative word?"[4] The imputation of identity to the ego is not only with respect to some strong evaluation. It is through a word spoken to us as an affirmation of being, the ground of our hope, in response to moral fault and the problem of evil. What does this claim of Ricoeur's mean for ethics and the appearance of subjectivity? That is the question I am pursuing in the following pages, realizing that in examining it we are traversing ontological, moral, and religious concerns.

This brings us to the fundamental difficulty I want to isolate and to circumvent in Ricoeur's philosophy. While he helps us think about the appearance of moral identity, Ricoeur's thought, I contend, raises its own difficulties with regard to reflection on the good. As we will see, he can only speak of premoral goods and what I call a hyperethical good, that is, those goods basic to life and a good that is beyond the dictates of morality. This is because Ricoeur understands ethics simply in terms of obligations and assessments of actions with respect to the appearance of moral identity. Yet when we ask about the idea of the good, the strong evaluation, implied in his philosophy about what it means to be human, we see that the self in its agency is the symbol, if not the ground, of the good. It is this symbol that gives rise to thought about the good, because the self is a clash between the search for happiness and the demands of duty. And it is this problematic that determines his philosophy of religion and his construal of the summum bonum.

While I intend to follow Ricoeur with respect to the reflexive character of all our discourse about the good, I part company with him over this axiological point. That is, I intend to contest his account of the problem of the self as determining the content of claims about the good and our affirmation of being. In order to do so, I want to specify the meaning of responsibility: a concept, we will see, important to Ricoeur's own thought but not sufficiently explored by him. The next step in our reflections, therefore, is to turn to Ricoeur's account of the appearance of moral identity. As noted above, in order to do this we must traverse the linguistic, moral, and religious dimensions of his philosophy.

SELF, TIME, AND LANGUAGE

Ricoeur's philosophy charts the emergence of the moral identity through the aporias of time and action. He begins with the claim that the human is a duality seeking unity.[5] We are mediating beings, both finite and free, and the drive to mediation is found in thinking, willing, and feeling. However, we have no direct introspective access to the self determined by its duality or to the mediations of thought, action, and affection. What self-understanding we attain is won by interpreting works that figure our condition: specifically, symbols, metaphors, and narratives. In this essay, we will focus on his treatment of narrative.

Narrative, Ricoeur holds, is the mimesis of human action through the act of making a plot.[6] It renders meaningful the prefigured but intelligible order of temporal action by configuring discordant events into a unity, a mythos. The act of making a plot is a synthetic act of the productive imagination; it creates meaning by displaying a possible world in which I can dwell. Likewise, reading is a synthetic act that brings unity to the fragmentariness of temporal existence. The act of reading (mimesis$_3$) intersects the world of the text (mimesis$_2$) and the lived world of the interpreter (mimesis$_1$), thereby refiguring life. Yet in this act narration transgresses its own linguistic structure because of aporias that inhere in temporal experience. These aporias are important, since they mark the transition from narrative to ethics.

The first aporia involves the unity of identity within the diversity of actions. By means of the narrative act we understand ourselves as the subject of our actions; we gain what Ricoeur calls a "narrative identity" as an answer to the question of "who" is acting. This "who" has its identity at three levels: through an imputation of it as the author of its deeds; in interaction with others marked by cooperation and conflict; and, due to the evaluation of these acts and interactions.[7] These distinctions are crucial for Ricoeur's ethics.

The second aporia of temporality concerns the unity of time itself, or "history." Drawing on Kant, Ricoeur argues that we achieve this unity through the imaginative idea of one history and human solidarity that serves as an ideal to guide thought and action. This provides a practical, not a theoretical, answer to the unity of history, a task to be undertaken rather than something to be known. Like the first aporia of identity, this one is not overcome or dissolved; it remains, while being rendered productive through the idea of history.

The first two aporias show the importance of freedom for the possibility of meaningful identity and history. But is it possible to make an affirmation of freedom in time? Ricoeur notes that time itself remains inscrutable. We do not have the experience of the unity of time needed for knowing what time is. This, then, constitutes a third aporia, one between our search for meaning and the inscrutability of time, that is parallel, we will see, to the aporia between duty and happiness. This temporal aporia is rendered productive, Ricoeur claims, by limiting theoretical knowledge and driving us back to the practical tasks of personal identity and working for solidarity.

This marks a transition from narrative to ethics through a question at the limit of reason, a question about the reality of freedom, which, as we shall see, correlates with another limit question concerning evil. Facing the inscrutability of time, we can ask about the affirmation of freedom within time, a freedom that is the condition for identity and social solidarity. Regarding evil, the question will be about the good of that freedom. The inscrutability of time, in other words, opens the space of the question of what is normative for freedom.

SELF, ACTION, AND DUTY TO OTHERS

I have argued that the transition from narrative to ethics is made by Ricoeur through the aporias of temporality that raise the question of the norms for identity and solidarity as well as the question of an affirmation of freedom as their condition. Ethical analysis, Ricoeur claims, concerns a duality: the teleological, or goal-oriented, structure of action in virtue ethics and obligations about human interaction found in deontological ethics. His general task is to show how these two modes of moral reflection are interrelated. But more specifically, Ricoeur is concerned in his ethics to explore the tripartite relation of the self, the solicitude of the Other, and the demands of justice required by the institutional mediation of life.

For Ricoeur "the question of identity is precisely that of 'who' acts."[8] Moral identity is not a selfsame substance through time.

Rather, it is born of promise making and also faithfulness with respect to actions. The self "does not merely consist in the self-designation of humans as the owners and the authors of their deeds; it implies also the self-interpretation in terms of the achievements and failures of what we called practices and plans of life. I suggest that we call 'self-esteem' the interpretation of ourselves mediated by the ethical evaluation of our actions."[9] Self-esteem accompanies the norms of success or excellence with regard to goal-oriented action.[10] This corresponds to narrative identity, which, we saw, returns us to practical life and thereby to achievements and failures open to evaluation. We fail or succeed, Ricoeur avers, in our practices and their goods, both of which are set within individual life plans. We esteem the self thanks to teleological evaluations of actions and their outcomes. For Ricoeur, this is the concern of an ethics of virtue.

How is this to be related to an ethics of duty? Ricoeur argues that all action is also interaction; it has a dialogic structure. Following Emmanuel Levinas, Ricoeur speaks of the "solicitude" of the other person. The confrontation between the esteem of the self based on actions and life plans with the claims of others requires a moral limitation on the pursuit of individual goods and plans of life; it requires the institution of distributive justice. Why is this the case?

Ricoeur argues that human interaction is asymmetric because "someone exerts power over somebody else; thus interaction does not merely confront agents equally capable of initiative but agents and patients as well."[11] Realizing this, Ricoeur claims that there is moral obligation because there is violence. This is confusing. Violence plainly cannot be a source of moral obligation or moral distinctions, since to speak of something as wrong (e.g., violence) is already to employ moral concepts. Ricoeur seems to be arguing that negativity discloses the real source of obligation in persons. As he notes elsewhere, the "person is manifest only in the practical act of treating it as an end and not merely as a means."[12] Violence against persons, a denial of them as ends in themselves, paradoxically manifests the source of obligation. A parallel might be drawn between the relation of violence to obligation, on the one hand, and the act of the productive imagination in narrative and metaphor, on the other: both disclose something through a negation. In this case, however, the negation is not the clash between literal and nonliteral predication definitive of semantic innovation; rather, violence is what reveals moral obligation.

According to Ricoeur, there are three affirmations disclosed by the negativity of violence. First, reciprocity must be affirmed as the condition necessary to grasp the asymmetry of moral relations. All interaction entails acting and suffering. Next, the presence of the victim discloses that in the inequality of the exercise of power is an affirmation of equality as the limiting condition on human action. Finally, insofar as we confront violence as what ought not to be, freedom is affirmed despite the difference between what is and what ought to be. Here we have the answer to the third aporia of temporality isolated above. We can affirm freedom as a moral idea, since it is the condition for the task of personal identity and social solidarity. Ricoeur's argument sets out, then, from a negation within human interaction (violence and the victim) in quest of the source of obligation and respect in equality and reciprocity as generic features of action.[13] Respect accompanies the obligation to see the Other as an agent equal to myself, who bears reciprocal rights and duties amid relations of power.

Despite his turn to violence rather than to desire as what must be overcome in morality, Ricoeur does follow Kant in claiming that the principle of morality as such can be formulated by the Golden Rule. Ricoeur puts it like this: "Do not do to others what you would hate to have done to you."[14] He claims that this formulation places evaluations of premoral goods, what we love and hate in our practices and life plans, within the deontic demands on action. Specifically, Ricoeur argues, following John Rawls, that this formulation of the Golden Rule entails a concern for distributive justice.[15] Premoral goods are thus to be distributed with respect to a principle grounded in human interaction. Deontic norms protect, promote, and determine the distribution of basic goods in the face of actual evil. This also means that the good in ethical discourse properly so-called is controlled by the needs and rights of others who claim us in their humanity and who may become our victims. "The notion of fundamental human goods," Ricoeur insists, "is substituted at the same place as the concept of humanity in the Kantian reformulation of the Golden Rule."[16]

Ricoeur's ethics is oriented to goods of practices and life plans even while insisting on the rights of the Other. The ethics is a post-Hegelian Kantianism in the sense that our participation in social life requires protecting the freedom of individual life plans while also asking about the just distribution of premoral goods. His specification of the Golden Rule articulates the conceptual form of the ethics. It relates obligation and respect between acting persons to the evaluation of purposive actions and self-esteem. As Ricoeur writes: if "self-esteem was the subjective correlative to the ethical evaluation of actions, then respect is the subjective correlative of moral obligation."[17]

Esteem and respect are coemergent with the self as acting and interacting with others. Ricoeur claims that these imputations of esteem and respect are constitutive of human identity. They are grafted onto the theory of purposive action and asymmetrical interaction. Narrative identity and even the practical idea of history are the linguistic forms of this "grafting on" and imputation with reference to action. We can say, then, that moral identity arises out of an aporia of action—action as purposive and interactional and thus the clash between happiness and duty—by means of a linguistic imputation of "who" is acting.

As noted above in the discussion of narrative identity, this logic of imputation is crucial to Ricoeur's argument. It means that the subject is not the sole origin of moral norms; rather, moral identity arises through the interpretation of action. This coheres with the basic concern of Ricoeur's philosophical project. "Subjectivity," he writes, "must be lost as the radical origin if it is to be retained in a more modest role. . . . the act of subjectivity is less what starts than what completes."[18] This "act" is an affirmation of being in time made linguistically through metaphor and narrative and ethically by means of the dual imputation of esteem and respect to persons under the Golden Rule. It is a response to the "thing of the text" as a possible way of being in the world and to the solicitude of the other. This means that the self founded on this affirmation is primordially in response to what presents itself. Ricoeur insists that with "this style of 'response to . . .' hermeneutics opposes the idealism of ultimate self-responsibility."[19] Later in this essay I will extend this theme of responsiveness, finding in it a direction for theological and ethical reflection beyond the confines of Ricoeur's moral philosophy.

Here, however, we must note that in Ricoeur's ethics human interaction and dialogically generated intersubjectivity are ultimately set within a teleological theory of action and goods. The ethics of duty is encompassed in a larger trajectory of the realization of freedom. We might surmise that this is because subjectivity completes our claims about meaning and value. The goods of basic actions and life plans order and give content to formal, deontic claims arising from interaction with others. Ricoeur further claims, like Kant, that the ethical cannot answer its own aporia of the clash between happiness and duty or between the despair that comes from failure and evil. The moral self is brought into question with respect to its final good. Thus, while the ethical provides the criteria for claims about narrative identity and the ground for the affirmation of freedom in time, it cannot ground an affirmation of that freedom amid evil. This is the transition point from ethics to the philosophy of religion.

SELF, THE GOOD, AND RELIGIOUS HOPE

Ricoeur argues that amid the failure and guilt that often characterize the moral life, the question is asked about the affirmation of being. This is a limit question, one parallel to the third aporia of temporality. And like that "limit," what Ricoeur seeks is some affirmation of being in freedom. As a limit question, this is a religious question. Indeed, religion is defined by the aporia of duty and happiness in the face of actual evil. In this respect Ricoeur is engaged in a radical form of questioning, since what is at stake is an affirmation or denial of life.

Ricoeur claims that the question of hope is disclosed in and through negation: the imputation to the self of the weight of its deeds, its failure, violence, and guilt.[20] This negation opens the question of the highest good and the possible regeneration of the will. This returns us to the teleologic grounds of his argument noted before, since hope seeks a fulfillment of the self beyond evil. The ethical aporia can be rendered productive only by an affirmation of being as a gift that breaks beyond the structure of human temporal activity. For Ricoeur, hope is grounded on the gift of a word spoken to the human as a promise of fulfillment. It does not have the promissory, obligatory character of ethical obligations found in human interaction. Yet while this is so, the word is not a transformation of the moral as defined by premoral goods and duties; it is the establishment of a new motivation for the moral life through the regeneration of the will.

We can say that hope for Ricoeur is a hyperethical good that founds obligation on gift rather than on equivalent regard.[21] The good here is not ordered by the needs of others, as is the case in "morality," but fulfills the self who encounters its own evil. Because hope is an affirmation of being in spite of moral evil, it is not a premoral good but arises out of the claims of morality in and through which the ego-as-self is constituted. Yet hope is not a moral good, since it overcomes guilt with the word that human existence is a gift. Hope is the affirmation of being amid the inscrutability of evil correlate to the imaginative judgment of freedom in narrative.

The crossing point of the religious and the moral, then, is the self. The "self," the transcendental ego endowed with a personal identity, is both a moral reality and in hope a symbol of a hyperethical good. By limiting the domain of the moral to the imputation of identity under the norms of esteem and respect, Ricoeur charts the intensification of the moral as the opening to the religious. He insists that the religious with its logic of superabundance and gift exceeds the moral logic of equivalence based on debt.[22] Like Kant on the summum bonum, Ricoeur asserts a good beyond morality that redeems the self and its aspirations. And also like Kant, he defines religion with reference to the problem of evil and the antinomy in morality of duty and happiness.

Through the word, the religious offers the final response to the moral problem of the self. It donates a possibility, a hyperethical good, in which I can dwell and thus specifies the axiology of Ricoeur's philosophy. In religious terms, this possibility is the eschatological event of the resurrection, an event that includes all reality. "To recognize the Resurrection of Jesus Christ," Ricoeur writes, "is to enter into the movement of hope in resurrection from the dead, to attain the new creation ex nihilo, that is, beyond death."[23] This eschatological event is the affirmation of being in spite of evil. It is the ultimate answer to the most serious question, as Ricoeur puts it, of time and narrative. At issue is whether or not "philosophical reflection on narrativity and time may aid us in thinking about eternity and death at the same time."[24]

Thus, by moving from narrative through ethics to the religious we see that self-identity has a double-meaning structure; it is symbolic. The "self's" semantic element is in the grafting on of its narrative identity. This imputation is the way to bring to language the ego's rootedness in freedom as a divine gift. Freedom and the divine Word are the nonsemantic conditions of identity, since they are not simply given in language but come to language in the self who acts. In fact, Ricoeur notes that "the symbol hesitates on the dividing line between bios and logos. It testifies to the primordial rootedness of Discourse in Life. It is born where force and form coincide."[25] The "self" is the figure for the unity of finitude and freedom amid the ambiguity of time. Put differently, narrative and moral identity are the ways the ego is given a self; this self imputed to the ego is symbolic.[26] Let me specify what this means, since it is integral for understanding the self as a symbol of the good in Ricoeur's thought.

Ricoeur argues that there are three dimensions of symbolism. The cosmic dimension of traditional symbolism is a reading of the sacred on the world. As we have seen, the question of narrative identity and historical solidarity was for Ricoeur precisely the question of how to read the human and its well-being on the inscrutability of time as the horizon of the meaning of being. This raised the question of the possibility of an affirmation of freedom as necessary to identity and history. This affirmation was made, I argued, through the moral imputation of self-identity. That imputation is the oneiric dimension of the symbol. It is concerned, as Ricoeur puts it, with what is manifest in the "psyche," the soul or the self. What is manifested in the self, we saw, is freedom and the moral reality of the human. Thus, through the aporias of temporality I demonstrated the interrelation and yet the distinction of the "cosmic" and the "oneiric" dimensions of the self as symbol.

This leads us to the poetic dimension of symbolism and also confirms my claim that the self for Ricoeur is the symbol of the good. He notes:

> Cosmos and Psyche are the two poles of the same "expressivity"; I express myself in expressing the world; I explore my own sacrality in deciphering that of the world. Now this double "expressivity"—cosmic and psychic—has its complement in a third modality of symbols: poetic imagination. . . . As M. Bachelard excellently says, [the poetic image] "puts us at the origin of speaking being;" "it becomes a new being of our language, it expresses us in making us that which it expresses."[27]

The human is instituted by a word spoken to it as a possibility for its being a self in freedom. This creativity of the word is what constitutes the possibility of the self and in grace fulfills the self beyond evil. The self is a poetic symbol of this "speaking being" because being is expressed through the human. Ricoeur insists that the cosmic, oneiric, and poetic dimensions of the symbolic are not separable. In terms of our argument, this unity-in-difference is seen in the self as relating its narrative, ethical, and religious dimensions. As a symbol of the origin of speaking being, the self is correlate to a transcendent synthesis of morality and happiness that is received through the eschatological word. The highest good for Ricoeur is this transcendent synthesis grasped in hope that opens the possibility of an affirmation of being in spite of our limits. This is why the self is the fit object of interrogation about the meaning of the good; it alone expresses this affirmation of being. The human is properly the subject matter of philosophy even as moral and sacred worth are imputed to reality through their relation to freedom.

THE APORIA OF THE GOOD

I have charted in Ricoeur's thought the return of the self to the center of philosophical concern through an aesthetic judgment about time in narrative and a teleological one in moral and religious discourse concerning action. This self is not the origin of normative claims, as in most Kantian ethics, but an end, a gift. Yet, this also exposes the tension at the heart of Ricoeur's philosophy, a tension that arises at the intersection of the two points in his thought where talk about the good is introduced: the ethical and the religious. The self, we might say, appears in Ricoeur's philosophy precisely within the space of this tension. In a way similar to Ricoeur, I want to intensify this insight in order to render it productive for further theological ethical reflection.

The discourses of the good in the ethical and religious levels of Ricoeur's thought require and yet clash with each other and thereby specify the central problematic of Ricoeur's ethics. I will call this the aporia of the good. The self as an ethical task inscribes its good within the claims and rights of other persons thanks to the principle of morality (the Golden Rule), even as this self calls for an affirmation of being amid evil. And yet given the asymmetrical character of interaction, human goods can never be realized entirely in time. Is an affirmation of the human good and morality possible?

Ricoeur finds the answer in religious discourse. The religious asserts the self as gift. And yet in doing so, religious discourse qualifies the moral relations that gave rise to the self—that the rights of others are the context for pursuing our goods. The good in religious discourse is, then, understood as the fulfillment of the self, making the specifically moral conditions that constitute identity, that is, the conditions that give rise to our ascription of "who" is acting, a means to this end. This is to instrumentalize others as a means to self-identity and thus, on Ricoeur's own terms, is immoral. The religious answers the moral, but in doing so seems to qualify conditions Ricoeur holds are needed for the self to appear as a self: actions subject to norms of justice and rights. This is why, we might surmise, Ricoeur, like Kant, wants to differentiate moral and religious claims.

On this score it helps little to argue that the relation to other persons is now founded on gift rather than on demand. That has to do with the motivation of the self to regard of the other rather than with the status of the other person qua their otherness and the question of their good. Similarly, Ricoeur's endorsement of the kingdom of ends with respect to the highest good does not obviate the fact that to specify the ends in question (i.e., respect for persons) one must detail the idea of the self. It would seem, then, that Ricoeur must mediate any conception of the good through the narrative inscription of the self on time, the ethical manifestation of freedom in the self, and the self as expressivity of original being. Any perception of the value is mediated through the idea of the self. But this is not, we must note, simply the reflexive, hermeneutical claim that we cannot circumvent the fact that it is we who have perceptions of value. It also bears on the very content of what one means by the good.

Admittedly, this is a curious priority of the self. The self does not reign in Ricoeur's thought as a given good but as the symbol of a promised good. This is the deepest trajectory of his "Poetics of the Will." Whereas for Kant art is a symbol of morality, for Ricoeur self-identity constituted through narrative identity, moral imputation, and grace is the symbol of the good. Thus, while Ricoeur escapes a subjectivism about the origin of meaning and moral norms, he does not escape it in his discourse about the good. But why should this bother us? In concluding this discussion I want briefly to sketch a possible theological response to this question. In part this requires dislodging the definition of religion from the Kantian problem of happiness and duty as the space in which the self appears. It also entails specifying further what we mean by responsibility.

RESPONSIBILITY AND THEOLOGICAL ETHICS

Thus far in our inquiry I have attempted to elucidate why for Ricoeur the self is the fit object for interpretation, in order to understand what we mean by the good. This is the case, I have argued, because self-identity appears within an aporia basic to his conception of the good, that of fulfillment and of duties to others. But we have reason to question Ricoeur's ethics on this point. Surprisingly, we must consider the relation between claims about moral identity and theological discourse. More specifically, we must raise the question of perspective. What do I mean?

Philosophers often argue that radical reflection entails an evaluation of our beliefs about the highest mode of life where, in principle, none of those beliefs is unrevisable. As noted before, they carry out this reflection from the perspective of the self as a question to itself.[28] Yet, it seems equally clear that we can ask whether or not that self—the self as questioner—is not open to yet another interpretive perspective. In fact, we can ask, which self should be examined?

This query is not as curious as it might initially sound. As we have seen, Ricoeur admits that there are layers or dimensions of identity—narrative, moral, and religious. Each of these, presumably, could serve as the entrance point for thinking about the self and the good. Ricoeur also acknowledges the possibility of a different perspective on the self in his claims about the word spoken to the human. The self that is the object of interpretation would then be the one known in response to the divine. Self-knowledge would entail understanding oneself as one is known. Theologians tend to adopt this perspective. It is why they use adjectival expressions to speak of the self—the natural self, the self as sinner, the self in grace—because the self is known as it exists in relation to the divine and to others.

The reason theologians make the shift in perspective denoted by such adjectival expressions is one Ricoeur, in fact, shares: the self is not a self-constituting source of the good, but, at best, a medium, or symbol, for thinking about the source of the good. In fact, sin as a theological concept refers to the attempt by the self to be the constituting source of the good. But this, of course, is precisely what the image of the self as radical questioner entails for some thinkers. To constrict our evaluation to the self-in-sin is, on this reading, simply inadequate for interpreting the human or the good. There must be a radical transformation in our perspective on the self if our humanity or the good are to be properly understood. Theologians in this century have even argued that in the light of the divine Word, the fallen, natural self is a remainder concept; it cannot provide us with insight into what it means to be human or the good.[29] The question of which self to examine while arising in theological reflection poses, then, the question of perspective within ethics.

I admit, of course, that this might initially be peculiar to theological reflection or to a philosopher, like Ricoeur, who listens to religious discourse. But the fact that the question of perspective originates in theological reflection ought not to demean its significance for ethics. It does not violate rational discourse to take up questions that arise from religious traditions. My contention with Ricoeur, then, is ultimately about perspective, whether or not he has in fact taken with utter seriousness the shift in viewing human life that theological reflection entails.

Now, by asking which perspective on the self we ought to adopt, we are undertaking nothing less than a "moral ontology." We are raising the question of the meaning of being human and the standard of conduct by examining what is sensed and discovered in our interactions with others in the light of theological discourse. This line of inquiry requires, as Charles Taylor notes, that we treat moral sensitivities "as our mode of access to the world in which ontological claims are discernible and can be rationally argued about and sifted."[30] I have already isolated the sensitivities important to Ricoeur's work by noting the various negations that have moved our inquiry from narrative through ethics to religious hope. The ontological import of these sensitivities (e.g., guilt) and their contrasting affirmations (e.g., hope) as well as the aporias that evoke them are a clue to how Ricoeur understands what it means to be human. As we have seen, what it means to be a self is to be a transcendental ego endowed with personal identity achieved and received through narration, moral imputation, and a word spoken to us. That is how the self appears.

Because of this, Ricoeur challenges, as we saw, an idealism of ultimate self-responsibility, where the self constitutes its identity in responding to itself in thinking, willing, and feeling. Radical reflexivity, where the self questions itself, is necessary but not sufficient for examining the appearance of the self's identity. Such reflexivity left to its own devices could imply, in theological reflection and in Ricoeur's mind, a form of sin. Thus, Ricoeur wants to claim that we are most primordially constituted in response to a word spoken to us and not simply by our aims and purposes.

However, at this juncture we must ask: Is responsiveness to the Word basic to Ricoeur's moral reflection? Does it in fact warrant a shift in his perspective on the human? Does it actually alter our understanding of the appearance of moral identity? While Ricoeur's ethics is open to a religious answer to a human need, it is not, I submit, transformed by that answer. Neither in its conceptual structure nor in its account of the good is Ricoeur's philosophy of the will defined by a response to the divine. No doubt Ricoeur makes this argument, as any Kantian would, to ensure that morality is not infested with nonmoral motives, even while providing some religious answer to the human search for happiness.

The difficulty here, I am suggesting, is that the solicitude of the other and the ineffability of God are interpreted within the dilemma of freedom as Ricoeur conceives of it. But this is to constrict our conception of the good; it potentially blinds us to the noninstrumental value of others. This is why Ricoeur's account of the good should bother us. He rightly insists on our necessary role in understanding the good but then collapses what counts as a sufficient account of the content of the good into answering the problem of the self, the aporia of happiness and duty. A theological ethics that learns from Ricoeur but questions his work on this axiological point must seek therefore to articulate what is sensed and discovered in the human response to the divine and others. It must elucidate a different hermeneutic of moral identity. And this entails, ultimately, a changed idea of religion and thus the primal human dilemma. Let me conclude by merely outlining what this might mean for a theological ethics.

Religious faith, I contend, entails convictions about and sensitivities to powers or a power to which human beings must appropriately respond if existence is to be meaningful. We come to be within a space of interaction. To constrict the range of those relations is to distort our perception of the good. These relations are morally relevant even as the moral life is central to any appropriate response to these powers. Theological ethical reflection does not begin, therefore, with what Ricoeur has called the "night of power" as the crisis of radical evil within the trajectory of freedom.[31] It begins with the call of being in the solicitude of the Other sensed and discovered within patterns of interaction. The self from this perspective is not simply the subject that affirms being or questions itself, no matter how radical that questioning appears to be. It is not the self that asks what it can know, what it ought to do, and what it can hope for. The self that is the object of interpretation is one interacting with and responding to other powers and their claim to goodness.

What one means by *God,* given this account of religious sensibilities, is not the coming one whose reign is the transcendent synthesis that answers the moral antinomy. That is, God is not conceptualized with reference to the priority of the future in our temporal being and with respect to the problem of evil. God is encountered in and through all others, the one to whom we must relate come what may. And because we must understand others in relation to the ineffable God, one's perception is transformed to recognize their inherent worth. Here theological discourse does not simply answer the moral problematic as Ricoeur understands it. Rather, theological discourse specifies the ultimate character of reality and its claim on us. It is a moral ontology in the radical sense.

I am not making the ad hominem claim that Ricoeur's moral philosophy falters because it is not a theological ethics in this spirit.[32] The point is that if one wants to escape the idealist self, a moral ontology must begin and end with responsiveness to the claim of others uttered in their being. Theological discourse radicalizes and protects this insight, since it argues that in the totality of our being on earth, in time, and with others we are encountering the ineffable God whose being and goodness cannot be inscribed within the human project. In all of our interactions, then, we are also interacting with the divine. I grant, of course, the theme of response in Ricoeur's own texts, specifically with respect to the solicitude of the Other and the "thing of the text." Yet a theological ethics allows us to conceptualize responsibility in a way not limited to the imputation of binding claims on the self and our debt to the victim. It is not, as it seems to be for Ricoeur, simply another way of speaking about moral accountability.[33]

A theological ethics radicalizes our idea of responsibility because it expands the scope of morally relevant relations to what Ricoeur sees as "non-moral" goods and to the encounter with the divine. This is because the primordial, constitutive act that creates life is indeed an asymmetrical interaction, and radically so, but it is not violent. As we have it in the myth of creation, "And God saw that it was good." What warrants this shift in perspective is not, as Ricoeur argues, the surplus of religious discourse that philosophy can attempt to approximate. This shift is wrought by what is sensed and discovered in our actual encounters with others. That is, in the light of this theological claim about the gratuitous character of being, we see that there is a power to which we must relate appropriately if the goodness of others is to be rightly acknowledged and served.

In theological terms, grace, not violence, is the primordial origin of our sense of ourselves as responsible beings; Creation and not the Fall is the fundamental backing of our moral claims. Ethical norms are not generated simply in reaction to violence; they are to formulate our response to the goodness of beings. Moral sensitivity thereby grounds an understanding of our interaction with others as a medium for the encounter with the divine. That interaction is the symbol of the good. Of course, this is to agree with Ricoeur that we cannot circumvent the self; we are, after all, agents who interpret our lives and our world. But the norm of that interpretation is determined, not through the negativity of guilt and violence that sparks the longing for hope, but in terms of the immediate goodness of the being of others recognized irrespective of merit or vice. If Kant insisted on respect for the humanity in persons, this ethics requires the acknowledgment and service of the goodness in beings. Such a response to others is what theologians mean by love. From this love arises the confession, *esse qua esse bonum est* (being as being is good).

This shows us the difficulty in Ricoeur's understanding of the Golden Rule: he focuses on duties pertaining to actions and the protection of premoral goods rather than on the reciprocity of love as a claim about who one is in relation to the being of others. This focus reflects his understanding of the "moral" and the teleological orientation of his thought. In a theological perspective, we are to love as we have first been loved. This is not a claim about the motivational ground for responsibility, as Ricoeur seems to hold. It is, rather, rooted in the being of others in their relation to the divine. Again, the religious is not a hyperethical response to the aporia of happiness and duty. What the religious means for the moral life is a radical transformation of our apprehension of and concern for reality to an inclusive concern for others and the divine. The religious life is an imitation of the divine through the creative recognition of and response to the goodness of others. The unavoidable fact that we are necessarily the ones who recognize and respond to others does not thereby mean that a sufficient account of the good can be restricted to the dilemma of our being and doing. On the contrary, it is by knowing the goodness of others and by serving this goodness in love that we rightly understand ourselves.

What I am arguing is that a way beyond the aporia of the good in Ricoeur's thought is found when we take with utter seriousness his own claim that the self is constituted in response to something spoken to it. Theologically construed, this "word" is spoken not simply in the message of salvation or religious symbols but in the being of things. The theological is not determined by the ethical problematic of the self; it is a transformation of our perspective on self. In our response to the being of others, we sense that the primordial relation in which we exist is indeed asymmetrical but not violent. This realization is the subjective correlate to what theologians mean by revelation. And this is the self that a moral ontology needs to examine, a task beyond the scope of the present inquiry.

CONCLUSION

In this essay I have explored Ricoeur's contribution to a theological and ethical account of the self. I have also sketched a line of thought that attempts to extend his ethics by considering responsive interaction as the clue to the meaning of being human. Yet I have done so to the point of theologically transforming the axiology that his philosophy articulates. This transformation, I have been arguing, is integral to the task of theological ethics. More importantly, this transformation in our understanding of the goodness of being is crucial if we are to grasp what it means to be selves in a world with others.

NOTES

1. See Paul Ricoeur: "Approaches de la personne," in *Esprit* 160 (March–April 1990): 115–30; "The Teleological and Deontological Structure of Action: Aristotle and/or Kant," in *Contemporary French Philosophy,* ed. A. Phillips Griffith (Cambridge: Cambridge University Press, 1987), pp. 99–111; "Fondements de l'Ethique," *Autres temps: Les cahiers du christianisme social* 3 (1984): 61–71; "The Human as the Subject Matter of Philosophy," in *The Narrative Path: The Later Words of Paul Ricoeur,* ed. T. Peter Kemp and David Rasmussen (Cambridge, Mass.: MIT Press, 1989), pp. 89–102; "The Problem of the Foundation of Moral Philosophy," trans. R. Lechner, *Philosophy Today* 22, no. 3–4 (1978): 175–92. Although it appeared too late to be considered in this essay, also see Ricoeur's Gifford Lectures published as *Soi-même comme un autre* (Paris: Editions du Seuil, 1990). For works on Ricoeur, see T. Peter Kemp and David Rasmussen, eds., *The Narrative Path: The Later Works of Paul Ricoeur* (Cambridge, Mass.: MIT Press, 1989); John Van Den Hengel, *The Home of Meaning: The Hermeneutics of the Subject of Paul Ricoeur* (Washington, D.C.: University Press of America, 1982); and David E. Klemm, *The Hermeneutic Theory of*

Paul Ricoeur: A Constructive Analysis (Lewisburg, Pa.: Bucknell University Press, 1983). I have made some of the argument of this essay in my *Mimetic Reflections: A Study in Hermeneutics, Theology, and Ethics* (New York: Fordham University Press, 1990).

2. Paul Ricoeur, "Freedom in the Light of Hope," in his *Essays on Biblical Interpretation,* ed. Lewis S. Mudge, trans. Robert Sweeney (Philadelphia: Fortress Press, 1980), p. 168.
3. See Charles Taylor, *Sources of the Self: The Making of Modern Identity* (Cambridge, Mass.: Harvard University Press, 1989), esp. pp. 3–24. For other discussions of the self, see Susan Wolf, *Freedom within Reason* (Oxford: Oxford University Press, 1990); Harry Frankfurt, *The Importance of What We Care about: Philosophical Essays* (Cambridge: Cambridge University Press, 1988); and also Frankfurt, *The Inner Citadel: Essays on Individual Autonomy,* ed. John Christman (Oxford: Oxford University Press, 1989).
4. Paul Ricoeur, "The Language of Faith," trans. R. Bradley De Ford, in *The Philosophy of Paul Ricoeur: An Anthology of His Work,* ed. Charles E. Reagan and David Stewart (Boston: Beacon Press, 1978), p. 237.
5. On this, see Paul Ricoeur, *Fallible Man,* trans. Charles A. Kelbley (Chicago: Henry Regnery, 1965), and of particular interest for my argument is Ricoeur, "Negativity and Primary Affirmation," in his *History and Truth,* trans. Charles A. Kelbley (Evanston, Ill.: Northwestern University Press, 1965), pp. 305–28.
6. See Paul Ricoeur, *Temps et récit,* 3 vols. (Paris: Editions du Seuil, 1983–85). This appears in English as *Time and Narrative,* trans. Kathleen McLaughlin and David Pellauer, 3 vols. (Chicago: University of Chicago Press, 1984–88). For convenience, reference will be made to the English translation. For helpful discussions of this work, see Stephan Strasser, "Zeit und Erzählung bei Paul Ricoeur," *Philosophische Rundschau* 34, no. 1/2 (1987): 1–13 and David Pellauer, "*Time and Narrative* and Theological Reflection," *Philosophy Today* 31 (Fall 1987): 262–86.
7. See Ricoeur, "Approches de la personne," pp. 124–27.
8. Ibid., p. 127; my translation.
9. Ricoeur, "The Human Being as the Subject of Philosophy," p. 99.
10. For a discussion of the clash between these two norms see Alasdair MacIntyre, *Whose Justice? Which Rationality?* (Notre Dame, Ind.: University of Notre Dame Press, 1988).
11. Ricoeur, "The Human as the Subject Matter of Philosophy," p. 99. Ricoeur agrees with Alan Gewirth that morality requires that we see the patient also as an agent who commands respect. Gewirth's form of ethical rationalism is based on the generic structure of action and the rights of freedom and well-being. Ricoeur too, I am suggesting, looks to the generic features of action and interaction, but within a concern for self-understanding. See Alan Gewirth, *Reason and Morality* (Chicago: University of Chicago Press, 1978).
12. Paul Ricoeur, "Freedom in the Light of Hope," p. 170.
13. As Ricoeur notes, the task "is to start from some paradigmatic norms recognized and assumed by most people, and from them to proceed backwards to the source of obligation" ("The Teleological and Deontological Structure of Action," p. 106). Ricoeur relies on Alan Donagan, *The Theory of Morality* (Chicago: University of Chicago Press, 1977). For a challenge to Ricoeur's attempt to mediate these positions, see Hans-Georg Gadamer, "The Hermeneutics of Suspicion," *Man and World* 17 (1984): 313–23.
14. Ricoeur, "Approches de la personne," p. 126. Ricoeur attributes this formulation of the Golden Rule to Hillel in his "The Human as the Subject Matter of Philosophy." See also Immanuel Kant, *Critique of Practical Reason,* trans. Lewis White Beck (Indianapolis: Bobbs-Merrill, 1956).

15. Ricoeur, "The Teleological and Deontological Structure of Action," p. 110. Ricoeur's turn to violence is also made in response to Hegel. See his "Ethics and Culture," trans. David Pellauer, in Ricoeur, *Political and Social Essays*, ed. David Stewart and Joseph Bien, trans. Donald Siewert et al. (Athens: Ohio University Press, 1974), pp. 243–70.
16. Ricoeur, "The Human as the Subject Matter of Philosophy," p. 100.
17. Ricoeur, "Phenomenology and Hermeneutics," *Nous* 9 (1975): 94.
18. Ibid., p. 95.
19. See Paul Ricoeur, "Guilt, Ethics, and Religion," in his *The Conflict of Interpretations: Essays in Hermeneutics*, ed. Don Ihde, trans. Willis Domingo et al. (Evanston, Ill.: Northwestern University Press, 1974), pp. 425–39.
20. Ricoeur has made this argument in an unpublished lecture titled "Beyond Autonomy and Heteronomy" given at the University of Chicago in the spring of 1987. See Van Den Hengel, *Home of Meaning*, pp. 247–60, for an explanation of the self as gift.
21. On this see Ricoeur, "Guilt, Ethics, and Religion," pp. 425–39.
22. For recent discussions of Ricoeur's significance for theology, see David E. Klemm, "Ricoeur, Theology, and the Rhetoric of Overturning," *Journal of Literature and Theology* 3 (1989): 267–84. And see also William Placher, "Paul Ricoeur and Postliberal Theology: A Conflict of Interpretations?" *Modern Theology* 4 (1987): 35–52.
23. Ricoeur, "Freedom in the Light of Hope," p. 159.
24. Ricoeur, *Time and Narrative*, 1:87.
25. Paul Ricoeur, *Interpretation Theory: Discourse and the Surplus of Meaning* (Fort Worth: Texas Christian Press, 1976), p. 59.
26. On this notion of how the ego receives a self, see Ricoeur, *Interpretation Theory*, p. 95.
27. Paul Ricoeur, *The Symbolism of Evil*, trans. Emerson Buchanan (New York: Harper and Row, 1967), p. 13.
28. See Charles Taylor, "Responsibility for Self," and Gary Watson, "Free Agency," in *Free Will*, ed. Gary Watson (Oxford: Oxford University Press, 1982), pp. 111–26, 96–110.
29. I am thinking of the Roman Catholic theologian Karl Rahner and of the Reformed theologian Karl Barth, although others could be mentioned. See Karl Rahner, *Foundations of the Christian Faith*, trans. William V. Dych (New York: Seabury, 1978), and Karl Barth, *Church Dogmatics*, 12 vols., ed. G. W. Bromiley and T. F. Torrance (Edinburgh: T & T Clark, 1956–69).
30. Charles Taylor, *Sources of the Self*, p. 8.
31. See Ricoeur, "Freedom in the Light of Hope," pp. 178–80.
32. I am also not arguing here, as some philosophers and theologians do, that the only adequate ethics is some form of a divine command ethics. For a discussion of this, see Philip Quinn, "The Recent Revival of Divine Command Ethics," *Philosophy and Phenomenological Research* 50, supplement (Fall 1990): 345–65.
33. The literature on responsibility is extensive. For works that I have found helpful, see H. Richard Niebuhr, *The Responsible Self: An Essay in Christian Moral Philosophy*, Introduction by James M. Gustafson (New York: Harper and Row, 1963), and Hans Jonas, *The Imperative of Responsibility: In Search of an Ethic for the Technological Age*, trans. H. Jonas and D. Herr (Chicago: University of Chicago Press, 1984).

HERMAN RAPAPORT

FACE TO FACE WITH RICOEUR AND LEVINAS

IN AN ESSAY entitled "Toward a Hermeneutic of the Idea of Revelation," Paul Ricoeur speaks of a "pretension of consciousness," that, in his view, constitutes itself as perhaps the "most formidable obstacle to the idea of revelation." Consciousness, Ricoeur tells us, would like to posit itself at the origin of meaning, while "hermeneutics brings about the abandonment of this pretension." No doubt this thesis is precisely what Martin Heidegger was advancing in *Being and Time* when he undertook the project of *Dasein* analysis. Heidegger knew quite well that it was problematic to allow consciousness to, in Ricoeur's words, "set itself up as the standard of meaning." And Ricoeur is merely following in Heidegger's wake when he writes that "understanding then is the complete opposite of a constitution for which the subject would have the key." In considering Jean Nabert's *Désir et Dieu,* Ricoeur wants to turn to a consideration of testimony or witnessing in which there is an "abandonment or letting go of the absolute claim to self-consciousness." To let go is at once an ethical and a speculative act, Ricoeur says, because it allows for something else to come to pass, namely, an originary affirmation of the absolute. It is "this movement of letting go which bears reflection to the encounter with contingent signs of the absolute which the absolute in its generosity allows to appear." These locutions, of course, are not very Heideggerian, but fall rather within a metaphysics of granting and bestowing. Ricoeur wants to know how the absolute is witnessed by us in such a way that an avowal of the sacred can be detected. And he insists that such an avowal cannot come to consciousness by way of experiential accounts in which a narrative takes the place of originary affirmation, or by means of symbols that are too quickly turned into "ideal forms of signification."[1] Both the narration of experience and the invocation of symbols obstruct our understanding of the absolute insofar as consciousness uses them to lay claim on the sacred. One might suppose that for Ricoeur, then, laying such a claim could only be legitimized by a suspect hermeneutics that would establish an articulation of those external signs by means of which the absolute is said to grant being. Further, one might suppose that for Ricoeur a hermeneutics of testimony would be something radically other than exegesis of self and of external signs.

Still, for Ricoeur testimony gives rise to a critical activity that involves interpretation. Ricoeur argues that we have to develop a criteriology of the divine that necessitates a certain hermeneutics of testimony, and that we have to pay attention to how we can judge the difference between true and false testimony. Then too, he is interested in the dialectic of the witness and of the things seen. "To be a witness is to have participated in what one has seen and to be able to testify to it."[2] That sentence is already problematic, in light of Ricoeur's previous arguments, because it hypostasizes a subject and therefore runs the risk of reinstating the very pretensions of consciousness Ricoeur criticizes at the outset. Yet, as Ricoeur might point out, he is fated to such contradictions as a philosopher with a Hegelian bent who likes to map out a number of superpositions. And hence none of the considerations of testimony should be identified with a sovereign consciousness.

This tragic destiny of truth outside of us in a wholly contingent history may accompany the letting go by means of which reflection abandons the illusions of a sovereign consciousness. Reflection does so by internalizing the dialectic of testimony from which it records the trace of the absolute in the contingency of history. The three dialectical moments of testimony—event and meaning, the trial of false testimony, and testimony about what is seen and of a life—find their echo, their reverberation, in the movement of consciousness that renounces its sovereignty.[3]

To give testimony or to bear witness must necessarily mean the relinquishing of that sovereignty through which a historical event is laid claim to by the pretensions of a consciousness, which is to say, a consciousness that would apprehend historical events as narratives with a certain closure. That is, for Ricoeur historical testimony and self-consciousness are necessarily not to be thought of as essentially compatible. In privileging historical testimony over self-consciousness, Ricoeur turns to a passage from Kant's *Critique of Judgement* on the imagination in which that faculty is said to aesthetically enlarge a concept even as it functions within the framework of an established idea or representation.

> Historical testimony has the same structure and the same function. It, too, is a "presentation" of what for reflection remains an idea; namely, the idea of a letting go wherein we affirm an order exempt from that servitude from which finite existence cannot deliver itself. The Kantian relation between an idea and its aesthetic "presentation" well expresses the kind of relation we are seeking to formulate between originary affirmation (which would require an impossible total mediation between self-consciousness and its symbolic experience) and its historical presentation in testimonies whose meaning we have never exhausted.[4]

Historical testimony, in other words, is a presentation akin to the Kantian imagination that is exempt from a servitude to the finite, a presentation that has let go of a certain self-conscious notion of existence. Originary affirmation—the absolute affirmation of the absolute—is never reducible to a total or closed relation between self-consciousness and symbolic experience, though it is given embodiment by a historical presentation that has a meaning we cannot exhaust. It is this relation between historical testimony and originary affirmation that produces what Ricoeur calls revelation. Kant is necessary here, because Ricoeur wants to say that in terms of reading Scripture, revelation is nothing less than an opening up of the imagination in place of obedience. Here, once more, we sense a falling back into a somewhat familiar Cartesian framework, however modified by Kant.

An interesting feature of Ricoeur's analysis is the way in which he considers the notion of textuality. At the close of the essay, for example, he speaks of the subject as being positioned in front of the text, and of the world as such having been transformed into a power. Throughout this essay, the text is viewed as some kind of thing to be interpreted. But if we turn to Emmanuel Levinas, who has also thought about witnessing and history, we notice that for him "language is perhaps to be defined as the very power to break the continuity of being or of history." In other words, for Levinas, language is what bears witness to the nonsovereignty of self-consciousness.[5] This is a position also maintained by Martin Heidegger, Maurice Blanchot, Georges Bataille, Jacques Lacan, and Jacques Derrida. And one might say that this position is perhaps one of the defining features of a poststructuralist orientation.

For Ricoeur, however, it is not so much language as reflection and a certain way of experiencing the world that breaks with the continuity of being or of history. This orientation stems from his close ties to a Hegelian thinking that focuses on experience, in Ricoeur's view, rather than on language, since experience is actually less likely than language to constitute itself as sovereign, thanks to the dialectics of consciousness. Levinas, of course, holds on to such a dialectics as well when he discusses the relation between the subject and the radical alterity of the Other. And, it is in terms of this dialectics that the subject experiences revelation by refusing to grasp the Other in his negative resistance. Levinas says that one does not struggle with a faceless god, but responds to his expression and to his revelation. The revelation occurs in terms of what Ricoeur calls letting go, and what Levinas would see as refusing sovereignty over the face of the Other. The face speaks to the subject only under the condition that the sovereignty or totality of self-consciousness has given way to something else, what Levinas calls infinity. It is there that language would break with the continuity of being and history and that language functions in terms of witnessing and giving testimony.

For Levinas, revelation is the moment when language can be experienced as that which breaks with sovereignty, the moment when the pretension of consciousness is dismantled and the Other comes into view *as* Other. Whereas in Ricoeur the revelation occurs largely as a response to something—for example, a poem—for Levinas the revelation comes the moment that we experience the limitations or discontinuities of response. At one point in *Totality and Infinity,* Levinas specifies that most poetry is exactly antithetical to revelation. What is wanted is prose, the rupture and commencement, the breaking of rhythms that enrapture interlocutors.[6] Ricoeur's imaginary overdeterminations would be much too beguiling and binding for Levinas, and especially suspect, given that they depend upon a poetic text. For Levinas, language permits revelation only in the sense that it is irreducible to consciousness, whereas for Ricoeur language is that through which consciousness imagines and lets itself go or achieves release. Consciousness does this, however, only because it is capable of reconstructing all the potentialities available in narrative and symbols.

Toward the end of Levinas's *Otherwise Than Being*, we read that the witness has a consciousness of the "Here I am" who bears testimony to the Infinite, but who does so without thematizing that to which it bears witness. According to Levinas, witness is irreducible to representation, narration, and thematization. "There is witness, a unique structure, an exception to the rule of being, irreducible to representation, only of the Infinite. The Infinite does not appear to him that bears witness to it. On the contrary, the witness belongs to the glory of the Infinite. It is by the voice of the witness that the glory of the Infinite is glorified."[7] Without doubt, Levinas's inference is that the witness cannot testify in terms that we would recognize as historical. This point was already made by Ricoeur, of course, though in Levinas it has been greatly radicalized. There is revelation here, but unlike Ricoeur's imaginative free play, it is of an order that cannot be represented. "No theme, no present, has a capacity for the Infinite," Levinas writes.[8]

I suspect this notion of the Infinite will make little sense to a reader unfamiliar with Heidegger, because it is keyed to the Heideggerian notion of concealment or oblivion in which being and representation is forgotten. In other words, for Levinas the Infinite marks an extremely unstable state in which exteriority and interiority, identity and difference, are no longer determinable. This is not surprising, since the Infinite suggests the concealment of all finitude, a concealment that, for Levinas, is experienced as glory. Moreover, in the coming to pass of the Infinite as what Heidegger would call dis-appropriation, the ethical comes about as comprehensible only outside of a Western humanist tradition. This disappropriative moment is what Levinas calls heteronomy, and it is textually inscribed in the Talmud as a conflict of interpretations that is profoundly alien to what Ricoeur calls the pretensions of consciousness. Indeed, such textual heteronomy touches on a notion of revelation that discloses a commandment that is not reducible to a metaphysics of addresser and addressee. Only in terms of what Ricoeur calls the letting go and of what Levinas views as the Infinite does this commandment come forth insofar as the commandment marks the rift or fracture that opens "the closed order of totality, of the world, or equally in the self-sufficiency of reason which is its correlative."[9] In terms of contemporary Continental philosophy, Levinas is suggesting that the commandment can only be grasped as something that breaks with the horizons of universalization. Obedience to the commandment cannot be "assimilated to the categorical imperative, where a universal suddenly finds itself in a position to direct the will."[10] For the commandment is the trait of the Infinite, the heteronomous, and of the revelation of Otherness.

Finally, Levinas has pointed to a number of writers with whom he finds much philosophical compatibility. Among them are Celan, Blanchot, Jabes, Kierkegaard, and Agnon. In a surprising turn to poetry, Levinas writes of Paul Celan:

> One finds that for Celan the poem situates itself at a pre-syntactic and pre-logical level (as is, certainly, *de rigeur* today!), though, one that is also pre-disclosive: up to the moment of pure touch, contact, capture, or grasp, which is, perhaps, a giving to the outstretched hand. A language of proximity for proximity, it is older than that of the truth of being that it probably supports and carries. Of the earliest languages, its response preceding the question, its responsibility being directed toward the one who is next, it makes possible all the wonder of giving thanks to its for-the-otherness.[11]

Because Celan's language of proximity precedes the truth of being, Levinas can invoke a dialogical relation between addresser and addressee which implicitly anticipates the Cogito. Most importantly, however, such language (or poetry) precedes the truth of being as heteronomous—even to the point of disclosing the inhuman.

Paul Celan, in his essay "Der Meridian," speaks of this, in the context of Georg Buchner, as a *furchtbares Verstummen* ("terrible silencing"), which partitions or cuts off word from breath.[12] That is, Celan considers poetry to be something terrifyingly inhuman and thinks of it from the standpoint of a brief moment when our breathing shifts or reverses itself and we are momentarily suffocated. For in that heteronomous moment something other than being comes to pass. Something alien to the subject occurs—"Dichtung: das kann eine Atemwende bedeuten" ("poetry: that can mean a reversal of breath").

One of Celan's suggestions is that in this reversal of breathing, poetry dis-appropriates the "I" and makes it a stranger or an Other. Moreover, in this moment of reversal, perhaps akin to what Heidegger called the turn, poetry discloses an abyss, an *Abgrund* that is a meridian or apogee, a place "wo die Person sich freizusetzen vermochte, als ein—befremdetes—Ich" (where the person is able to be set free, as an—estranged—"I").[13] It is here that the person can be released, let go, detached, only to be recognized as an astonished and estranged "I." This would develop Celan's view that perhaps poetry, like art, leads the "I" toward self-forgetting or, to use a stronger term, oblivion. As in Buchner, this self-forgetting comes at the expense of telling narratives and of constructing totalizing histories, something "Der Meridian" focuses on in numerous examples where Buchner's writing breaks off and narrative goes under. Similarly Celan's own poetry is, to say the least, extremely fragmented, its individual words fractured or dismembered as if, here too, word and breath were cut off from one another, confession and history asphyxiated.

Yet the Infinite comes to pass in the particles of suffocated speech, in what Levinas calls the pre-syntactic, pre-logical, and pre-disclosive. Such language witnesses or testifies, then, as *Atemwende,* as that which is inhospitable to our persistence as human beings and is therefore radically other. In itself, this is a revelation or disclosure of the Other that Derrida has formulated as "il y a la Cendre," the coming to pass of a *Dasein* exterior to the Heideggerian *Dasein,* which is to say, a *Dasein* that problematizes the opposition of human/inhuman, of life/death.[14] But such a revelation would be radically alien to a thinker like Ricoeur, for whom language is essentially addressed, if not to our obedience, then to our imagination. Nothing could be less compatible with Levinas, Celan, and also Derrida than the following sentence by Ricoeur: "We must say that the imagination is that part of ourselves that responds to the text as a Poem, and that alone can encounter revelation no longer as an unacceptable pretension, but a nonviolent appeal."[15]

NOTES

1. Paul Ricoeur, "Toward a Hermeneutic of the Idea of Revelation," in his *Essays on Biblical Interpretation,* ed. Lewis S. Mudge (Philadelphia: Fortress, 1980), pp. 109–11.
2. Ibid., p. 113.
3. Ibid., pp. 113–14.
4. Ibid., p. 116.
5. Emmanuel Levinas, *Totality and Infinity,* trans. Alphonso Lingis (Pittsburgh: Duquesne University Press, 1969), p. 195.

6. Ibid., p. 203.
7. Emmanuel Levinas, *Otherwise Than Being: or, Beyond Essence,* trans. Alphonso Lingis (The Hague: Martinus Nijhoff, 1981), p. 146.
8. Ibid.
9. Emmanuel Levinas, "Revelation in Jewish Tradition," in *The Levinas Reader,* ed. Séan Hand (Oxford: Blackwell, 1989), p. 205.
10. Ibid., p. 206.
11. Emmanuel Levinas, *Noms Propres* (Paris: Fata Morgana, 1976), p. 60 (my translation). Levinas's syntax in the original is very attenuated.
12. Paul Celan, "Der Meridian," in his *Gesammelte Werke,* vol. 3 (Frankfurt am Main: Suhrkamp, 1983), p. 195.
13. Ibid.
14. Jacques Derrida, *Feu la Cendre* (Paris: Des Femmes, 1987).
15. Ricoeur, "Toward a Hermeneutic," p. 117.

MARK I. WALLACE

RICOEUR, RORTY, AND THE QUESTION OF REVELATION

> I believe that being can still speak to me.
>
> (Paul Ricoeur, *The Symbolism of Evil*)

> [The culture of liberalism] would be one in which no trace of divinity remained, either in the form of a divinized world or a divinized self.
>
> (Richard Rorty, *Contingency, Irony, and Solidarity*)

INTRODUCTION

Is THE LITERARY TEXT an echo chamber in which the sounds of its own voice reverberate within a closed structure, or is it an open-ended environment in which the voice of "being" can be heard by the reader? It is remarkable that at a time when the referential intentions of the literary text are said to be an illusion, when the verdict on the text is that its aesthetic play is centripetal and not directed outward toward the world, some philosophers like Paul Ricoeur can suggest that the text makes an ontological claim about possible modes of existence, new ways of being in the world for the reader.

Ricoeur's biblical interpretation theory is a species of his realist notion of the text, and is best understood as an exercise in rhetorical or poetic reasoning. This is because his theory examines the argumentative styles and surplus of meaning characteristic of the mixed genres within the Bible. It is also because his hermeneutics seeks to account for the argumentative force of the Bible: its strategies of *persuasion* by which the reader is called upon to become a disciple of the biblical texts' distinctive ways of being in the world.

One of Ricoeur's important contributions to the current discussion is his proposal for a *figural ontology* that can provide the underpinning for a balanced understanding of biblical revelation. Classic texts like the Bible that interweave history and fiction, description and imagination, are revelatory because they place one's everyday perceptions of reality in abeyance by opening up new ways of being human, novel redescriptions of self and world, that are fertile and transformative. By wooing the reader to effect an *epoché* of conventional reality, the Bible challenges her to risk inhabiting the figurative space and sometimes dangerous world of its own poetic universe. This is the rhetoric of revelation in Ricoeur's hermeneutic: the analysis of the text's power to solicit the reader to wager her life on the values and ideals the text projects. Through a nonviolent appeal to the reader's imagination, the Bible provides an angle of vision that so increases one's capacity to see the world differently that it can be said, in Ricoeur's parlance, to "remake reality." The primary meaning of *fictio*, then, is *facere:* the text's ability to remake the world through its powers of imaginative redescription.[1]

In this essay I explore Ricoeur's confidence in the power of poetic texts to set forth a world in relation to his analysis of the competing modes of discourse and temporality within the Bible. Ricoeur maintains that a synchronic study of different biblical genres—in this case we will look at narrative and wisdom writings—illuminates the reality of time itself for readers who risk trusting in the Bible's powers of disclosure. I consider this Ricoeurian gesture of trust against the backdrop of Richard Rorty's suspicion of such an orientation as a vestige of Western philosophers' ahistorical conviction that classic literary texts (such as the Bible) are sources of transcendent meaning and truth. Toward the end of the paper I place Ricoeur and Rorty into conversation with each other on this and related issues, and conclude with some summary comments concerning the question of text-mediated revelation in Ricoeur's thought.

PRIVATE TRUTH, STRONG POETS, AND PUBLIC SPACE

Richard Rorty was recently lauded as the most important American philosopher in a generation.[2] This accolade is an index to Rorty's status as a thinker who has successfully translated the often arcane vocabularies of Anglo-American and Continental philosophies into a sensible and readable idiom. Such praise also points to Rorty's success at synthesizing traditional philosophical language with current work in a variety of nonphilosophical disciplines such as culture criticism, new historicism, literary theory, and social thought. The result is a truly integrative post-philosophical perspective that stresses the fragile tasks of practicing democratic conversation and appropriating the communal values embodied in literature and art over and against the time-honored philosophical quest for rational certitude and moral absolutes. Rorty's irritation with the pretensions and irrelevancies of high philosophical culture, and his concern for relocating intellectual life and moral reasoning within the contingencies and ironies of daily lived existence, has spoken volumes to people who long ago abandoned the classical notions of truth and morality they inherited but have been left with little in their place. Rorty's posture as a self-avowed dilettante and apologist for conversation and community is an attractive alternative to the flight from ambiguity and historicity so characteristic of many philosophers' quest for certainty.[3]

Rorty writes in the wake of the death of God, the distrust in language as a medium of representation, and the demise of the transcendental self as a source of epistemically privileged beliefs. He begins one recent book with the claim that "about two hundred years ago, the idea that truth was made rather than found began to take hold of the imagination of Europe."[4] For Rorty, language is not a royal road to a self-subsistent Truth or God that exists independent of human mind and lies ready-made for discovery through the right philosophical vocabulary. Language is not a reliable medium for mediating the relationship between the knowing subject and the so-called objective world outside of the subject; rather, language is a coping device that meets particular needs under certain conditions and circumstances. "Think of the term 'mind' or 'language' not as the name of a medium between self and reality but simply as a flag which signals the desirability of using a certain vocabulary when trying to cope with certain kinds of organisms."[5]

The old subject-object, inner-outer schema is an unhelpful remnant of classical coherence and correspondence theories of truth—theories that cannot account for the highly volatile factors of passion, desire, and power in deciding upon what is and what is not deemed "truth" or "knowledge" or "morality" by particular communities of interpretation. The question is not, "Is this language true to reality?" but "Is this language efficacious in meeting certain needs and performing certain functions for a thoroughly contingent and perspectival group of inquirers?"

If truth is a matter of constructing a vocabulary that one finds useful for coping with lived experience, then selfhood consists of developing a set of metaphors and terms that allows one to craft a self-definition freed from the received wisdom of past traditions. Rorty asks us to write our lives as fictions that have overcome the inherited descriptions of the world that impede our progress toward free and responsible self-actualization. Borrowing from Nietzsche, he maintains that the journey toward selfhood is marked by the exclamation "Thus I willed it!" over and against one's allegiance to the putative certainties of the philosophers.[6] Authentic individuality is a product of aesthetic self-creation in defiance of the inherited assumptions of the philosophical mandarins; the strong poet, the maker of fiction, the artist who spins out worlds—these are the true individuals.

Platonists, Kantians, and Christians have blinded thinkers to the sheer contingency and perspectival nature of their traditional visions of the self. On the one hand, the philosophers and theologians have upheld the spiritual quest for a core self or deep common essence that all persons share. The discovery of this generic human nature—what Plato and Christians call the soul—is championed as a universal reference point for making decisions about truth and moral obligation. On the other hand, this core self is said to be in communion with a power greater than ourselves, a transpersonal reality like Plato's Ideas or the God of Jews and Christians that can provide a further warrant for adjudicating competing truth claims and moral judgments.[7] This trust in the invisible world of the soul and the reality of God is inimical to the development of liberal inquiry and Nietzschean self-construction. "For in its ideal form, the culture of liberalism would be one which was enlightened, secular, through and through. It would be one in which no trace of divinity remained, either in the form of a divinized world or a divinized self. Such a culture would have no room for the notion that there are nonhuman forces to which human beings should be responsible."[8]

The strong poet is an ironist. She realizes that there is no noncircular justification for the vocabulary she uses as basic and fundamental in the process of forging her self-identity. Rorty acknowledges, therefore, that while the private task of constructing "true" individuality is of a piece with a thoroughgoing historicism and nominalism, this ironic mind-set is generally irrelevant to the public task of promoting genuine human solidarity. On the surface it seems that the sense of solidarity and community with other people—the necessary social glue for maintaining stable human society—is not aided by the acquisition of this or that vocabulary for the process of self-creation. Writing the script of one's life ("Was that life? Well then! Once more!"[9]) is not the uncovering of the "true self" or the "real world"—the realities that Platonists and Christians and liberals have used as the fiber and substance of moral and social order. But implicit in the process of inventing a private vocabulary as one's own is the recognition of the value of free and democratic public space for the realization of opportunities for self-creation. My private vocabulary is "none of your business," as Rorty says, but together we share the need for common space for making our vocabularies workable—we share a "common selfish hope, the hope that one's world—the little things around which one has woven one's final vocabulary—will not be destroyed."[10]

This communal need and shared hope for moral-aesthetic "space" for creating one's private worldview provides Rorty with a negative ethic for answering the public question "What provides the social bonds for maintaining human community?" His answer is not the positive ethic of the historic philosophies and theologies that uphold the universal ideal that insofar as all people possess an inner light or are bearers of God's image, social organization has a sure foundation upon which to reconcile differences and to build community. Rather, his answer is the negative ethic of bourgeois individualism: the acquisition of a private vocabulary implies the importance of public institutions and spaces for making this acquisition possible and fruitful. "Without the protection of something like the institutions of bourgeois liberal society, people will be less able to work out their private salvations."[11] There can be no nonrhetorical argument for the necessity of Western liberal institutions and structures, but if, as Rorty argues, the proper desideratum is the right to invent one's private sense of selfhood independent of previous assumptions, then such institutions will be necessary for the working out of the "self" one has chosen.

BIBLICAL REVELATION, GENRE ANALYSIS, AND CONTROVERSIES ABOUT TIME

The problem of language as a medium of presence, the notion of individual authenticity, and the need for communal space for enabling the project of selfhood are issues that drive Ricoeur's thought as well as Rorty's. But the differences between the two authors center on the "fundamental gesture" most characteristic of their respective philosophies.[12] Whereas Rorty operates with a basic suspicion of all previous (quixotic) appeals to a transcendent power outside of human experience, Ricoeur begins with a presumption of sympathy toward the claims to truth addressed to the reader in her interactions with the world of the text. Later we will consider the implications of these competing gestures, but first, what is the character of Ricoeur's conviction that a text can be a medium of epiphany in the life of the reader?

An initial response to this question is served by noting Ricoeur's distinction between general, poetic revelation and specific, biblical revelation. In reference to general revelation, Ricoeur suggests that whenever a figurative text effectively proposes a world that the reader may inhabit—that is, an imaginary environment wherein one's primordial belongingness to all being can be realized—it can be said to be revelatory. Poetic discourse is revelatory insofar as it manifests and restores the reader's sense of belonging to a more primitive world of connections, a world where the reader can realize her ownmost possibilities before she learns to oppose herself as a subject over and against other objects under her control. The aim of poetic, nondescriptive discourse is to entice the reader to abandon her own sense of everyday selfhood in order to be comported to the "larger self," the more expansive vision of reality, that the text projects beyond the plane of ordinary, manipulable existence.[13] This is the rhetoric of revelation in figurative discourse: the appeal to the reader to risk being appropriated by the new modes of being in the world that the text imagines.

The literary text's manifestation of one's primordial rootedness to all life is coextensive with the revelatory function of the biblical texts as well. "Thus this areligious sense of revelation helps us to restore the concept of biblical revelation to its full dignity. . . . If the Bible may be said to be revealed this must refer to what it says, to the new being it unfolds before us."[14] Ricoeur's location of biblical revelation under the rubric of general poetic revelation frees his hermeneutics from any tribal or parochial apology for the qualitative superiority of biblical poetics over and against other modes of imaginative discourse. Yet such an integration of biblical and general revelation does not undermine the wager of certain faith communities that the manifestation of the divine Other in, say, Jewish and Christian scriptures is more adequate to their sense of belonging to the Whole than that which is provided by nonbiblical forms of disclosure. It simply means that there is no extracommunal reason outside the community's shared values that can ground its collective presupposition that the Bible's appeal to its common life is more disclosive of its deepest possibilities than any other such appeal.

On the one hand, therefore, Jewish and Christian scripture is one of the great poems of human existence, as Ricoeur notes, but on the other hand, insofar as its poetic vision is centered by the authority of the divine voice, it is an extension beyond, and, finally, a disturbing subversion of general revelation and figurative discourse. For Ricoeur the Bible maintains a dialectical relationship to the areligious revelatory power of figural literature as such: it is at one and the same time both a general example and a unique expression of this literature. Biblical texts attest to the reader's relatedness to all life, indeed, but they also warn against any facile expressions of that relatedness in terms of a diffuse nature sacrality or extrascriptural sources of inspiration. In the conflict between the one and the many, it is the one that is emphasized in biblical discourse; in the tension between the iconoclastic proclamation of the Word in the community and the ubiquitous presence of the sacred in the world, it is the tradition of the Word that is privileged within the sacred cosmos.[15]

Ricoeur's mediation of the poetry/Bible polarity has the advantage of understanding biblical discourse as a type of poetic expression in general—even if that discourse is a unique example of, or a judgment upon, the general expression. If, then, the Bible is a species of the poem (at least on one level), how does it work? What enables its different literary genres and theological itineraries to mesh with the reader in such a way that the presentation of new possibilities, of a new world, can be said to be the result?

Revelation, according to Ricoeur, is engendered by the different modalities of discourse within the biblical intertext. The opening to new possibilities of existence emerges through the confluence and clash of the Bible's diverse literary genres. Instead, then, of abstracting philosophical concepts from the Bible's rich fermentation of meaning, Ricoeur focuses on the intertextual dynamics embodied in the originary literary expressions of religious faith.

Though Ricoeur uses a variety of conceptual and philosophical tools to analyze the plurality of biblical discourses, his approach does not sit well with current trends in philosophy of religion.[16] Here we note a significant difference between his rhetorical model for analyzing originary scriptural discourses and the analytic model of Anglo-American philosophy of religion. It is the difference between the hermeneutical task of understanding a religious symbol or idea as a possible mode of experience and the philosophical attempt to justify the cognitive claims of religious thought.[17] While Western philosophy of religion interrogates the question of God's existence and identity through formal *arguments* that are indifferent to the image-laden language of confessional and scriptural traditions, Ricoeur's rhetorical model analyzes the rich *descriptions* of God within the Bible through a literary-philosophical analysis of the text's crisscrossing patterns of meaning. Mainstream philosophy of religion asks whether the *truth* of certain formalized, second-order propositions can be apodictically demonstrated (e.g., Does God exist? Is the soul immortal? Are theism and evil incompatible?), whereas Ricoeur's rhetorical approach focuses on the question of the *meaning* of certain figural depictions of God, self, and world within the first-order discourse of particular traditions (e.g., How is God present and absent within biblical narratives? Can the testimony of the prophets be trusted? Is selfhood a present possession or a future gift?).

Ricoeur maintains that the rhetorical approach avoids the ontotheological siren calls of Western thought that have lured thinkers about religion into a certain metaphysical comfort by convincing them that, because they have mastered the standard analytic arguments and proofs *for and against* religious belief, they have therefore finished the task of thinking about religion. Ricoeur's alternative is to sidestep this "temptation" altogether. His point is that the reality of God is, not a deliverance of universal reason (as Kant, Plantinga, Swinburne, and others maintain), but, rather, the supreme figure within a series of texts that invite the reader to think and live alongside their creative mimesis of the world.

The identity of the Divine is rendered through the polyphonic discourses of the Bible. The rhetoric of the Bible is not an incidental facade that needs dismantling in order to extract a series of speculative concepts. Rather, this rhetoric constitutes a generative poetics that "names God" through the interplay of the Bible's conflicting and complementary modes of discourse. "The naming of God, in the originary expressions of faith, is not simple but multiple. It is not a single tone, but polyphonic. The originary expressions of faith are complex forms of discourse as diverse as narratives, prophecies, laws, proverbs, prayers, hymns, liturgical formulas, and wisdom writings. As a whole, these forms of discourse name God."[18] Far from the textual identity of the divine life being indifferent to the originary discourses of the Bible, Ricoeur maintains that God is "named" through the intersections between this plurality of discourses—from narratives to laws and from wisdom to apocalyptic writings. It is beyond the scope of this essay to examine the status of all these genres in Ricoeur's thought. Instead, I will consider two of the genres—narrative and sapiential writings—that Ricoeur studies in the context of his overall biblical hermeneutics. Ricoeur offers a structural and synchronic analysis of these two genres (as he does their companion types) in order to reveal the models of time they constitute. A synchronic study of these modes of discourse illustrates both the *intertextual dynamics* of biblical revelation and the *temporal structures* that underlie the message, the revelation, that address the reader as she considers the working of these discourses on one another. I will begin with Ricoeur's understanding of narrative temporality and then take up the vision of time within wisdom discourse.

The temporal structure that mediates the message of biblical narrative is successive, cumulative, anticipatory, chronological. Narrative configures discrete events under the control of a chronological configuration; it uses the powers of emplotment to organize disparate occurrences in terms of a story with a particular sense of an ending.[19] The plot maker combines and arranges her data into a single overarching chronology—an account with beginning, middle, and end—in order to persuade her reader that this narrative uncovers the untold story waiting to be told, the hidden temporal logic, that underlies the random occurrences of everyday existence. The narrative conception of time, then, is totalizing and chronological: it depends on the power of the productive imagination (in Kantian terms) to schematize into a meaningful totality the seemingly unrelated data of temporal existence. Narrative transforms all history into tales about the flow of time. Quoting from Kant's first *Critique,* Ricoeur contends that our capacity for narrative configuration is "an art hidden in the depths of the human soul" that organizes events into a historylike *Zeitroman* of successive plot and character.[20] The narrative temporality of the Bible projects a world of coherent events and meanings. The Yahwist, for example, uses the theological devices of genealogies and covenants in order to generate a narrative identification of the God of the Hebrew tribes.[21]

A cumulative comprehending of God is accomplished by tracing the acts of God within time and space. Israel's God is a God of the fathers and mothers, a God who, generation after generation, provides continual support through the community's "time" of testing and suffering. Like Rahab's scarlet thread, clues are given in history that can guide the struggling community to safety in spite of the dangers that surround it. This-worldly existence is now charged with sacred purpose because it is the place where the divine faithfulness is being worked out—in spite of the prima facie evidence to the contrary.[22]

The events of Exodus and Sinai offer a certain temporal security to the Hebrews who, without these events, would have found themselves adrift as victims of someone else's history and chronology. In this way the terror of the eternal return of the same, the terror of forever being relegated to the role of bit players within another nation's autobiography, is stemmed by Israel's collective memory of a God whose abiding presence guarantees the community's safe journey through the chaos and meaninglessness of cyclical time.

Ricoeur's biblical narratology makes a similar claim with reference to the Gospel stories. His exegesis of Mark highlights the interpretative function of this particular Jesus story. He borrows from Robert Alter the classification of the Bible's narratives as "historical."[23] Like the other biblical-story traditions, the Gospels use a particular verisimilitude to create a historylike account of Jesus' mission and identity. This feature is evident on the surface planes of Mark's narrative, where elements of episodic history and theological necessity are continually crisscrossing. At the same time, Jesus is both the innocent victim of Judas's treason and the disciples' abandonment (who does suffer as a contingent consequence of their betrayal) and the heavenly Son of Man (who must suffer on behalf of humankind in keeping with the divine masterplan). "To explicate this gospel means looking for the indications of the equation it posits between its christology of a suffering Son of man and the story of the betrayed Jesus."[24] In a manner analogous to the "Who is Yahweh?" question of the Hebrew Bible, Mark's art "foments" (*fomentent*) a narrative description of the identity of Jesus: he is the fully human and divinely promised suffering servant. Ricoeur argues that this twofold identity of Jesus as eternal Christ and historical human being is generated by the complicated temporality of Mark's Gospel, in which aspects of historical contingency (Jesus suffers) and eschatological necessity (Jesus must suffer) are fictively interwoven.[25]

As the Hebrew Bible is structured according to the ticktock rhythm of its narrative temporality, so the Christian Bible is rooted in a configuration of events that renders Jesus' identity both historically credible and a fulfillment of the divine promise. The monumental time of the master biblical story brings together the Hebrew Bible's narratives of divine deliverance and the Christian scripture's double description of the God-human Jesus in founding the identity of the biblical communities of faith and interpretation.

On one level, Ricoeur accords narrative literature a certain primacy in the polysemy of biblical revelation because it functions to identify the founding events that trace the divine presence at the origins of Israel and the church. "In this sense, we must say that naming God is first of all a moment of the narrative confession. God is named in 'the thing' recounted."[26] Narrative is the literary form that organizes the "polyphony of point and counterpoint" within the other modes of discourse into a "fragile analogical unity."[27]

Yet there is a danger to assigning primacy to biblical narrative in a manner that insulates it from its intersections with other genres. To engage the Bible solely from the perspective of its putative mainstream genre, narrative, is to compress the tensions and surplus of biblical meaning into a totalizing master story immune from the irony and pathos of daily experience. Disconnected from its collision with other literatures, the time of progressive narrative can degenerate into a disengagement with the forces of history that result in the victimization and destruction of individuals and communities. And religious communities formed by narrative, secure in the occult knowledge of the divine plan, can often slip into an insensitivity toward the specific and the discordant—those events that resist subsumption under the logic of the supreme plot.

The temporality of the wisdom writings challenges this narrative insensitivity. In part this is a result of the temporal dialectic characteristic of wisdom: while wisdom possesses a certain achronology through its interest in the always-the-same, it is still preoccupied with the meaning of time for communities that suffer from the unfulfillment of their narrative schemas.[28] Thus the temporal structure of wisdom is the time of the everyday and the immemorial that is, in many respects, uninterested in the emplotted time of the narrative. "This time of the everyday ignores the great events that make history. It is the time of the 'everyday.' And this time without events does not get narrated."[29] Wisdom does not offer a time line that is punctuated by sequential events. Instead, it offers a temporal awareness of people's confrontations with ageless limit questions: What is the meaning of death? Why is joy so transitory? How should one live one's life? Why do the innocent suffer? Where is God amidst the vagaries of existence? Through proverbs, wise sayings, and cries of lamentations, wisdom provides spiritual and affective resources for the perennial questions that are not answered in the "great events" of history and narrative.

Far from this mode of discourse being confined to a body of writings we technically refer to as "wisdom literature," Ricoeur contends that the questioning of the sages, prophets, and disciples conveys a sensibility about time that permeates and extends beyond the storied discourse of the scriptures.[30] The pain and bewilderment articulated by the wise ones—Qoholeth (Hebrew name for the Book of Ecclesiastes), Job, Jeremiah, Jesus—are summarized in terse questions—"Why me?" and "How long?"—that supersede the boundaries of the covenants remembered in the community's sacred stories. This gives wisdom temporality a universal and ahistorical character because the problems it addresses are the concerns of all people at all times.

Yet sapiential discourse engenders interest not only in the time of the everyday but also in the time of the arbitrary and peculiar. The anonymous occurrences that erupt and shatter a life generally cannot be accounted for by the incipient triumphalism of narrative coherence. The specific and ironic outbreakings of radical evil within the life of a people who had trusted their God to deliver them from such evil overflows the bounds of narrative identity. Unwarranted suffering exposes the insufficiency of a deuteronomic or evangelical reassurance that living the Torah or the Gospel will guarantee the faithful person's safe passage through the terrors of time and history. On the contrary, wisdom insinuates that life—even a life of obedience and fidelity—carries no assurances except that benign trust in a formulaic obedience undergirded by a master story is destined for disappointment and disillusionment.

In narrative discourse God is named as the Deliverer who saves the people from their enemies; in wisdom God is a problem to be struggled with and against vis-à-vis the Divine's prima facie abandonment of the community in times of trial. Thus the speculative aporia of philosophical theodicy (either God or evil, but not both) that emerges in reaction to unmerited suffering and evil is not answered by a formal theological solution but by the practical and cathartic responses offered by wisdom. "Wisdom does not so much speak of what ought to be done as of how to endure, how to suffer suffering."[31] Wisdom relocates the theodicy aporia on the level of practical experience (rather than theoretical knowledge), and thereby dissolves (rather than solves) the aporia and renders it "productive." "It is to this aporia that action and the catharsis of feelings and emotions are called upon not to give a solution but a response, a response able to render the aporia productive."[32]

The theoretical aporia is made practically productive because its dissolution liberates a therapeutic and purgative response to radical negation. The hope of wisdom is that one will discover some comfort in a life wagered on the temporal and religious values embodied in sapiential writings. The praxis of mourning one's losses, expressing anger toward God, learning solidarity with other victims of suffering, and discerning the overturning power of irony in all things provides a modicum of solace in and through life fractured by pain and suffering. Thus wisdom permits those who are alienated believers on the fringes of synagogue and church to belong again even if they cannot believe again in the interruptive God of the biblical narrative's salvation history.

The time of wisdom, then, is different from the time of narrative. Wisdom resists the narrative temptation to provide a supralapsarian temporalization of evil where evil is located at the origins of creation as a punishment of sin and, by virtue of that location, the problem of evil is thereby solved (theoretically speaking) in terms of the logic of punishment. This logic of punishment (evil and death are the outcome of an originary fall from grace) provides a temporal archaeology that is linked to a temporal teleology in the Bible's narrative genre.[33] In this fashion radical evil is assigned not only a beginning but also an end: it is the power of the enemy, a power that will be destroyed when the covenantal community is vindicated by God in the preordained endtime. Evil is no longer a surd when it can be emplotted on a time line that explains its first occasion and its preestablished fate; it is no longer inscrutable when it can be inserted into the plot of a totalizing narrative. And yet, as we have seen, it is this very totalization that wisdom resists: narrative's episodic structuring of evil into a meaningful whole is insensitive to the grief and pain that cannot be subsumed under any divine master story.

Ricoeur's *Time and Narrative* alludes to the dismantling effect of wisdom discourse in an argument structured according to a new understanding of the interdependence of time and narrative. In this study he maintains that time is humanized to the extent that it can be thematized in a narrative mode, and that narrative is meaningful insofar as it sheds light on our temporal experience.[34] This working thesis is highly elucidative of certain aporetics of time that Ricoeur examines in this work. But in the last few pages of *Time and Narrative* he offers his own immanent critique of the thesis and the project in general through a brief consideration of wisdom literature. Wisdom challenges the impulse to systemization characteristic of narrative discourse; it challenges the chimera of the supreme plot that binds together the disparate events cobbled together by the storyteller and the historian. Consider the following: "There is another way for time to envelop narrative. This is by giving rise to the formation of discursive modes other than the narrative one, which will speak, in another way, of the profound enigma. There comes a moment, in a work devoted to the power of narrative to elevate time to language, where we must admit that narrative is not the whole story and that time can be spoken of in other ways, because, even for narrative, it remains inscrutable." Wisdom literature is best equipped to express the "grief that is ceaselessly reborn from the contrast between the fragility of life and the power of time that destroys" because wisdom "goes right to the fundamental without passing through the art of narrating."[35]

After interweaving narrative and time into a near-seamless whole, Ricoeur, with remarkable honesty and humility, pulls apart the fabric by inserting the temporal problematics associated with wisdom writings. He concludes that narrative meaning is only partly successful, because wisdom reminds us that time, finally, remains opaque and inscrutable. Thus the reader of wisdom is taught that grief and irony, even divine betrayal, lie close to the heart of the narrative schemas within the Bible.

RICOEUR AND RORTY IN DIALOGUE

To this point we have considered the projects of Rorty and Ricoeur in relative isolation from one another. Now we can turn to a dialogue between Rorty's historicist philosophy and Ricoeur's rhetoric of revelation. Thus far we have seen that a text for Ricoeur is revelatory insofar as it has the power to project a vision of temporal reality that bursts the everyday assumptions of the reader. Revelation is a feature of the world of the text, the "opening up" of new possibilities for existence. In the conjunctions and controversy between narrative and antinarrative, we have examined how the reader is invited to adopt, and even to find some consolation in, the solutions to the problems of time these genres project. Thus, against the grain of current deconstruction, the world of the text for Ricoeur is not the self-contained and indeterminate play of tropes *within* the text that suspends all claims to referring to the "real" outside of the text, but is instead the subject matter *in front of* the text that potentially can liberate a more humanizing temporality that prepares the reader for the fragilities and vagaries of existence.

To suggest an awkward label, Ricoeur is a postmodern realist—a philosopher who celebrates the play of figurative discourse and deferred meaning, but a philosopher who takes seriously the text's capacity to render transparent certain aspects of our lived experience. In the play between text and reader, aesthetic discourse illuminates features of reality—especially temporal reality—that remain concealed apart from the powers of the literary imagination. In this regard Ricoeur's realism is out of step with the regnant forms of literary theory, new historicism, and postpositivist philosophy that are practiced today. A better representation of the current zeitgeist is Rorty. We have seen that, in the story Rorty tells, the text has no truth value because it is a private extension of the author's "in here" perspective, not the royal road to an "out there" reality. Rorty's therapeutic prescription for curing our metaphysical hunger for noncontingent truth, our nostalgia for pure presence, is the medicine of deconstruction; the cure is found in the unrestricted, dionysian practice of transforming the world of the text into an environment for poetic self-creation and democratic dialogue.[36] The remedy is to come of age and to recognize that truth is made, not found, that reality is constructed, not discovered, and that language is the house (or prison) we live in, not the window through which we catch glimpses of another world.

Though Ricoeur's interest in preserving the figural ontology, the reality claims, of literary and biblical fiction would be questioned by Rorty's nominalist pragmatism, it does not follow that there are not significant areas of agreement between Ricoeur and Rorty. Both authors offer alternatives to analytic philosophy's stress on the powers of the knowing subject to form incorrigible representations of mind-independent reality. And, correspondingly, they each turn to imaginative literature (Mann, Proust, and the Bible in the case of Ricoeur; and Orwell, Nabokov, and Proust in the case of Rorty) for accounts of human rationality and moral authenticity that are lacking in Anglo-American propositional philosophy. But here the similarities end. Ricoeur seeks to preserve the links between the language of the text (web of signifiers) and the vision of the world projected in front of the text (a quasi-transcendental signified) in order to set free the text's powers of ontological redescription. Rorty, on the other hand, maintains that such an effort is misguided because it is bound to an old inner-outer vocabulary that is no longer useful for a model of rationality that is right for our time—a model that champions contingency and irony rather than universality and metaphysics.

Ricoeur maintains that many contemporary theorists (like Rorty) operate with a false alternative between truth as found (the old vocabulary) and truth as made (the new-historicist mode). His approach seeks to overcome this opposition by way of a middle course between the Rortian-Nietzschean decree against literature's truth-bearing function, on the one hand, and the quest for universal certainty in foundationalist philosophy, on the other.[37] Wisdom literature, for example, provides trustworthy and potentially healing resources for a performative encounter with unjust suffering, but it does not ground these resources in any metaphysical system. A life of ironic faith can be a balm in times of trouble, but such a faith does not claim a direct purchase on reality as such. In this way, Ricoeur's biblical genre analysis challenges the boundaries between poetic-imaginary discourse and literal-descriptive language. All fiction productively discovers and creates. Insofar as the reader discovers existential possibilities within sapiential discourse, she is empowered to invent a life that is a recovery of those very values and possibilities.[38] Perhaps on this level Rorty would not object to Ricoeur's formulation. But Ricoeur insists that the text's powers of description-invention are linked to its capacity to reveal something "other"—what William James calls the "more"—that can support and undergird one's journey to wholeness and selfhood in the midst of disabling pain. Ricoeur acknowledges that such a belief is a fragile act of trust in the powers of literary disclosure that cannot be demonstrated by appeals to rational formulas or empirical proofs. But to thereby insist, as Rorty does, that such a presumption of alterity is a rearguard metaphysical quest for ahistorical foundations and certainties is an unfair accusation.

Moreover, such a charge betrays, I believe, Rorty's vestigial attachment to the canons of positivist philosophy that he purports to have disavowed. Rorty's historicism has its roots in analytic-empiricist thought, and I suspect his inability to accommodate the possibility of text-mediated transcendence is a vestige of this intellectual provenance. Postmodernism and empiricism part company at a number of places, but on this issue there is committed agreement: the gods are dead, and human experience is devoid of any epiphanic moments where something more or something new is made visible to the interpreter. The legitimacy of a life lived as a wager on this possibility is the fundamental disagreement between Rorty and Ricoeur.

Whereas Rorty in vintage Enlightenment form champions the exigency for throwing off the shackles of authority and convention, Ricoeur takes his cues from the hermeneutical attention to certain time-tested literary "voices" that come to the reader from the past through the medium of particular traditions. Nodding to Ricoeur, I suggest that Rorty-like appeals to self-construction exercise a certain tone deafness to the rootedness of these appeals in a historical tradition, namely, the empirical and Enlightenment ideal of the human subject as the supreme arbiter of meaning and truth. Rorty (by way of Nietzsche) may posture as an inventor of new worlds and new vocabularies, but his strident individualism is of a piece with a long-standing Western emphasis on the Self as the final tribunal for all claims to truth.[39] Thus we should ask whether a Rortian decree against the text's referential intentions, its vision of the real, is a form of hermeneutical violence that disallows the very plurality of meaning that it purports to serve. True to his empiricist and Enlightenment pedigree, Rorty emphasizes the self-enclosed immanence of figurative discourse. But this stress is false to the experience of many who feel addressed by certain claims to attention that come to them from the past, including those claims mediated by religious classics like the Bible. Rorty's historicism echoes a familiar refrain: his so-called plurality at the expense of openness to possible transcendence is as old as Western philosophy's turn to the privileged subject as the source for truth.

The concern in this paper has been to examine the dynamics of biblical revelation in Ricoeur against the backdrop of Rorty's historicism. We have seen that for Ricoeur, while the Bible is intertextual and polysemic, it is more than a ceaselessly oscillating exercise in contingency or *différance* because it says something about something that is of decisive significance for the reader. Indeed, in the controversy between the concordance of narrative and the discordance of wisdom, the Bible rhetorically presses onto the reader a vision of certain temporal structures that can be used as resources for a more complete understanding of existence. Scriptural literature is oriented beyond itself to a life of possibilities in which the sequential coherence of narrative and the immemorial irony of wisdom is dialectically intertwined. It is in this manner that the Bible speaks to us about what is fundamental to being human: by connecting narrative and wisdom, the Bible imagines a world in which time, if not completely understood, is now partially humanized through the powers of emplotment (so narrative) and the avowal of radical evil (so wisdom).

Human experience possesses intimations of an origin and a destiny that cannot be accounted for by a thoroughgoing historicism. To disallow this possibility under the banner of Nietzschean self-creation is to slide into self-referential incoherence: after the assertion that all knowledge is contingent and perspectival, the absolute claim is smuggled in that certain basic beliefs and experiences cannot possibly be true. This tacit intolerance of genuine plurality is specific to the orienting fundamental gestures that govern the differences between Ricoeur and Rorty. Beyond Rorty's Enlightenment dedivinization of the world for the sake of human flourishing, Ricoeur asks whether an apprenticeship to the wisdom and "authority" of particular sacred texts is not a more authentic mode of liberation than "strong textualism." He asks whether the reader might profit from wagering her existence on the hope that the biblical rhetoric projects a discordant-concordant temporality and ontology that is ultimately more satisfying and transformative than Rortian self-creation. At the end of *The Symbolism of Evil,* Ricoeur writes, "I believe that being can still speak to me."[40] If he is right, then the wager of biblical rhetoric will be won for any reader who risks inhabiting its imaginative universe.

NOTES

1. Paul Ricoeur, "The Function of Fiction in Shaping Reality," *Man and World* 12 (1979): 135.

2. See L. S. Klepp, "Every Man a Philosopher-King," *New York Times Magazine*, December 2, 1990, p. 117.
3. See Richard Rorty, "Pragmatism, Relativism, and Irrationalism," in his *Consequences of Pragmatism* (Minneapolis: University of Minnesota Press, 1982), pp. 160–75, and Rorty, *Philosophy and the Mirror of Nature* (Princeton, N.J.: Princeton University Press, 1979), pp. 315–94.
4. Richard Rorty, *Contingency, Irony, and Solidarity* (Cambridge: Cambridge University Press, 1989), p. 3. Cf. his "Solidarity or Objectivity?" in *Objectivity, Relativism, and Truth* (Cambridge: Cambridge University Press, 1991), pp. 21–34.
5. Rorty, *Contingency, Irony, and Solidarity*, p. 15.
6. "[Nietzsche] thinks a human life triumphant just insofar as it escapes from inherited descriptions of the contingencies of its existence and finds new descriptions. This is the difference between . . . thinking of redemption as making contact with something larger and more enduring than oneself and redemption as Nietzsche describes it: recreating all 'it was' into a 'thus I willed it' " (Rorty, *Contingency, Irony, and Solidarity*, p. 29).
7. For a contemporary and nonfoundational expression of this view, see Charles Taylor, *Sources of the Self: The Making of the Modern Identity* (Cambridge, Mass.: Harvard University Press, 1989). For Taylor's reaction to Rorty's criticisms of his and similar realist positions, see Charles Taylor, "Rorty in the Epistemological Tradition," in *Reading Rorty: Critical Responses to "Philosophy and the Mirror of Nature" (and Beyond)*, ed. Alan R. Malachowski (Oxford: Basil Blackwell, 1990), pp. 257–75.
8. Rorty, *Contingency, Irony, and Solidarity*, p. 45.
9. The quote is from Friedrich Nietzsche, *Thus Spake Zarathustra*, trans. R. J. Hollingdale (New York: Penguin, 1969), p. 178. The Nietzschean character of Rorty's thought is pervasive. Rorty uses Nietzsche to argue that the ideal individual has complete ownership of her identity because she constructs her life out of the raw materials of lived existence, not the ephemeral ideals of otherworldly philosophies. The ideal life is an artistic exercise in self-invention, the courage to say "once more!" to the imaginary invitation to live one's life over again.
10. Rorty, *Contingency, Irony, and Solidarity*, pp. 91–92.
11. Ibid., pp. 84–85.
12. The phrase belongs to Ricoeur in his mediation of the debate between Jürgen Habermas's critique of ideology and Hans-Georg Gadamer's hermeneutic of tradition. See Ricoeur, "Hermeneutics and the Critique of Ideology," in *Hermeneutics and the Human Sciences*, ed. and trans. John B. Thompson (Cambridge: Cambridge University Press, 1981), p. 63.
13. Paul Ricoeur, "Toward a Hermeneutic of the Idea of Revelation," in his *Essays on Biblical Interpretation*, ed. Lewis S. Mudge (Philadelphia: Fortress Press, 1980), p. 108.
14. Ricoeur, "Revelation," p. 104.
15. See Paul Ricoeur, "Manifestation and Proclamation," *Blaisdell Institute Journal* 11 (1978): 13–35. For a related perspective, cf. Erich Auerbach, *Mimesis: The Representation of Reality in Western Literature* (Princeton, N.J.: Princeton University Press, 1968), chaps. 1, 2, 7. For an alternative reading of Ricoeur that stresses the manifestation of the sacred rather than the proclamation of the Word in his writings on religion, see Kevin J. Vanhoozer, *Biblical Narrative in the Philosophy of Paul Ricoeur: A Study in Hermeneutics and Theology* (Cambridge: Cambridge University Press, 1990), pp. 165–78.
16. Representatives of these trends include, among others, the Reformed epistemologists Alvin Plantinga and Nicholas Wolterstorff and British analytic philosophers such as Anthony Flew and Richard Swinburne.

17. For a model similar to Ricoeur's, cf. Merold Westphal, *God, Guilt, and Death* (Bloomington: Indiana University Press, 1984), esp. pp. 1–13.
18. Paul Ricoeur, "Naming God," *Union Seminary Quarterly Review* 34 (1979): 215–27.
19. "Accordingly, to follow a story is to understand the successive actions, thoughts and feelings as displaying a particular *directedness.* By this I mean that we are pushed along by the development and that we respond to this thrust with expectations concerning the outcome and culmination of the process" (Ricoeur, "The Narrative Function," in *Hermeneutics and the Human Sciences,* p. 277).
20. Ibid., p. 287. See Ricoeur's discussion of three novels about time—Virginia Woolf's *Mrs. Dalloway,* Thomas Mann's *Magic Mountain,* and Marcel Proust's *Remembrance of Things Past*—as paradigmatic of the temporality of narrative discourse, in Paul Ricoeur, *Time and Narrative,* trans. Kathleen McLaughlin and David Pellauer, 3 vols. (Chicago: University of Chicago Press, 1984–88), 2:100–160.
21. "By binding patriarchs to one another through a genealogical tie and by establishing a correspondence between the promises made to the patriarchs and the promises made to Israel as a whole . . . the Jahwist composes a cumulative history accompanied by a cumulative comprehending of 'Who is Jahweh?' " (Paul Ricoeur, "Temps biblique," *Archivo di filosofia* 53 [1985]: 29; my translation).
22. Ibid., pp. 27–32.
23. Paul Ricoeur, "Le récit interprétatif: Exégèse et théologie dans les récits de la Passion," *Researches de science religieuse* 73 (1985): 18.
24. Ibid., p. 30.
25. See my "Parsimony of Presence in Mark: Narratology, the Reader, and Genre Analysis in Paul Ricoeur," *Studies in Religion/Science Religieuses* 18 (1989): 207–12.
26. Ricoeur, "Naming God," p. 220; cf. Ricoeur, "Temps biblique," p. 27.
27. John W. Van Den Hengel, *The Home of Meaning: The Hermeneutics of the Subject of Paul Ricoeur* (Washington, D.C.: University Press of America, 1982), p. 233.
28. Ricoeur, "Temps biblique," pp. 32–35.
29. Ibid., p. 32.
30. "Wisdom is not just contained in the wisdom writings. Overflowing the framework of the Covenant, its mediation bears on the human condition in general. It is directly addressed to the sense and nonsense of existence. It is a struggle for sense in spite of nonsense. Unjust suffering has a central place here to the extent that suffering itself poses its enigma at the juncture between the order of things and the ethical order" (Ricoeur, "Naming God," pp. 221–22).
31. Ibid., p. 222.
32. Paul Ricoeur, "Evil, a Challenge to Philosophy and Theology," *Journal of the American Academy of Religion* 53 (1985): 644.
33. Paul Ricoeur, "Time and Narrative in the Bible: Toward a Narrative Theology," unpublished Sarum Lectures, given at Oxford University, 1980.
34. Ricoeur, *Time and Narrative,* 1:3 and passim.
35. Ibid., 1:3, 3:272–73.
36. See Richard Rorty, "Philosophy as a Kind of Writing: An Essay on Derrida," in *Consequences of Pragmatism,* pp. 90–109.
37. See Ricoeur, *Time and Narrative,* 3:157–79, and cf. Rorty, *Contingency, Irony, and Solidarity,* pp. 73–95.
38. See Paul Ricoeur, *The Rule of Metaphor: Multi-Disciplinary Studies of the Creation of Meaning in Language,* trans. Robert Czerny, with Kathleen McLaughlin and John Costello, S.J. (London: Routledge and Kegan Paul, 1978), pp. 303–13.

39. In this sense, Rortian deconstruction is best understood, not as postmodernist, but, as I have learned in conversations with Stephen Dunning, as a variation on unhappy modernism. Rorty's ascription of supreme value to the task of forming personhood continues the modernist turn to the subject (albeit the subject now understood as the strong poet of Nietzsche rather than the empirical tabula rasa of Locke).
40. Paul Ricoeur, *The Symbolism of Evil,* trans. Emerson Buchanan (New York: Harper and Row, 1967), p. 352.

DAVID E. KLEMM

THEOLOGICAL HERMENEUTICS AND THE DIVINE NAME

Ricoeur and the Cross of Interpretation

WHAT IS THE RELATIONSHIP between hermeneutics and the divine? The question is ancient. Humans have ever ventured to interpret powerful manifestations of meaning as divine. In so doing, they name God. The ancient question is also unsettling, because traditionally in interpret*ing* what I understand as divine I am thereby interpret*ed* by the divine. In naming God, I am named by God. In religion and theology, hermeneutics has ever been the two-sided art of mediating between two originating points of interpretation: on one hand, the absolute subject, the *I,* which enters human existence in finite linguistic acts of human understanding (but never completely); and the countervailing absolute subject, *God,* which likewise reveals itself in language and existence by appearing indirectly both in sacred texts and in the natural world (while also concealing itself). Traditionally speaking, hermeneutics has both deciphered the plight of human life in the light of divine power and discerned the meaning of divine life for the human lot.

In the Jewish and Christian traditions, to understand the divine took the specific form of interpreting the biblical texts. As reader or hearer of the biblical Word, I interpret the biblical stories to understand God as final agent of narrated events. At the same time, God also speaks through the Bible and interprets me by placing my character within the singular plot running from creation to final judgment.

The formal structure of reciprocal interpretation is the same when interpreters turn to the Book of Nature, rather than the Bible, to decipher the intelligible structure of the universe: in construing the God of nature, the interpreter is at once the interpreted. How so? In contemplating the structure of nature, I form the idea of God by tracing observed causal relations back to an unknowable but intuitable first cause, superlative and unique in being, identical with the good, the beautiful, and the true. The idea of God provides the eternal standard for thinking, acting, and feeling. As guide to the blessed life, however, the idea of God also interprets the interpreter by functioning as the unescapable norm for critical self-scrutiny for all rational agents. Interpretation of the divine is thus unsettling in both biblical and natural theology, for it engages the interpreter in a reciprocal activity of ultimate seriousness: it is both the action and the passion of the interpreter.

For modern critical thought, the question about the relationship between hermeneutics and the divine is unsettling in a different way. As heirs of a theological tradition, we *should* understand how hermeneutics relates to the divine, but we have lost the forms of language and existence that once immediately displayed the reciprocal relationship between I and God. How can we speak about theological meanings when we can no longer appeal biblically to an absolute subject of history or metaphysically to an absolute object of knowledge? We have long lived with radical historical criticism, which acknowledges that textual meanings (including those occurring in the Bible) and our own interpretive stances are historically conditioned.[1] Likewise, we take for granted the ineluctability of the hermeneutical circle as an element in the structure of understanding, an element that means that any sign presenting itself to understanding has always already been interpreted and thus conditioned through personal preunderstandings.[2] Surely these insights of modern hermeneutics demolish all pretense of understanding narrated meanings in the Bible or the structure of the natural world as manifestations of an absolute subject or object ("God").[3] The modern critical principle of knowing imposes a test of rigorous separation between subject and object, and this separation appears to break the reciprocity through which the absoluteness of the divine appeared.

In *The Symbolism of Evil,* Ricoeur suggests that by letting go what is lost, we can perhaps recover the sense of the divine in our language and existence in a second naïveté. Ricoeur acknowledges that "something has been lost, irremediably lost: immediacy of belief." Yet he claims that we can "aim at a second naiveté in and through criticism. In short, it is by interpreting that we can hear again."[4] Turning to the Bible in its textuality, Ricoeur gives new voice to the ancient name "God" through his many occasional writings on biblical narrative. My question is whether Ricoeur's proposal enables the inquirer merely as inquirer to be interpreted by the divine or whether his proposal reaches only as far as a predisposed confessing community, which has already decided on the biblical identity of the divine name. Is theological hermeneutics a special hermeneutics of the Bible, or can we also articulate a theological dimension of general hermeneutical theory as such? How do Ricoeur's writings answer this question?

It is true that Ricoeur has consistently focused his attention on the special hermeneutics of the Bible. That fact alone, however, does not rule out the possibility that theological hermeneutics is nonetheless more than biblical hermeneutics alone. Ricoeur's work on biblical hermeneutics fulfills the important task of making Christian faith more intelligible both for insiders and for outsiders. The claim of this paper is that Ricoeur himself has not fully worked out the theological implications of the hermeneutical activity as such. However, Ricoeur's hermeneutical theory provides resources for articulating the theological dimension of interpretation. In this paper, I shall try to work out one way of disclosing this possibility.

In his essay "Naming God," Ricoeur makes an interesting suggestion, which he himself does not carry out, concerning the hermeneutical act of naming God that could be developed for this purpose. Briefly, Ricoeur claims that something in the name God, precisely as a name, overturns particular intentional acts of interpretation, opens the mind to what is other than itself or its world, and discloses theological meaning.[5] I understand this claim to imply that the biblical naming of God can itself reveal the necessary bridge between theological hermeneutics construed as biblical hermeneutics and theological hermeneutics more universally conceived. The enactment of the biblical name of God signals the self-transcending of a special theological hermeneutics toward a universal theological hermeneutics.

In this paper, I pick up on Ricoeur's suggestion, which Ricoeur allows to lie dormant through his decision to develop theological hermeneutics more or less exclusively as biblical hermeneutics. In so doing, I shall follow the systematic structure of Ricoeur's thought rather than his self-restriction to biblical texts. The possibility I develop here is thus consistent with the intentions of Ricoeur's own hermeneutical theory. I shall explore the divine name as it is given positively in the Bible against the horizon of intelligibility itself to show how it can give rise to a theological form of reflexivity that outflanks the old division between biblical and natural theology without falling back into a form of ontotheology. I hope to show that theological meaning discovered in the divine name necessarily breaks free of the biblical text in which it is inscribed and refigures itself in new acts of naming God. Moreover, by following the direction of meaning inherent in the name of God, we can recover the double sense in which interpretation of the divine name is both something I do and something I suffer.

Let me begin by identifying three moments in the dynamics of our interpretation of the divine name. The three moments are themselves hermeneutical constructs: three possible modes of reciprocally relating interpretation to the divine. These three moments correspond analogically to Ricoeur's analysis of threefold mimesis in *Time and Narrative.* As hermeneutical constructs, however, each moment possesses within itself the full threefold mimesis while displaying a predominance of one of the three mimetic elements. I shall trace a progression through these moments, focusing on the interactions within a coherent structure including these paired elements: first, the two countervailing subjects—the *I* or subject of human interpretative activity and the one divine subject named *God;* second, the interrelated fields of temporality in which human and divine subjects are manifest—*existence* and *language.*

I follow Ricoeur in relating these elements as follows: the I, as apodictic and inescapable atemporal origin point of thinking, willing, and feeling, is systematically elusive for reflection. The I, however, appears temporally as a phenomenon in language either directly (in saying "I") or indirectly (as implied author of meanings in language). In its temporal appearance in language, the I enters existence as a mode of being that is here. In saying or understanding the word *I,* the I exists here: saying the word *I* brings the subject into existence as what is, strictly speaking, *not*-I but an individual self here. All language that can be traced back to an I of utterance refers to a mode of existence as a possibility for the appearance of the I.

"Naming God" refers to the activity in which I utter the name God and thereby bring God into language and existence. The one named God remains systematically elusive for reflection, but appears as a word whose meaning is here in the temporal act of naming. Naming God in this sense is thus similar to using the pronoun I (as opposed to using a common noun or a proper name): it shows what one is talking about. Moreover, "naming God" is something I do: in the act of naming God, I am being named by God in that I appear here as absolutely dependent on and transformed by God—the infinite subject and ground of my being as an I that *is* here. The question is: Does the name God manifest the divine being only within the world of biblical texts, or is the name the trace of an absolute otherness that breaks out of the world of biblical texts to show itself in the act of interpretation itself?

SYMBOLIC MANIFESTATION

In "Manifestation and Proclamation," Ricoeur locates the first moment of interpreting the divine at the site of the hierophany: the enigmatic disclosure of the sacred on elements of the world—on the heavens, on the sun and moon, on the waters and vegetation, on mountains and caves.[6] I interpret the first moment as a preunderstanding of the divine, preceding the distinct linguistic articulation of the name.[7] I and God, existence and language tend not to be clearly distinct. All seem to converge on the religious symbol as the prefiguration of divine name.[8] According to Ricoeur, as a figure of discourse the religious symbol is deeply "bound" up with specific forms of ritual action (which I do), with the sacred time and place of manifestation (in existence and language), and with the superreal (*surréal*) power (of God) whose absence and presence appears on the concrete symbolic material.[9] Through this threefold adherence, the prefigured order of ritual action both articulates and is articulated by the divine through symbolic manifestation.

This first moment in the dynamics of the divine name is analogous to mimesis$_1$ as Ricoeur defines it in *Time and Narrative.*[10] To draw out this analogy, I focus first on the temporality involved in the manifestations of meaning in existence and language, and second on the form of the subject's appearance. In Ricoeur's analysis, mimesis$_1$ signifies a prefigured time of practical understanding. The mode of temporality is that of Heidegger's ordinary being-within-time (*Innerzeitigkeit*).[11] The form in which subjectivity appears is that of the facticity of everyday existence.[12] How are time and subjectivity shaped in the encounter with the divine within existence and language at this first moment? My claim, following Ricoeur's use of limit language, is that in religious contexts the mode of ordinary time and the form of everyday existence are driven to their limits, where they are heightened in meaning and doubled in structure.[13]

Ritual time is both the overturning of ordinary being-within-time and its intensification into sacred time. Sacred time is the other of profane time; yet by institutionalizing ritual action, humans incorporate it into the flow of ordinary temporal experience. Thus ordinary time both remains itself and becomes its Other—sacred time. Likewise, the interpreting subject doubles itself through symbolic manifestation. In ritual action, the subject belongs to the event, and is not clearly distinct from the appearing symbol.[14] The agent in ritual both remains identical with itself and identifies ecstatically with the agency disclosed through the symbol. I turn now to the second moment in the dynamics of divine name.

SACRED SCRIPTURE

Ricoeur locates the second moment in the dynamics of interpreting the divine name at the site of the text. According to Ricoeur, Judaism, Christianity, and Islam break with the hermeneutics of symbolic manifestation in emphasizing the authoritative text proclaimed as the Word of God.[15] With this moment, the divine actualizes itself as logos freed from adherence to the sacred cosmos. Moreover, the four elements in the interpretive structure reach different configuration: a distinction in principle emerges between existence and language, on one hand, and between saying I and naming God, on the other hand.

How do we account for the movement from symbolic manifestation to sacred scripture? Ricoeur leaves this question open, but the divine name suggests an answer: An infinite power of negation resident in the divine name prefigured as sacred symbol drives the movement from cosmic hierophany to Word of God. The symbol both manifests the divine (it is the existence of God in time) and conceals the divine (God is other than the symbol). The power of negativity is the power of the name God to differentiate its manifest meaning from the material of the symbol. We see this power in the difference between the particular cosmic sign and the self-manifesting universal meaning of the symbol: the meaning of the divine is always *more* than the concrete symbol as signifier can show. That is why the symbol infinitely gives rise to thought.[16]

When the divine name appears as text, the tension between the concrete element of the religious symbol and the divine power symbolized in it becomes serious. The Word is precisely the otherness of worldly things taken as concrete symbols: Language is the negation of perception. The negation involved, however, is what Hegel calls determinate negation.[17] In overturning the form of symbolic manifestation, the Word of God preserves some of its substance. Numinosity and the structure of self-manifestation, for example, are transferred from the natural symbol to the Holy Writ.

With the divine name configured as sacred scripture, we reach the analogue of mimesis$_2$. According to Ricoeur, mimesis$_2$ marks the passage from the prefigured order of action to the textual configuration of narrative structure.[18] Mimesis$_2$ enjoins the temporal mode of historicality (*Geschichtlichkeit*), for this mode of timing appears through the emplotment of discrete events into a whole. The biblical narrative conforms to this pattern by bringing together discordant episodes into a whole.

Most of Ricoeur's work in religious and theological hermeneutics falls under this second moment of interpreting sacred scripture. Treating the Bible as an autonomous poetic work, Ricoeur analyzes a variety of discursive forms to show how they function metaphorically to project possible worlds of the text.[19] The divine name serves as "the coordinator of these various discourses," but not by subsuming them under an ontological concept or by supplying a single image. The name God unifies the biblical texts by designating the final agent of the single act of deliverance differently configured in these discourses.[20] The hidden God actualizes its being in the various namings of God as the unique God, whose name can be shared by no other. According to Ricoeur, "It is the naming of God by the biblical texts that specifies the religious at the interior of the poetic."[21] Ricoeur analyzes textual forms from both testaments to exhibit the religious function of the divine name. The textual forms name God differently in that each one temporalizes time differently in the act of naming the unnameable subject revealed and concealed in biblical texts.

According to Ricoeur, Old Testament texts name God differently in narrative, prescriptive, hymnic, prophetic, and wisdom discourses. Narrative discourse names God in the third-person past tense as an actor in founding events for a community. Prophetic discourse names God in the first-person future tense as the voice behind the prophet. Prescriptive discourse names God as righteous giver of the law who demands holiness. Wisdom discourse names God as hidden preexistent wisdom, who addresses those who ask about the meaning of existence. Hymnic discourse names God in the second-person present tense, as one who may respond to praise, supplication, and thanksgiving.

Likewise, New Testament texts deploy different forms of discourse to announce Jesus as parable of God: Ricoeur analyzes the discourse of parable, eschatological saying, proverb, gospel, epistle, liturgical formula, and so on. The many modes of discourse display similar textual strategies to refer the reader to Jesus construed as embodiment of the divine name. Techniques of paradox, intensification, and extravagance function to overturn ordinary reference to possible modes of being. Through the incarnate name, the discourses converge on the approach of new being, the impossible mode of being made possible through the one Jesus names father.

Taken together, the biblical texts show the capacity to name God through the diverse temporal forms of the text. The name God functions as a limit expression within each of the temporal forms, such that God is named in time and yet time is assigned to God. We see this overturning and intensifying of time in mimesis$_2$, in that the Bible is figured both as the history of a people and as divine salvation history.

The I or subject of interpretation is likewise doubly construed at the religious limit of mimesis$_2$. The I of the reader in principle detaches itself from the prefigured order of action and is textually configured within the plot in alienated forms. For example, the true I is biblically configured in some New Testament texts as the Christ. It is a doubled I, however. The I inscribed in the text as the Christ is both the estranged I of the reader/hearer (I find myself in the Christ) and also the estranged I of the divine Word itself (my true I is assigned to the Word of God as Christ).

While the biblical naming of God is the unifying figure for the diversity of biblical texts, it is evident that one named God eludes any single act of naming or any set of acts. The name God in the Bible, like the cosmic symbol that prefigured it, does manifest a reality. But the reality it manifests also remains unmanifest through the name, wholly Other. This recognition marks the transition to the third moment in the self-manifestation of the divine name.

DIVINE NEGATION

Ricoeur does not himself isolate a third moment in the dynamics of the divine name. But he does say that "the referent 'God' is not just the index of the mutual belonging together (*appartenance*) of the originary forms of the discourse of faith. It is also the index of their incompleteness. It is their common goal, which escapes each of them."[22] I want to explore the dimension of meaning in the divine name that escapes even its unifying function. By isolating this dimension, I locate interpretation at the site of divine negation.

With this step, the power of negativity residing in the divine name manifests itself more fully: the divine name negates its connection with any symbol or textual name.[23] The name of God may initially reveal itself as a self-transcending name in the Bible. But once the name God has a standing in common discourse, it frees theological meaning from its adherence to the biblical text and frees it for disclosure in universal structures of existence.[24] Once again, the pattern is determinate negation that both cancels and preserves the antecedent biblical meanings. With the third moment, the paired elements I and God on one side and existence and language on the other side once again converge, but without erasing recognition of their differences.

The third moment in the dynamics of the divine name is the analogue of mimesis$_3$, the moment of reading as appropriation.[25] According to Ricoeur, mimesis$_3$ testifies to the impossibility of locating meaning solely in the internal structures of the text. As the world of the text intersects with the world of the reader, meaning is returned to the soil of lived existence. How are the forms of time and subjectivity transformed through mimesis$_3$?

According to Ricoeur, the act of appropriating meaning actualizes *Zeitlichkeit* as my own temporalizing of coming to be, having been, and making present. The I as subject of appropriation recovers itself from textual estrangement by accepting its own responsibility for the temporalizing of time. Because self-recovery of one's being in time is never complete, never perfect, always in medias res, mimesis$_3$ confronts us with what Gadamer calls the negativity of hermeneutical experience: the experience of human finitude in existence and language. According to Gadamer, to experience in the genuine sense is to recognize that one is not master of time and of the future.[26]

With the third moment we also find an extraordinary doubling in the domain of subjectivity. As the I appropriates the divine negativity found on the name, the theological meaning disclosed there appropriates the I in the truth of its own negativity. The felt negativity of hermeneutical experience correlates with the negativity found on the divine name: both are interpretations of the divine. In thinking the name God in its negativity, I am thinking my own negativity as God's thinking of me. To fill out this claim, I must refer to the role of feeling in Ricoeur's figural ontology.[27]

Under Ricoeur's analysis, feeling is the locus of both an intentional act aimed at something exterior to the self and an inward affection of the self by its own mode of belongingness to beings and being through desire and love.[28] By means of feeling, action and passion can converge. In authentic feeling, I set the divine at a distance and the divine reaches me. What are the feelings accompanying interpretations of the divine name? To answer this, I follow Ricoeur's frequent allusions to Kant's third *Critique:* Intensified feelings of the *beautiful* and *sublime* accompany the first two moments in the dynamics of the divine name.[29]

According to Kant, in judging a representation as beautiful, I articulate a felt state of harmony between imagination and understanding. The feeling of the beautiful is associated with the pleasure that arises in the act of judging a singular representation: "This rose is beautiful." The feeling of pleasure mediates the form of the given representation with an emergent harmonious play between the cognitive faculties of imagination and understanding: the image seeks a concept, but none can satisfy the mind's interest in the image. Pleasure in the beautiful sustains peaceful contemplation of meanings hovering between image and thought.[30]

Let us depart now from Kant, but think analogously to the reflective judgment of the beautiful in the direction of Ricoeur. In the case of the symbolic manifestation of the divine name, I judge a representation as holy. In making the judgment, the feeling of pleasure in the beautiful is driven to its religious limit. The religious symbol arouses infinite delight in the power and meaning displayed in the living cosmos.[31]

According to Kant, in judging a representation as sublime, I articulate the mind's inability to form an image or to find a concept for presentations of the pure ideas of reason. Sublime presentations strike us as absolutely great or powerful. To say that a mountain or a moral act is sublime is to articulate the feeling accompanying a manifestation of the hidden unifying principle of nature in its majesty.[32] A feeling of pain initially arises from the discord and subsequently resolves itself into a negative pleasure in a higher correspondence between the inadequacy of any image or concept to present the unity of things and the unity itself.[33]

Departing again from Kant by means of Ricoeur, in the case of the biblical narrative I analogously judge the biblical narrative as sacred. Making this judgment drives the feeling of the sublime to its religious limit. For Kant the ideas of reason are purely formal. The Bible adds content in naming God as both giver of a just law for human freedom and the final agent in redeeming human weakness. The biblical naming of God also presents a heightening of meaning in both subjectivity and temporality: I am subject both to autonomous law and to God's redemptive activity. I interpret the text, yet am interpreted by the text as both guilty and forgiven. Ricoeur makes this clear when he says that, "The word 'God' says more than the word 'Being,' because it presupposes the entire context of narratives, prophecies, laws, wisdom writings, psalms, and so on."[34] Through the taking up of specific forms and material of discourse, the name God in the Bible approaches the reader through feelings evoked by metaphorical projection.

In the Bible, God is named in various modes of discourse, but they name God differently. The clash among acts of naming God cannot be resolved by forming a single image of the one named. The productive imagination cannot synthesize the episodes of divine naming as it can synthesize the acts of naming one's friend. By naming God variously, the biblical texts point to a reality that both unifies and eludes any and all of the modes of naming. The name God overturns the naming of God, while nonetheless naming God as the unnameable.

Taken together, the various acts of naming God name God as not the God named in any individual act. The name God overturns or defeats the poetic imagination in act and thus refers it to the infinite background against which it projects meaning. In this way, the name God makes present the unnameable limit of the imagination: the meaning and the reality of the name God converge. The name God does not fail to name; the name manifests the reality named. How so? The acts of naming God are taken up into the infinite background of naming, which assumes presence when named. This unnameable presence, linked to the name God, reverses the direction of naming to interpret my existence as reader or hearer. The intensified feeling of the sublime is not yet the feeling accompanying the moment of divine negation, however. To approach the third moment, I must go beyond Kant and turn to Schleiermacher and the feeling of *absolute dependence.*

Under Schleiermacher's analysis, the feeling of absolute dependence is itself the determinate negation of the feeling of the sublime.[35] How so? For Schleiermacher, self-consciousness includes felt awareness of the interaction between the feeling of freedom accompanying the self's activity and the feeling of dependence accompanying the self's receptivity.[36] To be human is to be an active mediator between these forms of action and passion. But according to Schleiermacher, one point in feeling transcends the act of mediating, opening the I to divine activity. The absolute moment does not occur in the feeling of freedom, for every conscious act has an intentional object that limits the subject.[37] However, the absolute moment does occur in the feeling of dependence. The feeling of absolute dependence occurs precisely in the realization of the impossibility of absolute freedom. The feeling of absolute dependence is the feeling of the sheer givenness of reason itself.[38] If the feeling of the sublime accompanies awareness of our rational destiny, the feeling of absolute dependence is its determinate negation. It is the feeling that the whole of our rational activity is dependent on an unnameable otherness.[39]

Schleiermacher names this otherness God: an otherness that strictly means no conceivable objective correlate at all. In so naming God, Schleiermacher follows the rhetoric of the divine name, whose own negative power leads hermeneutics from the unifying biblical name to divine nothingness as felt. The divine name breaks out of biblical language and breaks into human existence. In appropriating the divine name as divine negation, the textually estranged subjectivity comes back to itself through the infinite power of negation. In assenting to divine negation, I assent to the openness and finitude of my own being. This overcoming of estrangement through a divine letting go is both action and passion, will and grace. Appropriation of the divine name becomes appropriation by the divine name: the I suffers nothingness as beyond its control yet most deeply its own. Let me briefly connect the doubleness in interpreting the divine more generally with hermeneutics.

THE CROSS OF INTERPRETATION

We can picture the three moments in the hermeneutics of the divine as a kind of ascent from symbolic manifestation through sacred scripture to divine negation. At the pinnacle, however, the divine name dictates an enabling command for the inquirer to return, to descend through reflexive repetition back into the worlds of textual meaning and prefigured action. Schleiermacher was aware of this return, for he combines divine negation with the received meanings from the biblical text and its appropriation in the religious practices of the community. Following Ricoeur, we may construe the ascent as moving from the first naïveté to criticism and the descent as moving from criticism to the second naïveté. What is the necessity for this descent?

The answer is twofold: both hermeneutics and the divine name demand the descent. For Ricoeur, the hermeneutics of language and existence aims at self-understanding. Self-understanding demands something more than appropriation of the formal and empty "I think" against the background of divine nothingness. To reclaim the fullness of its being, the estranged self must mediate meanings through the works and acts that are signs of its own act of existing.[40] Moreover, the power of negativity in the name of God negates even its own self-negation, sending the interpreter back to its trace in language and existence. In so doing, the divine name names the interpreting I as heir of a tradition, whose theological meaning indwells the entire structure of interpretive activity.

In the descent, language and existence are transformed by theological meaning, for the divine name accompanies every act of interpretation, relativizing it. Every meaning is what it is and it is not that: The biblical text is and is not the Word of God; the natural symbol is and is not divine manifestation. Everything remains what it is, but is crossed out by the awareness of divine negativity.

With the return from divine negation, it is possible to name God anew. In this case, the divine name names both the interpretive act and the interpreted divine. I call that figure the cross of interpretation (see fig. 7). The cross of interpretation symbolizes the whole hermeneutical process through which the symbol gives rise to thought. And it provides criteria for judging relationships between hermeneutics and the divine. When divine negativity is felt in the negativity of hermeneutical experience, the cross of inter-

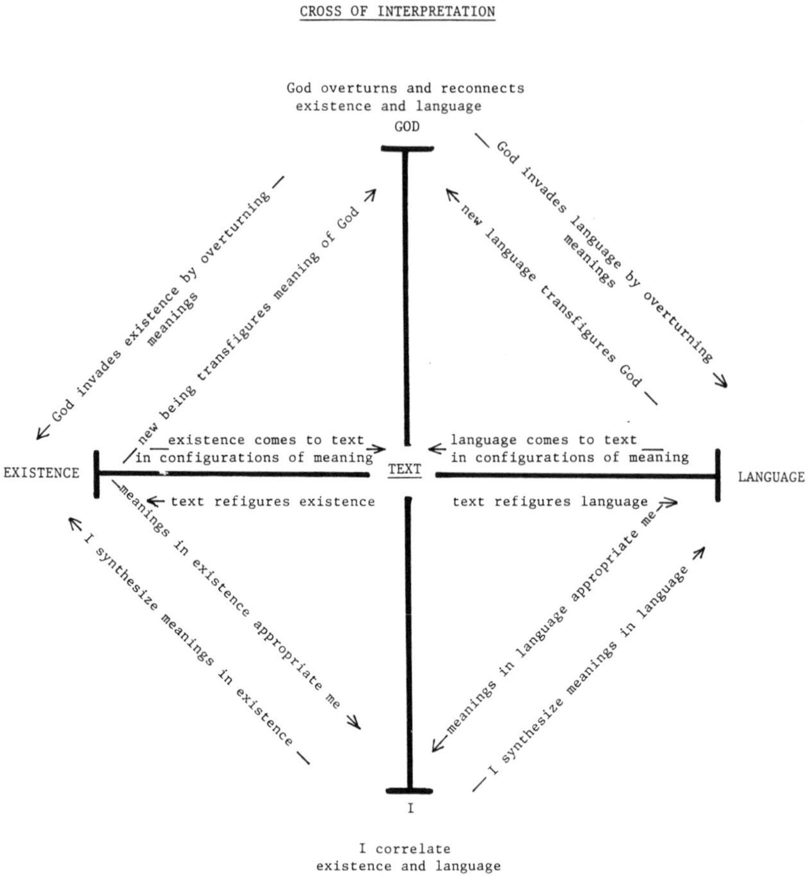

The Cross of Interpretation in Ricoeur's hermeneutics as constructed by David E. Klemm.

pretation becomes a symbol. It shows that the activity of interpreting the divine is itself a trace of the divine name.[41] It is an unusual symbol, because it is both reflexive and dynamic. Let me explain.

The cross of interpretation is reflexive in that the symbol symbolizes my thinking about the symbol. Its content is precisely the felt openness to what is other than thought. The cross of interpretation is both produced by the imagination for a universal community of interpreters and received historically through a particular community. The cross of interpretation is also dynamic, because it gathers together the different moments in the dynamics of the divine name. The symbol tells the story of the divine name by moving from its initial manifestation in the sacred cosmos to its inscription in sacred scripture to its breaking through textual forms, and finally to the openness of its hermeneutical destiny as unnameable name.

The divine breaks into the cross of interpretation where interpretive syntheses break down and reveal the dependence of the I on something other than itself. The divine also shows itself in the open horizon against which we discern meanings. Let me be clear. I am not asserting that failure or breakdown *is* divine, but that we discern the divine name when confronting hermeneutically the absolute dependence of our desire to be and effort to exist. For example, in the hermeneutics of existence, as Ricoeur spells it out in *Fallible Man*, the divine name shines through the structures of existence in the failures to perform theoretical, practical, and affective syntheses. In the hermeneutics of texts—as Ricoeur writes in *Interpretation Theory*, the *Rule of Metaphor*, and elsewhere—the divine name shines through linguistic structures in the breakdowns of literal predication, metaphorical predication, and the relations between parts and whole. In the reciprocity between time and narrative, the divine name shines through temporal structures in the aporia of temporality and in the ultimate inability for narrative to heal those aporia. Breaks and failures of interpretation not only enable the divine to shine through, they prompt new meanings, which arise from the ashes of the old.

Grounding the cross of interpretation is the feeling of faith seeking understanding in interpretive activity, the faith of the second naïveté. This is faith that the ultimate inability to name God nonetheless names God when we understand and affirm that inability in response to the divine name. It is a faith conferred by the name of God, which names us as the ones ever striving and ever failing to name God. This faith is twofold: it trusts that the movement of the self-transcending name of God leads us to insight and not to nothing; it accepts the openness of hermeneutical inquiry as a gift of the divine name.

Ricoeur's hermeneutics enables us to see that the cross of interpretation is the final site of human action and passion. The cross is the place of the human struggle to discern theological meaning in the divine name and the place of divine struggle to reveal human meaning in the divine naming. Our lives are such that we suffer the cross: it is ours actively to bear. Yet the divine life is such that

God's name is inscribed on the cross: this name suffers our actions and transforms them. The cross of interpretation, inscribed with the divine name, enacts the double genitive in the relationship between hermeneutics and the divine: it bespeaks our interpretation of the divine and the divine interpretation of us.

NOTES

1. Hans-Georg Gadamer, "The Problem of Historical Consciousness," *Graduate Faculty Journal of the New School of Social Research* 5 (1975): 2–51.
2. See Martin Heidegger, *Sein und Zeit,* 12th ed. (Tübingen: Max Niemeyer, 1972), paragraphs 31–33.
3. Ricoeur writes, "This double renouncing of the absolute 'object' and the absolute 'subject' is the price that must be paid to enter into a radically non-speculative and pre-philosophical mode of language" ("Naming God," *Union Seminary Quarterly Review* 34 [1979]: 220.
4. Paul Ricoeur, *The Symbolism of Evil,* trans. Emerson Buchanan (New York: Harper and Row, 1967), p. 351.
5. In "Naming God" Ricoeur asserts that biblical texts do have both sense and reference, that there is a unified reference among the many biblical modes of discourse, and that the reference is disclosed in the act of naming God (see "Naming God," p. 217).
6. Ricoeur cites and builds on the achievements of Mircea Eliade, Gerardus Van der Leeuw, Rudolf Otto, and other phenomenologists of the sacred in setting forth his theory of religious symbols. (See "Manifestation and Proclamation," *Blaisdell Institute Journal* 12 [Winter 1978]: 13–21. See also Ricoeur, *The Symbolism of Evil,* pp. 3–24; Ricoeur, *Interpretation Theory: Discourse and the Surplus of Meaning* (Fort Worth: Texas Christian Press, 1976), pp. 53–69.
7. Ricoeur himself likens the hierophany to "the condensation of an infinite discourse" in which "manifestation and meaning are strictly contemporaneous and reciprocal" (*Symbolism of Evil,* p. 11).
8. Ricoeur articulates the semantic structure of the religious symbol as a double-meaning expression: "Symbolic signs are opaque, because the first, literal, obvious meaning itself points analogically to a second meaning which is not given otherwise than in it" (*Symbolism of Evil,* p. 15).
9. "Manifestation and Proclamation," p. 15. Cf. Ricoeur's statement: "Symbols have roots. Symbols plunge us into the shadowy experience of power" (Ricoeur, *Interpretation Theory,* p. 69; see also p. 58.
10. Paul Ricoeur, *Time and Narrative,* vol. 1, trans. Kathleen McLaughlin and David Pellauer (Chicago: University of Chicago Press, 1984), pp. 54–64.
11. Martin Heidegger, *Sein und Zeit,* 6th ed. (Tübingen: Max Niemeyer, 1970), par. 78–83.
12. In agreement with Ricoeur's criticism of Heidegger, I am resisting the move to equate *Innerzeitigkeit* with inauthenticity. Hence I use the term *everyday or factic existence.* See part 2 of section 4 in *Time and Narrative,* volume 3 (1988).
13. Ricoeur's most basic formula for identifying the religious within the poetic or ordinary uses of language is that religious expressions are limit language. He writes, "this is not a supplementary form of discourse. . . . It is rather a question of an indication or a modification that undoubtedly affects every form of discourse through a sort of passing over to the limit. In this way, it constitutes a short summary of the naming of God" ("Naming God," p. 223). By speaking of a

religious limit disclosed in the moment of symbolic manifestation, I follow Ricoeur's claim against Heidegger that we can confront the primordial in ways other than resolute anticipation of death.

14. According to Ricoeur, "to manifest the 'sacred' *on* the 'cosmos' and to manifest it *in* the 'psyche' are the same thing" (*Symbolism of Evil*, p. 12).
15. Ricoeur, "Manifestation and Proclamation," p. 13.
16. See Ricoeur, "Manifestation and Proclamation," p. 15. See also Ricoeur, *Interpretation Theory*, p. 57.
17. See G. W. F. Hegel, *Phenomenology of Spirit*, 2 vols., trans. J. B. Baillie (New York: Macmillan 1910), and *The Logic of Hegel*, trans. William Wallace, 2d ed. (Oxford: Oxford University Press, 1982).
18. Ricoeur, *Time and Narrative*, 1:64–70.
19. For Ricoeur, the "autonomous work," is distanciated from the author's intentions, the shared world of interlocutors, and the original audience. Textual meaning must be worked out by explicit methods of interpretation.
20. Ricoeur, "Naming God," p. 222.
21. Ricoeur, "Naming God," p. 219.
22. Ricoeur, "Naming God," p. 222.
23. To be sure, Ricoeur acknowledges the self-transcending name of God. But he confines this linguistic self-transcendence to the dynamics of the biblical text, and he restricts theological hermeneutics to biblical hermeneutics.
24. Behind this interpretive move stand the theological projects of several thinkers. The most important, in reverse chronological order, are those of Robert P. Scharlemann, Thomas Altizer, Karl Rahner, Gerhard Ebeling, and, of course, both Schleiermacher and Hegel.
25. Ricoeur, *Time and Narrative*, 1:70–87.
26. Hans-Georg Gadamer, *Wahrheit und Methode*, 4th ed. (Tübingen: J. C. B. Mohr, 1975), pp. 338–442.
27. Ricoeur has often said that his theory of metaphorical reference has an ontological bearing. Through metaphor and narrative, I understand a world I might inhabit and into which I project my ownmost powers. To see the world as open to new meaning is an increase in possible being. Being as possibility rests on the poetic power of "seeing as," but the poetic capacity to "see as" in turn rests on the power to "feel as" the meanings in texts and actions suggest. (Paul Ricoeur, "The Metaphorical Process as Cognition, Imagination, and Feeling," *Critical Inquiry* 5 (1978): 143–59.)
28. Paul Ricoeur, *Fallible Man*, pp. 127–33.
29. Ricoeur frequently refers to Kant's *Critique of Judgement* in discussing his view of symbol. "Le symbole donne à penser" refers to Kant's doctrine of the aesthetical presentation of the idea by the productive imagination. (Paul Ricoeur, "Manifestation and Proclamation," p. 15. Immanuel Kant, *Kritik der Urteilskraft*, par. 49.)
30. Kant, *Kritik der Urteilskraft*, Einleitung, VII, par. 9.
31. The religious symbol—for example, a sacred fire—combines an intuited form with a formless energy, a power of negativity, which threatens to consume its own structuring principle. Aesthetic pleasure and contemplation are heightened to religious desire and worship. (Compare *Kritik der Urteilskraft*, par. 22.)
32. Kant, *Kritik der Urteilskraft*, p. 169 (pars. 25, 28).
33. Ibid., pars. 23, 27.
34. Ricoeur, "Naming God," p. 222.
35. Schleiermacher breaks from Kant by means of Kantian analysis when he claims there is more at stake in feeling than Kantian feelings of the agreeable, beautiful, morally good, and sublime. I take this to be consistent with Ricoeur's own modification of Kantian faculty psychology in his philosophical anthropology in *Fallible Man*.

36. Friedrich Schleiermacher, *Der Christliche Glaube,* vol. 1, ed. M. Redeker (Berlin: DeGruyter: 1960), pp. 24–27, par 4.1–4.2.
37. Ibid., 1:27, par. 4.3.
38. See Konrad Cramer, "Die Subjektivitätstheoretischen Prämissen von Schleiermachers Bestimmung des religiosen Bewußtseins," in *Friedrich Schleiermacher, 1768–1834: Theologe, Philosoph, Padägoge,* ed. Dietz Lange (Göttingen: Vanderhoeck & Ruprecht, 1985), pp. 129–65.
39. Schleiermacher, *Der Christliche Glaube,* 1:28, par. 4.3.
40. See Paul Ricoeur, "Existence and Hermeneutics," trans. Kathleen McLaughlin in *The Conflict of Interpretations: Essays in Hermeneutics,* ed. Don Ihde (Evanston, Ill.: Northwestern University Press, 1974), p. 17.
41. See Hans-Georg Gadamer, *Wahrheit und Methode,* 4th ed. (Tübingen: J. C. B. Mohr, 1975), pp. 338–442.

PART IV

CONCLUDING REFLECTIONS

DAVID E. KLEMM

INDIVIDUALITY
The Principle of Ricoeur's Mediating Philosophy and Its Bearing on Theology of Culture

A MEDIATING PHILOSOPHY—that is how Paul Ricoeur describes his thought in its development over the years.[1] The essays in this volume confirm the insight: in questioning Paul Ricoeur, each author focuses on at least one of Ricoeur's problems of mediation. For example, in raising fundamental issues in interpretation (part I), Robert Scharlemann deals in part with the possibility of making and encountering poetic mediations between lived time (psychological time) and objectively measured time (cosmic time) in his discussion of textuality. Gerald Bruns also concentrates on mediations in language, specifically those between philosophy and poetry (logos and mythos): Are they poetic or philosophical in character?

In the essays on history and narrativity (part 2), Hans Kellner, André Gaudreault, Philip Rosen, and Michèle Lagny, focus in part on mediations between historical and fictive narratives. Dudley Andrew considers mediations between the organic and intellectual functions of reason as well as between private and public meanings. John Van Den Hengel reflects on mediations between the Jesus of history and the Christ of faith within the context of time and narrative.

In the essays on the nature of existence and the being of God (part III), Bernard Dauenhauer and Fred Dallmayr focus on the possibilities for political mediations between ethics and economics, reason and power, polity and policy. Pamela Anderson analyzes the mythico-poetic resources for ethical mediations between personal identity and communal identity. William Schweiker takes up the question of the relation between ethical mediations between duty and happiness and theological mediations between the idea of the Good and a word spoken to me. Religious and theological mediations between universal and particular presentations of the divine are further explored in the essays by Herman Rapaport (with regard to mediating between universal originating affirmation and particular historical testimony, subject and sign), Mark Wallace (with regard to mediating between general poetic revelation and the specific revelation of God in the Bible), and David Klemm (with regard to mediating between the universal meanings of the name God and particular acts of naming God).

Clearly Ricoeur's central questions are posed as questions of mediation. By *to mediate,* broadly speaking, Ricoeur means precisely the comprehending anew, through the rule-governed freedom of critical interpretation, what has already been given to experience and has already been comprehended unreflectively in a given language. Meanings in texts and actions are mediated unities, fragile yet resilient syntheses; they express and reflect the restless human desire to be and effort to exist. Individual meanings arise from the human will to grasp and receive an understanding of truth, goodness, and beauty in actual life, no matter how fragmentary and fleeting the insight might be.

As fragile mediated unities, meanings express what Ricoeur calls the "*pathétique* of 'misery' ": Human beings live their lives in the midst of disproportionate contraries. Figuratively speaking, humans stand between the infinite cosmos and the finite earth. The *pathétique* of misery stems not merely from the human position as intermediary in the world, however, but from the fact that the human is "intermediate within himself, within his *selves,*" and must mediate between the disproportional sides of his own being, as a noncoincidence of the self with itself.[2] Human experience is stretched between infinite reason and finite sensibility—between an open universality, which can appear contrariwise either as the ordering ground of being or as the threatening fixed structure of fate, and a given particularity, which can likewise appear either as source of concrete vitality or as the merely transitory and ever disappointing.

"Fallible man" brings about fallible meanings. As the essays in this volume attest, meanings in texts and actions, whether highly particularized interpretations or articulations of universal ontological structures, are disputable and thus vulnerable. Myths, once solid and strong as the positive basis of certain cultures, often lie broken and helpless, discarded by fallible man for lack of market value. Critical discourse, once the beacon of hope for enlightenment and freedom, strikes many as the villain itself, tool of Western imperialism. What are the grounds for hope, given the fragility of all things mediated?

Ricoeur's answer is that the basis for hope is given in the first principle grounding all mediating activity. Interpretive activity makes manifest the ground of human hope, the basis of both human freedom and belongingness to nature. Meanings in texts and actions are never merely futile cries in the night, because even the cry of futility displays the ground of hope. What is the first principle of interpretive activity and how does it appear in cultural life, generally speaking? Herein we broach Ricoeur's possible contribution to theology of culture.

The first principle of Ricoeur's hermeneutical thought can best be expressed as *the principle of individuality.* It is given clear philosophical articulation by Schleiermacher in his lectures on dialectic in ways that are particularly striking for their correspondence with Ricoeur's thought. Readers of Ricoeur know that in his rehabilitation of text-based hermeneutical theory, Ricoeur is in a significant sense the Schleiermacher of our time.[3] But in addition, through his engagements in dialogue and dispute, Ricoeur revives in practice the Platonic art of dialectic, so assiduously studied by Schleiermacher. Schleiermacher provides the modern theory of dialectic as a "presentation of the principles of leading an artful conversation in the domain of pure thinking."[4] Ricoeur, whether influenced directly by Schleiermacher or not, appropriates the same set of principles. Dialectic, for Schleiermacher, is essentially a search for the universal principles and conditions under which differences between disputing voices in dialogue are brought to their unity in knowing. Dialectic is a conversation about conversation to show in principle how disagreement can be overcome by referring both parties of a formal dispute to the lawfulness of knowing, expressed as the "truth." As such, dialectic is a knowing about knowing, or a *Wissenschaftslehre* (science of knowledge).[5] It provides the theoretical basis for all other sciences, including hermeneutics. My claim in this conclusion is that to grasp

Schleiermacher's formulation of the first principle will aid us in understanding Ricoeur.

Recall that prior to Ricoeur, Schleiermacher himself accomplished something like a "post-Hegelian Kantianism." How so? Schleiermacher positioned himself between the critical philosophy of Kant and the absolute idealism of Hegel precisely in his presentation and defense of *individuality* as a first principle enabling dialectical mediations between thinking and being.[6] Let me explain.

Kant, in *The Critique of Pure Reason,* showed that human knowledge is a synthesis of a manifold of sensible intuitions (*Anschauungen*) by means of a concept (*Begriff*). Human knowledge brings together sensible content with intellectual form. Human knowledge thus implies a formal (or ideal) principle of abstract universality and a material (or real) principle of concrete particularity, both of which are applied in every case of knowing. If so, under what principle can we know about knowing? In what sense, if any, do we know the unity of the formal and material elements of knowing, apart from any specific case of knowing involving any specific empirical content or psychological circumstances? The question about the ground of knowing is a question about self-knowledge, for I am the origin point, the principle, of both conceiving and intuiting, thinking and perceiving. As the agent whose act of knowing synthesizes the ideal and the real, I am the ground of knowing. Knowing about knowing is knowing the I. Is self-knowledge possible, however?

According to Kant, we have no knowledge, strictly speaking, of the unity of the self. The self is a pure idea, a necessary thought without possible exhibition in sensible intuition. Moreover, Kant denied that human beings are capable of an "intellectual intuition" of the unity of the self, a nonsensible seeing of the unifying principle itself. We must presuppose the unity of the self; but we cannot know it, because the unity of the self cannot appear through the forms of intuition (space and time). The first principle of knowing is unknowable because unintuitable. Kant's critique thus displays the finitude of human knowing with respect to the first principle. It highlights the difference between the formal requirements for knowing (synthesis of intellectual form and sensible content) and the first principle of knowing (the unity of intellectual form and sensible content), while demonstrating the formal necessity of presupposing the unknowable unity. This claim is the basis for the charge that Kant's transcendental idealism leaves reality bifurcated between thinking (categories of the understanding), and being (intuitions of objects in time and space) and thus cannot in the end explain the fact of knowing.

Hegel, by contrast, appropriates Fichte's claim in the *Science of Knowledge* (1794) that human beings do possess knowledge of the self as I and thus of the first principle of the unity of the ideal and the real. Fichte claimed that the ground of all knowing is the being of a subject that posits itself unconditionally as being self-posited.[7] Unconditional positing is the being of the I: the I is an act of unconditional self-positing that is also the accomplished deed of having been self-posited. Moreover, the I is given to human knowledge through a paradigmatic intellectual intuition, which makes possible every particular instance of knowledge in experience.

According to both Fichte and Hegel, in presenting to mind the synthesizing activity itself, in thinking about thinking, the self produces an intuition of I through which the unity of the self's being appears under conditions of time and space. The self knows the first principle of knowing, the principle of unity, because the self as subject is always already a unity of positing (formal thinking) and something posited (being as given in phenomenal appearance), and the self knows itself as subject. This claim is the basis for the charge that the speculative idealism of Fichte and Hegel too easily unifies reality and thus cannot account for the difference between sensible content and intellectual form (Does the I produce the sensible content?).

Schleiermacher stands with Kant, Fichte, and Hegel in regard to his human cognition of the first principle of the unity of knowing. Schleiermacher conceives of the self as a structural unity composed of principles of universal subjectivity (the necessary source of intellectual functions), particular personality (source of organic functions such as sensation and emotion), and a unifying principle (source of determinate individuality), which grounds actual syntheses of subject and person, intellectual form and organic content, thinking and being, the ideal and the real.[8] Schleiermacher likewise holds that in "immediate self-consciousness," humans do have an original "intuition" of the primordial principle of the unifying activity, an intuition that makes possible any actual cognitive synthesis.[9] Concerning this primordial intuition, Schleiermacher stands between Kant on the one hand and Fichte and Hegel on the other hand. Schleiermacher claims less than the absolute idealist position, for Schleiermacher claims that the intuition of the self is not purely an *intellectual* intuition, self-produced in thought when thought thinks itself, as it is for Fichte and Hegel. But Schleiermacher's notion of intuition claims more than the critical philosophy, for the intuition of the self is not merely an idea of pure reason. In distinction from Kant and Hegel, Schleiermacher's notion of intuition is determined by the *principle of individuality,* the principle of the *unity* of the intelligible and the sensible (universal and particular) as this unity *appears* to the self through the unifying unity of the intellectual and organic functions of reason.

Intuition for Schleiermacher is an individual "thought-thing" (*Gedankending*), neither purely intelligible nor purely sensible, but a mediated unity of both intellectual and sensible components. "Intuition" of the self is Schleiermacher's term for the cognitive awareness of the ground that makes any object of knowing possible but cannot itself be a temporal-spatial object of knowing. More importantly for the study of Ricoeur, intuition for Schleiermacher refers to the capacity of *language* to bring the universality of thought and the particularity of reality together into a knowable individual unity.[10] The word is itself a unity of thought and thing, and words that disclose the synthesizing power of words enable the intuition in question. Words about words disclose something nonarbitrary about the ground of all finite knowing, i.e., the unity of the self, for the word and the self share the structure of individually combining intellectual and sensible elements. Nonetheless, the self as the ground of knowing remains transcendent to the participants in actual conversations under conditions of time and space.[11]

According to Schleiermacher, language as "thought-thing" lets us "see" or understand the meaning of being a self as a unifying unity. How so? Robert P. Scharlemann has brought clarity to this point independently of Schleiermacher, but in such a way that it enables us better to interpret Schleiermacher. Scharlemann points out the instantiating power of certain words and thus makes evident what Schleiermacher means by an "intuition."[12] According to Scharlemann, in understanding what is meant when someone says the word *I,* one intuits the being of the self as a finite unifying of thought and perception. The being of the self only *is* as the word *I* is understood; the understood word *I* allows the being of the self to appear.

The being of God, the absolute identity of thinking and being, is similarly intuited through language, even as language. For

Schleiermacher, genuine dispute presupposes the absolute identity of thinking and being as source and goal of knowing beyond dispute. The idea of an *Urwissen* (the original knowledge presupposed by dispute) functions for Schleiermacher as a *regulative idea* for thinking and willing in the Kantian sense: it serves as a limit concept to confine human knowledge to possible experience and its necessary conditions. At the same time, however, in a more Platonic than Kantian sense, the intuited absolute identity of thinking and being functions as a *revealed symbol* of the source of constructive human reason, a source that is sought for and desired by all human intentional activities as their ultimate transcendent ground and goal.[13]

Again, Scharlemann's analysis of instantiating words can assist us in interpretation: The word *God* allows us to intuit the being of God, for when someone understands the meaning of the word *God,* the word itself manifests the being that is neither any subject, nor any object, but the absolute ground of the possibility of every thing, hence not nothing either.[14] Such seeing is always, for Schleiermacher, structured through the principle of individuality: we intuit the being of the self and the being of God only in understanding the universal meanings that appear in unity with particular words given in particular historical languages.

My claim in this essay is that Ricoeur's thought is thoroughly consistent with the principle of individuality as analyzed by Schleiermacher. Consequently, Ricoeur accomplishes many things, including these: (1) Ricoeur deepens Schleiermacher's insight into the nature of *language* as the concrete medium making possible intuitions of the self and God in their individuality; (2) Ricoeur extends the analysis of language to include its *metaphorical function* of creating new meaning through dialectical criticism of the old; and (3) Ricoeur develops a *narrative theory* showing how this form of language mediates between time and eternity to grant and receive meaning in human existence. These are significant achievements. I want briefly to review them with regard to their first principle and to show how Ricoeur might contribute thereby to theology of culture by establishing rules for a new intuition of the self and God through narrative literature.

1. For both Ricoeur and Schleiermacher, language is the medium in which principles of universal subjectivity and particular being are brought together and distinguished in their unity. Language is the domain of mediated unity between freedom and nature, eth-

ics and physics. The very nature of language is to be the individualizing individual. Language individualizes all thought and being; as "thought-thing" (*Gedankending*), it is itself individual. Its first principle is the principle of individuality.[15] Ricoeur's theory of the text as discourse fixed as writing extends Schleiermacher's hermeneutics by showing the semantic autonomy of the text as an individual with a meaning and intention distinct from authorial intention.[16]

2. Ricoeur shows how the metaphoric process underlying all language is a figural shaping of possible being through the power of creative imagination. Metaphoric creation of new meaning occurs through the semantic tension between opposing interpretations of a single sentence. The imagination works through the tension between opposites to create a new image on the basis of a mediating resemblance. In the clash, the individualizing capacity of language makes possible a new meaning, refiguring being. Living metaphors are reflexive and point to the individualizing activity of language itself. Metaphor discloses possible modes of being human, by bringing to light individual ways of connecting thought and being. Metaphor refers to *being-as*, which is grasped and received beyond the opposition of being and nonbeing.[17]

   In its disclosure of the individuality of meaning, and in the productive capacity of individual meaning to comprehend anew the unifying unity of one's own human being as mediator, the working of metaphor allows us to "intuit" (in Schleiermacher's sense) the nature of human being, according to Ricoeur. But according to Ricoeur, individualized meanings of given sentences are always fragile mediations, imperfectly grasped due to the linguisticality of all thinking and experiencing. Understanding, mediated through discursive judgment, is always something less than absolute knowing.

3. Schleiermacher, of course, already understood the temporality of human being through his linguistic intuition of the temporal act underlying all mediations, and Heidegger analyzed the existential structure of the human being that I am in terms of its temporal meaning. Ricoeur, however, makes a major and original contribution by correlating such phenomenological analyses with a thoroughgoing theory of narrative discourse. Ricoeur's theory of narrative makes explicit the correlation between time and language: "Time becomes human time to the extent that it is organized after the manner of a narrative; narrative, in turn, is

meaningful to the extent that it portrays the features of temporal existence."[18] According to Ricoeur, narrative expresses human temporality and presents the nature and meaning of being in time for individual intuition and interpretation.

Narratival portrayals of temporal experience reply both to the abstract unknowability of the universal form of time and to the concreteness of particular discordant temporal incidents and actions. The narrative mediates between the opposites by making unity out of diversity. The mediated unity is neither an abstract generic unity nor one more particular occurrence in time. The narrative combines particular episodes into a whole through the act of emplotment. The plot unifies and synthesizes the manifold of episodes without either sacrificing the particulars to an abstract universal or allowing the particulars to escape their accountability to the presupposed idea of unity.

In its emplotment, the narrative is an individual. The plot unifies (while preserving the distinction between) the universal and the particular, the ideal and the real, by bringing discordant events together into a single story oriented toward a concrete "end" through which a universal meaning presents itself. Moreover, the plot unifies universal and particular in a medium different from the conceptual medium of universality or the sensible medium of particularity, but a unified composite of both: the word.

Ricoeur's narrative theory gives analytic precision to our interpretations of human temporality, which cannot be known as an object as such, but which comes to language as narrative. Reflection on narrative manifests the *social dimension* of human being in time: narratives mediate not only between discordant dimensions of individual life but also when read or told as shared stories, between individuals within a community as well as between communities. Moreover, reflection on narrative discloses the *ethical* orientation of human being in time toward the good: when read or told, narratives redescribe possibilities for human *action* within the community and thus raise questions about the proper purpose and means of action. In particular, Ricoeur's narrative theory shows with technical precision the concrete role of narrative in the formative act of becoming a self within a community. According to Ricoeur, the personal identity of the self is paradigmatically presented in narrative, for narrative embodies the same complex temporal structure as an actual self.

Autobiography plays a paradigmatic role in displaying the linguistic process of becoming a self. On the basis of the shared structure of individuality between language and self, the self can find and construct its personal identity in the individual "connectedness of a life" narrated in autobiography.[19] In telling the story of one's own life, one is at once author, narrator, personage, and reader of the narrative. I am I as the individual self in whom all my narratival voices converge.

With his conception of narratival identity, Ricoeur successfully mediates between, and offers a plausible alternative to, two competing figures of the self. On the one hand, Ricoeur considers the "exalted" subject as it appears in the philosophies of transcendental subjectivity associated with Descartes, Fichte, and Husserl. On the other hand, Ricoeur considers the "humiliated" subject as it appears in the rhetorics of illusional subjectivity associated with Nietzsche and his current followers in deconstruction.[20] Each of these figures is one-sided in that either the principle of universal subjectivity or the principle of particular personality is given privileged position and the other is subordinated to it.

According to Ricoeur, whose view is consistent with Schleiermacher, a theory of the self must account for both of these independent principles of experience and it must resist the temptation to reduce either one to the other. We must presuppose the unity of the opposing principles, but direct cognitive access to the unity is not possible under conditions of time and space. Nonetheless, precisely in the poetic mediation between the ideal and the real, the self understands and intuits the *unity* of the ideal and the real as the *meaning* of its own being. In this understood meaning or intuition, however, the self has only the ideal of the unity of its being, not the concrete reality. The self understands a meaning not yet fully appropriated, as an ideal not yet realized, therefore as a *task* to be completed in order for the ideal of the unity to become concretely real. The task is oriented toward the good in itself or God—the absolute ground or unity of thinking and being, conceived as source and goal of all mediating activity.

At this point, we see clearly the issue of theology of culture. According to Schleiermacher (and by virtue of their shared first principle, according to Ricoeur), immediate self-consciousness (as the awareness of the sheer identity of the ideal and the real in the finite structure of the self) presents an analogy to the sheer identity of the ideal and the real in the structure of the absolute ground—God.[21] Immediate self-consciousness is awareness of the *Nullpunkt*, the unifying unity of opposite elements, the essence of the self, and the integrated foundation of the mediating activities of the self from which "the temporal life" (*das zeitliche Leben*) arises. The mediating activities are determined by time, but in the unity of the *Nullpunkt*, time is negated.[22] The two are joined when the intuited negation of time in the *Nullpunkt* is mediated in time through language. No *concept* of God can define this unity, for it includes opposing elements that cannot be conceived together but can only be named as one through language: In reflecting on the feeling and intuition of the active element of the self's positing of itself as self-positing, the self grasps its *identity* with absolute unity of thinking and being; this element gives rise to the *speculative* relation to God. And in reflecting on the feeling and intuition of the passive element of the self's having been posited as self-positing by something entirely other than itself, the self grasps its absolute dependence on and *difference* from the absolute unity of thinking and being; this element gives rise to the *religious* relation to God.[23] Theological intuition as such must include both speculative and religious elements together in a unity.[24]

For Schleiermacher and Ricoeur alike, to name God is to invoke the principle of the absolute yet individual unity of the ideal and the real. In saying God, we present a linguistically mediated unity in time and space. In saying God, we affirm the necessity of the first principle of all finite thinking and being; and we affirm the impossibility that anything nameable can actually present the first principle. God, as the highest good, is, as Plato says, "the cause of knowledge and truth," "the source not only of the intelligibility of the objects of knowledge, but also of their being and reality; yet it is not itself that reality, but is beyond it, and superior to it in dignity and power."[25] God is therefore no thing we can mediate. Yet, as the source and goal of all mediating, God cannot be discounted as nothing either. On the grounds of their shared principle of individuality, Schleiermacher and Ricoeur agree about God: if God is the absolute unity of the self (finite unity of intellectual and organic functions) and the world (finite unity of reason and being), then *God is God as absolute individual.* God is God as absolute unity of universal subjectivity and given reality. God is God as the unity of abstract ideal and the concretely real. In principle, for both Schleiermacher and Ricoeur, God is the idea of what must appear as particular reality, and yet what cannot be identified with any particular reality. For both Schleiermacher and Ricoeur, the actual unity of universal and particular occurs in the word—language. God is God as the word God, yet the word *God* is not God.

By its nature "theology of culture" is a reflection on those works (or Schleiermacher's "thought-things") that disclose God in and through linguistically mediated unities of meaning and being. All three principles are necessary for theological analysis: a principle of the universality of thinking, a principle of the particularity of perceiving, and a principle of the unity of universality and particularity in the divine ground. Paul Tillich used these three principles in his theology of culture, with special success in the interpretation of expressionist painting.[26]

According to Tillich, reason acting under the universal principle of *autonomy* grasps the form of the painting (self-portrait, landscape, still life, etc.); reason acting under the particular principle of *heteronomy* receives a representation of the content of the painting (the things that are seen through the form); and reason acting under the individual principle of *theonomy* grasps and receives the depth content or import as a third dimension of the work. The depth dimension of the work is distinct from its ideal form or real content; it speaks through the third medium of language and evokes a new speaking in response.

The work of art or culture is given a theological voice through the suggestive power embodied in the tensions and connections between form and content in the painting or artwork. The work speaks of God when it presents the ground of being in an individual meaning (a feeling, intuition, and thought) that appears *on* the subject matter (form and content) in such a way that it cannot be detached *from* the subject matter and still appear, but which is nonetheless something other than the subject matter. The depth dimension of a cultural work, when it appears, makes the form and content seem accidental in what they have to communicate in relation to its own individual disclosure of the ground of being. When the depth dimension appears, the work speaks with urgency and holiness; the viewer or reader is grasped by an ultimate concern about being anything at all.[27]

Both Schleiermacher and Tillich are primarily theologians. They make explicit the structure of their respective theologies of culture. In principle, however, their theologies of culture are not different from that of Ricoeur, although Ricoeur has not focused in the same way on questions of theological interpretation of culture. Ricoeur is a philosopher who listens to the biblical Word and who testifies to the Word within the community of listeners. Ricoeur applies his philosophical hermeneutics to biblical texts, but he reserves distance from the office of theologian, in both its biblical and its philosophical forms.

Nonetheless, Ricoeur makes a contribution to theology of culture in his analysis of poetic discourse, especially by giving us models for reading narrative discourse theologically. Ricoeur's many occasional writings on biblical discourse collectively present a paradigm for the disclosure of God in a text. The general rule for interpreting a poetic text is given by analogy to the process of understanding metaphor at the sentence level: Let the tensional interplay between universal form and particular content generate a feeling and image of an individually presented *possibility to be* beyond the given world of ordinary discourse. A religious text, according to Ricoeur, proceeds similarly by way of the model of metaphoric overturning of literal meaning and creation of new meaning through the productive power of language, but with a difference. Certain biblical texts show the capacity to manifest the depth dimension, which precedes the split between thinking and being, or, as Ricoeur says, to manifest the "limit" dimension of reality, through the polyphonic naming of God running through the Bible. The name God turns the interpretive activity of projecting the world of the text into a metaphor for God's being.

Biblical texts refer to God as the ground and goal of any possible world of the text because the name God stands at the center of a cluster of limit-expressions that manifest in the unity of the word as "thought-thing" or living "symbol" the absolute unity in difference of thinking and being. *The name God can do so when its position within an individual text both enables the reader to identify the voice speaking from the world of this text as not other than the divine voice itself and to recognize at the same time that the divine voice is not the same as any particular voice speaking in the text.* Ricoeur gives detailed analyses of the capacity of biblical texts to disclose God through the tensional interactions within and between the texts.

As we have seen, for Ricoeur, narrative mirrors what human being is, namely, a fragile mediation between the potential meaninglessness of cosmic time (*chronos*) and the potential meaningfulness of lived time. Narrative universalizes particular temporal experiences by connecting them sequentially through plot and referring the sequence to eternity; narrative particularizes the intimidating horizon of cosmic time by drawing the end and limit of lived time into temporal perspective through particular episodes. In the biblical narrative, Ricoeur shows how intertextuality functions to bring two semantic fields together into a metaphoric clash: narrative forms interact with forms of legal and prescriptive discourse, prophecy and hymn, and wisdom discourse to refer the name of God to an individual voice speaking through the transitions between forms and the tensions between content and those forms.[28]

The gospels in particular reveal narrative devices for presenting God for reflection in texts. The New Testament texts are tales about time.[29] In them the nature of human being in time is disclosed, as it is in any narrative text, in its relation to eternity taken as the negation of my being in time in death. However, the New Testament texts reveal another possibility than being toward death in time's relation to eternity. Through the narrative emplotment of time and eternity, and the use of the converging names Jesus Christ and God as limit expressions, time can be understood to bear a different relationship to eternity. The narrated life of Jesus manifests a being-toward-God by his understanding of present time as the time in which the endtime is immanent, the eternal is present now. Biblical time is time that negates while confirming the difference between time and eternity.[30] In the times of decision and of testimony to the truth in faith, as these moments are structured by the narrative itself, the divine joins the human, God is in time, and time is lived as beyond care and anxiety, beyond the threat of death, as the time of eternal life.

Ricoeur makes no attempt to account for the fact that this particular text or set of texts—the Bible—is able to do this. It appears to be a given fact for Ricoeur that the Bible can mediate God within a community of listeners in the Western culture, and Ricoeur makes no explicit efforts to search out this power of disclosure in nonbiblical texts. In principle, however, Ricoeur's hermeneutics, which culminates in its narrative theory, can be applied to cultural products other than the Bible, in which there is no explicit naming of God. How so?

If to be God is to be other than anything named as God, then it is possible that names other than God can present God. The hermeneutical task for a theology of culture applied to narrative would be to find in other texts individual linguistic equivalents to the naming of God in the biblical texts. The equivalent might not appear as a name at all, but could be any meaning appearing in a text that renders present the depth of being by presenting concretely what it means to be in the time of carefree, anxiety-free being. Such a project might best apply to the modern stream-of-consciousness novels that Ricoeur also considers to be tales about time, narratives that both configure time by taking it to a limit in eternity and refigure time as the time of hope grounded in an intuition of the unity of time and eternity.[31] In *Time and Narrative,* volume 2, Ricoeur's analyses of Thomas Mann's *Magic Mountain,* Virginia Woolf's *Mrs. Dalloway,* and Marcel Proust's *Remembrance of Things Past* show how the stream-of-consciousness novels render a vision of eternity in time by experimenting with the distensions and interruptions of human consciousness in time and by breaking down the formal difference between internal time-consciousness and the impersonal passage of cosmic time.

To pursue such an agenda in theology of culture would be to follow the direction of Ricoeur's own questions about meaning in texts and actions, and it would retrieve Schleiermacher's earliest agenda for theological interpretation given in his speeches on religion: to reflect on the feeling and intuition of the eternal in the temporal, the infinite in the finite, and thereby to give glory to God.[32]

NOTES

1. See Richard Kearney, "Paul Ricoeur," in *Dialogues with Contemporary Continental Thinkers,* ed. and trans. Richard Kearney (Manchester: Manchester University Press, 1984), p. 32. See also Paul Ricoeur, "On Interpretation," in *After Philosophy,* ed. Kenneth Baynes, James Bohman, and Thomas McCarthy (Cambridge, Mass.: MIT Press, 1987), pp. 374–76. References to the human being as mediating abound in Ricoeur. For example: "Man is not intermediate because he is between angel and animal; he is intermediate within himself, within his *selves.* He is intermediate because he is a mixture, and a mixture because he brings about mediations. His ontological characteristic of being-intermediate consists precisely in that his act of existing is the very act of bringing about mediations between all the modalities and all the levels of reality within him and outside him" (*Fallible Man,* rev. trans. by Charles A. Kelbley [New York: Fordham University Press, 1986], p. 3).
2. Ricoeur, *Fallible Man,* p. 3. See especially chap. 1, "The *Pathétique* of 'Misery' and Pure Reflection."
3. See Paul Ricoeur, "Schleiermacher's Hermeneutics," *Monist* 60 (1977): 181–97.
4. *Friedrich Schleiermachers Dialektik,* ed. Rudolf Odebrecht (Darmstadt: Wissenschaftliche Buchgesellschaft, 1942), p. 5, my translation. For a helpful study of the dialectic, with particular attention to the Platonic and Kantian references in Schleiermacher's doctrine, see Karl Pohl, "Die Bedeutung der Sprache für den Erkenntnisakt in der 'Dialektik' Friedrich Schleiermachers," *Kant-Studien* 46, no. 4 (1954–55): 302–32.
5. For a discussion on the connection between a conversation about conversation

and a knowing about knowing, see Maciej Potepa, "Die Frage nach dem Subjekt in der Hermeneutik Schleiermachers," in Manfred Frank et al., eds., *Die Frage nach dem Subjekt* (Frankfurt am Main: Suhrkamp, 1988), p. 129.

6. See Heinz Kimmerle, "Das Verhältnis Schleiermachers zum Transzendentalen Idealismus," *Kant-Studien* 51, no. 4 (1959/60): 410–26, for a discussion of the status of Schleiermacher's principle of individuality relative to various schools of transcendental idealism.
7. Johann Gottlieb Fichte, *Grundlage der gesamten Wissenschaftslehre* (1794; rpt. Hamburg: Felix Meiner, 1988), 1:97.
8. For current use of this terminology, with special reference to Schleiermacher among the German idealist philosophers, see Manfred Frank, *Das individuelle Allgemeine: Textstrukturierung und -interpretation nach Schleiermacher* (Frankfurt am Main: Suhrkamp, 1977), pp. 87–144; Manfred Frank, *Die Unhintergehbarkeit von Individualität* (Frankfurt am Main: Suhrkamp, 1986), pp. 116–31.
9. This interpretation of Schleiermacher's doctrine exceeds his own strict wording. Schleiermacher says that "that thinking in which the organic activity is predominant is *perception;* that (thinking) in which the intellectual activity rules and the organic only accompanies we name *thinking in the narrow sense;* that (thinking) where both stand in equilibrium we designate through the word *intuition.* Of such thinking we cannot notice whether it has taken its beginning from the organic or the intellectual side" *Friedrich Schleiermachers Dialektik,* p. 157; my translation and emphases. Schleiermacher also says that immediate self-consciousness presents us with this moment of equilibrium or unity, "die aufhebende Verknüpfung der relativen Gegensätze" (the synthesis which overcomes the relative opposites) (ibid., p. 289). I infer, with other supporting textual evidence, that in immediate self-consciousness humans have an original intuition of the unifying activity.
10. Schleiermacher is quite explicit about the *Sprachgebundenheit* (language-dependence) of all thinking and perceiving. There is no thinking apart from the concretion of thought in language. And reciprocally, "alles Reden ist ein erscheinendes Denken" (all speech is an appearance of thought). "Rede und Denken stehen also in einer festen Verbindung, sind eigentlich identisch. Das Denken ist nicht ohne Rede möglich, und dies ist die Bedingung der Vollendung des Denkens" (Speech and Thought are thus in a tight connection; they are in fact identical. Thought is not possible without speech, and this is the condition for the completion of thought) (*Friedrich Schleiermachers Dialektik,* p. 127).
11. Ibid., p. 270.
12. See, for example, Robert P. Scharlemann, *Inscriptions and Reflections: Essays in Philosophical Theology* (Charlottesville and London: University Press of Virginia, 1989), pp. 41, 67.
13. *Friedrich Schleiermachers Dialektik,* pp. 11–12, 281–82.
14. Scharlemann, *Inscriptions and Reflections,* p. 48.
15. Consider the elementary structures of meaning and being, as they are held in common by Schleiermacher and Ricoeur. The first principle of both meaning and being is the individual mediated unity of universal and particular elements, each of which is underivable from the other. The mediated unity occurs neither in the medium of pure thinking nor in that of pure perceiving, but in the third medium of language. For example, the *meaning* of a sentence occurs through the linguistic connection of particular subject, universal predicate, and the individualizing copula, distinct from the universal and particular elements it connects. Likewise, the *being* of a natural object is an individualized connection in the real object between universal thought and particular perception, a connection that shows itself only in language through meaning.
16. Paul Ricoeur, *Interpretation Theory* (Fort Worth: Texas Christian University

Press, 1976), p. 29. Texts, especially poetic texts, have a privileged ability to disclose possible modes of self-understanding through the projected world of the text. This is possible because the *being of a human* is likewise an individual connection and a connecting activity between a universal element (the universal subject indicated as *I*) and a particular element (a unique person). At all levels, the mediating activity of connecting and distinguishing is always an individualizing activity, according to both Schleiermacher and Ricoeur.

17. See Paul Ricoeur, *The Rule of Metaphor,* trans. Robert Czerny (Toronto and Buffalo: University of Toronto Press, 1977), study 8, esp. p. 313.
18. Paul Ricoeur, *Time and Narrative,* vol. 1, trans. Kathleen McLaughlin and David Pellauer (Chicago and London: University of Chicago Press, 1984), p. 3.
19. See Paul Ricoeur, *Soi-même comme un autre* (Paris: Editions du Seuil, 1990), for a thorough discussion of personal identity as narratival identity, especially pp. 139, 167.
20. Ibid., pp. 15–27.
21. *Freidrich Schleiermachers Dialektik,* p. 288.
22. The German text reads: "In dem Übergang ist die Zeitform gesetzt, in der Identität ist sie negiert" (ibid., p. 286).
23. See the study by Hans-Richard Reuter entitled *Die Einheit der Dialektik Friedrich Schleiermachers: Eine systmatische Interpretation* (Munich: Christian Kaiser Verlag, 1979), chap. 5 ("Selbst"), pp. 210–64, esp. pp. 236–47. Cf. pp. 286–94 of the Odebrecht edition of the *Dialektic.*
24. This sentence runs against the letter of Schleiermacher, who makes some problematic statements about the necessity of holding apart the speculative and dogmatic conceptions of God. On systematic grounds, this will not do. In principle, Schleiermacher is driven to think them both together.
25. Plato, *The Republic,* trans. Desmond Lee, (London: Penguin Books, 1987), pp. 308, 309.
26. See Paul Tillich, *Writings in the Philosophy of Culture/Kulturphilosophische Schriften,* ed. Michael Palmer, vol. 2 of *Main Works/Hauptwerke,* (Berlin, New York: De Gruyter-Evangelisches Verlagswerk GmbH, 1990). Palmer's introduction, "Paul Tillich's Theology of Culture," is very helpful; see pp. 1–33. See also Robert P. Scharlemann, "Tillich and the Religious Interpretation of Art," in *The Thought of Paul Tillich,* ed. James Luther Adams, Wilhelm Pauck, and Roger Lincoln Shinn (San Francisco: Harper and Row, 1985), pp. 156–74. Recent discussion of Tillich's theology of culture can be found in *Religion et culture: Actes du colloque international du centenaire Paul Tillich, 1986,* ed. Michel Despland, Jean-Claude Petit, and Jean Richard (Quebec and Ottawa: Les Presses de l'Université Laval, Les Editions du Cerf, 1987).
27. See especially, Scharlemann, "Tillich and the Religious Interpretation of Art."
28. See Paul Ricoeur, "Naming God," *Union Seminary Quarterly Review* 34, no. 4 (1979): 215–27, as well as Ricoeur, "Towards a Hermeneutic of the Idea of Revelation," *Harvard Theological Review* 70, no. 1–2 (1977): 1–37.
29. A very helpful analysis can be found in Kevin J. Van Hoozer, *Biblical Narrative in the Philosophy of Paul Ricoeur: A Study in Hermeneutics and Theology* (Cambridge: Cambridge University Press, 1990), esp. p. 190.
30. See Paul Ricoeur, "Temps biblique," *Archivio di filosofia* 1 (1985): 22–35.
31. See Van Hoozer's discussion of this point in *Biblical Narrative,* pp. 216–18.
32. Friedrich Schleiermacher, *On Religion: Speeches to Its Cultured Despisers,* trans. with an introduction by Richard Crouter (Cambridge and New York: Cambridge University Press, 1990), second speech.

WILLIAM SCHWEIKER

HERMENEUTICS, ETHICS, AND THE THEOLOGY OF CULTURE

Concluding Reflections

"IN THE END, I do not know what man is. My confession to myself is that man is instituted by the word, that is, by a language which is less spoken *by* man than spoken *to* man. . . . Is not The Good News the instigation of the *possibility* of man by a creative word?"[1] In the passage that heads these reflections, Paul Ricoeur claims that inquiry into life exposes the human as that being who cannot answer the question of its own existence but is constituted by a word spoken to it. My task in this conclusion is to explore this point further and what it means for theological-ethical reflection on culture. I will not attempt a detailed interpretation of Ricoeur's thought. The various essays in this volume have undertaken that task with grace and skill. Rather, my concern is to isolate basic issues and fundamental themes facing all forms of humanistic inquiry—to clarify, as it were, the most pressing issues before us.

I argue that theological ethical reflection can decisively aid us in examining the texture of human existence. That is to say, theological ethics is a way of interpreting the world and human life that seeks to provide insight and guidance for how we ought to live. I realize that this is not a conviction widely held by humanists, or, for that matter, by theologians. Given this, I offer a twofold thesis for these concluding reflections. First, I contend that Ricoeur's philosophy has resources for rehabilitating the theology of culture, that is, a form of theological reflection not limited to explicating the beliefs and practices of specific religious communities. It does so, interestingly, by provoking us to examine the relation between ethics (in the comprehensive sense of normative inquiry into how we should live) and theological reflection. What we are concerned with, then, is an interpretation of our moral world, or culture, from a theological point of view. Yet I also argue, second, that undertaking such theological ethical reflection on human life is itself integral to the rejuvenation of humanistic thought, since it reopens the question of human existence in a most radical form. A theological ethics of culture provides the means to understand, question, and transform the political and linguistic forces that improperly attempt to constitute human life and thus falsely answer the question of human existence. In the name of the word, to use Ricoeur's term, theological ethics of culture critiques and protects the words, the forms of discourse and patterns of interactions, important for individual and social life, that is, for our moral world. To see why this is the case and what it means for theology and for the various humanistic disciplines is the subject of the following pages.

I will develop the argument by progressing through three distinct but related levels of reflection. These levels cohere with the basic outlines of Ricoeur's philosophy and also, we will note, the theology of culture as practiced earlier in this century. I begin with the debate about the symbolic, or language, important to the theology of culture and current hermeneutic reflection. This debate turns on the status and creative power of language itself. It is one that touches the basic question of human identity. Thus, I will show, second, that these debates about language turn on a deeper question that surrounds human life, specifically the relation of human identity to the moral conditions for human community. In terms of a theological ethics of culture, we enter here, via the problem of the symbolic, the question of what ought to determine the shape of human identity. Earlier theologians of culture, like Paul Tillich, spoke of this ought, or law, in terms of theonomous existence, that is, a mode of life whose normative determination is not simply self-generated (autonomous) or imposed by others, even by God (heteronomous), but which arises out of the depths of existence. Drawing on Ricoeur, I attempt to specify the norms that can and should govern the imputation of human identity, norms that arise out of the temporal shape of human action and interaction rendered meaningful through narrative. In this way, normative reflection coheres with and yet deepens the earlier discussion of language. In and through these questions about language and the norms for action, I will, finally, reach the basic theological question. That is, if symbols give rise to thought, as Ricoeur insists, and human action and identity transpire in relations governed by norms and goods, then claims about the divine cohere with and transform these dimensions of human existence, our lives as interpreters and agents. In Ricoeur's mind, the word spoken to the human in and through the words that structure human life is the creative instigation of the possibility of our existence. Theological reflection on the moral world, or culture, must consider this Word and the possibility of human existence it instigates. Put in strictly theological terms, this allows us to conceive of faith as a primary affirmation of life that founds the possibility of our being agents in the world. In this way, I will show the import of theological reflection for humanistic inquiry.

THE SYMBOLIC AND THE CRITIQUE OF THEOLOGY

The theology of culture and hermeneutics share at least this much. Each mode of reflection holds that we understand through the act of interpretation. Furthermore, theologians, philosophers, and social critics would agree that the problem of understanding is universal simply because ambiguity surrounds all of human life. This is certainly the case with cultural life. By culture I mean, initially at least, that second reality—a *Welt,* as the Germans put it—imposed on our surrounding environment through human action that is important for the formation of distinctively human forms of life. Any culture, therefore, is a response to the problem of the formation of human identity, coupled to the basic dynamics of human association, and deeply historical and contingent. In this sense culture forms our moral world and may be examined from the perspective of ethics.

The theology of culture attempts the interpretation of culture from a specifically religious point of view. As Langdon Gilkey has recently put it, this mode of reflection seeks "to understand what is happening in contemporary culture and in the sequence of events that make up contemporary history" and to do so by examining "the *religious* dilemmas of cultural life."[2] Implicit in this definition of the theology of culture is some idea of religion, what distinguishes it from other human phenomena, and its relation to culture and history, that is, to the culture-creating power of human beings, including the writing of "history" and the acting and suffering of persons and communities through time. Given this, a theology of culture, as I understand it, is uniquely concerned with the relation that does and ought to obtain between the religious and human moral existence, our power to act in the world.

In order to carry out such reflection, earlier theologians of culture, like Tillich, drew on specific ideas of language and symbols. Symbolic forms, they held, point to or express a depth dimension of human existence, a depth from which a particular myth or symbol derives its existence and its meaning. As Tillich liked to put it, a symbol, as opposed to a sign, participates in that to which it points. This depth that is a symbol's referent might be consciousness itself, or, as Tillich insisted, the ground of the relation of self and world. Myths and symbols, in other words, point to some ground and power of "being" that is the unconditioned element in all conditioned relations of the self to itself, to others, and to a cultural world riddled with possibilities and limiting conditions. The "unconditioned," insofar as it is basic to the meaning of existence, is a matter of concern to us, even of ultimate concern.

Armed with this conception of the symbolic, Tillich defined *religion* with respect to those structures that condition human life in the world, that is to say, with respect to culture. "Religion as ultimate concern is the meaning-giving substance of culture, and culture is the totality of forms in which the basic concern of religion expresses itself. In abbreviation: religion is the substance of culture, culture is the form of religion. . . . He who can read the style of a culture can discover its ultimate concern, its religious substance."[3] In this view, religion is an attitude and response to the depths of existence that necessarily comes to cxpression in determinate cultural forms. Again, the symbolic points to something, and this something (call it "being" or the "sacred") is important for the very meaning of our humanity. To be authentically human is to have a proper relation to this "depth." Theologians were quick to point out that this relation is established by the sacred and not by the human. As Tillich noted, we are grasped by ultimate concern. He made the point in this manner in order to counter the usual psychological and Marxist criticisms that religious ideas are simply projections of human desires.

Put differently, theologians held that culture per se is religious even though cultures express their religious substance differently.

Religion is the life and vitality of culture; *culture,* so defined, is open to interpretation from a theological point of view. Inherent in this conception of the symbolic, religion, and culture was the conviction that human beings cannot answer the question of their own existence. As Tillich put it, "The answer cannot be derived from the question. It is said *to* him who asks, but it is not taken *from* him."[4] This requires, in other words, a turn to some revealed answer to the human dilemma, a dilemma expressing itself in cultural forms. The theologian's task, therefore, is to correlate the revealed and salvific message of the Christian community to the existential questions found in a culture.

These ideas are now being challenged, and with good reason. The criticism turns on the relation between this conception of religion, the symbolic, and the construal of human existence in a theology of culture. First, there are philosophical criticisms. The "end of man," as Michel Foucault championed it, and the critique of logocentrism by Jacques Derrida seem to undercut the claim that to be a self entails a constitutive relation to something of ultimate concern and that this something is beyond, before, or outside of the symbolic system that discloses it. Meaning is produced in the difference between signs in a system and the constant deferral of any reference to a nonsystemic "reality." Likewise, forms of human identity, as Foucault argues through his analyses of prisons and asylums, are constituted by the discursive practices and relations of power operative in institutions. Much as language does not point beyond itself, human identity is not referable to some transcendental subject. Given this, can we speak theologically of culture and its depths?

In addition to these philosophical criticisms, there is, second, a set of criticisms of the theology of culture that center on the idea of religion and its constitutive relation to authentic human existence. Philosophers of religion, like Wayne Proudfoot, or theologians, such as George Lindbeck, question the possibility and validity of speaking about religion as a sui generis phenomenon. Religion is not the depth of culture; it is not "ultimate concern" or an experience of the holy, as Rudolf Otto called it. These thinkers insist that we must look to the religions and not to the religious, examine the life and discourse of specific communities and not some ostensively universal dimension of human existence that modern thinkers called religion. The theology of culture does not recognize this fact, and, thus, fails to see that it is not theology at all.

Behind these criticisms of the very possibility of a theology of culture is to be found an interrelated philosophical and theological problematic. Philosophically the question turns on the relation that obtains between a theory of language and human identity. Is identity constituted by linguistic forms to the extent that we can reduce the self into the myriad discursive patterns operating in a social order, whether that order is a religious community, the rise of the asylum, or Western logocentric culture? Is Richard Rorty correct, for instance, when he claims that "human beings are centerless networks of beliefs and desires" and that their "vocabularies and opinions are determined by historical circumstance" of the communities they inhabit?[5] Ricoeur insists that "language is only the locus of the articulation of an experience which supports it, and that everything, consequently, does not arrive *in* language, but only comes *to* language."[6] It is this claim that is now challenged philosophically and must be addressed by a theological ethics of culture.

Given the criticism of religion, the theological issue is related but distinct from this philosophical point. Is theological reflection concerned with what arrives *in* the discourse of a specific community and the capacity of that arrival to determine a form of life? Can we speak of the divine with respect not only to what arrives in a determinate form of discourse (the Christian scripture, for instance), but also what comes to expression in the symbols, myths, and narratives of a culture? Is it still possible to speak of *homo religiosis* so that we might examine culture as a whole from a theological point of view? Or is it the case that such a reflection is always, in the final analysis, simply another form of sociology? We might surmise that this criticism of the theology of culture is related to the previous philosophical one. They return us to primal questions. What and who is the human? By what word or words are we constituted? Is this constitution in some sense a matter for theological reflection?

I have been arguing that in much current humanistic inquiry there is a challenge to previous ways of understanding the relation between human capacities for creative expression and actual cultural forms, especially language. Language, it is argued, does not express human consciousness or refer to an extralinguistic world. We are concerned with what arrives *in* forms of discourse (whether this is God or the self) or with the ways in which linguistic systems are projective of meaning through the constant deferral of any fixed signified. Given this, the theology of culture as previously undertaken seems impossible because it defines religion with respect to the depth structure of existence expressed through symbolic, cultural forms.

However, we must note a simple fact. Since any theory of language is a claim about meaning, it entails some conviction about those for whom events, signs, persons, texts, have import. My contention is that it is precisely with reference to this "for whom" that theories must be adjudicated. This is a moral question basic to our world situation. The primal social and cultural problematic of our time centers on the relation between the dignity of individual life and the various linguistic, economic, and political totalities that endow human life with identity. Human life is increasingly determined by forms of discourse and relations of power that operate without reference to a human origin or a human end. We exist within economies and systems of meaning-production. As John B. Thompson has argued, in a world of technology and mass communication, systems of meaning are in the service of relations of power and domination.[7]

To put this differently, our cultural situation is one in which the production and dissemination of meaning is used for political and economic ends. Art, education, and literature are increasing subsumed into the mechanisms of a technological social structure and are expressive of that structure. This has profound effect on the shape and texture of human life, both individual and communal. The critics of the theology of culture and its presuppositions are making particular claims about this sociocultural situation, and these claims are dominating humanistic studies. What is needed is clarity about what these arguments really entail. This requires that we acknowledge that theories of language, or the symbolic, are not self-adjudicating, and, thereby, pose further questions for moral inquiry.

NORMS AND IDENTITY: THE HUMAN VULNERABILITY

The philosophical and theological criticisms of a theology of culture and its idea of the symbolic noted above express more than a simple rejection of one way of carrying out cultural analysis. The clash between the theology of culture and its critics forces us to raise anew what Jürgen Habermas has rightly called the specific human vulnerability: that we individuate ourselves through socialization.[8] Human identity is itself a second actuality dependent on cultural life. We come to be as selves through the appropriation of the rules, values, and forms of discourse of our communities, that is, with respect to the aspects of what Ricoeur in his narrative theory has called "mimesis$_1$." The self not only lives in a moral world, it is, primordially, a moral being. The relevant questions are then these: What degree of self-transcendence do we have from our social wholes in the constitution and direction of our lives? What norms ought to guide our lives? More forcefully, how are we to understand the dignity of human beings? How these questions are answered determines the way in which a thinker or school of thought adjudicates between competing theories of language and meaning. There are, in other words, moral and political questions at the root of any theory of culture simply because human association is basic to cultural forms.

This way of putting the matter is basic to my critical appropriation of Ricoeur's thought. As others have noted, there is in much contemporary thought a three-way debate over how to understand the moral conditions of human community.[9] There are, first, those who hope to specify Kantian-like rights needed for the protection of individuals and communities. This is seen, for instance, in the discourse of human rights in the United Nations and also in the tradition of Roman Catholic social encyclicals, but also, philosophically, in the discourse ethics of Habermas, Karl Otto-Apel, and others. Next, there are also thinkers, such as Alasdair MacIntyre and theologians like Stanley Hauerwas, who see the liberal project as a failure and seek some alternate community: the university in MacIntyre's case; the gathered church for Hauerwas. Finally, others, such as Rorty and Jeffrey Stout, seek to further liberal democracy, but without Kantian or universal moral appeals.

The later two kinds of positions represent Hegelian options in the sense that moral norms and moral identity are community specific, the stuff of objective spirit, or *Geist.* Of course, the current Hegelians do not believe in Hegel's claims about "spirit," but they do agree that our identity and our norms are communal endowments. Because of this, the norms and values of our communities are not, in the first instance, heteronomous; they are not imposed on us externally, since we appropriate them in becoming who we are. They shape our very dignity. As Rorty himself puts it, there is no human dignity that is not derivative from "the dignity of some specific community, and no appeal beyond the relative merits of various actual or proposed communities to impartial criteria which will help us weight those merits."[10] What is at stake here is nothing less than human dignity and the norms for judgments about the exercise, promotion, and protection of that dignity within a society. What we must insist upon is the intimate relation that exists between an understanding of social and political existence and some theory of language and the constitution of human identity. When we draw this connection, what do we see?

The poststructuralist and sociolinguistic theories of language previously noted, along with the criticisms of the theology of culture they entail, share a common political and even moral assumption. This is the case despite the fact that they reach radically different conclusions. The common assumption is this: identity, insofar as we can speak of it, is without remainder the product of some social and linguistic totality. Thinkers differ, and radically so, about which totality ought to concern us, whether it is liberal democracy or the fate of being, for instance. But the picture, again in Rorty's terms, is "of the self as a centerless and contingent web" constituted by its relation "to those with similar tastes and similar identities."[11] The self is a social functionary whose meaning and constitution is to be understood within some linguistic and social whole. Accordingly, different identities are the product of different languages. A liberal democrat pleads for tolerance but also knows that those with different visions of life, especially religious ones, simply appear mad.

The degree of difference between forms of identity can, of course, be debated. But the point remains. In the postmodern context, identity is a function of membership; what we mean by human identity is that which is assumed or imputed by a community and its discourse to the individual. There is no act of the self discoverable through phenomenological analysis prior to or at the telos of the totality that endows it with identity. From this perspective, the self as an arche, an origin, of its actual identity was the invention of Enlightenment thinkers who foolishly believed they had to provide rational foundations for their criticisms of previous views of life, especially those that centered on divine commands and the rights of kings. Strong arguments for autonomy are simply not viable. The autonomous self, we are told, is a chimera, an impossible fantasy. What identity we have is rooted, finally, in our communities and their several languages. What protests and denunciations we undertake are always internal to those communities, undertaken with their tools and on their behalf. At best, we are what Michael Walzer has called "internal critics."[12] Our lives and our criticisms are in the service of, responsible to, the social whole of which we are a member. All norms, all means for the adjudication of claims, are solely political in character.

Once this judgment about the conditions of human association is made, the scholar's task is to trace the ways in which subjects are constituted. Doing so accomplishes two interrelated things. First, by specifying how and in what ways the self is constituted by a discursive totality—a prison system, the logocentric discourse of the West, the *Gestell* of technology, patriarchy, the narratives of particular communities—one confirms the functional character of identity, that it arrives *in* forms of discourse, as I put it above. Thus, one must ask about power relations, discursive patterns, and the self-subverting character of language, and not about actual persons. The economy of meaning has reference to human life only insofar as it is productive of specific identities. It is this economy and not human life that is the subject matter of inquiry; humanistic reflection is transformed into the study of discursive structures and relations of power.

Second, this examination of the constitution of the self means a radicalization of internal criticism. Little wonder that from Heidegger's destruction of metaphysics to Derrida's deconstruction of logocentrism the thinker is quick to point out that one cannot, finally, escape the discourse one is attempting to subvert. What more complete totality can be conceived than that of Being or Text? What more complete task for the philosopher to undertake than to be the internal critic of that totality? (Were these not all claims of Hegel?) One undoes the totality from the inside by showing what it effaces or forgets, like the question of the meaning of being (as Heidegger put it) or examining how it deconstructs itself (in Derrida's words) in the face of its own claims to totality. But one remains bound to the totality, one's philosophical activity and identity is defined by it and in its service. This argument has led to the unified readings of history in much of twentieth-century Continental philosophy—either as the history of the question of being or as its deconstruction. Such thinking is neither heteronomous nor autonomous; it is animated by the subject matter that the thinker follows, as Heidegger might say. This is, as he rightly saw, the piety of thinking—a theonomy without God.

Thus, the various criticisms of the theology of culture, and the specific idea of myth and symbol at its heart, are more basically determinate answers to the vulnerability of the human species, ones that emphasize the identity-engendering power of various totalities (the church, language, being). Thinkers celebrate or criticize this fact and thus take varying postures on our current cultural dilemma. After all, if contemporary history and culture are the story of the forgetfulness of the meaning of being, one has a different assessment of our situation than if this history and culture are seen as a call to authentic membership in the Christian community.

I realize that this is an ironic conclusion to reach. Deconstructionists, sociolinguistic theologians, and the various new Hegelians all claim to be critics of totalistic thinking, that mode of reflection they identify either with Enlightenment moral universalism or with the defunct project of ontotheology. Yet when we ask, as Ricoeur bids us to ask, about the constitution of human identity—what word or words normatively form who we are—then something else comes to light. What is happening in our culture is that the question of human existence is being answered with respect to various totalities, which, so it is argued, constitute who and what we are and to whom or what we are responsible. The self is no longer a culture-creating power imposing a world on its environment; the self is a product of social and linguistic processes. What is normative is then the social totality, and the self is more lived than living.

It is hardly surprising, therefore, that the theology of culture has become problematic in the present intellectual scene. For some thinkers God is the name for that totality that we must deconstruct but that we can never finally escape. According to this reading, theology, as Mark C. Taylor and others argue, has the task of simply tracing out the meaning of the modern death of God and the deconstruction of theology into all areas of culture. At best, we can speak about what is at the margins, the breaks and disruptions of a totality, as somehow a negative epiphany of the sacred. This conclusion, it should be noted, means that any criticism of cultural and social totalities is irrational in the sense that it exceeds the rationality of the system. One might surmise that this is why deconstructionist theologians are enthralled with the discourse of negative theology. For sociolinguistic theologians, one can only speak theologically by means of the discourse of a specific Christian community of which the thinker is a part. The relation of God and self is such that we must stick with our communal narratives, since these render forth precisely this relationship. For these theologians, one's critical posture with respect to culture means that the rationality of one's judgment is always community specific. In a word, the critique of the symbolic noted in the first section of this conclusion, coupled with these arguments about the moral and political conditions for human identity, means that theological reflection is either finished, irrational, or provincial. Theology of culture's aspiration to public and intelligible discourse is no longer possible.

Again, I insist that each of these approaches to theology and to culture is a specific answer to the vulnerability of the human species. Each also entails a claim about the rationality of our norms for judgment about those social, historical, and linguistic totalities that inform and direct our lives. Each reflects some Hegelian-like option for understanding our cultural situation. The "for whom" of these positions, in other words, is a linguistic or social totality. Scholarly inquiry, ironically, has then jettisoned the notion that there is a human act at the beginning or the end of any bearer of meaning.

Are these the only plausible responses to human vulnerability? I do not think that they are. I also do not believe that the alternative to them is a form of Kantianism currently under criticism. As Rorty puts it, such a Kantianism holds "that there are such things as intrinsic human dignity, intrinsic human rights, and an ahistorical distinction between the demands of morality and those of prudence."[13] In light of Ricoeur's work, I contest the idea that claims about human dignity and rights are, by the nature of the case, somehow ahistorical. In a critical appropriation of Ricoeur, it is possible to attempt a post-Hegelian return to Kant with respect to the specific human vulnerability. Mindful of biblical overtones, what I argue can be put as a maxim: humans were not made for language, but language was made for human beings. But who or what is the human? On returning to this question, I can directly engage Ricoeur's hermeneutic project.

NARRATIVE AND ACTION

Ricoeur raises anew the question of the human as that for whom systems of meaning, including political and social realities, are to be evaluated. His philosophy is concerned with the problem of the human search for wholeness mindful of the dualities intrinsic to existence. This enables him, I contend, to examine the ways in which we seek wholeness, and thus open cultural interpretation at its most pressing level, while also insisting on the limits to any answer we might fashion for ourselves. This provides tools for the interpretation of culture. It also specifies norms for the judgment of community and human character. These two claims mean that human identity and norms for judgment are indeed linguistically and socially constituted, but they derive their intelligibility and binding character from the dynamics of human freedom.

In order to show this, I want to explore Ricoeur's account of the threefold mimesis. It allows us to draw together reflection on language and the specific human vulnerability. I want to isolate the intentional structure of the mimetic act. By this I mean the coconstitutive relation between the objective conditions of intelligibility in the order of action and the imaginative act rendering action meaningful through figuration. Isolating this structure is important for seeing what Ricoeur's hermeneutics might contribute to a theological-ethical interpretation of culture. In doing so, I am also retracing the argument above about language and moral identity. It is important, however, for my position that I center on mimesis and narrative. Doing so makes problems of human action and agency, and thus ethics, basic to an interpretation of culture.

For Ricoeur narrative is the mimesis of human action through the act of making a plot. It renders meaningful the prefigured but intelligible order of temporal action by configuring discordant events into a unity, a mythos. Any narrative draws its intelligibility from what Ricoeur calls mimesis$_1$, that is, the prefigured order of action itself: structural attributes distinguishing action from natural motion; the symbolic mediation of actions in rules and norms for human behavior; and the temporal character of action. This preunderstanding of narrated time provides the anchoring for narratives in the literal world of human conduct, our bodily openness to the world, and norm-governed interaction with others. The making of a plot is, then, a synthetic act of the productive imagination in the face of the diversity of lived time. It is creative of meaning by displaying a possible world in which a reader can dwell. Reading is also a synthetic act that relates a narrative and its world to actual life. It brings unity to temporal existence. The act of reading or interpretation (Mimesis$_3$) intersects the world of the text (Mimesis$_2$) and the lived world of the interpreter (Mimesis$_1$) thereby refiguring life.

It is important to note that there is a synthetic act at both ends of narrative, as it were. The productive imagination acts in making a plot; reading, as a different employment of the imagination, is the act of appropriation. Narrative and its appropriation is an answer to the search for (temporal) wholeness, one that, interestingly enough, mediates that wholeness through the unreal, the fictive, but that is measured by a human act at its beginning and its end. The unreality of figuration, we can say, places a limit on the possibility of a total mediation of the human problem, of freedom and finitude, and, for Ricoeur, language and being. Later I will explore the significance of the fictive refiguring the real and what this means for a theological ethics of culture.

Here I must stress the phenomenological correlation of the intelligible order of action and the imaginative construction of meaning. For Ricoeur, a symbol has a double-meaning structure. It has semantic and nonsemantic elements. In this respect a narrative is symbolic in character, as is that identity we achieve and receive through the narrative act. This coheres with Ricoeur's basic philosophical claims that the human is a being who mediates finitude and freedom. The self is the figure for the unity of finitude and freedom in the individual amid the ambiguity of time. This is why the human dwells poetically on earth and it shows us that our narrative identities owe themselves to some linguistic or symbolic mediation.

However, making this point does not answer the critics, since, as we have seen, it is precisely this account of identity that is in question. In this respect, Ricoeur's work implies, I think, two lines of argument important for ethical and theological reflection. These arguments are dependent on the relation between intelligibility and meaning we have isolated in the narration of human action; they link the symbolic and the normative. The first argument is this. Ricoeur's account of symbol, metaphor, and narrative does not entail the romantic or idealist claim that the self expresses itself in linguistic forms. One does not, in other words, examine cultural works in order to uncover the subjectivity expressed therein. Like the positions explored above, Ricoeur too argues that identity is imputed to an individual through linguistic ascription. Insofar as they are meaningful, our identities, we might say, are achieved and received rather than expressed. The I does not create itself or its world. Second, this does not mean, as it does for certain poststructuralist thinkers, that identity is explainable solely in terms of linguistic patterns or codes. This is because meaning claims are dependent on some intelligible order, which, in the case of narrative identity, is the prefigured structure of human action. The importance of this ought not to be overlooked. It means that one can specify norms entailed in any imputation of a meaningful identity with respect to conditions of intelligibility. These norms are neither irrational nor simply community specific.

Ricoeur makes this point in his analysis of the asymmetry of violence born of human interaction and the teleological character of all purposive acts. So, for instance, any imputation of identity that reduces human action to mere happenings or physical motion ought not to claim our assent, whether that imputation is the claim that human beings are simply preference-driven consumers or that the self is a trace in a linguistic system. Similarly, any account of identity that violates norms and rules of social welfare that arise from the solicitude of the Other for our respect or from the very temporal conditions of life stands under the censure of this account. Ricoeur is clear that these deontic norms are revealed amid asymmetrical relations of power in human interaction. There are moral demands, as he notes, because there is violence in the world. An encounter with what ought not to be transforms our perception of what is.

Ricoeur's idea of narrative, as I have stressed, means that identity is not the simple expression of a prefigured "I." The self is achieved and received through narrative configuration with respect to counterfactual *oughts* that govern the imputation of moral responsibility. Yet the self, for all of that, is not open to infinite manipulation simply because meaningful identity itself figures intelligible conditions of action. According to this reading, the self as an actor, an agent, is also a criterion for judging various answers to the specific human vulnerability. It is not a foundation or an origin of those norms, but a teleological good with respect to the ends of action. Put more generally, Ricoeur holds that subjectivity "must be lost as the radical origin if it is to be retained in a more modest role. . . . the act of subjectivity is less what starts than what completes."[14] What is completed in the self is a specific answer to human vulnerability, one that entails norms and limitations for what can count as a viable form of identity. Later I will argue for a theological transformation at this level of reflection, a transformation that moves beyond Ricoeur's thought.

Thus, self-identity is achieved and received through social discourse and narratives. The self, in this respect, does not found, but rather completes, linguistic and social forms. In a genuine sense, human identity does arrive *in* language, and this seriously qualifies previous idealistic theories of subjectivity and the ideas of culture they supported. Yet, such identity, if it is to be viable, must cohere with two distinct but related sets of criteria for judging responses to human vulnerability. I have noted deontic claims that arise out of the order of action and the solicitude of the Other to our respect, and, also, a teleological norm mediated by narrative configuration, that is, the "self." These norms concern human dignity (the "self") and basic rights (what ought not to be violated) against which social reality is measured. They are not, as Rorty seems to hold, ahistorical. In fact, they arise out of the very act of configuring temporal experience, whether in fiction or history.

Attending to Ricoeur's account of narrative in this way might help to rejuvenate cultural and historical studies within moral inquiry because it places at the center of reflection the question of what it means to be human and how we should live. Yet it raises again the question of what constitutes the human as that being for whom linguistic and social systems are to be evaluated. It is this question that requires theological reflection.

RECONCEIVING THE THEOLOGY OF CULTURE

Thus far I have made several interrelated claims. First, I engaged the criticisms of previous theories of symbol and what those theories meant for religion and also for human existence. In the light of Ricoeur's narrative theory, I have argued that myths, symbols, and narratives are not expressive of the I, but that human identity is constituted through the fictive unreality of the text. Next, I have argued that the specific human vulnerability is that we are individuated through socialization. Human identity is achieved and received with respect to some community, its discourse, and the norms that direct its life. How a thinker understands the dialectical relation of self and community provides, so I have argued, the terms for that thinker's adjudication of the adequacy of theories of language and human identity. We have seen that various "Hegelianisms" dominate humanistic inquiry and also the criticism of the theology of culture. These positions challenge modern theories of ethical autonomy by stressing the way in which human dignity and values are imputed to the individual by a community. While granting the Hegelian point that human identity is always social in character, I have, following Ricoeur, isolated norms that arise within human action and interaction. This post-Hegelian return to Kant with respect to the moral conditions for human association and identity is to test and limit the spiritual, almost theonomous, power of the social whole.

Finally, at each juncture of this argument I have also stressed that a basic human drive is toward wholeness. This drive is never fully achieved, since it is always undertaken through metaphor, narrative, and symbol. Because there is an act of the productive imagination at either end of narrative figuration, such figuration never escapes the specific limitation of human existence, that we are incomplete. Ambiguity surrounds human life because of the dualities that permeate existence, dualities that thinking, willing, and feeling cannot finally mediate. This enables us to grasp the dialectical character of human identity (individuation through socialization) within historical communities and their languages even as we realize that the mediation of human identity is through imaginative works that disclose freedom and its norms.

Now we must ask, What does it mean that persons and communities seek wholeness through the work of the imagination? How does this relate to theological ethical reflection? What is the relation, in other words, between narrative, the moral conditions of identity, and religious reflection? My wager is that attending to these matters allows us to reclaim the best insights of defining religion as ultimate concern, but without its problems. In order to understand this, we must grasp the relation of freedom and faith in a primary affirmation of life constitutive of human existence. Freedom and faith are disclosed, we will see, by the fictive world of the text and the actuality of evil in the world. Because faith and freedom voice a primary affirmation of being as good, they are basic to reconceiving the theology of culture.

Recall that in Ricoeur's account, what a text discloses in front of itself is a *possible* way of being in the world. That this world is a possibility signals the way in which it escapes complete determination by any actual form of life. Yet it also specifies the human act that could complete that world: that one decide actually to exist in this possibility. The mediation of the human drive for wholeness through the unreality of myth, symbol, and metaphor instanciates the human as a free being, an agent who must decide to actualize a way of being in some determinate range of possibilities, some possible moral world. Freedom is the phenomenological correlate to symbol, narrative, or myth. Our freedom is entangled with symbolic forms while under the demand to actualize some mode of life. The relation of freedom and language means, in other words, that the only way to self-understanding is through the interpretation of those myths, symbols, and narratives that provide possible ways of being in the world.

However, the world in which I may dwell is always a second possibility with respect to the actual conditions of life. Those conditions are marked by real violence and evil. The inscrutability of evil, that we must approach it via symbol, does not obviate its facticity. The asymmetry of power in human interaction too often leads to the death or silence of other persons; the failure of the acting self to achieve its ends too easily results in despair. While the possible world of the text discloses freedom, the actual world of moral existence raises the profound question of whether or not and to what extent we can affirm life and its possibilities amid real violence and evil.

These two points about the human as a free interpreter forever barred from complete identity with itself and as an agent in a world of fault and evil mean that our existence is not simply constituted by the communities in which we live. Our lives also entail a judgment, one that cannot be made for us by others or by our communities. Not only do we make judgments about possible courses of action, we also, in so acting, make some judgment, an affirmation or denial, of existence in all of its contingency and fallenness. But denial and affirmation are not equally primordial options. In every judgment to actualize some possibility, existence is affirmed. This is, if I might call it such, the testimony of freedom, that free action testifies to the affirmation of life. This affirmation, this faith, enables one to see the sheer contingency of existence as good, even as this insight helps to regenerate the will in the service of life.[15] It is, to use a theological concept, the event of grace, the Good News, as Ricoeur puts it, of the possibility of human existence by a creative word.

It is this primal affirmation of existence, the testimony of freedom, that requires theological reflection. It is a recasting of the definition of religion as ultimate concern through a philosophy of the will and thus ethics. How are we to understand this primal affirmation that permeates our lives as self-interpreting agents? Does it simply issue forth from the self, the human? The assumption that it does or that the constitution of our lives is explainable in terms of our social totalities leads to the forms of idolatry found in all attempts at a total mediation of the human problem. These attempts confuse the unreal with the real, whether this is through the supposed total mediation of a self-identical I, thinking within the fate of being, or the claim that there is nothing outside of the text. Faith is the affirmation of life without such total mediation; it protects us from the pretense of mistaking any answer for the final answer, any social god for the divine.

As stated in the epigraph of this essay, Ricoeur insists that the decisive revelation is "the instigation of the *possibility* of man by a creative word." The apprehension of the possibility of our existence as itself a gift transforms the real—our actual lives marked by fault, violence, and evil—when in our action we enact an *affirmation* of being. Thus, it is amid being agents in relation to others and our environing world that we encounter a divine Other as what endows existence with meaning and value. The testimony of freedom in response to this word has then its own double meaning, its own symbolic structure. Examining this structure constitutes the task of the theology of culture. And insisting on this symbolic character is what a theological ethics of culture contributes to humanistic inquiry. What do I mean?

In response to the specific human vulnerability of individuation through socialization, every culture answers with respect to its beliefs, values, and language in tension with the affirmation of existence an intentional act of human agents instanciates. That is to say, each culture has a semantic element through which persons and communities are endowed with identity and a nonsemantic element, the affirmation of existence in action. This is why I have, in the course of these concluding reflections, explored the interrelation of language and human vulnerability. Yet here we must note that this affirmation is not simply expressed through the semantic dimensions of culture, as the early theology of culture might have argued. This affirmation exists in a tensive relation with a culture's beliefs, values, and language forms. It founds the person as an incomplete project whose life transpires amid the moral conditions and limits of human association. That is, this affirmation of life is entailed in any response to the solicitude of others for our respect and is endorsed in striving for the good. It is the root of our sense of justice. Freedom, we might say, becomes meaningful through the discourse of a community; that discourse is not binding outside of its coherence with an affirmation of existence and sense of justice.

A theological ethics of *culture,* I am suggesting, examines this correlation of freedom and language in specific historical situations. It understands and criticizes culture as a productive, even a metaphoric, clash between free action and the myths, symbols, and narratives that present ways of being in this world. Culture is not simply the form of a religious substance; it is a conflict-riddled enactment of human vulnerability against the background of a primary affirmation of life and the demand of justice. Yet, how is this a *theology* of culture? How is it not simply a construction of the theologian's imagination or an odd form of sociology? Since a theological ethics of culture is, as I claimed at the outset, the interpretation of culture from a particular perspective, this question really is about the angle of vision such interpretation entails.

Actually, I have attempted to adopt this interpretative perspective throughout this conclusion with respect to the themes addressed and the way of addressing them. A theological ethics of culture as I conceive it must examine the interrelation of claims about meaning (and thus theories of language and cultural production) with the specific human vulnerability (and thus social analysis and political theory) from the perspective of the human as the one who in its identity and action affirms life as a gift. To be sure, theologians will weight differently the respect to which the symbols and narratives of a specific community aid in this task. Yet they all seem to agree that religious discourse, like all figurative or symbolic forms, transforms our perception of the real. Specifically, religious discourse transforms the fault-ridden character of human existence and thus enables a primary affirmation of life. The theologian examines culture attentive to the affirmation of life that shines through the ambiguity of human existence. The theologian claims, then, that her or his reflections on the name God and the experience of the sacred is precisely about that reality which is not reducible to our words or our social and individual identities, but which creates existence and empowers the affirmation of life endowed with a sense of justice.

So conceived, this form of reflection helps to examine the "for whom" against which theoretical reflection must be measured. It transforms the claim about the human good found in Ricoeur's philosophy, since it argues that in judging theories by a human measure, we, in fact, also affirm life itself and, in so doing, affirm the divine. God is that which evokes and grounds the testimony of freedom. God is that in relation to which all claims to meaning and value in human action and association are measured and judged. Given this, the community in which we dwell is the open, temporal reality of freedom and life itself under the claims of justice. It is this community of life that is the scene of our search for wholeness and freedom. This transforms any anthropocentric theory of value into an affirmation of the goodness of existence despite the actuality of evil and ignites a theocentric freedom in the service of others and our world.

CONCLUSION

In this conclusion I have attempted to rehabilitate the theology of culture.[16] I have done so with respect to fundamental issues and theoretical debates shaping the direction of humanistic inquiry. The wager has been that a theological ethics of culture might join in rejuvenating humanistic inquiry while retaining its distinctive task. And what is that? It is often said that in our day thinkers have given up on the ancient task of seeking wisdom, of probing the questions that fill the human heart. The task facing us is to reopen the endless inquiry into who we are and how we should live. By responding to this task, I believe, one confronts not only the ambiguity of existence but also, surprisingly, its affirmation.

NOTES

1. Paul Ricoeur, "The Language of Faith," trans. R. Bradley De Ford, in *The Philosophy of Paul Ricoeur: An Anthology of His Work,* ed. Charles E. Reagan and David Stewart (Boston: Beacon Press, 1978), pp. 237–38.
2. Langdon Gilkey, *Society and the Sacred: Toward a Theology of Culture in Decline* (New York: Crossroads, 1981), p. x.
3. Paul Tillich, "Aspects of a Religious Analysis of Culture," in his *Theology of Culture,* ed. Robert C. Kimball (Oxford: Oxford University Press, 1959), p. 43.
4. Ibid., p. 49.
5. Richard Rorty, "The Priority of Democracy to Philosophy," in his *Objectivity, Relativism, and Truth: Philosophical Papers,* vol. 1 (Cambridge: Cambridge University Press, 1991), p. 191.
6. Paul Ricoeur, "Ethics and Culture," trans. David Pellauer, in *Political and Social Ethics,* ed. David Stewart and Joseph Bein (Athens: Ohio University Press, 1974), p. 262. See also his "Religion, Atheism, and Faith" and "Guilt, Ethics, and Religion," in his *The Conflict of Interpretations: Essays in Hermeneutics,* ed. Don Ihde (Evanston, Ill.: Northwestern University Press, 1974), pp. 440–67, 425–39.
7. John B. Thompson, *Ideology and Modern Culture: Critical Social Theory in the Era of Mass Communication* (Stanford, Calif.: Stanford University Press, 1990).

8. Jürgen Habermas, *Moral Consciousness and Communicative Action*, trans. Christian Lenhardt and Shierry Weber Nicholsen, introduction by Thomas McCarthy (Cambridge, Mass.: MIT Press, 1990), p. 200.
9. See Richard Rorty, "Postmodern Bourgeois Liberalism," in his *Objectivity, Relativism, and Truth*, pp. 197–202.
10. Ibid., p. 197.
11. Rorty, "The Priority of Democracy to Philosophy," p. 192.
12. See Michael Walzer, *Interpretation and Social Criticism* (Cambridge, Mass.: Harvard University Press, 1987). For an interesting discussion of the problem of responsibility for social totalities, see William Horosz, *The Crisis of Responsibility: Man as the Source of Accountability* (Norman: University of Oklahoma Press, 1975).
13. Rorty, "Postmodern Bourgeois Liberalism," p. 197.
14. Paul Ricoeur, "Phenomenology and Hermeneutics," in *Nous* 9 (1975): 94.
15. On this, see Ricoeur's essay "Freedom in the Light of Hope," in *Essays in Biblical Interpretation*, ed. Lewis S. Judge (Philadelphia: Fortress Press, 1981), pp. 155–82.
16. I wish to thank Lois Malcolm for helpful comments on this concluding essay.

DAVID JASPER

A RESPONSE TO ROBERT SCHARLEMANN

My response to Professor Scharlemann's fine paper does not presume to be critical, for his argument is persuasive and beautifully constructed. What I wish to do is to attempt to reply as a literary critic to a philosopher, each having a common concern for theology. I do not wish to repeat his proposals but to scrutinize their implications from a different perspective and perhaps ask questions, therefore, for the consequences of the kind of interdisciplinarity represented by Paul Ricoeur.

Jacques Derrida, in "The White Mythology," cites a passage from Anatole France's "Garden of Epicurus":

> the metaphysicians, when they make up a new language, are like knife-grinders who grind coins and medals against their stone instead of knives and scissors. They rub out the relief, the inscriptions, the portraits, and when one can no longer see on the coins Victoria, or Wilhelm, or the French Republic, they explain: these coins now have nothing specifically English or German or French about them, for we have taken them out of time and space; they are now no longer worth, say, five francs, but rather have an inestimable value, and the area in which they are a medium of exchange has been infinitely extended.[1]

Against these "metaphysicians," Derrida is defending what Scharlemann calls the textuality of a text that "is an articulated body that localizes a being in the world." I respond most readily to this defense of the particularity of textuality, as well as to (1)

Scharlemann's critique of Ricoeur's essay "Qu'est-ce qu'un texte" ("What Is a Text?" 1970)—which is primarily concerned with interpretation and not textuality; (2) his revision of Ricoeur's sense of metaphor as unitive of being and nonbeing "in the service of making a new reference to reality"; and finally (3), his suspicion of the poetic reprise of history in the context of the discussion of threefold mimesis in *Time and Narrative,* volume 1.

What is striking about Scharlemann's argument is the radical possibility that it offers for a theological restatement that avoids the essentially conservative limitations of Ricoeur's proposals made in the face of the aporias of temporality. His argument provides, furthermore, a remarkable defense of Derrida's critique of phonocentrism in the light of Jürgen Habermas's criticism of Derrida in *The Philosophical Discourse of Modernity* (1985).[2]

Like Scharlemann, Derrida consciously employs and distances himself from Heidegger's later philosophy, and particularly from what he describes as its "metaphorics of proximity."[3] Derrida, with a brutality uncharacteristic of Scharlemann, explodes metaphysical thought from the inside by employing the strategy of the literary critic upon the philosophical text and overturning its basic conceptual hierarchies, its claim to be a redescription of the reality of being there in the world and its foundational relationships. Habermas describes Derrida's procedures as follows: "Derrida proceeds by a critique of style, in that he finds something like indirect communications, by which the text itself denies its manifest content, in the rhetorical surplus of meaning in the literary strata of texts that present themselves as non-literary. In this way, he compels texts by Husserl, Saussure, or Rousseau to confess their guilt, against the explicit interpretations of their author."[4] Texts, in other words, are brought to confess their textuality. Paul de Man, in *Allegories of Reading,* goes so far as to say that to the extent that metaphysics or philosophy is "literary," its deconstruction is impossible. Its particularity, then, one might say, is irreducible, and, in de Man's words, "it at least establishes a somewhat more reliable point of 'reference' from which to ask the question."[5] In his discussion of Rousseau's *Social Contract,* de Man explores at length what Scharlemann would describe as "the unique voice of a text, . . . [which] cannot be abstracted from the text itself." This unique voice clearly undermines the authority of Rousseau's legislative discourse: the *Social Contract* is a theoretical description of the state that disintegrates as soon as it is put into motion.[6] Habermas concludes that, "the constraints constitutive for knowledge of a philosophical text only become accessible when the text is handled as what it would not like to be—as a literary text."[7]

I take Scharlemann's contention that textuality means that the literary work is "another form of being there in the world" to be another version of Derrida's purposely paradoxical statement that any interpretation is inevitably a false interpretation, and any understanding, a misunderstanding. In his essay "Being, 'as not': Overturning the Ontological,"[8] Scharlemann makes a distinction between an ontological entity, a religious entity, and a theological entity. He summarizes this distinction as follows: "an 'ontological' text is a text that both carries a thought-sense and also is the world that sense signifies; a 'religious' text is that same unity of meaning and signified except that the meaning is an image instead of a thought; and a 'theological' text is a religious or ontological text that is overturned so as not to be what it is or to be what it is not."[9] The textuality implied in this theological mode is very different from the poetic meditation that, as Scharlemann describes it, Ricoeur proposes between the temporality of the psychological and the cosmological. It is a textuality that embraces the temporal overturning of Colossians 3:1–2, and offers an "authentic" theological possibility for "indwelling" the resurrection narratives of the New Testament.

Precisely because I am so persuaded by Scharlemann's argument, I find myself less than satisfied with his references to Bultmann and the idea of kerygma in the 1941 essay "The New Testament and Mythology."[10] This essay can hardly anticipate the notion of textuality insofar as kerygma is actually recoverable through a hermeneutic of demythologizing.[11] Bultmann's procedures of interpretation actually *deny* the textuality of the New Testament texts by moving through them in order to clarify the ontological structure of human existence. If it is by this means that we encounter kerygma as "the materiality of [Jesus'] living presence," then this theological program has engaged in no radical overturning, no escape from the essentially "poetic mediation" of Ricoeur, no possibility of a new temporality that allows us to "dwell within" the resurrection narratives.

Like many people, I was much exercised some years ago by the long notorious review of *Time and Narrative* by Professor J. Hillis Miller in the *Times Literary Supplement* (October 9, 1987, pp. 1104–5). Miller, with characteristic bluntness, challenged Ricoeur's presuppositions about language and denied that there is such a thing as an "experience of being in the world and in time" prior to language. Scharlemann, more elegantly, has developed this criticism in the direction of textuality. He has begun the crucial task of theological reconstructions after Derrida, and not in terms of a kind of Jewish mysticism (as Habermas characterizes Derrida), but of a rereading of New Testament texts in terms of their particular substance, their textuality. It is a radical task between literature and theology never addressed by Bultmann in this way. Indeed, I am hard put to identify any predecessors in the history of New Testament criticism: perhaps that is the fate of a genuine indwelling.

NOTES

1. Anatole France, "Le jardin d'Epicure," quoted by Jacques Derrida, in his *Marges de la Philosophie* (Paris: Editions de Minuit, 1972), p. 250; my translation.
2. Jürgen Habermas, *The Philosophical Discourse of Modernity,* trans. Frederick Lawrence (Cambridge: Cambridge University Press, 1987), pp. 61–84.
3. Jacques Derrida, *Marges de la Philosophie,* quoted ibid., p. 162.
4. Habermas, *Philosophical Discourse of Modernity,* p. 189.
5. Paul de Man, *Allegories of Reading* (New Haven, Conn.: Yale University Press, 1979), p. 131.
6. See Edgar McKnight, *The Bible and the Reader* (Philadelphia: Fortress Press, 1985), pp. 89–91.
7. Habermas, *Philosophical Discourse of Modernity,* p. 189.
8. Robert Scharlemann, "Being 'As Not': Overturning the Ontological," in his *Inscriptions and Reflections: Essays in Philosophical Theology* (Charlottesville: University Press of Virginia, 1989), pp. 54–65.
9. Ibid., p. 57.
10. Rudolf Bultmann, "The New Testament and Theology," in *Kerygma and Myth: A Theological Debate,* ed. Hans Werner Bertsche, trans. Reginald Fuller (London: S.P.C.K., 1953), pp. 1–44.
11. See Lynn M. Poland, *Literary Criticism and Biblical Hermeneutics: A Critique of Formalist Approaches* (Chicago: American Academy of Religion, 1985), p. 31.

DONALD G. MARSHALL

RESPONSE TO GERALD BRUNS

I WANT TO START with a word or two about Paul Ricoeur's work. Ricoeur's great strength, I would claim, is his responsiveness to the currents of thought in the contemporary intellectual world. This is not quite syncretism, as though he had just cobbled together bits and pieces from every current system of thought. Ricoeur's career gives the impression of someone working through his own line of reflection, but doing so with his ears open to what the people around him are saying. In taking up the themes, issues, and critiques he hears, he is not just co-opting or defensively absorbing them. Each encounter—whether with psychoanalysis or Marxism or analytic philosophy—subtly or not so subtly transforms even his most basic ideas. His encounter with Freud, for instance, transformed Ricoeur's focus on the concept of consciousness as it had dominated a philosophical line from Descartes to Husserl. Ricoeur did not just abandon his own theme or become a convert parroting his master.

To borrow the terms Ricoeur says are the basic structure of Jesus' parables, he went through a threefold process.[1] First came *finding*, the *encounter* with the other. Second came *reversal*, a conversion that is hard to characterize, since it is a reorientation that simultaneously holds to continuity and also takes one's thought in a new and unexpected direction. And finally, there comes *decision*, acting along that new direction. This last stage emerges in those strangely moving interpretations Ricoeur offers of the thinkers he encounters—Freud, Nietzsche, Marx, and so on. These are classic hermeneutic exercises, representations of another thinker's ideas that strengthen their argument, as Plato would say, and thus acknowledge their least-restricted validity. But at the same time, in the process of commenting there is a discovery of fresh possibilities in one's thinking, and so a recovery of something further to say that is one's own. The other thinker's discourse is not simply submitted to; yet Ricoeur accepts a responsibility to speak in that other person's terms. Only by doing so can he show that he really does understand, that he has opened himself to the other's reflective situation so that he can speak for their ideas almost better than they could themselves.

I think this capacity is Ricoeur's great virtue, and it lays bare the sense in which his is a thoroughly hermeneutic kind of thinking. He is not obsessed with his own idea, but seems really to believe that his idea will only come into its own insofar as it opens itself to the ideas of others. This does not seem to me a widespread virtue in our era. We tend to prize stubborn thinkers who get a deep insight and will not let go of it. In Isaiah Berlin's terms, we distrust the fox, who has many ideas, but we are impressed by the hedgehog, who has only one, but a great one. This valuation may be a symptom of living in a scattered era swept by all kinds of fashion. Those who stay put amid the cultural flux end up setting the agenda. Doing so strikes us as the ethics, or even the piety, of thinking.

This attitude deserves some reflection. I believe it is too one-sided to attribute integrity and seriousness to the hedgehog while condemning the fox as vacillating and superficial. In fact, two ethical stances come into conflict here, stances that could be figured under various terms: responsiveness and steadfastness, ecumenism and fidelity, diversity and integrity, integration and purity. It cannot be that one of these is right and the other wrong. Yet both demands cannot be satisfied at once. If Hegel is right, we have the potential for tragedy, a conflict of two rights—and *tragedy* may not be too dramatic a term for a clash of intellectual temperaments, considering the historical consequences of ideologies in our time. Contemporary thinkers pride themselves, perhaps prematurely, on their critique of power. Yet when two thinkers encounter each other, some are ready to say that the one who changes as a result of the encounter is "weak" and the one who remains impervious to influence is "strong."

What are the hermeneutic consequences of this predilection for thinkers who stick to one idea and push it to its last extreme? This question lies at the heart of Gerald Bruns's paper. It is a genuinely hermeneutic question, because it calls, not for an answer that would dispose of it, but for a response that deepens our grasp of the question and of the thinking it opens. To put it most directly: Is the aim and task of interpretation really to understand something?

Bruns figures this question under the rubric of the ancient quarrel between philosophy and poetry. Poetry, it seems, doesn't explain anything. It is remarkably thoughtless and irresponsible. Given deep-seated and, I expect, universal cultural presuppositions, we cannot help figuring thoughtless irresponsibility as a sort of pleasure, so that it seems as though poets are having quite a good time. What this means is that they find the world and words highly interesting. They take an interest in the mere existence of things, and for them, words themselves are things and not "means of communication" that cooperatively disappear into the function of meaning something. Bruns describes one way of regarding what is going on in such a case: things get out of hand, out of control. Or maybe more precisely, it is we who are out of control.

Plato recognized the peculiar attraction of this state of affairs, but in the long run, he would have none of it. This is not just an epistemological question. Plato does frequently ask what knowledge poetry can give us, but even before that, we must ask what function knowledge serves according to Plato. The answer is not that it gives us justified beliefs about the world around us, but that it gives us a firm standpoint that justifies our refusing to interest ourselves too much in what goes on in the world around us. This is philosophical knowing's ethical function. Ethics here is not just rules of conduct. It means shaping a character that keep its shape against the deforming pressure exerted by the flow of experience. Poetry makes us too interested in, too responsive to, experience—that is what he means when he says it "waters the passions" (*pathê:* not just "feelings," but any submission to alien influences).

The point for Plato, then, is, not to understand poetry, but to control it—to write it only under the strict supervision of this sort of philosophical knowledge or ethical character. But Plato loved poetry and could not help writing it, so it took Aristotle, who was not thus passionately self-divided, to show how this control could be done effectively. The secret is to regulate, not the content, but the form. Indeed, the Aristotelian philosopher's great skill is abstracting and codifying forms—of tragedies, arguments, organisms, anything. Thus philosophy learned not to bother expelling poetry, but instead to neutralize its baneful influence by regulating its form and ignoring its content, its real substance. That is to say, it refused on ethical grounds to interpret—to understand and open itself to—what poetry says.

But what does poetry say, and why should we expect it to conflict with the ethical? To discern the answer that modern thinkers symptomatically find themselves giving, we can draw on Kierkegaard's contrast in *Fear and Trembling* between the aesthetic and the ethical.[2] The aesthetic is the immediate, the sensate, the psychical, feelings and desires, the individual. The ethical is the universal. It takes the form of a principle. Our duty is to control our wandering and wavering individuality and to act on principle. By doing so, we will make ourselves intelligible, Kierkegaard says, to ourselves and others. That a man should kill his own daughter is unintelligible. But if Agamemnon sacrifices Iphigenia in the name of his duty as leader of the whole people, then we can understand what he is doing, painful though it be. Of course, Kierkegaard thinks dialectically, so he does not leave it there. Beyond the ethical is the religious. The first immediacy of the aesthetic turns into a second immediacy, one where the single individual enters into an absolute relation to the absolute that is higher than the ethical universal. Kierkegaard remarks in passing that the religious "is the only power that can rescue the aesthetic from its battle with the ethical" (p. 93).

The particular relevance of this to hermeneutics and the issue of understanding seems to me to come out in Kierkegaard's discussion of "the secret." In the aesthetic, keeping something hidden increases the tension, generates "inwardness," makes things "interesting." By contrast, the ethical requires disclosure. It demands the clarity of concepts and principles and the open examination of one's action to see whether it is justified. From the point of view of ethics, concealment looks like lying, and poets lie all day long—not that they're *trying* to mislead you, it's just that they cannot help it. They're always saying things that are *pseudos*, misleading; poetry is a way of not saying what you mean exactly.[3] But the ethical insists that you say exactly what you mean.

For Kierkegaard, the hidden or secret is recovered at the stage of the religious. The question is whether Abraham is justified in not telling Sarah or Isaac about the sacrifice God has required of him. That his silence increases the dramatic tension and interest of the story is acceptable from the aesthetic point of view. It is intolerable from the ethical point of view. But from the religious point of view, it again becomes acceptable, because Abraham dwells in relation to the paradox. With infinite resignation, he has given up Isaac, the very thing that makes his life worth living. Yet in faith, he expects to get Isaac back again. This double movement simply cannot be put into words. To attempt to do so draws faith back into the ethical, trivializes it, and deprives the individual of the depth and seriousness, the greatness, that only the passion of faith can grant. As Kierkegaard says, "if I cannot make myself understood when I speak, then I am not speaking. This is the case with Abraham" (p. 113). How could he say to Isaac, "I am going to sacrifice you, as God has commanded me to do, but I have unshakable faith that . . ."—that what? The relief of speaking, Kierkegaard says, is that it "translates me into the universal" (p. 113), so that I make myself intelligible. But Abraham cannot speak, because "he cannot say that which would explain everything (that is, so it is understandable)" (p. 115). "Speak he cannot; he speaks no human language. . . . he speaks in a divine language, he speaks in tongues" (p. 114).

Likewise, I infer, the poet speaks in a way that cannot be understood, and he comes into his true vocation only when his unintelligibility is not merely playing with secrets for aesthetic effect, but bringing us one by one into an absolute relation to the absolute. Johannes de Silentio, the pseudonymous author of *Fear and Trembling,* repeatedly insists he cannot understand Abraham, he can only admire him. He does not himself claim to make the movement of faith. He fulfills the poet's humbler task: he remembers Abraham and transforms him by admiring, loving, and delighting in him. But decidedly he does not understand him, and his book does not make him intelligible.

Now here is the decisive question. Hans-Georg Gadamer says that "Being that can be understood is language."[4] This is a phrase that irritates a spectrum of commentators from Marxists to Heideggerians. Language, they say, cannot make being understandable. Language itself, so far as it has being, is not understandable. Understanding is not how we stand in relation to being.

I want to acknowledge that I feel the force of the insight behind this objection. Yet some questions arise in my mind. The first is, How are we to understand this word *understand?* There runs through Bruns's paper a language that seems to think of understanding as getting a grip on something, pinning it down, putting it in its place where we can get hold of it whenever we want it. I think this is not what Gadamer, at least, means by *understanding.* When Ricoeur understands Freud, he has not pinned his back to the mat. It is something more like Jacob wrestling with the demon of the Jabbok. Jacob ends up with a dislocated hip, a blessing, and a new name, Israel. He will never be the same, though he will not be somebody else exactly. In Ricoeur's spirit, we certainly do not want to quibble over the term. Perhaps *understanding* is the wrong word for this peculiar outcome that is the aim of the hermeneutic activity. But is there a better word?

Second, what is at stake in Kierkegaard's promise that the religious will rescue the aesthetic from its battle with the ethical? Is not this a very—dare one say—postromantic assertion? I *think* one could ask not absurdly whether Plato, still less Aristotle, could even understand what we call the religious, and I at least would be interested in hearing the answer. Was romanticism bound to generate both the aesthetic and the religious in a pincer movement to smash the ethical? To put it differently, is a category of transcendence intruding into the realm of finitude? If so, could this seepage have anything to do with the closure of the Hebrew and Christian canon? I mean, do we need to acknowledge some split in hermeneutics between sacred and profane that does not correspond to the separation of biblical from nonbiblical?[5]

Let me return to my opening concern about the relation of the hermeneutic to the ethical in modern thought. The call for "conversation" (or its more technical-sounding cousin "dialogue") has become a cliché that spans the work of thinkers as diverse as Michael Oakeshott, Martin Buber, Hans-Georg Gadamer, and Richard Rorty. The aim of conversation, if not "understanding" exactly, may at least be "coming to an understanding" with another about something.[6] This conception has all the earmarks of humanism, pluralism, and democratic process, where the ethical issues are the diversity of voices admitted to the conversation and the good faith of the participants in listening attentively to each other. Kierkegaard, of course, would reject the term out of hand. Conversation is mediation, and a person's relation to God admits no mediation. To borrow terms from Hans Kellner, When does the immediate become the unmediable, and what are its claims when it does so? Recently, the term *Other* (with a capital letter) has provided a way to point to this question without quite committing oneself to anything in particular. Kierkegaard would have unhesitatingly called this "Other" God. Heidegger calls it Being and later "the fourfold." Levinas calls it "the face." For many, it is the holocaust, the Shoah, in whose wake understanding and language have been ruined, so that to say anything trivializes and betrays. In

The Symbolism of Evil, Ricoeur himself confronted the immediate unintelligible in the shape of evil.

The conflict here is the more intense and perhaps the more irresolvable because the contest is over what "the Other" is and how we must stand in relation to it. Are we to enter into conversation and negotiate an understanding? Or must our response be Abraham's "Here I am," followed by absolute fidelity and obedience? I recognize that the very way I have stated the case already implies room for hermeneutic maneuver: the "Other" ranges through several appearances from sheer evil to the source of the infinite ethical, and thus undergoes the differentiation that makes negotiation possible.[7] The accusation that runs from Kierkegaard to Levinas is that those who insist on understanding are complacent self-deceivers incapable of the passion of faith. On the other hand, to insist that the "Other" would be effaced or disfigured by any effort to understand runs its own risks of self-deception.[8] One such is the substitution of ad hominem accusation for reflective mutual inquiry—not a promising example of what respect for the Other will yield in practice. Moral authority claimed by invoking an "Other" that is left blank (the night in which all cats are grey, as Hegel says) can become just an alibi, too.

I cannot claim to decide. Even to begin engineering an exchange, as I have done, presupposes the possibility of dialogue and therefore the primacy of hermeneutics. Perhaps the only way to end is just to pose again the fundamental question: Do we still want to say that the aim of interpreting—indeed of human existence itself—is understanding?

NOTES

1. Paul Ricoeur, "Listening to the Parables of Jesus," in *The Philosophy of Paul Ricoeur: An Anthology of His Work,* ed. Charles E. Reagan and David Stewart (Boston: Beacon Press, 1978), pp. 239–45, esp. 240–41.
2. Page numbers that follow in the text citations are from Kierkegaard, *Fear and Trembling* and *Repetition,* ed. and trans. Howard V. Hong and Edna H. Hong (Princeton, N.J.: Princeton University Press, 1983).
3. I take the phrase from J. L. Austin, "Pretending," in *Philosophical Papers,* ed. U. O. Urmson and G. J. Warnock (Oxford: Clarendon, 1961), pp. 201–19, esp. 219–an essay highly relevant to poetry. In the *Sophist,* Plato takes up the closely related problem of the image and greatly deepens the polemical and somewhat sophistical line of thought in the *Republic,* book 10. Images, he argues, do not merely conceal what they depict but reveal that every thing is also self-concealing. But logos—words and thinking—is a kind of imaging. The risk is

that we will be unable to separate the real from the unreal, and thus the true from the false. See Stanley Rosen's illuminating commentary, *Plato's Sophist and the Drama of Original and Image* (New Haven, Conn.: Yale University Press, 1983). The point is that poetry is not just on holiday from the ethical life, but that it makes the ethical life impossible by hollowing out its necessary presuppositions.

4. Hans-Georg Gadamer, *Truth and Method,* rev. trans. Joel B. Weinsheimer and Donald G. Marshall (2d ed.; New York: Continuum, 1989), p. 474. Jürgen Habermas expressed the Marxist critique by insisting that labor, above all, had a reality that stood outside language and offered grounds for a critique of linguistic distortion. See his "The Hermeneutic Claim to Universality," trans. Josef Bleicher, in *Contemporary Hermeneutics: Hermeneutics as Method, Philosophy, and Critique,* ed. Josef Bleicher (London: Routledge, 1980), pp. 181–211, and Gadamer's reply, "The Universality of the Hermeneutical Problem," in *Philosophical Hermeneutics,* ed. and trans. David E. Linge (Berkeley: University of California Press, 1976), pp. 3–17, as well as *Truth and Method,* pp. 545–48. The Heideggerian critique of Gadamer is implicit in Gerald Bruns, *Heidegger's Estrangements: Language, Truth, and Poetry in the Later Writings* (New Haven and London: Yale University Press, 1989).
5. I do not mean this to sound too cryptic. The point is that the closure of the canon fixes a text that inevitably grows more alien with the passage of time. Hans Frei's *The Eclipse of Biblical Narrative* (New Haven, Conn.: Yale University Press, 1974) traces the emergence of historicist biblical scholarship out of this alienation—a scholarship that was anathema to Kierkegaard. Schleiermacher attempted to face reality by fashioning a unified hermeneutic that integrated the historical and divinatory without privileging the biblical text. Friedrich von Schelling asserted that poetry was the vehicle of religious insight and substituted the universal syncretism of myth for the exclusivity of the Bible. In his conception of the book as spiritual instrument, Mallarmé sought a book that could be for the modern world what the Bible was for the ancient. Contemporary thought replaces "the book" with the open working of textuality—to echo the series of puns (*l'ouvre, l'oeuvre, livre*) that guides Maurice Blanchot's *L'Espace littéraire* (Paris: Gallimard, 1955). Such a text, precisely by its disseminative refusal of closure, remains the site of the "unnameable," as Beckett titles one of his unclassifiable works (a title that hovers in an irreducible, strange, and undecidable proximity to the unnameable God). Many in our age seem convinced that only these texts and the self-vexing thinking they sponsor have any claim to seriousness. *Tout le reste est littérature.*
6. This illuminating suggestion was one contribution by Joel Weinsheimer to our "Translators' Preface" to Gadamer's *Truth and Method,* p. xvi.
7. To cite the *Sophist* once more, Plato pursues the motif of the destruction of all logos by those who hold to their integrity and refuse to weave words into discourses, which, though never strong enough to ensure insight, are yet the only way to it.
8. For a sympathetic reading, yet also critique, of Levinas, see David E. Klemm, "Levinas's Phenomenology of the Other and Language as the Other of Phenomenology," *Man and World* 22 (1989): 403–26. I raised some reservations about another powerfully extremist modern thinker in "The Necessity of Writing: Death and Imagination in Maurice Blanchot's *L'Espace littéraire,*" *Boundary 2,* no. 14 (1985–86): 225–36, esp. 234–35.

MORNY JOY

RESPONSE TO HANS KELLNER AND HERMAN RAPAPORT

Response to Kellner

THE FRAGILITY OF HUMAN LIFE, the fragility of language: Is it futile to attempt to understand and express awareness of this fragility? Are such attempts to be couched in language that is ironic, realistic, or optimistic? What are mere words in the face of fate?

While Hans Kellner does not dispute Ricoeur's endeavor to reconcile our past and our present by means of narrative sequences, he questions the spirit in which this task is done. In one sense this is a temperamental difference, but it indicates a profound dissimilarity in attitude toward history and the role of narrative. Kellner discerns an unthematized preoccupation with death (with "mortographies," as he calls them) in Ricoeur's discussion of historians—death as the obvious limit of historical consciousness, but death also as the presiding genius of the game of life. Is all narrative just a stopgap, a reassurance in the face of inevitable defeat? Or does narrative serve some other purpose? Kellner sees *Time and Narrative* as an edifice built on a twofold anxiety—anxiety in the face of death, but also anxiety about the end of the narrative era, when the wellspring of affirmation and imagination has run dry.

In contrast, Ricoeur's treatise can be read as a work of affirmation and hope, namely, that despite the adversity, erosion, even erasure, of human efforts (i.e., the discordance of human existence), new insights can continually be discerned and woven into the record of life known as history. It is not in any volume of *Time and Narrative* but in a reflection on Hannah Arendt's *The Human Condition* that Ricoeur makes his own profession of hope in this connection.

This acknowledgment of the frailty of a history that we don't "make," sounds like an ultimate memento mori. Our mortality is, so to speak, reasserted at the end of our travel. What, then, remains to *the thinker*—not the political animal—in front of death? The exaltation of birth, of a new beginning. Only natality—perhaps—escapes the illusion of immortality on the part of mortals who think eternity.[1]

Of primary importance for Ricoeur in this exercise of natality or being in the world is the cultivation of an identity, both personal and social. This identity is the result of a relationship to words and to narrative by which we discern what Ricoeur calls initially (after Heidegger) "our ownmost possibility," and more recently "a possible world I might inhabit." "For some years now I have maintained that what is interpreted in a text is the proposing of a world that I might inhabit and into which I might project my ownmost powers."[2] It is the formation of this identity, which Ricoeur terms "narrative identity," and the responsibility we assume for its linguistic mediations that constitute for Ricoeur a primary ethical duty.

This hermeneutical idea of subjectivity as a dialectic between the self and mediated social meanings has deep moral and political implications. It shows that there is an *ethic of the word,* that language is not just a concern of logic or semiotics, but entails the fundamental moral duty that people be responsible for what they say.[3]

As Kellner observes, Ricoeur does indeed invoke an anamnestic imperative in connection with history, both because he asserts that human life is worthy of record (especially that of the defeated and the forsaken) and because such records are conveyors of alternate visions of the world. This is not to say that Ricoeur subscribes to a facile conventionalism along the lines of learning from past mistakes. But he does have an optimism that is at odds with Kellner's reading of Braudel as a "satire on language" and his stress on the limitations of all human efforts to contain in words events and past experience. Yet Ricoeur's heuristic and positive attitude does not result from an ignorance of the inefficacies and inexactitude of language. In *The Rule of Metaphor,*[4] Ricoeur explores the "thingness" of language; the event that is discourse. He comments on the ambiguity or the equivocity of words, but he chooses instead to focus on polysemy as the basis of metaphor and the locus of creative potential in language (and ultimately in life). This is always Ricoeur's tendency, i.e., to emphasize the creative, positive element rather than to dwell on the scattershot that is all too evident in word and world. And even with the telling of the tale, the awareness that things could be otherwise will always haunt Ricoeur. Not only does he hold that we are subject to the effects of past deeds that influence us in ways we can never completely appreciate, but also that we can never predict the course of future events from past deeds and occurrences. Ricoeur would contend that even our best efforts to organize the future on the basis of past experiences cannot account for all possible ramifications. What happens is always something other than what we expected. Even our expectations change in largely unforeseeable ways (*Time and Narrative,* 3:257). It is only at the end of volume 3 of *Time and Narrative* that Ricoeur gives the rationale for such an immense and disparate study: he places the enigma of time in the context of the search for identity in time and place.

The mystery of time is not equivalent to a prohibition directed against language. Rather, it gives rise to the exigency to think more and to speak differently. If such be the case, we must pursue to its end the return movement, and hold that the reaffirmation of historical consciousness within the limits of its validity requires in turn the search, by individuals and the communities to which they belong, for their respective narrative identities. Here is the core of our whole investigation, for it is only within this search that the aporetics of time and the poetics of narrative correspond to each other in a sufficient way (*Time and Narrative,* 3:274).

It then becomes apparent that Ricoeur's principal intention has not been to arrive at a clearer definition of time, but rather to encourage the personal appropriation by a reader of the type of identity (i.e., narrative identity) that is consonant with the vicissitudes of our time-bound existence. In fostering this awareness, Ricoeur acknowledges that the days of a grand synthesis in the service of *Geist* are over. Hegel's "cunning of reason," whereby the present at once incorporates the past and projects the future is described as "a magician's trick that does not work" (*Time and Narrative,* 3:205). At the same time, Ricoeur acknowledges that the days of grand narratives have passed. "There is no plot of all plots capable of equating the idea of one humanity and one history" (*Time and Narrative,* 3:259). In addition, there is no timeless ahistorical Self to be deciphered. There is instead a narrative self, a provisional and plausible identity, sufficient for self-examination and reflective deliberation.

As I understand Ricoeur within the present philosophical climate, his dialectical mediations set a course between philosophical systems that try to define truth in watertight compartments, on the one hand, and postmodern postponements that send us off on interminable journeys, on the other. Ricoeur's self-critical hermeneutics affirms that narrative can provide a structure appropriate for understanding and discussing notions of self and experience within our world that is at once limited yet infinite.

Yet in deference to and admiration of Kellner's analysis, I would also want to pose the question: What is the cost of narrative? What is it that is omitted in its discursive portrayals? Initially one might be tempted to answer, poetry. Yet in the essay "Toward a Hermeneutic of the Idea of Revelation," Ricoeur states: "If to understand oneself is to understand oneself in front of the text, must we not say that the reader's understanding is suspended, de-realized, made potential just as the world itself is metamorphosized by the poem? If this is true, we must say that the imagination is that part of ourselves that responds to the text as a Poem, and that alone can encounter revelation no longer as an unacceptable pretension, but as a nonviolent appeal."[5]

It would be too long a digression in this context to discuss Ricoeur's expansion of the role of narrative to include all aspects of Aristotle's poetics,[6] but it is a question that is of great importance if one is to appreciate Ricoeur's vision of the panorama of narrative. Is it an all-inclusive mode? Or does Ricoeur, in his adaptation of poetics to narrative read into narrative itself, in the guise of imagination, a hidden hand at work in all our creative efforts? It is the answer to this question, I believe, that is at the source of Ricoeur's and Kellner's different approaches to history as narrative.

RESPONSE TO RAPAPORT

Professor Rapaport's discussion is almost exclusively based on one of Ricoeur's early essays, "Toward a Hermeneutic of the Idea of Revelation." This is a pity, since in "Manifestation and Proclamation,"[7] another essay written around the same time, Ricoeur specifically answers many of the criticisms that Rapaport has identified. However, it is in *Time and Narrative* (3:116–26) that Ricoeur compares his own usage of the term *trace* with that of Levinas. Had Rapaport studied these two other texts, his evaluation of Ricoeur in comparison with Levinas might have been very different.

Levinas and Ricoeur have a profound respect for each other. Though their orientations are different, they have always referred to each other with admiration. In *Time and Narrative,* vol. 3, Ricoeur singles out Levinas's article "The Trace of the Other," stating: "Yet I cannot overestimate how much my investigation of the role of the trace in the problematic of the role of reference in history owes to this magnificent meditation" (p. 124).

So what are the differences between Ricoeur and Levinas, particularly on the question of the trace? Professor Rapaport does not pursue this obvious point of comparison regarding the trace at all, being content to locate Levinas's disclosure of the trace in "the pre-syntactic, pre-logical and pre-disclosive." In contrast, he declares that, for Ricoeur, any disclosure is linguistically mediated. This indeed is true at one level, and Ricoeur himself would not contest such a description. However, I feel there are finer distinctions to be made by a more complex and nuanced comparison of the work of the two scholars.

In "Manifestation and Proclamation," Ricoeur distinguishes two forms of revelation: as manifestation or hierophany and as proclamation (where specific sacred texts are paradigmatic for a tradition). Ricoeur examines the likelihood of the mutual exclusion of the two forms by reason of their different relations to language, but he also focuses on the ways in which they can intersect. Ricoeur's reading of the sacred and its symbolic forces works toward a dialectic of manifestation and proclamation (a typical Ricoeur procedure). Though Ricoeur allows that epiphanies—dear to the heart of Eliade and the cornerstone of Levinas's contemplation of the trace—need not be expressed verbally, he holds that they can have symbolic and verbal repercussions. Thus, while their interaction does not preclude their being distinct forms of revelation, it also illustrates succinctly the circuity involved when natural symbols (or manifestation) are incorporated into a literate religious worldview by proclamation: "Of course, something like a creation story is necessary if symbolism is to come to language, but the myth that recounts it returns in a way to nature through the symbolism of the ritual where the element becomes once again immediately meaningful, as may be seen in the ritual of immersion, emersion, ablution, libation, baptism, etc." To understand this process, Ricoeur believes that a hermeneutics of symbols is needed, so that the latent meanings may achieve full appreciation. Hermeneutics and its reverberations do, in fact, presume a thematization that Ricoeur feels does not diminish, but rather enhances, the sacredness of symbolism. Rapaport, interpreting Levinas, feels this resort to language and consciousness detracts from the uniqueness of the experience of the sacred, which he believes ultimately eludes any representation. However, I feel that Rapaport does not do Ricoeur sufficient justice by implying that a reliance on linguistic structures (however disciplined) precludes any realization of the sacred. I believe that a subtle and discrete analysis of the different forms of revelation, i.e., of manifestation and proclamation, would avoid such an impasse.

In a similar vein, I would hold that although the respective uses of the word *trace* by Levinas and Ricoeur could easily be accounted for by a simplistic and exclusionary reading of manifestation and proclamation, Ricoeur's own discussion in *Time and Narrative*, vol. 3, points to a richer interrelationship than Rapaport allows. In concluding his discussion of the motifs of history, Ricoeur declares: "Under the impetus of a text from Levinas ['The Trace'], we were able to conclude our meditation on a deliberately enigmatic note. The trace, we said, signifies without making anything appear" (p. 156).

Now Rapaport (and other Levinas scholars) may read this as a trivialization of the theory of the trace. For, as we know, according to Levinas, the paradigmatic trace is the human face that manifests the Other in all its mystery. This is not a relationship of discourse, but in fact a revelation of the Infinite, which evokes the absence and inscrutability of the Absolute. Such an unveiling, in a Heideggerian way, only testifies to the utter transcendence and the elusive nature of the Other. "A trace is the insertion of space in time, the point at which the world inclines toward a past and a time. This time is a withdrawal of the other. Superiority does not reside in a presence in the world, but in an irreversible transcendence. . . . Only a being that transcends the world can leave a trace. A trace is a presence of that which properly speaking has never been there, of what is always past."[9]

Levinas's ethic is based on our responsibility to the face of the

Other, which is neither sign nor symbol, but the locus of the trace of the ever-elusive Other. "It is in the trace of the other that the face shines."[10]

Yet Ricoeur's own explorations of the trace in history, of the passage of what has passed, of what has not or cannot be present, bears the imprint, even in its seemingly secular quest, of the profound contemplation of Levinas. Ricoeur concedes that narrative (as history) may be inadequate to its task of reconstructing the past from the records and archives now present. And he does so in a way that pays homage to Levinas and evokes the infinite vistas of Ricoeur's own journey: "I would rather leave open the possibility that in the last analysis there is a relative Other, a historical Other, that in some way the remembered past is meaningful on the basis of an immemorial past" (*Time and Narrative,* 3:125).

It is in this relationship to the other, with its connotations of absolute responsibility and humility that Ricoeur and Levinas most resemble each other. For Levinas, God as Other can only be intimated through our allowing ourselves to be open to the same vulnerability in another human being. This ontological deference calls into question not only the traditional primacy of being but also the categories and assumptions that have sustained it. It is not surprising then that this radical orientation favors the encounter rather than the spoken word or the written text.

Ricoeur, in comparison, is more indebted to the Greek legacy and the primacy of the rational. Nevertheless, he will concede the limits of rationality, particularly in regard to our ability to interpret the Other in textual recounting. Ricoeur advocates a non-egoistic, nonnarcissistic, nonimperialist attitude before a text. Such a demeanor will not impose a meaning on the text, but it lets the text reveal a world wherein I can project my own most possibilities. This form of revelatory truth as instanced by texts has distinct implications for biblical scriptures as well. The resonances of being can only be heard, in Ricoeur's portrayal, by those whose respect before a text allows the expression of its originary impulse.

It is this disclosive element of texts that Ricoeur names the "poetic." However, he does not mean poetry in the narrow sense of the term. In *The Rule of Metaphor,* Ricoeur deliberately extends the domain of Aristotelian poiesis. Ricoeur there links the span of meaning of praxis and poiesis so that poiesis now refers to a dynamic and creative activity inseparable from the designs of being. It is in this connection too that Ricoeur incorporates his idea of imaginative response, which is his own idiosyncratic reading of the Kantian productive imagination, not just the aesthetic one that Rapaport charges. So Ricoeur does not restrict revelatory insights to poetry alone, as Rapaport intimates. In the context of Scripture, all texts, whether prose or lyric, are poetic; all such texts have the potential to disclose being, insofar as the hearer/reader does not impose the prescriptions of a sovereign consciousness. And this brings us back full circle.

Ricoeur's polyphonic and polysemic model of revelation draws a careful distinction between manifestation and proclamation. Manifestation would refer to an originary event: God's mark that is in history before being in speech, a revelation that evades any form of control by language or knowledge. Of this event, Ricoeur would say: "The God who reveals himself is a hidden God and hidden things belong to him."[11] On this score, both Ricoeur and Levinas are in agreement. Where they differ is that for Levinas the trace of this encounter with a disclosing/concealing Absolute can only now be discerned in the face of the Other. Revelation retains its manifestative element as an ethical imperative enjoining the same reverence toward the Other that one would have toward the Absolute. In contrast, Ricoeur focuses on the movement from revelation as an originary event to its transcription. This will, of course, involve testimony or proclamation. In this regard, Ricoeur admits that an interpretative process occurs, as it must when words are used as a medium. However, Ricoeur laments the psychologizing of the word *inspiration* as it has been used in connection with this process. What is needed, Ricoeur remarks, is "an authentic pneumatology." The transcription, however, does not mark the end of the line, for there is a further interpretive step. This is that of the reader of the word, whose world can be radically reordered by the reception of a sacred text. It is here that hermeneutics ultimately finds its place. It is here that meaning attempts to decipher the traces of the Absolute in the events recounted. It is here also that Ricoeur insists on abandoning any rational pretensions to plumb the depths of the Absolute: "It is precisely this movement of letting go which bears reflection to the encounter with contingent signs of the absolute which the absolute in its generosity allows to appear."[12]

Rapaport, I feel, makes too easy a comparison and contrast of Ricoeur and Levinas. It may be that Ricoeur emphasizes the linguisticality of revelation, but he is aware that, at its best, it is but imperfect mediation. Words relate an event that, for both Ricoeur and Levinas, surpasses our wildest imaginings, our profoundest thoughts.

NOTES

1. Paul Ricoeur, "Action, Story, and History: On Re-reading *The Human Condition,*" *Salmagundi* 60 (1983): 72.
2. Paul Ricoeur, *Time and Narrative,* trans. Kathleen McLaughlin and David Pellauer, 3 vols. (Chicago: University of Chicago Press, 1984–88), 1:81. Citations of this source will hereafter appear in the text.
3. "Interview with Paul Ricoeur," in *Dialogues with Contemporary Continental Thinkers,* ed. Richard Kearney (Manchester: Manchester University Press, 1984), p. 32.
4. Paul Ricoeur, *The Rule of Metaphor: Multi-Disciplinary Studies of the Creation of Meaning in Language,* trans. Robert Czerny with Kathleen McLaughlin and John Costello, S.J. (London: Routledge and Kegan Paul, 1978).
5. Paul Ricoeur, "Toward a Hermeneutic of the Idea of Revelation," *Harvard Theological Review* 70, no. 1–2 (January–April 1977): 37.
6. See Study 8 in Ricoeur, *The Rule of Metaphor,* pp. 303–13, and especially the footnotes on pp. 365–67.
7. Ricoeur, "Toward a Hermeneutic of the Idea of Revelation," pp. 1–37; Ricoeur, "Manifestation and Proclamation," *Blaisdell Institute Journal* 12 (Winter 1978): 13–35.
8. Ricoeur, "Manifestation and Proclamation," p. 19.
9. Emmanuel Levinas, "The Trace of the Other," in *Deconstruction and Theology,* ed. Mark Taylor (Chicago: University of Chicago Press), p. 359.
10. Ibid.
11. Ricoeur, "Toward a Hermeneutic of the Idea of Revelation," p. 25.
12. Ibid., p. 32.

JAMES F. MCCUE

RESPONSE TO PAMELA ANDERSON, WILLIAM SCHWEIKER, AND FRED DALLMAYR

REFLECTION ON ETHICS AND POLITICS has to traverse much more terrain than it once did. When Aristotle reflected on ethics or on political life, he had little uncertainty about how one should act; and the world about which he thought, the Greek polis, was in principle smaller than Johnson County, Iowa. And for Kant matters weren't so very much different.

For both, the problem was how to make sense of what they somehow already knew. It is a very different problem that confronts us. For our world is not the polis, it is not even the nation-state, organized by a code of law, a set of institutions, and a history. It is the fluid globe. And we literally do not know what to do. What is virtuous action? How are we to treat other humans as ends? These questions are far more perplexing to us than they seem to have been to either Aristotle or Kant.

Yet, at the same time, the very foundations of thought have lost whatever stability they once might have had, and it seems impossible to discuss issues of ethics and politics seriously without, as it were, starting all over again with basic issues of the self, of sociality, of language, and of action. Hence, any discussion of ethics and politics is likely to prove unsatisfactory for perhaps 90 percent of the participants: either it will be distressing for the superficiality with which it simply bypasses all the basic questions and pontificates on matters political, or it will never get to the point that it sheds any light on the issue that is, after all, paramount—How shall we act? Either one does not dive deep enough, or one never comes up.

This problem is especially difficult as I try to pull together the three papers before me. I am much more at home with the issues and the discourse of the Dallmayr paper, and will, I recognize, give my principal attention to it. Yet obviously, the issues raised by William Schweiker and by Pamela Anderson are fundamental to any Ricoeurian discourse about ethics and about politics.

Let me consider the Anderson paper first. The concern of her paper parallels some of the concerns of the papers in this volume dealing with history and fiction. At the end of her analysis, she expresses the concern that "the potentially distorting and mystifying power of Ricoeur's transcendental idealist conception of the productive imagination in the narrative constitution of self-identity" is not adequately guarded against. This concern echoes some of the concerns expressed in other essays in this volume that Ricoeur is, somehow, too optimistic, too acquiescent in the self-righteousness of tradition. What we want to consider is whether this is systemic or merely a matter of Ricoeur's personal disposition.

Anderson cites a passage from *Lectures on Ideology and Utopia* to show that for Ricoeur "the distorting function [of ideology] covers only a small surface of the social imagination." Much has already been said about Ricoeur's optimistic tendencies, and we see them again here. I agree that Ricoeur is much too glib in the passage she cites. He separates too radically ideology as legitimate communal self-identity and ideology as mask for the will to power. To a significant degree the former inescapably implies the latter. And he surely is too quick in limiting the "area" of ideology as mask to such modest proportions. But I wonder if she is right in seeing this as a consequence of his transcendental idealism. I wonder here if she does not confuse two things: an optimistic tendency that shows itself in many ways in Ricoeur's thought and the actual structure of his analysis. I grant that the tendency is there, but it seems to me that what we see here has really very little to do with Ricoeur's transcendental idealism, and could be corrected, if correction is needed, without any wholesale recasting of his thought.

Is reflective judgment sufficient to ensure the truth and justice of the forms of praxis, as well as the norms governing action, constituted by what is assumed to be the mythico-poetic imagination? she asks. Once again, there is surely a problem here about truth and justice and the forms of communal life. What do *truth* and *justice* mean with reference to praxis? And how does one reach and establish norms in this domain? I share the implicit criticism that Ricoeur is too little bothered by the difficulties here. In principle, he seems to be open to a quite radical critique of ideology, but because in the matter at hand he is criticizing the simplism of Marx's and Lenin's critique of bourgeois ideology, he gets bogged down in an antithetical oversimplification himself. It is unclear, however, that these problems are particularly rooted in Ricoeur's Kantian anthropology. The "forms of praxis," by which I suppose Anderson means societally endorsed and interpreted patterns of action, are problematic whether they are constituted by Ricoeur's "mythico-poetic imagination" or wherever they come from.

I have a similar problem with the Schweiker paper: it seems to me to identify real problems but to ascribe them to fictitious causes. He argues, first, that Ricoeur's ethical and religious anthropology is ultimately rooted in the modernist self, a self that, of course, none of us wants to be caught with. He then sketches, as an alternative, an anthropology and an ethics that are appropriately postmodern.

I have difficulty with the whole argument, though I have to acknowledge that part of my difficulty may be a certain foreignness to the idiom of discourse: I don't speak Ricoeur at home, speak it with a pronounced accent when I do speak it, and don't speak some of it at all. Nonetheless, it seems doubtful to me that Ricoeur's conception of the religious is basically subject centered. There may be an analogy between Ricoeur's position and the Augustinian-Calvinist doctrine of grace that seems to lie at the root of the conception of the religious that Schweiker cites. But that he is rigidly committed or even inclined to the latter by the former seems a gratuitous assertion. One could draw on certain other of Ricoeur's religious symbols—the Kingdom of God, for example, as used in "The Project of a Social Ethic"—that would not confine religion so exclusively to the project of the self.[1] In a general way, Ricoeur is simply not constrained to a noninteractional mode of analysis.

So far I have defended Ricoeur against his critics; and it may simply be that his faults here have not particularly interrupted my dogmatic slumber and that I have therefore not been a sufficiently critical reader. Let me, therefore, turn to the Dallmayr paper and to a more familiar terrain.

Dallmayr does a nice job of refocusing and repointing Ricoeur's

1957 essay "The Political Paradox." I agree with him that some of the ideas of the essay remain remarkably suggestive.[2] Dallmayr expresses two "qualms" in the concluding pages of his paper. Let me take issue with one and agree with and try to extend the second.

The first qualm is a concern over the role of a prepostmetaphysical metaphysics in Ricoeur's construal of the political paradox. Granted that Ricoeur's language is colored by the texts that he has made a part of himself, is it necessary to see any very substantive Hegelianism or Kantian noumena in his analysis of this paradox? One can talk about "the truth of polity"—in Rousseauian, i.e., pre-Kant and pre-Hegel, terms—along the lines of Rousseau's analysis: i.e., as what the citizen wills, or as that for the sake of which the citizen adheres to the general will. Similarly, one need not recur to Kant or Hegel (or Plato) to talk about the interaction of a certain ideal order with an only partially harmonious "reality." The fact that Dallmayr has to employ so many different ontologies (Augustine is called in, too) suggests that Ricoeur is really not working out of an articulated systematic base here.

Along similar lines, I think that Dallmayr overmetaphysicizes the issue of power and reason. In Ricoeur's essay, *power* tends to stand as a synonym for oppression or domination—thus representing the antipode to reason or rational accord, a move undercut by the postmetaphysical turn and by Hannah Arendt, Claude Lefort, and Michel Foucault. But is not Dallmayr here exaggerating the opposition between domination and reason? Ricoeur's point is that power is inseparable from the state, from polity, and that it always has the potential to become oppression or domination. One may agree or disagree; one may quarrel with Ricoeur's recurrent optimism; but it hardly seems an issue of premetaphysical and postmetaphysical turn.

Where I am entirely in agreement with Dallmayr is where he questions Ricoeur's equation of polity and state. Ricoeur remains too close to his texts in "The Political Paradox" and in many of his political essays, and identifies the Aristotelian-Hegelian model of the state as the state *tout court.* He has warned us in an essay written the year after "The Political Paradox" that "The real power of decision is often other than one might think; this is why one must always be doing new analyses to discover where the real power of decision lies. This is the real question." Yet he gives us no new analyses and does little with the question. Instead, he tells us in the same essay that: "The State has become for us the form of power at the interior of finite historical communities; it is the agent of a historical community, the mode of organization which makes it capable of making decisions; it is essentially a capacity for decision in a finite community."[3]

This identification of polis and state is problematic on two counts. The first is underscored by Dallmayr; I would want to add a second. First, it is simply fantastic to think of the state (or at least of most states) as being concerned with "moral and rational growth." Whatever may have been the case in Aristotle's Athens or Hegel's Prussia, most modern states are interested in such things only as instrumental to something more "important." If I might call on a distinction that Alasdair MacIntyre makes between "goods of excellence" and "goods of effectiveness,"[4] I would propose that states as we know them are interested primarily in the latter, and in the former only insofar as they serve the latter. The educational function of the state, for example, is largely and increasingly focused on competitiveness, and concerns itself with the values of classical (or any other) humanism only to the extent that these are seen as (still) having something to contribute to this ultimate state value.

This difficulty is compounded and clarified by the second, to which I referred earlier. Ricoeur, like many since the time of Kant, has expressed the hope that states would lose their ultimacy before the increasingly technological power of modern warfare destroyed us all. At the same time, he has acknowledged that this did not, in fact, seem to be happening. What he never gets into focus is that the modern state, especially in the post–World War II period, and perhaps especially since the early 1970s, has been losing control over certain functions that at least the more powerful states had seemed to possess.[5] His political thinking seems never to have been deeply subverted by political economy; but I would argue that increasingly the frcedom of self-determination of the state (always very limited in the case of weak or peripheral states) is constrained by the competitive pressures of the global economy. States are more than ever before in a situation analogous to that of a firm in traditional economic analysis: their options are seriously constrained by the dynamics of competition, and they will either heed these constraints or go under. The ability of states to domesticate the economy and to superimpose certain noneconomic values is under great pressure. It is not simply, I suspect that it is not primarily, postmodernist discourse that has decentralized the nation-state.

Dallmayr greets the recent collapse of Marxist regimes in Eastern Europe as a sign of the integrity of the political vis-à-vis the economic; and in "The Political Paradox" Ricoeur expands at length on this theme in response to the suppression of the 1956 Hungarian uprising. But this is to overlook an important part of the story. The modern state exists within what Joseph Schumpeter has aptly called the maelstrom of creative destruction that is the modern capitalist economy. What the changes in the Soviet Union and in Central Europe have shown, inter alia, is that no society (Albania may still count as an exception, but for how long?) can insulate itself from that maelstrom. One can just as appropriately look at recent developments there as demonstration that it is not possible to subordinate an economy to political norms and values. Viewed this way, there is a certain parallel between events there, Thatcherism in Britain, the partial dismantling of the New Deal here in the 1980s, and the abandonment of anything particularly socialistic by François Mitterand, the most popular and powerful French socialist in anyone's memory.

The ability to define ends, to decide basic matters about how a society is to live, is under constant pressure from the internationalization of the economy. The New Deal, Social Democracy, and practical Marxism all had in common the view that there was an ultimacy to politics, that it was the forum in which the ultimate values of a society were articulated, embodied, struggled over. The state was the instrument whereby we took command of our destiny and decided what we would be. In this respect it provided a rough analogue to the Aristotelian polis or the Hegelian state. All of these movements are presently in retreat; whether this is but a momentary relapse that will soon be righted or whether the recent past is the momentary relapse can hardly be decided. But I think it fair to say that Ricoeur's political thought proceeds as though this weren't happening.

My questions then to Paul Ricoeur, and to all of us, are the following:

1. If, as Dallmayr and I would both insist, the state is not the space in which humans become most richly and deeply human, what is that space? What are the communities that do what Aristotle ascribed to the polis? How are such communities to be identified and fostered? How do they relate to the state?
2. What is the political task? Is it, as Ricoeur sometimes seems to suggest, transformative? That is, is the task to reconstruct the

political world—along democratic socialist or even Christian socialist lines—so that it once again approximates Hegel's reason realized in the human being or the Aristotelian polis? Or is it, as Ricoeur sometimes also seems to suggest, especially in his addresses to Christian audiences, exemplary and oppositional: to create forms of life and interaction that contest the basic structures that are controlling in our public life? Or is it both, and if so what is the mediation between them?[6]

3. Are the frequently criticized features of Ricoeur's thought—a certain tendency toward optimism, a kind of "Cartesianism"—rooted in the very structure of his thought, and even in hermeneutics as the dominant method of his thinking? Or are these mere contingencies, merely a matter of personality, that others can easily leave behind in their appropriation of Ricoeur? Does the privileging of texts in Ricoeur create some of the tendencies noted? Does man-reading-text as the central paradigm have systemic repercussions?

NOTES

1. Paul Ricoeur, "The Project of a Social Ethic," trans. David Stuart in his *Political and Social Essays,* ed. David Stewart and Joseph Bien, trans. Donald Siewert et al. (Athens: Ohio University Press, 1974), p. 166. [Editorial note: A portion of James McCue's original response to William Schweiker's paper has been deleted because it pertained to sections no longer contained in the revised version of Schweiker's paper published in this volume. The central thrust of his critique, however, remains.]
2. It is, however, my impression that much of what Dallmayr calls to our attention could be found rather widely in the French non-Marxist Left of the 1950s. This is not a terrain that I know well, but I have in mind writers such as Albert Camus and Claude Julien. Surely the readers of *Esprit* and *Christianisme social* of that era would not have found these ideas surprising.
3. Ricoeur, "From Nation to Humanity: Task of Christians," trans. Hoke Robinson, in *Political and Social Essays,* pp. 139–40, 138.
4. Alasdair MacIntyre, *Whose Justice? Which Rationality?* (Notre Dame: University of Notre Dame Press, 1988), p. 32.
5. In their immediate pasts, the powerful industrial states were to a significant (albeit not an absolute) degree able to define social policy and to impose such definition onto a national economy. With all its limitations, for example, that was what the New Deal meant to most Americans: that there were choices, and that they were to be made through the political process. Mutatis mutandis, similar situations developed in the major Western European countries as well. Events of the past decade or two suggest that there is a progressive loss of control over issues of social policy: the inability of many states to determine levels of unemployment politically and the growing gap between rich and poor as working-class gains are eroded through an opening up to international competition are the kinds of developments to which I refer. Obviously, one must not be

dogmatic here. Developments are open to more than one interpretation. Still, the development of a deeply competitive international economy would seem to make it increasingly difficult to reinstitute and expand New Deal–type programs, and it is not clear how industrially developed states can remove themselves from the pressures of that economy.

6. If our relationship to the state is more complicated than the Aristotelian or Hegelian model would suggest, it may well be that some of Ricoeur's addresses to confessional audiences may have a broader relevance, for there dualisms and antitheses are more at home than where Aristotle and Hegel provide the paradigms, and eschatological motifs take over some of the functions of Kantian transcendentals, and nonstate agencies are seen in their political importance.

MARY GERHART

RESPONSE TO JOHN VAN DEN HENGEL, DAVID KLEMM, AND MARK WALLACE

One of the best ways to experience the instability of the text is to act as a respondent to conference papers! Nevertheless, since all three papers represent promising constructive projects, I will pose questions to each of the texts as I read them, attempting to enable them to think more or more productively in the light of different disciplines—here, specifically, literary analysis, philosophical theology, and philosophy of science.

One of the problems with philosophical theology as currently written and read is evidenced by the suspicion other religious scholars, literary critics, and philosophers have that philosophical theology *substitutes* itself as self-evident, literal meaning in place of originating texts. Paul de Man made this suspicion explicit when he located hermeneutics traditionally in the "sphere of theology . . . [and] its secular prolongation in the various historical disciplines." He explained his position by comparing poetics and hermeneutics: "Unlike poetics, which is concerned with the taxonomy and the interaction of poetic structures, hermeneutics is concerned with the meanings of specific texts." De Man summarized his suspicion in the following charge: "In a hermeneutical enterprise, reading necessarily intervenes but, like computation in an algebraic proof, it is a means toward an end . . . : the ultimate aim of a hermeneutically successful reading is to do away with reading altogether."[1]

This criticism of hermeneutics as traditionally practiced—i.e., to do away with reading altogether—may be too radical or even self-serving, given de Man's deconstructionist inclination. Nevertheless, it is useful in providing a common ground from which to question the papers of John Van Den Hengel, David Klemm, and Mark Wallace.

All three of the papers in one way or another acknowledge Paul Ricoeur's explicit affirmation of many genres, of their autonomy vis-à-vis the genre of philosophical discourse, and hence, of the need the interpreter has of mediating understanding (which is always already genred). For myself, this triple affirmation has been one of the distinguishing marks of Ricoeur's work. It discloses an insight about expressions that is analogous to the discovery that Ricoeur, building on I. A. Richards and others, made about metaphor—namely, that neither metaphor nor genre can be translated without remainder. Moreover, generic considerations enable interpreters to distance themselves for the purpose of seeing more or understanding better. Ricoeur's triple affirmation constitutes that which "goes without saying" for many less careful thinkers and, precisely *because* it goes unmentioned, contributes to unproductive conflicts of misunderstanding. My questions to each of the presenters pertains to the points at which Ricoeur's triple affirmation regarding genre informs—or fails to inform—their work.

I am in general agreement with John Van Den Hengel that Ricoeur's work on *Time and Narrative* affords us the opportunity to reassess issues, the treatment of which before was unrewarding or inconclusive. This opportunity is clearly present with respect to understanding the enigmatic, and in many ways unique, genre we call gospel. In his paper "Jesus between History and Fiction," Van Den Hengel suggests that, whereas Ricoeur previously appears to have slighted the historical question with respect to the genre gospel—having been influenced unduly by Rudolf Bultmann and Robert Alter—his work in *Time and Narrative* provides valuable resources for reconstructing the genre gospel as historical.

I am grateful to Professor Van Den Hengel both for his proposal and for his bibliographical research, especially in the first part of his paper, on Ricoeur's treatment of the issue before *Time and Narrative.* I also think that Van Den Hengel's conception of the role of liturgy and sacrament in the history of the reception of the Christic event could enrich Ricoeur's notion of manifestation and proclamation. Nevertheless, while I fully support his project of applying Ricoeur's new work on narrative from *Time and Narrative* to the Gospels, I am less sanguine that Van Den Hengel's ambition to make the gospel text a conjectural or institutional history along the lines of French historiography—history that, he wishes to claim, is at the same time a conjectural configuration of the event of Jesus—can or should be realized.

My first question is a request for clarification: How does Van Den Hengel define *history* and how does he understand Ricoeur to define *history?* In the paper, Van Den Hengel observes that Ricoeur follows Alter—and in a different way, Frei, who holds to the "history-like" character of the Gospels and who does not so much as index the term *fiction* in seeing the Gospels as fiction or midrash in historicized prose.[2] Van Den Hengel claims that these texts do not qualify as history for Ricoeur, although historiographic writing can be signified by other literary genres.

The present paper is Van Den Hengel's attempt to go in the opposite direction: namely, to support the claim that the Gospels are historical. He seems to agree that historical critical inquiry cannot reconstruct the life of Jesus, yet he cites Norman Perrin to claim a link with the "factual" history of Jesus. This history is an original structure and sequence of occurrences that occasion "the relation event-testimony." It is not a larger historical framework. But Van Den Hengel also thinks that the Gospels have a historical dimension beyond their being as an "event of meaning" and that it is appropriate to speak of the history of the reception of the Gospels. Yet he wants to consider the Gospels themselves "historical narratives."

Why does Van Den Hengel want the Gospels to be "historical narratives"? He has stated seven reasons and proposals concerning how the Gospels may be so reconstructed. But it is difficult for me to understand why these goals could not be fulfilled under the claim that the Gospels are historylike. And so another way of phrasing my question would be, Is the genre "history" extricable from the genre "narrative"? At some points in his paper, Van Den Hengel seems to suggest that history precedes or supercedes narrative. For example, he states that history must have a plausibility structure founded on the prenarrative structure of action and the conceptual network of action that stems from real human action. And later, he asserts that the historical genre calls therefore for a more differentiated refiguration of human action, presumably more than a narrative refiguration. And yet later he asserts that history is, not a reliving, reenacting, or rethinking of the actions of people, but a discovering of the schema, the framework, or the worldview within which such actions took place and can take place again. This overall schema of the Gospels (into which the actions of Jesus are inserted), for Van Den Hengel, is derived from the intertextuality with the figures of the Hebrew Scriptures.

What is missing? For Ricoeur, history and fiction are both forms of narrative and are constituted on three levels of mimesis. For reasons too lengthy to repeat here, Ricoeur emphasizes the common basis of fictional and historical narrative—that they are both results of the productive imagination. In his previous interpretation of Ricoeur, Van Den Hengel seems to have a different definition of history than the one implied in his present paper; in *The Home of Meaning,* he writes, "History is a type of story that proves the region of the possible. In history the imagination is made productive on the basis of the analogy of the intersubjective recognition of the other in history as another I."[3] To place the Gospels more on the side of history cannot, in Ricoeur's theory, involve placing the event "outside" narrative meaning. Nor does it involve removing the ambiguity and plurality that necessarily result from four different Gospel texts.

Is anything lost by refuting the claim that the Gospels are historical narratives? From his own ambivalence on this issue, my hunch is that Van Den Hengel is responding more to the demands of common sense than to those of theoretical plausibility—see, for example, his quoting with approval the *sensus communis* that Luke is history. But the genre of common sense is no less a problem than others. Nor is common sense necessarily common to all in ecclesial communities. From a feminist ecclesial standpoint, for example, to consider the Gospels as historylike (as distinct from historical) makes eminently good common, as well as theoretical, sense. For certain privileges have been awarded on positivist understandings of history that for feminists are difficult, if not impossible, to dislodge without something like Ricoeur's revised understanding of that genre.

David Klemm revises the classical question of how to decipher the plight of human life in the light of divine power and how to discern the meaning of divine life for the human life as follows: How can we speak about theological meanings, when we can no longer appeal either to an absolute subject of history or to an absolute object of knowledge? The shift from a question of "how" to a combination of two questions—"how" and "can we"—sets up an interesting tension in Klemm's claim that the theological meaning discovered in the divine name necessarily breaks free of the biblical text and refigures itself in a new act of naming God. Now, at first glance, this claim sounds strikingly like the target of de Man's criticism, viz., that hermeneutics attempts to do away with reading altogether. But Klemm's summary expectation, as suggested by Ricoeur, is that we can speak of the divine in our language and existence in the act of letting go. And the very expectation is a shift away from the modality of asseveration (which is the typical result from the act of dispensing with or substituting for literary genres).

I think that Klemm, in fact, does achieve a refiguration of the divine name by naming God beyond the biblical text and does so in a way that avoids either substituting for the genred text or dispensing with reading altogether. He does so in the manner of Ricoeur's best work, that is, by plotting a careful dialectic in progressive stages and by retaining the dialectical movement in the conclusion.

Therefore, while I do not question his project as conceived, there are two aspects on which I would like his clarification and further thought. Klemm states that sacred symbols are freed from adherence to natural signifiers and freed for textual inscription within the grand narrative of God's Word. I was somewhat surprised at this use of *grand narrative,* particularly when the citation to Ricoeur's essay "Manifestation and Proclamation" does not seem to require its use. Moreover, we have seen in the Van Den Hengel paper a reluctance on the part of Ricoeur when he questioned the historical concerns of the Christologies of Pannenberg, Moltmann, and Metz, who had attempted to find the meaning of the Jesus event by linking the history of Jesus into a larger historical framework (e.g., solidarity with the oppressed in history). Now it is true that the reference to "grand narrative" occurs at the transition from mimesis$_1$ to mimesis$_2$—and the freeing of the symbol as "bound" to the sacred cosmos into the symbol as sacred poetry. But just what is meant by the concept of grand narrative and how does it function (if it does) at the level of mimesis$_2$ and what happens to it in Klemm's dialectical move to mimesis$_3$?

Let me try to clarify why this is an issue. Some contemporary thinkers, like Lyotard, would claim that postmodernism eschews grand narrative as a means for legitimating contemporary meanings. Others, like Adorno and Jameson, think that legitimation is always done—even if it is denied by the legitimator—by means of a grand narrative (i.e., the story the thinker tells of how the world of meanings got to be the way it is now), and that it is better to make that story explicit rather than to pretend that it does not exist. Where does Klemm stand on this issue?

My second question is also one for clarification: How do we understand Klemm's use of *second naïveté* in the sentence: "Following Ricoeur, we may construe the ascent as moving from the first naïveté to criticism and the descent as moving from criticism to the second naïveté"? In *The Symbolism of Evil,* Ricoeur is usually taken to mean, by *first naïveté,* the immediacy of belief by a noncritical consciousness, and by *second naïveté,* that mediation of belief by a critical consciousness. But this understanding of Ricoeur might fail to heed his caution in *Freedom and Nature* to the effect that a critical attitude may be even more difficult to dislodge than the "natural attitude." In *Metaphoric Process,* my colleague and I take the danger of understanding by second naïveté into account as follows: "We may judge that our theoretical understanding is correct and that our experience is delusive, which, without further questioning, leaves us in a state of second naïveté."[4] It is not clear how Klemm understands second naïveté nor how he protects the concept from misunderstanding.

I am intrigued by Mark Wallace's argument that Ricoeur's "figural ontology" can show how classic texts—both historical and fictional—are "revelatory because they place one's everyday perceptions of reality in abeyance by opening up new ways of being human . . . that are fertile and transformative." He makes this argument in order to counter Richard Rorty's claim that texts refer only to themselves and have no truth value because they are "private extension[s] of author[s'] 'in here' perspective, not the royal road to an 'out there' reality." In many ways, Wallace's position on the revelatory function of fictional, as well as historical, narrative might address Van Den Hengel's concern for the historicity of the Gospels. My own question pertains to Wallace's distinction between religious and fictional texts. He thinks that Ricoeur does not go far enough in realizing the distinctively critical, even absolutist, function of scriptural revelation in relation to other modalities of poetic discourse. Wallace, by contrast, wishes to account for the exclusive, "iconoclastic" claims of the Bible vis-à-vis other forms of spirituality and religious discourse.

My hunch is that this concern is best handled dialectically, such as the way in which Klemm handled the notion of "Word of God" at the level of mimesis$_2$. Indeed, Wallace goes in this direction when he notices that the "different literary genres and theological itineraries . . . mesh with the reader in such a way that the presentation of new possibilities, of a new world, can be said to be the result." What does Wallace desire? Does he desire, following Auerbach, a unique and absolute function for scriptural revelation in relation to other modalities of poetic discourse? If so, then Wallace would have to deny what he presently affirms: (1) Ricoeur's refusal to abstract philosophical concepts from the Bible's fermentation of meaning and (2) Ricoeur's insistence on the intertextual dynamics embodied in the originary literary expressions of religious faith. An alternative approach, distinct from Klemm as well, would be to delimit the desire for a unique and absolute distinction between religious and poetic language by using one or more of the hermeneutics of suspicion as initiated by Marx, Freud, Nietzsche, or contemporary feminists.

In a current project, I attempt to extend the relationship of Ricoeur's genre theory to his theory of metaphor, particularly on the issue of his distinction between literal and nonliteral language. Although Ricoeur himself uses this distinction in his theory of metaphor—for example, when he writes that metaphoric meaning is built on the "ruins" of literal meaning—there are good reasons to regard the distinction as unhelpful, if only because it secretly supports our inordinate desire for literal and genre-free meanings in history, philosophy, and theology.

NOTES

1. Paul de Man, *Blindness and Insight: Essays in the Rhetoric of Contemporary Criticism,* intro. by W. Godzich, 2d ed. rev. (Minneapolis: University of Minnesota Press, 1983), pp. ix–x.
2. Hans Frei, *The Eclipse of Biblical Narrative: A Study of Eighteenth and Nineteenth Century Hermeneutics* (New Haven and London: Yale University Press, 1974).
3. John Van Den Hengel, *The Home of Meaning: The Hermeneutics of the Subject of Paul Ricoeur* (Washington, D.C.: University Press of America, 1982), p. 142n.
4. Mary Gerhart and Allan Russell, *Metaphoric Process: The Creation of Scientific and Religious Understanding,* with a foreword by Paul Ricoeur (Fort Worth: Texas Christian University Press, 1984), p. 38.

SELECT BIBLIOGRAPHY
NOTES ON CONTRIBUTORS
NAME INDEX
SUBJECT INDEX

SELECT BIBLIOGRAPHY

Ricoeur Works Cited

For a complete Ricoeur bibliography, see Frans D. Vansina, *Paul Ricoeur: Bibliographie systématique de ses écrits et des publications consacrées à sa pensée (1935–1984)* (Leuven: Editions Peeters, 1985).

Books

Fallible Man, trans. Charles A. Kelbley. Chicago: Henry Regnery, 1965. Rev. trans. with an Introduction by Walter J. Lowe. New York: Fordham University Press, 1986.

History and Truth, trans. Charles A. Kelbley. Evanston, Ill.: Northwestern University Press, 1965.

Freedom and Nature: The Voluntary and the Involuntary, trans. Erazim Kohák. Evanston, Ill.: Northwestern University Press, 1966.

The Symbolism of Evil, trans. Emerson Buchanan. New York: Harper and Row, 1967.

Les incidences théologiques des recherches actuelles concernant le langage. Paris: Institut d'Etudes Oecuméniques, 1969.

Freud and Philosophy: An Essay on Interpretation, trans. Denis Savage. New Haven, Conn.: Yale University Press, 1970.

The Conflict of Interpretations: Essays in Hermeneutics, ed. Don Ihde, trans. Willis Domingo et al. Evanston, Ill.: Northwestern University Press, 1974.

Political and Social Essays, ed. David Stewart and Joseph Bien, trans. Donald Siewert et al. Athens: Ohio University Press, 1974.

Interpretation Theory: Discourse and the Surplus of Meaning. Fort Worth: Texas Christian Press, 1976.

The Philosophy of Paul Ricoeur: An Anthology of His Work, ed. Charles E. Reagan and David Stewart. Boston: Beacon Press, 1978.

The Rule of Metaphor: Multi-Disciplinary Studies of the Creation of Meaning in Language, trans. Robert Czerny with Kathleen McLaughlin and John Costello, S.J. London: Routledge and Kegan Paul, 1978.

Essays on Biblical Interpretation, ed. Lewis S. Mudge. Philadelphia: Fortress Press, 1980.

Hermeneutics and the Human Sciences: Essays on Language, Action, and Interpretation, ed., trans., and intro. John B. Thompson. Cambridge: Cambridge University Press, 1981.

Time and Narrative. Vol. 1, trans. Kathleen McLaughlin and David Pellauer. Chicago: University of Chicago Press, 1984.

Time and Narrative. Vol. 2, trans. Kathleen McLaughlin and David Pellauer. Chicago: University of Chicago Press, 1985.

Lectures on Ideology and Utopia, ed. George H. Taylor. New York: Columbia University Press, 1986.

Time and Narrative. Vol. 3, trans. Kathleen Blamey and David Pellauer. Chicago: University of Chicago Press, 1988.

Soi-même comme un autre. Paris: Editions du Seuil, 1990.

Articles

"La Parole, instauratrice de liberté." *Cahier universitaires catholiques,* no. 10 (July 1966): 493–507.

"Bultmann." *Foi-Education* 37, no. 78 (1967): 17–35.

"Ebeling." *Foi-Education* 37, no. 78 (1967): 36–53, 53–57.

"Tasks of the Ecclesial Community in the Modern World." In *Theology of Renewal,* vol. 2, *Renewal of Religious Structures,* ed. L. K. Shook, pp. 242–54. New York: Herder and Herder, 1968.

"Qu'est-ce qu'un texte?" In *Hermeneutik und Dialektik,* ed. Rudiger Bubner, Konrad Cramer, and Reiner Wiehl, pp. 181–200. Tübingen: J. C. B. Mohr Paul Siebeck, 1970.

"Du conflit à la convergence des méthodes an exégèse biblique." In *Exégèse et herméneutique,* ed. X. Léon-Dufour, pp. 35–53. Paris: Seuil, 1971.

"Esquisse de conclusion." In *Exégèse et herméneutique,* ed. X. Léon-Dufour, pp. 285–96. Paris: Seuil, 1971.

"Evénement et Sens." *Archivio di filosofia* 41 (1971): 15–34.

"Sur l'exégèse de Genèse 1:1–2:4." In *Exégèse et herméneutique,* ed. X. Léon-Dufour, pp. 67–84, 85–96. Paris: Seuil, 1971.

"The Tasks of a Political Educator," trans. David Stewart. *Philosophy Today* 17, no. 2/4 (Summer 1973): 142–52.

"Listening to the Parables of Jesus." *Criterion* 13, no. 3 (Spring 1974): 18–22.

"Biblical Hermeneutics." In *Paul Ricoeur on Biblical Hermeneutics.* ed. John Dominic Crossan, pp. 29–148. Missoula, Mont.: SBL, 1975. No. 4 of *Semeia: An Experimental Journal for Biblical Criticism.*

"Le Dieu crucifié de Jürgen Moltmann." *Les quatres fleuves: Cahiers de recherche et de réflexion religieuses,* no. 4 (1975): 109–14.

"Phenomenology and Hermeneutics," trans. R. Bradley De Ford. *Nous* 9, no. 1 (1975): 85–102.

"Philosophical and Theological Hermeneutics," trans. David Pellauer. *Studies in Religion/Sciences religieuses* 5, no. 1 (1975): 14–33.

"History and Hermeneutics," trans. David Pellauer. *Journal of Philosophy* 73, no. 19 (1976): 683–95.

"Le 'Royaume' dans la parabole de Jésus." *Etudes théologiques et religieuses* 51, no. 1 (1976): 15–19.

"Toward a Hermeneutic of the Idea of Revelation," trans. David Pellauer. *Harvard Theological Review* 70, no. 1–2 (January–April 1977): 1–37.

"Manifestation and Proclamation," trans. David Pellauer. *Blaisdell Institute Journal* 11 (1978): 13–35.

"The Metaphorical Process as Cognition, Imagination, and Feeling." *Critical Inquiry,* 5, no. 1 (1978): 143–59.

"The Problem of the Foundation of Moral Philosophy," trans. David Pellauer. *Philosophy Today* 22, no. 3–4 (Fall 1978): 175–92.

"The Function of Fiction in Shaping Reality." *Man and World* 12, no. 2 (1979): 123–41.

"Naming God," trans. David Pellauer. *Union Seminary Quarterly Review* 34, no. 4 (1979): 215–28.

"Time and Narrative in the Bible: Toward a Narrative Theology." Sarum Lectures, Oxford University, 1980.

"The Bible and the Imagination." In *The Bible as a Document of the University,* ed. H. D. Betz with a foreword by Martin Marty, trans. David Pellauer, pp. 49–75. Chico, Calif.: Scholars Press, 1981.

"Mimesis and Representation," trans. David Pellauer. *Annals of Scholarship* 2, no. 3 (1981): 15–32.

"Action, Story, and History: On Re-Reading *The Human Condition.*" *Salmagundi,* no. 60 (Spring–Summer 1983): 60–72.

"Can Fictional Narratives Be True?" In *Analecta Husserliana: The Yearbook of Phenomenological Research,* ed. A.-T. Tymieniecka, vol. 14, pp. 3–19. Dordrecht-Boston-London: D. Reidel, 1983.

"The Creativity of Language" and "Myth as the Bearer of Possible Worlds," trans. Richard Kearney. In *Dialogues with Contemporary Continental Thinkers: The Phenomenological Heritage,* ed. Richard Kearney, pp. 23–45. Manchester: Manchester University Press, 1984.

"Fondements de l'Ethique." *Autres temps: Les cahiers du christianisme social* 3 (1984): 61–71.

"From Proclamation to Narrativity." *Journal of Religion* 64 (1984): 501–12.

"Geschichte als erzählte Zeit." *Evangelische Kommentare* 18 (1984): 45–46.

"Ethique et politique." *Esprit* 101 (May 1985): 1–11.

"Evil, a Challenge to Philosophy and Theology," trans. David Pellauer. *Journal of the American Academy of Religion* 45 (1985): 635–48.

"History as Narrative and Practice," trans. R. Lechner. *Philosophy Today* 29, no. 3 (Fall 1985): 213–22.

"Le récit interprétatif: Exégèse et théologie dans les récits de la Passion." *Recherches de science religieuse* 73 (1985): 17–38.

"Narrated Time," trans. Robert Sweeney. *Philosophy Today* 29, no. 4 (Winter 1985): 259–72.

"Temps biblique." *Archivio di filosofia* 53 (1985): 27–32.

"Ce qui me préoccupé depuis trente ans." *Esprit* 8–9 (August–September 1986): 227–43.

"Contingence et rationalité dans le récit." *Phänomenologische Forschungen* 18 (1986): 11–29.

"Ipséité/Alterité/Socialité." *Archivio di filosofia* 54 (1986): 17–34.

"Life: A Story in Search of a Narrator," trans. J. N. Kray and A. J. Scholten. In *Facts and Values: Philosophical Reflections from Western and Non-Western Perspectives*, ed. M. C. Doeser and J. N. Kraay, pp. 121–32. Dordrecht: Martinus Nijhoff, 1986.

"On Interpretation," trans. Kathleen McLaughlin. In *After Philosophy*, ed. Kenneth Baynes, James Bohman, and Thomas McCarthy, pp. 374–76. Cambridge, Mass.: MIT Press, 1987.

"The Fragility of Political Language," trans. David Pellauer. *Philosophy Today* 31, no. 2 (1987): 35–44.

"Individu et identité personnelle." In *Sur l'individu*, ed. Paul Veyne, J.-P. Vernan, et al. pp. 54–72. Paris: Editions du Seuil, 1987.

"Myth and History." In *The Encyclopedia of Religion*, vol. 10, ed. M. Eliade, pp. 273–82. New York, London: MacMillan, 1987.

"The Teleological and Deontological Structure of Action: Aristotle and/or Kant." In *Contemporary French Philosophy*, ed. A. Phillips Griffith, pp. 99–111. Cambridge: Cambridge University Press, 1987.

"Eloge de la lecture et de l'écriture." *Etudes théologiques et religieuses* 64 (1989): 395–405.

"The Human as the Subject Matter of Philosophy." In *The Narrative Path: The Later Works of Paul Ricoeur*, ed. T. Peter Kemp and David Rasmussen, pp. 89–102. Cambridge, Mass.: MIT Press, 1989.

"Approches de la personne." *Esprit* 160 (March–April 1990): 115–30.

Secondary Works on Ricoeur Cited

Dauenhauer, Bernard. *The Politics of Hope.* Foreword by Paul Ricoeur. Boston: Routledge and Kegan Paul, 1986.

———. "History as Source: Reflections on Heidegger and Ricoeur." *Journal of the British Society for Phenomenology* 20, no. 3 (1989): 236–47.

Gadamer, Hans-Georg. "The Hermeneutics of Suspicion." *Man and World* 17 (1984): 313–23.

Gerhart, Mary, and Allan Russell. *Metaphoric Processes: The Creation of Scientific and Religious Understanding,* with a foreword by Paul Ricoeur. Fort Worth: Texas Christian University Press, 1984.

Kemp, Peter T., and David Rasmussen, eds. *The Narrative Path: The Later Works of Paul Ricoeur.* Cambridge, Mass.: MIT Press, 1989.

Klemm, David E. *The Hermeneutic Theory of Paul Ricoeur: A Constructive Analysis.* Lewisburg, Pa.: Bucknell University Press, 1983.

———. "Ricoeur, Theology, and the Rhetoric of Overturning." *Journal of Literature and Theology* 3 (1989): 267–84.

Lacasse, Alain. *Temps et récit: Essai d'application de la thèse de Paul Ricoeur au film "Huit et demi" de Federico Fellini.* Master's thesis. Québec: Université Laval, 1988.

Pellauer, David. "*Time and Narrative* and Theological Reflection." *Philosophy Today* 31 (Fall 1987): 262–86.

Placher, William. "Paul Ricoeur and Postliberal Theology: A Conflict of Interpretations?" *Modern Theology* 4 (1987): 35–52.

Schweiker, William. *Mimetic Reflections: A Study in Hermeneutics, Theology, and Ethics.* New York: Fordham University Press, 1990.

Strasser, Stephan. "Zeit und Erzählung bei Paul Ricoeur." *Philosophische Rundschau* 34, no. 1/2 (1987): 1–13.

Van den Hengel, John. *The Home of Meaning: The Hermeneutics of the Subject of Paul Ricoeur.* Washington, D.C.: University Press of America, 1982.

Van Hoozer, Kevin J. *Biblical Narrative in the Philosophy of Paul Ricoeur: A Study in Hermeneutics and Theology.* Cambridge: Cambridge University Press, 1990.

NOTES ON CONTRIBUTORS

PAMELA ANDERSON is an assistant professor of philosophy at Roanoke College, Salem, Virginia. Pamela received a D.Phil. from Oxford University, England. Besides publishing this and another essay on Ricoeur, she has a forthcoming book entitled *Paul Ricoeur's Philosophy of the Will: A Reconstruction.*

DUDLEY ANDREW is Angelo Bertocci Professor of Critical Studies and director of the Institute for Cinema and Culture at the University of Iowa. His books include *André Bazin* and *Film in the Aura of Art.* His study of poetic realism will appear shortly.

GERALD BRUNS is William and Hazel White Professor of English at the University of Notre Dame. He is also the author of *Inventions: Writing, Textuality, and Understanding in Literary History* and *Modern Poetry and the Idea of Language.*

FRED DALLMAYR is Packey J. Dee Professor of Political Theory at the University of Notre Dame. A native of Germany, he has taught at a number of universities, among them Purdue University, the University of Georgia, Hamburg University, and the New School for Social Research. Among his publications are: *Beyond Dogma and Despair, Twilight of Subjectivity, Polis and Praxis, Language and Politics, Critical Encounters: Between Philosophy and Politics, Margins of Political Discourse,* and *Between Freiburg and Frankfurt: Toward a Critical Ontology.*

BERNARD P. DAUENHAUER is professor of philosophy and director of the Humanities Center at the University of Georgia. He is the author of *The Politics of Hope* and *Elements of Responsible Politics.*

ANDRÉ GAUDREAULT is professor of film studies, Laval University, Quebec. He is author of *Du littérataire au filmique: Systeme du récit.*

MARY GERHART is professor of religious studies at Hobart and William Smith Colleges in Geneva, New York. She is author of *The Question of Belief in Literary Criticism: An Introduction to the Hermeneutical Theory of Paul Ricoeur,* as well as of *Metaphoric Process: The Creation of Scientific and Religious Understanding* (with Allan M. Russell).

DAVID JASPER is professor and director of the Centre for the Study of Literature and Theology, Department of English, University of Glasgow, Scotland. He is editor of *Literature and Theology* and author of many books, including *Coleridge as Poet and Religious Thinker, The New Testament and the Literary Imagination,* and *The Study of Literature and Religion: An Introduction.*

MORNY JOY is professor of religious studies at the University of Calgary, Calgary, Alberta, Canada. She is author of many articles on Ricoeur and other current thinkers. She is currently working on a book relating Ricoeur to feminist thought on the self.

HANS KELLNER is associate professor of history at Michigan State University. He is author of *Language and Historical Representation: Getting the Story Crooked.*

DAVID E. KLEMM is associate professor of theology and ethics at the University of Iowa. Among his publications are *The Hermeneutical Theory of Paul Ricoeur* and *Hermeneutical Inquiry* (editor and contributor).

MICHÈLE LAGNY is professor of film studies, Sorbonne University, Paris III. She is author of *Visconti: classicisme subversion* as well as many articles.

JAMES F. MCCUE is professor of religion and chair of the program in global studies at the University of Iowa. He is author of many scholarly articles.

DONALD G. MARSHALL is professor and chair of the Department of English, University of Illinois, Chicago. He is author of numerous articles on literary criticism and hermeneutics.

HERMAN RAPAPORT is professor and chair of comparative literature at the University of Iowa. He is author of many publications, including *Heidegger and Derrida* and *Milton and the Postmodern.*

PHILIP ROSEN is professor of film studies in the Department of English at Brown University, Providence, Rhode Island. He is the author of the forthcoming *Past Present: Theory, Cinema, Historicity* and editor of *Narrative, Apparatus, Ideology: A Film Theory Reader.*

ROBERT P. SCHARLEMANN is Commonwealth Professor in the Department of Religious Studies at the University of Virginia. His previous publications include: *Thomas Aquinas and John Gerhard; Reflection and Doubt in the Thought of Paul Tillich; The Being of God; Inscriptions and Reflections: Essays in Philosophical Theology;* and *The Reason of Following: Christology and the Ecstatic I.*

WILLIAM SCHWEIKER is assistant professor of theological ethics at the Divinity School of the University of Chicago. He is author of *Mimetic Reflections* and many scholarly articles.

JOHN VAN DEN HENGEL is professor of theology at St. Paul's University, Ottawa, Canada. He is the author of *The Home of Meaning: The Hermeneutics of the Subject of Paul Ricoeur.*

MARK I. WALLACE is assistant professor of religion at Swarthmore College in Swarthmore, Pennsylvania. He is author of *The Second Naiveté: Barth, Ricoeur, and the New Yale Theology* and coeditor of *Hermeneutics, Narrative, and the Bible: An Anthology of the Religious Thought of Paul Ricoeur.*

NAME INDEX

Adorno, Theodor, 347
Agnon, Shmuel Yosef, 231
Alter, Robert, 137, 243
Althusser, Louis, 29, 35
Amos, 185
Ankersmit, F. R., 61
Apel, Karl-Otto, 299
Arendt, Hannah, 163, 167, 188, 191, 327, 338
Ariès, Philippe, 51, 52, 56–58
Aristotle, 2, 14–17, 28–33, 37–39, 42–44, 53, 63, 93, 160–63, 170, 179–83, 189–91, 320, 329, 332, 339–40
Artaud, Antonin, 27, 44
Auerbach, Erich, 50, 349
Augustine, 14–17, 38, 188–93, 62–64, 338
Aurenche, Jean, 70

Balzac, Honoré de, 29, 117
Bann, Stephen, 69
Bataille, Georges, 229
Baudelaire, Charles, 118
Bazin, André, 68–69, 123, 129, 130
Benjamin, Walter, 56
Berlin, Isaiah, 319
Bernanos, Georges, 69
Beylie, Claude, 119
Blamey, Kathleen, 64
Blanchot, Maurice, 42, 43, 229, 231
Booth, John Wilkes, 79
Bost, Pierre, 70
Braudel, Fernand, 52–59, 60–64, 112, 327
Bresson, Robert, 69, 70
Brooks, Peter, 118
Buber, Martin, 323
Buchner, Georg, 231–32
Bultmann, Rudolph, 14, 21–23, 136, 316–17, 344

Carné, Marcel, 115, 118, 129, 130
Castorp, Hans, 52
Celan, Paul, 231–32
Chaplin, Charlie, 126
Chaunu, Pierre, 51–52, 57
Chauvet, L.-M., 149
Collingwood, R. G., 68, 85
Cukor, George, 125

Danto, Arthur, 37, 43
Darwin, Charles, 85, 88
Debureau, Baptiste, 118, 124, 125
Deleuze, Gilles, 201
de Certeau, Michel, 68, 100
De Man, Paul, 315, 343
Derrida, Jacques, 21, 43–44, 229, 232, 301, 314
Descartes, René, 8, 284, 318
Dickens, Charles, 117
Duby, Georges, 109
Dufy, Raoul, 40–41

Ebeling, G., 136
Edison, Thomas, 77
Eliade, Mircea, 330
Epicurus, 179

Febvre, Lucien, 61
Fichte, Johann, 279, 284
Ford, Henry, 76–81
Foucault, Michel, 191, 198, 296, 338
France, Anatole, 314
Frege, Gottlob, 146
Frei, Hans, 142
Freud, Sigmund, 8, 34, 51, 64–65, 190, 198–99, 318, 322, 349
Frye, Northrop, 50

Gabin, Jean, 125–26
Gadamer, Hans-Georg, 2, 35–36, 264, 322–23
Genette, Gerard, 99
Gilkey, Langdon, 294
Gombrich, E. H., 61
Goodfield, June, 85
Gramsci, A., 192

Habermas, Jürgen, 298–99, 315, 317
Hauerwas, Stanley, 299
Havel, Vàclav, 188
Hegel, G. W. F., 18, 42–44, 54, 64, 163, 182–83, 186–91, 227, 261, 279, 299–301, 319, 324, 328, 338–41
Heidegger, Martin, 5, 6, 13–20, 30–32, 36, 39, 44, 51, 192, 226, 229, 230, 232, 282, 315, 323, 327, 331
Herodotus, 138
Hobbes, Thomas, 192
Hölderlin, Friedrich, 20, 30–31, 42
Homer, 28
Horkheimer, Max, 87
Howard, Trevor, 109
Husserl, Edmund, 6–8, 16, 17, 36, 63, 284, 315, 318

Jabes, Edmond, 231
James, William, 249
Jameson, Fredric, 38, 347
Jaspers, Karl, 6, 7
Jeancolas, Jean-Pierre, 115
Jesus Christ, 14, 22–24, 134, 214, 262, 287
Joyce, James, 44

Kant, Immanuel, 2, 5, 16–18, 28, 30, 37, 42–44, 60, 189–90, 197–99, 202, 205, 211, 214, 217, 228, 237, 241, 243, 264, 266, 278–81, 299, 335, 337, 338
Kermode, Frank, 112
Kierkegaard, Søren, 231, 321–24
Koestler, Arthur, 180
Koselleck, Reinhart, 86–87, 159

Lacan, Jacques, 229
Lacasse, Alain, 96
Lacoue-Labarthe, Philippe, 202
Lefort, Claude, 191, 338
Lemaître, Frédérick, 118, 124
Lenin, Vladimir, 186–87, 337
Lessing, Gotthold, 135
Levinas, Emmanuel, 40, 146, 210, 228–32, 323, 324, 330–33
Lévi-Strauss, Claude, 118–19, 198
Lindbeck, George, 296
Locke, John, 163
Lukács, George, 107
Luther, Martin, 38
Lyotard, Jean-François, 201, 347

Machiavelli, Niccolò, 185–86
MacIntyre, Alasdair, 299, 339
Mallarmé, Stephane, 44
Mann, Thomas, 51, 56, 98, 110, 249, 287
Marcel, Gabriel, 6–8
Maroger, Jacques, 41
Marx, Karl, 8, 29, 163, 177–89, 318, 337, 349
Medioli, Enrico, 110
Méliès, Georges, 90–96
Metz, Christian, 119
Metz, Johanne-Baptist, 143, 347
Michelet, Jules, 62
Mill, John Stuart, 163
Miller, J. Hillis, 316
Mitterand, François, 340
Moltmann, Jürgen, 143, 347
Morris, William, 71–73
Mulvey, Laura, 120

Nabert, Jean, 226
Nabokov, Vladimir, 249
Niépce, Joseph Nicephone, 68, 69
Nietzsche, Friedrich, 7, 8, 29, 62, 110, 113, 158, 190, 237, 249–51, 284, 318, 349
Nozick, Robert, 163
Nussbaum, Martha, 27, 37

Oakeshott, Michael, 323
Otto, Rudolph, 296

Pannenberg, Wolfhart, 143, 347
Paul, Saint, 14
Peirce, C. S., 69
Pellauer, David, 64
Perrin, Norman, 137, 143, 345
Pétain, Phillippe, 125
Pirenne, Henri, 61
Plantinga, Alvin, 241
Plato, 7, 26, 29, 39, 185, 237, 277, 281, 318, 320, 323, 338
Prévert, Jacques, 118
Proudfoot, Wayne, 296
Proust, Marcel, 98, 249

Ranke, Leopold von, 68–69, 76
Rawls, John, 211

Richards, I. A., 344
Rockefeller, John D., 76–80
Rorty, Richard, 29, 235, 236–39, 249–50, 297, 299, 300, 323, 348
Rousseau, Jean-Jacques, 181–83, 189–90, 315
Ruskin, John, 71, 79, 81

Sartre, Jean-Paul, 130
Saussure, Ferdinand, 315
Scharlemann, Robert, 280
Schifano, Laurence, 110
Schiller, Friedrich, 30, 123
Schleiermacher, Friedrich, 266, 277–89
Schumpeter, Joseph, 340
Semler, Johann Salomo, 21
Simiand, François, 61
Simmel, Georg, 83
Simon, Herbert, 165
Simon, Ulrich, 148
Socrates, 26–29, 185
Stalin, Joseph, 129
Stout, Jeffrey, 299
Strauss, D. F., 21, 22
Stravinsky, Igor, 111
Swinburne, Algernon Charles, 241

Taylor, Charles, 219
Taylor, Mark C., 302
Thompson, John B., 298
Thucydides, 138
Tillich, Paul, 3, 286, 293, 295
Tolstoy, Leo, 61
Toulmin, Stephen, 85
Trenet, Charles, 130
Turk, Edward Baron, 115

Urban, Charles, 90, 92

Viollet-le-Duc, Eugène-Emmanuel, 70, 73, 81
Visconti, Luchino, 92, 98, 102, 113
Voegelin, Eric, 134, 141
Von Rad, Gerhard, 134
Vovelle, Michel, 51–58

Wagner, Richard, 108–10
Wallace, Michael, 79
Walsh, Raoul, 79
Walzer, Michael, 300
Weber, Max, 166, 191
Weil, Eric, 163, 167
Wells, A. B., 78, 80
White, Hayden, 59–64, 68, 146
Wittgenstein, Ludwig, 44
Woolf, Virginia, 287

SUBJECT INDEX

Absolute dependence, 266, 269, 285
Action, 5, 8, 10, 36; and biblical texts, 137–49; divine and human, 140–41, 147; political, 157–58, 163–64, 169, 173, 186; temporal conditions of, 158–60. *See also* Praxis
Analogue, 54–55, 59, 63–64, 68
Appropriation, 8, 35, 129, 263, 266. *See also* Understanding
Architecture, 70–78; preservation, 71–78; restoration, 70–78
Art, 119, 121; and Kant, 217; work of, 13, 20–21, 31–32, 43, 119, 121
Autonomy, 286, 293–301
Axiology. *See* Good

Being: being in the world, 24, 36, 234; modes of, 13–14, 37
Bible, 50, 54, 133–35, 140–45, 228, 235, 240, 244, 256–65, 288; narrative genre, 235, 242–44, 288; wisdom genre, 235, 244–47, 288

Care (*Sorge, cura*), 20, 23–24, 56
Christ, 14, 135, 142–49, 262
Christology, 134–35, 145–50
Cinema, 68–69, 78–84, 90–96; French, 115–20. *See also* Film
Cinematograph, 90–96
Cross of interpretation, 267–70
Culture: definition of, 294–98; theology of, 3, 281, 286–89, 292–312

Dasein (being-there), 19–24, 36–37, 51–52
Death, 51–65
Distanciation, 35, 203; and biblical texts, 136–43

Divine, 206, 227, 241, 261. *See also* God
Duty, 209–13

Ethics, 319–20, 335; of conviction, 166–73; deontological (duty), 209–13, 306–7; and economics and politics, 162–68; and the mythico-poetic imagination, 196–203; of responsibility, 166–73; teleological (virtue), 209–13, 306–7
Evil, 7, 207–21, 245–47, 309–12; political, 178–93
Existence, 19; and language, 258–70. See also *Dasein*
Existentialism, 33, 130
Explanation, 2, 5, 8, 143

Faith, 308–12
Feeling, 264–66, 285–89
Figural ontology, 235, 248
Figuration, in film, 119; configuration, 50, 98; prefiguration, 50; refiguration or transfiguration, 50, 96, 161–62, 199, 200. *See also* Mimesis
Film: French cinema, 115–31; and historiography, 78–84; melodrama, 116–23, 131; poetic realism, 122–30; theory, 117, 121. *See also* Cinema
Freedom, 209–20, 266, 304–12

Gift, 213–17, 310
God, 14, 17, 137, 141, 221, 236, 243, 280–88, 302, 311, 321, 332; and divine negation, 263–66; naming of, 259–63. *See also* Divine

Golden Rule, 211–12, 222
Good: aporia of, 216–19; and being, 222–23, 284; hyperethical goods, 207; premoral goods, 207, 211; and the self, 205–7, 213–17
Gospels, 133–50, 345–46
Grace, 222, 246, 309, 337

Hermeneutics, 33–37, 118; Aristotelian, 37–38; biblical, 135–45, 257; definition of, 1, 8; of existence, 4; hermeneutical arc, 8, 136; Platonic, 39–44; of restoration and suspicion, 198; theological, 257
Heteronomy, 286, 293–301
Historical consciousness, 2, 17–19, 49, 62, 85; and Christology, 143, 147
Historical criticism, 135, 137, 143–46
Historiography, 67–69, 85–88, 95, 107, 120; in architecture, 70–78; of biblical texts, 134–50; and film, 78–84
History, 50–51, 115, 121, 208
History and fiction, 122; and biblical texts, 133–50; narrative in cinema, 90–96; and narrativity, 49–65. *See also* Narrative
Hölderlin lectures, 20, 30–31, 42, 192
Hope, 213–19, 277

I, 258–59, 279
Imaginary, 94, 109, 112
Imagination, 17, 24, 228, 232, 264; mythico-poetic, 195–203, 336–37; productive, 162, 197–203, 208–10, 265, 304–6, 336
Indexical sign, 69, 72–76, 81. *See also* Trace
Individuality, principle of, 277–89
Infinite, 230–32, 331
Intuition, 280–89

Jesus, 134–49, 214, 288
Judgment, reflective, 197, 200, 264, 336
Justice, 209–13, 311, 337

Kerygma, 15, 21–24, 316

Language, 228–32, 236, 239, 280–81, 328; debates and theories, 293–303; and existence, 1, 258–70, 347; political, 170–71
Lieutenance (standing for), 92–94
Limit-experience, 140
Limit-expression, 261, 287–88
Logos, 14, 17, 28–29, 32, 147, 149
Longue durée (long time span), 109, 112

Manifestation, 259–60
Memory, 50, 62–63
Metaphor, 15–16, 22–24, 59, 278–88, 305, 308, 349
Mimesis, 28, 37, 64, 208–9, 259–64, 299, 304–7, 315, 347–48; prefiguration, configuration, and refiguration, 161–62, 199, 200. *See also* Figuration
Moral identity, 205–23, 304–12
Moral ontology, 219–30
Myth, 3–5, 14–20, 22, 117, 140, 197, 201, 277, 295–98, 305–9; time of, 107–9, 112
Mythos, 14, 53, 201–2

Naïveté: first, 267, 348; second, 348
Narrative, 5, 9, 17, 53–55, 64–65, 121, 306–7, 345, 346; biblical, 133–43, 242–44, 261–63, 287–88; and cinema, 90–96, 108; narrativity in Ricoeur, 49, 53–55, 64–65; and self-identity, 196–97, 208–9, 305–9; and temporality in *Ludwig,* 98–113; theory of, 281–83. *See also* History and fiction; Time
Negation, 264–70

Other, 55, 59, 68, 71, 196, 209–11, 220, 229, 232, 240, 324, 331

Philosophy: moral, 205–23; and poetry, 26–46; political, 157–94; reflexive, 6–7; of religion, 241
Poetry: *Dichtung,* 20, 30; and philosophy, 27–44; poetic creation, 13, 15–19; *Poiesis,* 30
Politics, 335: and economics and ethics, 162–68; fragility of, 168–73; Marxist, 177–83, 185–88; as policy (*la politique*), 178, 183–93; as polity (*le politique*), 178–93, 338
Post-Hegelian Kantianism, 18, 211, 278, 293, 303, 308

Postmodernism, 163, 188, 191–92, 229, 337, 347; critique of myth, 201–3; Rorty and Ricoeur, 236–39, 248–51
Power: divine, 261, 346; and goodness, 220–23; political, 157, 163–64, 176–93; and violence, 210–11, 222
Praxis, 36–37, 196, 199, 202. *See also* Action
Psychoanalysis, 34, 119

Quasi, 54–55, 64, 96, 112, 146, 149

Religion, definition of, 295–98
Responsibility, 207, 217–23; ethics of conviction, 166–73; ethics of responsibility, 166–73
Revelation: as manifestation and proclamation, 330–33; as narrative, 235, 242–44, 288; as poetic discourse, 239–52; and testimony, 226–32; as wisdom, 235, 244–47, 288

Same, 55, 59, 68, 196
Scriptures. *See* Bible
Self, 17, 23–24, 283–85, 300, 306–7, 328, 337; self-identity (*l'ipseité*), 163, 195–203
Symbol, 3–5, 17–19, 117, 198, 287, 295–98, 305–9, 347; cosmic, oneiric, and poetic, 215; sacred, 260–62; the self as, 215–17

Temporality, 259–60, 315; and architecture, 69–82; in biblical narrative, 235, 242–47; and cinema, 81–84; and historiography, 67–69; 85–88. *See also* Narrative; Time
Testimony, 226–30. *See also* Word
Text, 5, 8–10, 33–37, 61, 120, 308
Textuality: in film, 79, 81; in texts, 13–24, 35, 314–17
Theology: biblical, 14, 256–58; of culture, 3, 281, 286–89, 292–312; deconstructionist, 302; narrative, 4; natural, 256–58; sociolinguistic, 302; theological ethics of culture, 293–312
Theonomy, 286, 293–301, 308
Time, 51–53, 56, 197; cosmic and lived (or phenomenological), 5, 9, 16–19, 67, 98–100, 106–9, 112, 147, 158–62, 287; and death, 51–57; historical, 14, 98–113, 147, 158–62; leisure, 82; mythical, 98–99, 108–9; private and public, 104–9. *See also* Narrative; Temporality
Trace, 67–68, 90–93, 122, 146, 160–62, 330–33; and architecture, 72–78; and film, 79–84, 122, 131; and historiography, 67–69; of Jesus, 146–48. *See also* Indexical sign

Ultimate concern, 295–98
Understanding, 5, 8, 36, 143, 264. *See also* Appropriation

Violence, 210–11, 222, 306–10; political, 186–93

Word, 214–15, 219, 223, 240, 294; biblical, 286–88; of God, 135–36, 214–23, 260, 348. *See also* Testimony